HOME-BASED TRAVEL AGENT

How To Succeed in Your Own Travel Marketing Business

Kelly Monaghan

HOME-BASED TRAVEL AGENT
How To Succeed In Your Own
Travel Marketing Business

Fifth Edition

Cover design by Foster & Foster, Inc.

For information contact
The Intrepid Traveler
P.O. Box 531
Branford, CT 06450

http://www.intrepidtraveler.com

ISBN 1-887140-61-1

Table of Contents

Dedication

To the men and women who have revolutionized the travel distribution landscape by becoming independent, outside travel agents while maintaining the highest standards of professionalism and ethics, this training program is respectfully dedicated.

Introduction

Travel! Adventure! Romance!

The three seem to go together naturally, don't they? So is it any wonder that thousands and thousands of people (maybe you?) dream of escaping from their humdrum lives to a new lifestyle that will let them sail the seven seas, climb the highest mountains, explore the four corners of the earth? A career that will actually let them get paid for doing something they love?

Of course there are any number of careers that involve travel on a regular basis. The military ("Join the Navy and see the world!"), the airlines, diplomacy, import/export, international trade, cruise ships — all these jobs involve travel. And chances are, if you've invested in this course, you've dreamed of having one of those jobs at some point in your life. Unfortunately, most people never get past the dreaming stage. After all, deciding that what you *really* want to do is be a jet pilot or the captain of the *Love Boat* is one thing. Doing it is something else again. Not just anyone can be a jet pilot. Or a ship's captain. Or a diplomat. There's a lot of specialized (and expensive) training involved. Age can also be a factor. After all, not too many forty-year-olds are accepted in the Army. Not too many twenty-year-olds are appointed ambassador.

Another problem with many of the more traditional travel-oriented careers is that the job, not you, determines where you travel. The military officer goes where the government decides (and often finds people shooting at him when he gets there). The airline pilot shuttles back and forth endlessly between City A and City B. The career foreign service officer develops an expertise in Latin America and never sees the Far East.

Small wonder, then, that many people see the travel agency business as an inviting alternative. Travel agents get to really *see* the world, they think. They can travel where they want, when they want, and they get all sorts of great discounts when they do! What a great job! But then the doubts start creeping in: It's a whole new career. It requires all sorts of specialized training. It means a major commitment to opening an office,

investing in fancy computer equipment, managing a staff. Ugh.

But don't throw in the towel just yet. There is a way for people to get into the travel agency business on their own terms. A way in which they can tailor the travel industry to them rather than the other way around. This course will teach you how to do that.

These aren't precisely "secrets," but I've learned that very few people are aware of how easy it is to get into the travel game, on your own terms, in your own time, at your own level of commitment.

Do you just want to go on the occasional tour with a bunch of your friends or fellow club members? There's a way to do that!

Do you want to be a travel agent but avoid getting bogged down in fighting for the lowest airfare in a crazy fare-war atmosphere? There's a way to do that!

Are you interested in dealing in luxury cruises and nothing but luxury cruises? There's a way to do that!

Are you looking for a part-time job that will cover the mortgage or pay the private school tuition or allow you to stay home with the kids? There's a way to do that!

Would you like to make your entire living in the travel industry? There's a way to do that!

Do you just want to "try it on for size" before making a firm decision on whether selling travel is right for you? There's a way to do that!

Would you like to take your time learning the travel business, never exceeding your comfort level? There's a way to do that!

Would you be interested in making a nice income just by showing other people and businesses how to save money on travel? There's a way to do that!

Do you have zero interest in selling travel but still wouldn't mind saving a couple of hundred dollars every time you and your spouse take a vacation? There's a way to do that, too!

The new world of travel

Today it is possible to get involved in the travel industry almost instantaneously, with little or no experience or training, and start learning the business through actual hands-on experience in selling travel. By the time you finish this course, you will have all the information you need to begin a money-making (part-time or full-time!) travel career just by sharing the fun and excitement of travel with your friends and neighbors.

This course is designed to set you on the road to becoming a thoroughly professional, full-time marketer of travel, but I want to make it clear at the outset that the new world of travel is like a sumptuous buffet. You can take as much, or as little, as you want.

Here are just some of the ways you can participate in the exciting and lucrative world of travel as a tour organizer or travel agent. Some are part-timer strategies; others can be done full-time and produce a respectable income. One or more of these options is bound to be right for you.

- ***Organize an educational tour.*** Many tour operators who target their tours to the educational market are eager to find people like you who will round up a group of school kids for a foreign tour. In exchange for your efforts, you will receive a free trip for yourself and perhaps a cash payment to help defray additional expenses. You can often get a free trip by signing up as few as six kids.

- ***Take your club on a tour.*** If you belong to a group — a bridge club, the Kiwanis, the Podunk Marching and Chowder Society — you can organize a tour. Most of the time you will be dealing through a travel agent, less frequently directly with a tour operator. In exchange for bringing in a group of people, you (and the other folks on the tour) will receive a cheaper rate. In addition, as the organizer you may be in line for a "tour conductor pass"; in other words, your friends not only pay less but you go along for free.

- ***Take a cruise.*** Many cruise lines offer programs similar to those offered by the educational tour operators — bring in enough couples and you cruise for free.

- ***Become a "finder" for a travel agency.*** Many travel agents will give you a finder's fee just for bringing in business. In this arrangement, you do none of the work of helping the customer decide which tour or cruise to take nor do you make the bookings. The travel agent does all that. You just get the customer through the door. But make no mistake, that is a valuable service and the travel agent will pay you a small cut of the commission. Typically you will get 20% of the commission (roughly 2% of the cost of the trip).

- ***Join a "referral agency."*** Referral agencies will give you up to 5% commission on the price of the travel product, just for a referral. They also promise access to extensive industry discounts and benefits, typically for an entry cost of around $495. The typical referral agency agent doesn't wind up making much money, but 5% is not a bad commission for simply handing out business cards.

- ***Become an outside sales representative for a travel agency.*** This is the core relationship in the home-based and part-time travel business. I believe that after you read this course and realize how easy it is to become an outside rep and how many advantages this relationship offers, you will become one as soon as possible. In this arrangement, you not only find the customer but you handle all the details of the booking as well. You will have to hand the booking over to the "host" agency so they can process it and collect the commission. In exchange for your doing most of the work, the agency will split the commission with you. A typical split is 50/50, but I'll show you how you can get even more!

- *Get you own IATA number and become your very own travel agency.* Thanks to recent changes in the travel distribution system, it is now possible to get most of the business benefits of a having a storefront travel agency at a fraction of the upfront cost. By getting your own IATA number (or other unique industry identifier) you can keep the entire commission, without having to split it with anyone.

These opportunities exist because of some very simple and easy-to-understand facts of economic life. Travel suppliers (tour operators, wholesalers, cruise lines) want to sell more of their "product." Travel agencies, which act as go-betweens for the travel suppliers, want to bring in more customers. There are a number of ways to do this: by offering a better product, by providing better service, by creating better advertising, or by finding new and better ways to market their products and services. It is this last category — marketing — that has created some very attractive opportunities for folks like you.

Every travel product, from the cheapest hotel room to the most luxurious round-the-world cruise, must be sold. That requires salespeople, and everyone in the business has them. The airlines have their reservationists, travel agencies have their sub-agents. At some point, everyone selling travel asks themselves some variation of the following question: "If I'm selling one million worth of product with 10 salespeople, why couldn't I sell two million with 20?" It's not that simple of course. Many things have to be taken into consideration when increasing your sales force: demand (doubling the number of reservationists will not double the number of calls coming in), overhead, salaries and benefits, training, and on and on. Still, the marketer can't shake the idea. "If I had more people selling for me, I'd bring in more money."

What, then, if they could bring in additional salespeople at no cost whatsoever? In fact, what if they could actually get people to pay them for the privilege of selling for them? What if they set it up so that these new salespeople would only get paid for the business they brought in? What if they "paid" these salespeople in free travel or through a discount instead of cash? The idea proved so attractive that more and more travel suppliers began experimenting with some variation on the theme. Cruise lines offered free berths to people who could sign up a bunch of friends to take a cruise. Tour operators who wanted to reach the multi-billion-dollar educational market made teachers their "sales force," offering free trips and cash stipends. Travel agents began to experiment with outside sales representatives — freelance, independent agents who sell tickets, tours, and cruises to their own customers and let the agency do the ticketing in exchange for a split of the commission.

Over the last decade or so, a number of social, business, and economic trends have given this trend a push:

- *The rise of the entrepreneur.* More and more people are deciding that the "traditional" career model just doesn't work for them. Instead of sticking with the same company for 30 or 40 years, they are opting out of the corporate world to start their own businesses. For many of these people, the size of the business or the money to be made is less important than the freedom they will have to set their own pace and be their own boss.

- ***The two paycheck family.*** Today this is less of a trend than an accomplished fact of our economic life. Beginning in the '70s, rampant inflation made the traditional one paycheck family more and more a thing of the past. Millions of women "returned" to the job market for that second paycheck. Many of them found they lacked the skills demanded by a more complex and technological workplace than the one they left to get married. Today's young mothers often count themselves lucky if they can afford a few months at home with their young ones before getting back to a full-time job. Many of these women (and some "house husbands," too) would give their eyeteeth for a money-making part-time career that would allow them time with the kids.

- ***The second-job syndrome.*** After the two paycheck family has come the two and a half paycheck family. More and more family units are taking on part-time jobs. Sometimes it is a simple matter of economic necessity. In other cases, people are "test-driving" new careers or seeing if they might want to ditch their regular job and start their own business. Still others have heeded the advice of financial gurus and turned an avocation into a sideline business to gain not just the extra income but the tax advantages of running a small business.

- ***Downsizing.*** Downsizing has been the norm for years now. First it was major corporations that slashed workers. Then it was the "new economy" dot-coms that were letting people go. Next came state and local governments starved by tax cuts of the revenue they needed to maintain service levels. There is no indication that this trend will do anything but continue, as the gap between the haves and the have nots increases. Many people are realizing that if they want to find a job that will last, they're going to have to create it for themselves. Indeed, some states have responded to this new reality by instituting programs that help the newly unemployed set themselves up in business.

- ***Computerization.*** The rise of the small, affordable, personal computer has made part-time and home-based businesses more attractive to many people. The efficiency offered by automation means that business opportunities that might have been seen as too time-consuming a few years ago are now seen as something that need take up only a few hours a week. Travel agencies, using the same cheap computers linked together in a network, have the computer power to maintain and track fairly large numbers of outside reps. Whereas ten years ago having an outside sales force might have seemed like an organizational nightmare, today it's more likely to be seen as a piece of cake.

- *The Internet.* The advent of an international computer network allowing cheap and virtually instantaneous communication between large numbers of people scattered over a wide geographical area has had a profound effect on all aspects of business. For travel suppliers it's meant a new way to distribute information and find and communicate with both travel agents and customers. For travel agencies it's meant that operating and communicating with an outside sales force has become even easier.

- *Franchising.* Over the last decade or so, franchising has boomed. Many of the entrepreneurs who start their own businesses do so under the comforting umbrella of a franchise. And the travel industry has not been overlooked. If you have the money, you can buy into your own travel agency. If you don't have the money, you can accomplish much the same end by becoming an outside sales rep. Think about it: You operate on your own (just like a franchise), have your own customers (just like a franchise), run your own business affairs (just like a franchise), but you still have an association with a larger entity that provides you with services (just like a franchise). And just as the franchisee pays a franchise fee, the outside sales rep for a travel agency splits the commission with the agency. Of course, legally speaking, being a franchisee and being an outside sales rep are two different things. Still, the two arrangements have much the same practical effect. More and more travel agencies are applying the franchise metaphor when they consider adding an outside sales operation and are, consequently, becoming more open to the idea of having independent reps bring them business.

- *Turmoil in the travel industry.* As you may know, in the 1990s, airlines began cutting and then totally eliminated commissions paid to travel agents. One result was that many storefront travel agencies went out of business. Suppliers of other travel products (cruises, tours, etc.) began wondering who was going to sell their products. These suppliers suddenly became much more open to the idea of using "non-traditional" channels (like home-based agents) to sell their wares.

The end result is that, today, becoming a player in the multi-billion dollar world of travel has never been easier — if you know how to go about it. This book and the home study course of which it is part will show you a number of ways to take advantage of the latest changes in the travel distribution system. However, you should be aware that there are other, more "traditional," ways to go about it.

The 'traditional' career paths

Of course, if you're the traditional type, you can always go out and start your own travel agency. These are the storefront travel boutiques that you see as you drive through your town. These are the places that are listed in the Yellow Pages under "Travel Agencies." Fewer people are starting storefront agencies these days for reasons that will become apparent as you progress through this course. Still, some people can't resist the lure of going into the business. But they are usually not rank beginners. They are usually people who have been working in the travel industry for some time, who know the ropes and figure they can make it on their own. Sometimes they start an agency from scratch. Sometimes they hook up with one of the growing number of franchise operations to get a head start. In any event, they put up quite a bit of their own money — $50,000 or more in most cases.

Like most small businesses, travel agencies have a high mortality rate. It's a competitive business that sometimes operates on distressingly low margins. When you factor in the high cost of overhead and payroll, it can be easy to lose money. Many would-be entrepreneurs find it's just not worth it and shut their doors in a year or two. However, a growing number of small agencies are closing their doors — not to go out of business, but to become home-based agencies using the strategies outlined in this course. They lose the high overhead while keeping their customers!

Another option is to get a job at a travel agency or a corporate travel office. You can always go to a travel school to get the minimum qualifications needed to land an entry-level job in an agency. For most people, this is the only option. Travel agencies like to hire people who already know how to use the GDS (global distribution system) they use to ticket flights, and this is precisely what the travel schools teach.

There are a number of drawbacks to this option, however:

- ***There is a great deal of competition for jobs.*** Look at the want ads. Over and over, you'll see they specify "two years SABRE experience" or "5+ years agency experience." That puts beginners at a distinct disadvantage. Most agencies have enough to do to make ends meet without worrying about bringing you up to speed.
- ***Entry-level pay is low.*** The typical starting salary in a small agency is $12,000 to $14,000. Of course, there is always the chance for advancement and many people in the industry make a good living. The median income for a travel agent in 1998 was about $23,000 a year and ten percent made more than $34,000.
- ***The work is far from glamorous.*** Most entry-level agency employees spend their days at computer terminals handling the nitty-gritty details of booking and ticketing point-to-point airline trips, the least lucrative aspect of the business. There is often little chance to meet with customers and share your excitement for the open road.
- ***The work is reactive rather than proactive.*** In the typical agency, the customer comes to you. As an entry-level

employee you have little opportunity to develop new business. Moreover, it is the customer, not you, who determines the kind of travel products you wind up selling.

- **The turnover is high.** Many people find after a few months that agency work is a lot harder and a lot less glamorous than they thought. You might be one of them. Even if you stick it out, you may find a constant stream of new faces at the office.
- **The payoffs are down the road.** Of course, as an agency employee, you are eligible for the benefits that come with being in the travel business (see *Chapter 10: Straight Talk On Travel Industry Benefits*), but in most agencies you will have to pay six months, a year, or more of dues before you get to take advantage of them. Also, many opportunities for free and reduced-cost travel are tied to agency volume. If your agency isn't big enough, or is having a bad year, your travel benefits may suffer accordingly.
- **Travel time is limited.** Even when new or low-level travel agency employees can qualify for free or low-cost travel, the time to take advantage of these deals is limited. Most agency employees get two weeks vacation, just as they would at a "regular" job.

This brief discussion is meant to be realistic rather than discouraging. Many people thrive in the agency atmosphere, have a lot of fun, sell a lot of vacations, have exciting careers, and become very successful. If you decide to go the traditional route, I would like to think that this course will prove helpful to you as you begin your climb up the career ladder. However, the main purpose of this course is not to tell you how to have a traditional career in the travel agency business. And if I have concentrated perhaps a little too much on the downside of the traditional path it's just to point up the positive aspects of becoming a home-based agent.

What's more, if you have your heart set on having a storefront agency, I'll show you a way to do that, too! The bad news is you won't be able to sell air (at least not without forming an alliance with another agency), but there are plenty of successful agents these days who don't want to sell air anyway. The good news is that, because you are not selling air in your new storefront agency, you will avoid all the financial burdens that go along with selling air (bonding, meeting Airline Reporting Corporation requirements, and so forth). But this is an advanced concept. It is possible but not required.

One size does not fit all

One of the most attractive aspects of the new travel marketing landscape is that it is very definitely not a one-size-fits-all proposition. You can design your travel career to suit your interests, your schedule, your working style and preferences, and your monetary goals. You can plan to work one hour a week or 80. You can plan to save money on just your own travel. Or you can plan to make money on the travel of a small circle of friends, or the travel of everyone in your neighborhood, town, county, or region. You can plan to earn pin money in a part-time travel business or you can set your sights on a full-time annual income of over $50,000. It's all doable and it's all up to you!

- **Become a part-time specialist.** Suppose you love taking cruises; you do it once a year and have cruised with several different lines. You are a natural to sell the joys and benefits of cruising to others. And if you want to specialize just in cruises — no short-haul airline tickets, no European tours — you should be able to find a travel agency that will be more than happy to handle all the cruise business you can bring in. Or perhaps you are lucky enough to be Irish and you know the "auld sod" like the back of your hand. You may want to specialize in travel to Ireland. You can use your special knowledge of the destination to add value to your services. You may even want to lead some special interest tours yourself, all the while earning a commission on every person you book.

- **Be a generalist.** You may decide that offering to book all types of travel for a select clientele will work best for you. If you know you can get a circle of family, friends, and neighbors to turn their travel needs over to you, you can get into the business quickly. There are some disadvantages to this arrangement which I will get into later, but it has the advantage of giving you a clear handle on your business. In other words, once you learn that Aunt Matilda spends $1,500 a year on travel, you can look forward to getting a steady cut of that sum.

- **Be a full-time home-based travel agent.** There's no law that says that you cannot spend every waking hour building your own, highly profitable travel business. It's pretty easy to earn a 7% commission; if you sell the right products, you can make 10% or 12% or 15%. In a few rare instances, you can make over 20% commission on some sales. Sometimes when you earn a free trip as a reward for your sales efforts, you have the option of taking that trip yourself — or selling it at full price and pocketing the entire fare! There are outside sales reps today who earn over $100,000 a year selling travel. Why not join them? If you have the drive and the commitment, there's no reason you can't.

- **Be a by-the-hour travel consultant.** Most people involved in selling travel are compensated by commissions. But I know some enterprising souls who, in addition to receiving a commission as outside reps, charge their clients an hourly fee for helping them plan their vacations! If you have special expertise, in-depth knowledge of specific destinations, or

provide special services like making reservations at little known restaurants in exotic climes, you may be able to charge up to $100 an hour for your services. This is not as far out a strategy as it might seem. Now that most traditional travel agencies are charging fees for airline ticketing, the traveling public is becoming accustomed to paying good money for a travel agent's expertise.

Is it for you?

Who should get into the travel agent game? Once you learn how easy it is to get started, to make sales, to make bookings, and to make money, the answer is simple and straightforward: *Everyone!* After all, even if all you want to do is save money on your own travel for business and pleasure, the information in this course will enable you to save many times the purchase price. If you're not convinced by now, I would like to think that by the time you have finished the course you will be. In fact, you may even find you're so excited by the possibilities that you'll start your travel agent career rolling *before* you've finished the course!

If you are reading this, you have no doubt made a commitment to become a home-based travel agent. Even so, take some time to consider these good solid reasons for joining the thousands of people who are having fun and making money as home-based travel agents. My guess is this list will spark your creativity and get you thinking about ways in which you can turn the information in this course to your personal benefit:

- *Are you a traveler?* If you love travel yourself, you have already mastered a major challenge for anyone in sales — you know your product. It is now a relatively simple matter to translate the knowledge and enthusiasm you already possess into powerful sales presentations that will bring you your first bookings and steady repeat business. In addition, you'll start saving money on your own travel instantly.

- *Are you looking for a low-investment part-time business?* Look no further. As I've already said, and will explain in detail later, you can become a travel agent today. And your initial investment can be absolutely zero (okay, maybe you'll use a stamp or two and make a few phone calls). I made my first several bookings with no business card, no stationery, no nothing!

- *Do you need a flexible schedule?* Here's a business that allows you to set your own hours like few others. You can chat with folks at work or call them at home at night. Work full-time one week and scale back the next. Whatever schedule works best for you, you can design a travel business to accommodate it.

- *Do you have a built-in audience?* Many professions offer their practitioners access to large groups of people — ministers, accountants, salespeople, the list goes on. All of these people come in contact with many people in the course of their work, people who are often prime prospects for any travel business. If you are in a position to reach a ready-made audience, you can prosper in the travel business.

- ***Do you belong to a club or organization?*** Clubs and other affinity groups represent superb opportunities to make major sales. If you get ten people in your club to go on a cruise with their spouses, that's a $30,000 to $40,000 sale.

- ***Are you a small businessperson?*** If so, why not make travel an add-on to your existing product line? Everyone who comes into your place of business can learn about the travel opportunities you have to offer. If you send catalogs or brochures to your customers on a regular basis you have already paid for the postage to send them a flyer about a great bargain on an upcoming tour or cruise. Or why not offer discounted travel to your employees as an extra benefit? You'll forego some or all of the commission, but the goodwill you generate will be hard to beat.

- ***Do you travel on business?*** Many people who travel on business pay their own way and then get reimbursed by their employer or client. As a travel agent, you can earn a commission on a lot of that travel, especially if it involves international travel. If you own your own business and spend a considerable amount of money on travel, then the prospect of saving 5% to 7% on your travel expenditures should make your bottom line sit up and take notice.

- ***Are you in sales?*** If you are, you've probably already thought of a dozen ways you can prosper in this business. Your existing sales skills will fit perfectly in a home-based travel business and you no doubt already have a large and ever-growing pool of prospects.

- ***Are you retired?*** Perfect. Not only do you now have the time to devote to learning about travel, but you are an integral part of the largest and fastest growing market for leisure travel. You can make a handsome income, and enjoy some wonderful fringe benefits, just by specializing in the travel interests and needs of folks just like you.

- ***Are you home with the kids?*** Here's a way to make a bit of extra money at the same time you're burping and diapering. Much of your business with customers can be conducted on the phone; your friends probably won't mind if you're bouncing junior on your knee while you talk to them. You can use baby's nap time to get on the phone and call the travel suppliers. It's a perfect scenario for the homemaker or house-husband.

- ***Are you committed to a full-time career?*** If you are not sure, the information in this course will show you how to test the waters for a minimal investment. If you find you love the travel business as much as you thought, great! You'll be ideally situated to maximize your income potential. If, on the other hand, you decide the travel business is not for you (it's not for everyone), you have the option of continuing on a part-time basis or getting out altogether without having spent a small fortune discovering you've made a wrong career turn.

- ■ *Are you <u>sure</u> you want to work in an agency?* Experience tells me that some people taking this course are currently employed in travel agencies. Many people thrive in an agency atmosphere, but many become bored and disillusioned with the rote work that taking orders and working the GDS often involves. The strategies outlined in this course will show you how easy it is to progress to the status of an agency owner — without the huge upfront investment and high overhead. In the process you will put yourself in a position to earn many times what you would make as an entry-level inside employee.

What's the catch?

If this is all sounding too good to be true, I know exactly how you feel. I felt the same way. In fact, I still feel that way. Part of me keeps wondering when I'll find "the catch." So far there doesn't seem to be one. But if I've pumped you up *too* much so far, perhaps it's time to bring you down to earth a bit.

If there is a catch to the new travel game, it's letting your goals outstrip your gumption. Another way of saying that is you've got to determine, first, what you want out of your travel business and, second, if you have what it takes in terms of skills, time, commitment, and intestinal fortitude to get it.

For some the goals were pretty simple. Some folks just want a way to make something they love — travel — more a part of their daily life. They're not looking to make selling travel their sole means of making a living. They're not going to be one of those $100,000 a year outside reps. They are looking to stretch their travel budget, to get more mileage out of their travel dollar. Or looking to supplement their income by sharing the joys of travel with others.

Others are looking for a steady but part-time business, one that will bring in a minimum dollar amount each year, while providing some travel benefits as well. These folks have set concrete financial goals (a crucial step to success) and they scale their business to meet those goals. If they make more money than they planned, that's fine, but if they find they are spending more time than they want on business, they can scale back quite easily.

Finally there are the go-for-the-gold types who want to take their business to the max. These people are goal-driven go-getters who are willing to put in the long hours to learn the industry and perfect their professional skills. They are most likely detail-oriented businesspeople who judge success more in dollar amounts than cruises taken or resorts visited.

One catch, then, is that you might not have a clear picture of where you're headed when you start out. Another is not having a clear picture of the realities of the journey. To help you guide your own thinking as you progress through this course, let me share some thoughts that may help you put all this in perspective:

- ■ ***This is no get-rich-quick scheme.*** Those who make large sums of money selling travel work very hard and earn every penny. How much money a person makes and how hard they have to work to make it, varies from person to person. Some people have more time to devote to their travel business than others. Some have more drive and determination than others. Some folks are natural salespeople; others will have to work harder to hone their skills. It may sound like a cliché, but how much money you make is up to you. I certainly can't predict how much you'll make, but I can guarantee you that if you think you can make a small fortune working just a half hour a day while watching television, you'll be disappointed.

- ■ ***It's a business.*** The statistics tell us that the majority of new businesses fail in a year or two. There's no reason to expect that your travel business may not meet the same fate. The saving grace is that, if you follow the strategies in this course, you will not lose more money than you can afford in a failed venture. Also, if you decide being independent is not for you, you should have enough of a track record to make you an attractive employee for a local agency. It's quite possible to use the strategies in this course knowing you'll earn just a few hundred dollars a year. If that's fine for you, then everything's okay. Of course, you can also seek to make selling travel a money-maker. And that's fine, too.

- ■ ***You have to be business-like.*** If you are working on a very casual part-tome basis maybe you can get away with being sloppy. Otherwise, you will have to run your business in a business-like manner. That means being organized, <u>establishing standard operating procedures, keeping impeccable records</u>, <u>counting your pennies, going after money due you, doing your taxes, and on and on</u>.

- ■ ***It's a service business.*** Whatever else you are selling, you are selling customer satisfaction. If you have never worked in a setting in which you had to "please the public," you may be surprised at how much people will expect from you and how readily they'll blame you for things over which you have no control. Believe me, if the toilet in the luxury hotel in Nairobi backs up and overflows, it's your fault!

- ■ ***Things go wrong.*** Most people who go into business have at least some bad experiences. I sure have. I certainly can't guarantee that you won't have some of your own. You may

Introduction

just accept problems as a natural part of life. I think that's a healthy attitude. On the other hand, you may decide that the kinds of problems that tend to come up in this business aren't worth whatever you're getting out of it. So be it. Later in the course, I'll talk about some of the things that can go amiss and some ways you can protect yourself.

- *It involves selling.* No matter how glamorous travel may be, to make money at it you have to sell. That means looking for new customers, finding out about what their travel needs are, presenting them with attractive options, answering their questions, dealing with their objections, and, above all, asking them to part with their hard-earned money. I happen to have a background in sales and marketing. In fact, over the years I have trained hundreds of salespeople in a variety of industries. I know from experience that selling is a skill and that like any skill it can be learned. I also know from experience that not everyone is cut out for selling. It's not so much that they *can't*, it's just that, for whatever reason, they find out they don't enjoy it that much. You may be one of those people.

So that's the downside. And I don't think that's it's really all that bad. If you've never run your own business before, you will learn new things, about yourself and the world at large, that will give you a deep sense of personal satisfaction. Yes, running a business is work, but it's not impossible work. Millions of people do it. With a little application so can you.

In this course I will share with you the fun, the excitement and the money-making possibilities of the travel business. I will also teach you the little "secrets" that will put you on an equal footing with the industry pros who are peddling those "Be A Travel Agent" business opportunities and several long steps ahead of other novice home-based agents who weren't smart enough to invest in this course. They will stumble about and make costly mistakes (just like I did!), while you are charting a smooth upward course towards success.

Should you be a "travel agent"?

That may seem an odd question to ask at this point. What I am really asking is, "Should you *call* yourself a travel agent"?

I use the term 'travel agent' throughout this course because it is a simple descriptive term and commonly understood. However, you should be aware that there is a trend, especially among home-based agents, to get away from using the term.

Why? One reason, I think, is that many home-based agents want to differentiate themselves from the traditional, storefront travel agent. Old-style travel agents pretty much tried to be all things to all people. Many, if not most, home-based agents specialize to at least some extent. For example, most do not sell cheap, point-to-point airline tickets, or do so only under protest. Many more are even more specialized.

That's why you will see more and more business cards identifying the bearer as a Travel Consultant. This term has been around for quite some time, actually. Originally, it was meant to convey the idea that the person with that title was more experienced and knowledgeable than a mere "travel agent." In fact, The Travel Institute, formerly known as the Institute of Certified Travel Agents (ICTA), confers the designation "Certified Travel Consultant" (CTC) on agents who meet its high standards and pass its rigorous tests. However, there is no law to prevent people from calling themselves Travel Consultants and many do, ICTA or no.

Since many people today see "Travel Consultant" as just a fancy term for travel agent, some agents are becoming even more creative. Here are some of the titles I've come across: Leisure Travel Specialist, Vacation Consultant, Cruise Consultant, Dive Travel Specialist, Hawaii Specialist. You get the idea. These titles tell the customer not just what to expect from this agent, but just as important what *not* to expect from that agent.

You can call yourself whatever you wish, of course. However, I suspect that once you have gone through this course and absorbed its principles, you will probably choose to focus and specialize your travel business to some extent. So as you read through the course suspend judgement about exactly how your business card will read. You might wind up saving yourself some money.

How this course is organized

In writing this course, I have assumed that you have relatively little experience in the travel industry, except as a consumer, and little or no background in selling.

Whether you plan to become a home-based travel agent on a part- or full-time basis, I think you will find the bulk of the material in this course both of interest and of use. Even if you have been working for a travel agency for five years, my guess is you will learn some new things from this course and, perhaps, decide to make some changes in the way you manage your career.

The course is organized in three main sections:

Part I: How to Profit as a Home-Based Travel Agent. In this section, I will lay out the opportunities that exist to get involved in organizing and selling travel on either a part-time or full-time basis. The material in this section will progress from the very basic to the fairly advanced. I cover everything from simple, one-off ways to sell travel without even becoming a travel agent to how to open your own travel agency with employees and a network of your own outside agents.

This information will allow you to construct your travel business on your own terms. Like I said, this is definitely not a one-size-fits-all proposition, so some of the material may not apply to your particular situation. You may only want to use some of the strategies discussed or you may want to do it all. It's up to you.

Throughout, I have tried to place an emphasis on doing things in the most cost-effective manner possible. You can spend a lot of money setting up your home travel business, but you certainly don't have to. I also try, whenever possible, to cut through the hype and tell you how the business *really* works.

Part II: The Craft of Booking Travel. In this section, I will provide you with guidance on how to research travel options and actually make bookings for a variety of travel products. This is where "the rubber meets the road," as it were, providing you with the day to day mechanics of running your travel business. Again, the emphasis is on streetwise strategies that aren't always taught in travel schools.

Part III: The Fine Art of Selling Travel. Next, I'll show you how to translate your enthusiasm for this new lifestyle into actual sales and put real cash in your pocket. You'll learn how to locate your very first customers, get to know their travel needs and preferences, use powerful benefits to sell high-ticket tours and cruises, and ask for their business with pride and confidence. This is a complete mini-training program in the classic core selling skills. It is patterned after sales training programs I created for some of America's most successful selling organizations.

There are two other elements of the course that are not included in this volume:

How to Choose a Host Agency. Even if you eventually decide you don't need one, you will probably start your home-based travel agent career by becoming an outside sales representative for an established travel agency, what is known in the business as a "host agency." Although host agencies are covered in *Part I* of the course, this section will give you a good introduction to the many choices available to you and guide you in choosing wisely. I urge you not to make a hasty decision or take shortcuts in making that decision. I provide an extremely thorough methodology for investigating any host agency business opportunity. Use it!

If you purchased this book as part of my home study course, you already have it. If not, you can purchase it at:

http://www.HomeTravelAgency.com/choosehost.html

How to Get Your Own IATA Number. More and more home-based agents are becoming truly independent by getting their own unique industry identifier. This step not only allows them to operate completely independent of a host agency, it even lets them start hiring their own employees or running their own network of outside agents. The various ways of making this major step are covered in this Special Report, along with my recommendation for the fastest, cheapest way to accomplish this goal.

If you purchased this book as part of my home study course, you already have it. If not, you can purchase it at:

http://www.HomeTravelAgency.com/getiata.html

In addition, there is another resource provided with the home study course that will prove invaluable as you start your career and well after. It is *The Travel Agent's Complete Desk Reference*. Again, if you purchased this book as part of my home study course, you already have it. If not, you can purchase it at:

http://www.HomeTravelAgency.com/deskref.html

How to use this course

There is a great deal of information in this course. You will not be able to absorb it all at once or in one reading. How you approach it is pretty much up to you. You can move at your own pace, reading at random, moving back and forth in the course. However, here are some suggestions.

I urge you to read through all of *Part I* before doing anything else. You can skim it if you wish and skip parts you don't feel apply to what you want to do with your business, but at least try to get a good overview of how the business works and what's possible.

By this point you may be eager to start looking into finding a host agency. Turn to *How to Choose A Host Agency* and begin your research. Request marketing materials and sample contracts from agencies that look interesting. I should add here that, for reasons I discuss in the course, you do not absolutely have to have a host agency. It's just that my personal feeling is that a host agency makes the most sense for beginners and that, even if you get your own IATA number, the services of a host agency can still be useful in certain circumstances. You, of course, are free to make your own decision.

While you're waiting for this material, you can go back and start studying *Part I* in more depth. Before you make any host agency decision, do yourself a huge favor and spend some time brainstorming how you want your business to look (i.e. what you will sell, to whom, and how). Make notes and expand upon them as your thinking evolves. If you are going into this business with your spouse, bounce ideas off each other and write down your insights.

Part II is more technical and will be most helpful as you reach the point when you feel ready to start making actual bookings for actual clients. This section may also be helpful as you look into host agencies, since you will want to get clear on exactly how they prefer you to make bookings through them. Because it is divided by travel product, you can quickly and easily refer to whichever chapter you need most at any given moment. This section has been designed for ready reference rather than armchair reading, but reading through it all will probably spark off some ideas.

Part III can be read at your leisure. You may even be tempted to skip it altogether but I would recommend against that. I am convinced that what separates successful from unsuccessful home-based agents is their willingness to see what they do as a professional process of *selling* to client needs.

Join a professional organization as soon as possible. I recommend the Outside Sales Support Network (OSSN) and I provide a downloadable discounted application form at

http://www.HomeTravelAgency.com/ossnapp.pdf.

Become active in your nearest chapter or take one of OSSN's low-cost cruise-seminars. This will get you excited about the benefits associated with your new profession, plug you into a great continuing education resource, and introduce you to a friendly bunch of more experienced fellow agents to whom you can turn for guidance.

Return to the course as often as you wish, but at least periodically. As you gain more experience, many things mentioned in the course will take on new meaning for you and spark more great ideas on how you can profit and prosper.

How to Profit as a Home-Based Travel Agent

Chapter One:

A Brief Overview of the Travel Industry

What you will learn

When you have completed this chapter, you will be able to:

- Describe a variety of ways in which travel products move from supplier to customer.
- Explain the relationship among base cost, gross margin, and retail price.
- List three ways in which travel agents are compensated.
- Describe the function of ARC, IATA, IATAN, and CLIA as gatekeepers in the travel industry.

Key terms and concepts

This chapter involves the following key terms and concepts:

- The travel agent is a middleman who facilitates the sale of a travel product from a supplier to a customer, adding value in the process.
- There is no *one* way of doing anything in the travel business.
- You do not need anyone's permission to sell travel. All you really need is to make the decision that selling travel is what you want to do. After that, any "bumps in the road" can be handled.
- Disintermediation is a fancy term for cutting out the middleman.

The history of travel

People have been traveling for as long as there have been people. Since our ancestors were expelled from the Garden of Eden (or climbed down from the trees of Africa, if you prefer) they have traveled far and wide, populating virtually every nook and cranny of the globe, some so remote that scientists are still scratching their heads over how they got there.

The first travelers went on foot or by primitive water craft. They probably traveled in small groups, so you might say that group travel is as old as mankind! But they certainly didn't travel for fun. Finding new territory on which to hunt and gather was a matter of survival and not a vacation.

Once humans became "civilized" (literally, when they started living in cities and villages), travel became more professional. As trade grew, caravans were organized to transport merchants and their goods over great distances. It was then that something resembling today's travel industry was born. Caravan leaders organized groups of merchants, providing guide service and some protection from bandits. Caravansaries, the truck stops of their era, popped up along trade routes, offering both travelers and pack animals shelter, food, and drink.

When sea-going travel became widely available there were captains who offered transport services to merchants and others. By the Greek era, people were traveling to broaden their education or just to see what there was to see. Herodotus, the Greek historian, was as much tourist as he was scholar.

Inns came into being, providing the same function as the ancient caravansaries on a smaller scale. Various provisioners catered to the needs of travelers, selling pack animals and supplies for the road.

Roman times saw the beginning of leisure travel in a form we recognize. In those days, the wealthy would travel for the sheer enjoyment of it, to see the wonders of the ancient world, all under the guise of deepening their wisdom. After the fall of Rome, during the "Dark Ages," the practice fell into disuse, only to be reborn as the "Grand Tour of Europe," a rite of passage for wealthy young European men of the 17th and 18th centuries. Then, as today in similar tours, the emphasis was on sites associated with the ancient world and the Renaissance.

By this time, the travel infrastructure was becoming more, well, *structured*. There were ships that sold passage, stage coach lines that linked major cities, toll roads, ferries, inns along the way, guides and bodyguards, hawkers of paintings and souvenirs, all looking to get a cut of the tourist's purse.

(The words "tourist" and "tourism," by the way, didn't come into widespread use until much later, in the 1930s.)

Modern tourism is generally agreed to have been "invented" in 1841, in England, by a young man named Thomas Cook. If the name sounds familiar, it should. The company he founded still exists!

Cook saw the potential of England's growing rail network and organized a trip to take people from Leicester to a temperance meeting in Loughsborough, 12 miles away. The roundtrip fare was a shilling. The outing was a roaring success and an industry was born. It has hardly looked back since.

The early twentieth century saw the beginning of motor car touring, commercial air travel, and the golden age of cruising, when luxurious ocean liners transported people in style from Europe to the Americas and beyond. The Thomas Cook Company and its many imitators performed the increasingly necessary function of helping the traveler coordinate the many elements that went into a trip. The travel agent came into his (and her) own.

The next major step (for our purposes) came in the 1950s and 1960s when the travel distribution system met the computer. A cruise line might have dozens of trips a year but a modern airline company had scores, even hundreds, each day. The computerized reservations systems (CRS) that were developed by the airlines in this period were a godsend. They enabled the airlines to sell and distribute thousands of airline tickets efficiently through hundreds of travel agencies scattered over large distances and keep track of the vast sums of money generated in the process.

The rise of the CRS did three things. It launched the computer era that is still unfolding before us; it made the travel agent a true professional in the eyes of the public; and it placed the airlines squarely at the center of the travel distribution system, giving them enormous power.

Today, computers are still a central feature of the travel distribution system, which would seem to give the edge to the "big guys," the ones with a large budget for technology. In fact, the CRS has be redubbed the GDS or global distribution system, which seems to suggest that the big guys think they control it all. This is true to some extent, but the rise of the *personal* computer has given the "little guy" (you and me) the means to compete effectively — if we know what we're doing and we do it cleverly enough. To a large extent, that's what this course is all about.

With the CRS came a more central role for the travel agent. Now, instead of traveling to the airport or some distant airline office, travelers could stop at the travel agency on Main Street to pick up their tickets, along with a lot of free advice. This marriage of convenience and added value was possible because the airlines compensated travel agents through commissions. As it became a "no-brainer" for people to purchase tickets through travel agents, travel agents prospered.

Gradually, other types of travel products became bookable through the CRS, which further added to travel agent income. But since the CRS was designed to serve the peculiar needs of the airline industry, the airlines wound up dictating, without really having to try, how travel could be sold and who could be a travel agent. This is changing now, as you shall see. But many of the attitudes, systems, procedures, and ways of doing business that still hold in today's travel distribution system were created in this era.

The history of the travel industry is a fascinating one and if you'd like to delve into it more deeply, I urge you to consult the bibliography provided in *The Travel Agent's Complete Desk Reference*.

The role of the middleman

Like any distribution system, the travel distribution system is about getting something from Point A to Point B. In this case the "something" is a travel product or service and Points A and B are not geographical locations exactly, but people — suppliers and travelers.

Originally, the relationship was direct. If you needed to take a train you went to the train station and dealt with the railway company. The relationship looked like this:

The traveler dealt directly with the supplier and vice versa. (The lines in all these diagrams indicate a two-way relationship.) Many times, the relationship can still look like that today. But what if you needed to get off the train and board a ship to continue your journey? Then you dealt with the steamship line. And if the dock was not convenient to the train station? Then you dealt with a livery company. The relationship became more complicated:

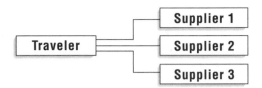

Thomas Cook, and all those who followed his lead, saw the wisdom of making the traveler's life simpler, by becoming a middleman. He created the first true "travel agency," in the process encouraging people to take trips they might not otherwise consider because of the hassle and unfamiliarity of making all these varying arrangements.

In the above scenario, the travel agency is pulling together a number of different products for the traveler's convenience. But travel agencies can provide another service, helping the traveler sort through a myriad of different options when making a single choice.

If the travel agency business grew out of a need to make the complex simple, it matured into an everyday convenience. Even if the traveler's need was very simple and straightforward — a plane ticket, a hotel reservation — it became increasingly convenient to deal with a travel agent who, at no additional cost to the traveler, offered superior knowledge and good advice. People went to travel agencies for very simple purchases:

In the early days, the Thomas Cook era, the "travel agent" took on the responsibility of making all arrangements with the suppliers. Some travel agencies still do this and you can, too, if you wish. Doing this, however, cuts down on the time available to find new customers and sell to them. So a further level of sophistication was added to the system.

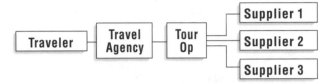

In this scenario, I have called the new player a "tour op" or tour operator. "Wholesaler," "incoming tour operator," and "destination management firm" are other terms that might be applied. This person or company, whatever the term, takes the responsibility of assembling travel "products" from a variety of suppliers and offering them, as a package and at a set price, to the travel agent who can then market that package to his or her clientele.

The list of suppliers (and products) that a "tour op" in this scenario might deal with can be extensive. It might include airlines, cruise lines, motorcoach companies, railway companies, hotels, restaurants, attractions (such as theme parks, museums, etc.), guides, visa expediters, caterers, and on and on. It all depends on how extensive and elaborate a "package" the tour op wishes to create.

It can also happen that there will be suppliers within suppliers, as it were, a scenario that might look something like this:

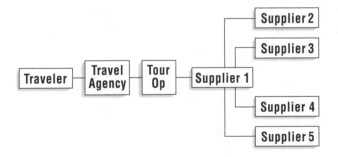

In this scenario, Supplier 1 might be a receptive tour operator in Italy, while suppliers 2 and 3 offer services in Florence and Suppliers 4 and 5 offer services in Venice. In addition, Suppliers 2, 3, 4 and 5 would have sub-suppliers providing some or all of the services they offer to Supplier 1.

Thus far I have been using the term "travel agency" in the corporate sense, to mean a business entity. A travel agency, of course, can consist of one person or many. But no matter how many travel agents are employed in a travel agency, they all represent one single entity, the travel agency.

Now let's add a new element: The independent home-based travel agent. This person is an independent contractor who is legally separate from the travel agency (that is, *not* an employee of the travel agency). The home-based agent finds customers for a travel agency and is compensated by the travel agency for that work with a portion of the commission due to the travel agency from the supplier. (Don't worry. All these terms and concepts will be explained in detail later. For now, just concentrate on the "big picture.")

In the diagram that follows, the independent, home-based travel agent is designated "HBTA."

At this point, things may seem to be getting a bit complicated, but this is just the beginning!

Variations on a theme

So far we have looked at situations in which the lines of communication are pretty simple and straightforward. They move in a straight line. Traveler goes to travel agent, who turns to tour operator, who calls on his many contacts. Or traveler deals with home-based agent who deals with travel agency, who… you get the idea. In the real world it can be and often is more complicated.

Because there are so many different elements in even the simplest of trips and because the consumer has so many choices of where and how to book, modern travelers often wind up dealing with multiple suppliers, sometimes by choice, sometimes by happenstance.

In a fairly common scenario, a traveler goes to a travel agent for an airline ticket, but when he arrives at the destination he rents a car in the airport and then drives around until he selects a hotel. That scenario could be diagrammed as follows.

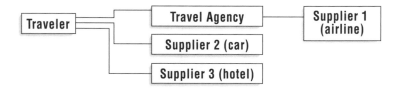

Similarly, a traveler might book a cruise through a travel agency but book his flight to the port of departure on the Internet adding on a few days after the cruise before his return flight — something the travel agent knows nothing about, by the way. On his return, the traveler might rent a car at the port and drive to a nearby resort to spend a few extra days "recuperating" from the cruise before returning home, making these arrangements directly with the suppliers.

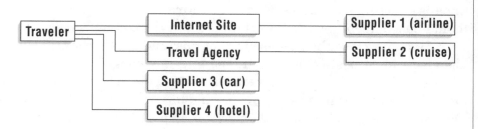

At this point, you may be asking yourself, "Why doesn't the travel agent sell the traveler these other elements of the trip?" An excellent question and one we will consider in due course. In many cases, the travel agency *should* be making an effort to get as much of the business as possible. However, there are very good reasons why a travel agency might want to let some of this business go. For now, however, let's concentrate on the many ways in which travel products can flow from supplier to traveler.

Let's add a home-based agent to the equation:

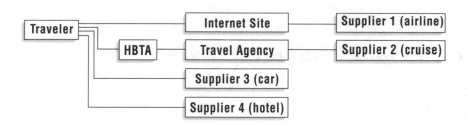

So far not a lot has changed. The home-based travel agent is pretty much a stand-in for the travel agency in the above scenario. Indeed, the traveler will no doubt think of the home-baser in just that way. Today, however, thanks to recent changes in the travel distribution system, the home-based agent has a lot more options. For example:

In this situation, the marketing-savvy home-based agent has recaptured some of the money left on the table in the previous examples. She (or he) is more than happy to let the traveler book his own airline ticket on the Internet. Why? Well, you'll learn the answer to that a little later.

The home-based agent has booked the cruise through a travel agency. Could she have done this directly with the cruise line? Absolutely. Sometimes, however, booking a cruise through a travel agency, even though it means splitting a commission, can be **more** financially rewarding for the home-based agent, as I will explain later in the course.

Here our clever home-based agent has anticipated the traveler's need or desire for a post-cruise "chill out" and has suggested an appropriate resort not too far from the port. She has also pointed out that the traveler doesn't need a rental car at the resort and has suggested a limousine transfer from dock to resort and then to the airport for the trip home, something that pampers the client, plays to his vanity, and probably costs less than renting a car. She then made these bookings directly with the resort and the limo company, without having to split the commission with anyone.

We could look at more variations on the fairly simple theme of supplier, middleman, and traveler, but I think the point has been made. There are many, many ways in which the traveler's needs can be met.

As you progress through this course, I would like to encourage you to think creatively about how you can meet the needs of your clients, all the while using the travel distribution system to your advantage. Never assume there is only one way of doing something. In some cases, that may be true, but in most situations there will always be another way of accomplishing the same goal.

How to make money in travel

When someone creates a travel product — a seven-day Caribbean cruise, for example — they have to decide how much to charge for it. In *extremely oversimplified* terms, they do this by figuring out what it costs them to supply that product (base cost) and then adding an additional sum (gross margin) to arrive at a selling price. Determining gross margin is a tricky business and can mean the difference between success and failure in any business. Set it too high and you will lose sales; set it too low and you will go out of business.

The most important thing to understand is that gross margin does not equal profit. Gross margin is used to pay for many things, including so-called "distribution costs" (commissions to travel agents, among other things). Only after all these things have been paid for can a business even begin to figure out if it has made a profit.

Another thing to bear in mind is that in the travel business things are priced on a unit basis. For example, every cabin on a cruise ship has a retail price. But it is rare that a cruise ship sets sail with every cabin occupied. And the captain can't say to the crew, "We're only half full, so you're only getting half pay." Thus, the gross margin per cabin must be set high enough to cover the fixed costs associated with those unsold cabins.

Another thing to remember is that after "profit" (if any) has been determined, there is another step. The government will want its share in the form of taxes. So a fairly common way for businesses to look at the world is like this:

Base Cost + Gross Margin = Retail Price

(Retail Price x Units Sold) – Cost of Making the Sale – Fixed Costs = Profit (Before Taxes)

Profit – Taxes = Actual Profit (also called "net profit")

People who are new to the business world are sometimes astonished at how high gross margin can be. It is not unusual for a U.S.-based tour operator to price a European tour at two times or more what they pay a European wholesaler. What the casual observer fails to realize is that, after all things are taken into account, — including any commissions paid to travel agents — a supplier's actual "profit margin" can be quite modest.

It follows, then (and this is worth keeping in mind) that the more a travel product changes hands, the higher the price. That's because each reseller must build in "margin" to cover his costs, everything from marketing to the electric light bill.

Disintermediation

Disintermediation is quite the buzz word in today's travel industry. It's just a fancy term for "cutting out the middleman," a phrase with which you are no doubt familiar. When you hear travel industry professionals use the word "disintermediation," the middleman they have in mind most often is the travel agent. The perfect example of this is when the airlines stopped paying travel agents base commissions and tried to drive consumer traffic to their web sites with the promise of lower fares.

But disintermediation cuts both ways. I just mentioned how price increases as a product changes hands. In the flow charts above, I demonstrated some ways in which the home-based travel agent can "disintermediate" various "middlemen" in a travel transaction. It might be a host agency, it might be a tour operator. As your career develops, you should always be looking for opportunities to do your own disintermediation — when it makes sense.

That's the key. Disintermediation for the sake of disintermediation doesn't make a lot of sense. It can be argued (and it has!) that when the airlines cut out travel agents, they didn't appreciate the consequences and wound up shooting themselves in the foot. In many cases, tickets are now being sold for less money than the airline would have received by selling through a travel agent, even after the travel agent's commission was deducted.

So before you jump at a chance to "go direct" and cut out your host agency, do the math. If you can make more money funneling a booking through a host (and often you can), then do it. If you can save a lot of time and hassle by doing so, then you might consider the commission split money well spent. Still, the principle remains valid. The more middlemen in a transaction, the greater the likelihood you are leaving money on the table.

How travel agents are compensated

I have already mentioned commissions paid to travel agencies by suppliers, but there are other ways for travel agents to make money. Let's consider them all.

Commissions

Most of the money earned by travel agents comes in the form of commissions. A commission is a percentage of the total sale that is paid by a supplier to the travel agency making that sale. Notice that I said "travel agency" and not "travel agent." It's an important distinction.

In a storefront travel agency with several travel agents, all monies received as commissions from suppliers are paid to the agency, not to the individual travel agents who work at that agency. The agency then decides how to compensate the agents it employs. Some agents will be paid a straight salary. The agency owner may use the money she received as commission from suppliers to pay that salary, but legally and practically speaking it is still a salary and not commission income. The salaried agent's income remains the same no matter how many bookings he makes.

Some travel agencies use a combination of fixed salary and commissions to compensate their agents. They do this to encourage agents to be more productive. If all agents are on straight salary, the agent selling twice as much as the person sitting next to him might rightly start to think he's working too hard. Adding commissions as an incentive thus makes sense to a lot of agency owners.

Finally, some travel agents are compensated solely on commissions. In the case of a one-person travel agency, the travel agency and the travel agent are one and the same. In larger agencies, the vast majority of commission-only agents are so-called outside agents. We will explore this type of arrangement in greater detail a little later.

The most important thing to remember about commissions is their variable nature. Commissions are stated as a percentage, not a fixed dollar amount. Ten percent of a $1,000 sale is $100, but 10% of a $5,000 sale is $500. Which sale would you rather make? Similarly, a 10% commission on a $1,000 sale is $100, but a 15% commission on that same sale is $150. Which commission rate would you rather have?

Commissions have one overwhelming advantage, especially for the home-based agent but for many storefront agencies as well. When you are selling on a commission basis, it is almost always possible to accept a customer's credit card as a form of payment. That is because you yourself do not need to have the ability to process credit cards (what is called having a "merchant account"). You pass on the customer's credit card information to the supplier. The supplier processes the card and then writes you (or the travel agency) a check for the commission due. Since most customers prefer to pay by credit card, especially for high-ticket items, the advantages for all concerned become rather obvious.

When you are paid on a commission basis, there are two basic ways to make more money: make more sales at the same rate of commission or earn a better commission on the same amount of sales. Generally speaking, it is easier to increase your commission rate than your sales volume. Ideally, you will want to do both — increase sales and the commission you are paid on those sales. This course will teach you how to do both.

Fees

Fees are charged mostly by agents selling airlines tickets. They are a replacement (and a partial replacement, at that) for the commissions that airlines no longer pay. But fees can be charged for other things, like making hotel reservations that pay no commissions, crafting customized itineraries, making restaurant reservations, and so forth.

Unlike commissions, fees are fixed dollar amounts. A travel agency will charge $25 for making, say, an airline booking regardless of the cost of the ticket. Fees typically vary according to the service being performed and, in theory at least, seek to represent a fair price for the agent's time, effort, and expenses incurred in providing the service.

Charging fees creates some practical problems for the home-based agent. Unless you have a merchant account, collecting them can be problematical. There are ways around this problem and we will discuss them in due course.

Buying at "net"

Some suppliers are willing to sell their products to travel agents on a net basis. That is, the price they quote the travel agent is not the "retail price," and does not include a commission for the travel agency or travel agent. The travel agent adds a markup to arrive at the retail price the customer pays. The customer does not know the price the travel agent is paying the supplier.

Buying "at net" is an increasingly common phenomenon in the travel distribution system and one you should pay particular attention to as you design your travel marketing business. The obvious advantage is that you can "set your own commission" or, perhaps more accurately, build in your own gross margin out of which you will realize a profit.

One example of buying at net is consolidator tickets, which are explained in more detail in *Chapter 12: Booking Airlines*. Most consolidator tickets are sold at net (a few pay a fixed commission of 8% or 10%, sometimes more). Since the buying and selling of consolidator tickets is such a simple and straightforward matter any markup is virtually pure "profit" (minus overhead, of course).

Many other travel suppliers are exploring selling to travel agents at net (a phenomenon sometimes referred to as the "merchant model" because that's how most retail merchants operate). If you can find the right product at the right net price you can add a considerable mark-up and still offer a very attractive price to the customer.

Buying at net and selling at a mark-up creates problems similar to those encountered when you are charging fees. Most likely you will have to collect the money due in the form of cash or a check and overcome some resistance from customers who would prefer to pay with a credit card.

Selling add-on services and products

It is possible to supplement your travel agent income by offering products and services that are complimentary to what you are already selling.

One travel agent I know adds value to his business while adding dollars to his bottom line by offering consulting services. Based on his intimate knowledge of Europe, primarily Switzerland and France, he charges his clients $100 an hour to help them plan their vacations. His services involve a great deal of personal attention and consultation, direct negotiations with hotels and other suppliers on the continent, and specific recommendations about restaurants, routes, and sights to see. He even drives his clients to the airport and picks them up when they return.

Of course, he also funnels all the commissionable elements through a travel agency with which he has an affiliation and earns a commission as well. This strikes me as a high-end strategy that will work only when you have developed extremely specialized experience and access to an affluent client base. However, as the industry in general becomes more comfortable with the idea of charging service fees, expect arrangements like this to become more common.

There are other ways to make additional money that even a beginner can implement. For example, you can offer house watching or pet boarding services to people you send on vacation. You can sell them guidebooks or specialty luggage. If you sell a special kind of travel, you can sell them special equipment, such as diving equipment and accessories. And you can charge them a separate fee for certain vacation planning services, even if you can't yet command a fee of $100 an hour.

Very few (if any) storefront agencies do any of these things. Home-based travel agents are limited only by their imaginations. Just make sure that whatever you do complies with local ordinances (pet boarding, for example) and that you have the proper insurance (when driving clients to the airport, for example).

Important points about compensation

Most storefront travel agencies state their size in terms of earnings. "We're a two million dollar agency," they'll say. Wow! They must be doing real well. Well, maybe. That two million refers to gross sales, but since the travel agency is compensated on a commission basis they actually make about 10 percent of that amount (less if they sell a lot of air, more if they sell very little air). So now they're down to about $200,000. Not bad, you might think, but out of that money they have to pay an awful lot of overhead. If the agency has four employees who earn $25,000 a year, that's more than $100,000 right there. More, because there are expenses (like payroll tax) associated with having employees. So when you hear about what storefront agencies are making, take it with a grain of salt.

In a somewhat similar fashion, a lot of home-based agents look at what they put into the bank over the course of the year and think of that as what they "made" that year, as if it were a salary. Not so. What you put in the bank is what a "real" business calls its gross sales. Only when you have deducted all expenses will you know what you really made. When you've finished this course, you will be way ahead of most home-based agents because you will think and act like a "real" business.

There are three main ways to increase your compensation.

- **Sell more.** This course is designed to help you learn how to do just that.
- **Sell smarter.** Increasing your commission level is the easiest and fastest way to boost your income. Remember that if you are earning 10 percent and can raise that rate to 12 percent, you have increased your gross income by 20 percent!
- **Spend less.** That is why this course always tells you the least expensive way to get things done.

How the travel industry is structured

The travel industry is vast. Estimates of the total annual value of the worldwide travel industry start at $400 billion and go up from there. And yet, the travel industry is remarkably unstructured. That's because there are so many different suppliers selling so many different types of products in so many different countries to so many people in so many other countries. It's hard to rein it in. In some ways the modern travel business is remarkably like the marketplaces of the ancient world, a place where merchants and buyers from distant lands gather to trade the humble products and fabulous treasures of their homelands.

In the United States, it is remarkably easy to sell travel. So easy, in fact, that many people have a hard time believing it.

To sell travel in the good old U.S. of A. (Canada, too!) you do not need to pass a test. You do not need a certificate. You do not need to be registered in most states. You do not need a license (except in Rhode Island). You do not need accreditation. You do not need a special number. A lot of people will tell you that you need one or more of these things and they'll be sincere in telling you that. But they are wrong. All you really need is a desire to sell travel and an understanding of how the system works. And that I will give you in this course.

Now, you can get many of these things (numbers, certificates, accreditations, and so forth), and there are good reasons to get many of them, but I want to make it crystal clear that you do not need any of them to get started. You may *never* need any of them. And since I have already promised to help you spend as little money as possible to become a travel agent, I want to encourage you not to get any of these things unless and until you really need them to grow your business.

All that being said, there have been attempts to control the travel industry. Many countries make it illegal to sell travel unless you are the owner or employee of an "accredited" travel agency. The reason given for these laws is that they protect the consumer, but my personal feeling is that they exist to reduce competition and discourage initiative. Even in the United States, some states have thrown up "barriers to entry" in the form of registration fees and the like. These laws may be annoying but they are not a sincere attempt to control who can and cannot be a travel

agent. No one gets turned down as long as they pay up. All the state wants is your money. Think of it as an extortion racket and you'll get the idea.

There have been other, less sinister, attempts to impose some order on the travel industry. That's simply because the industry is so large and complex that it only makes sense for all concerned to try to make it easier to do business.

Suppliers have a need to distribute their products to the broadest possible market. All of them do that directly. You can call up any airline, cruise line, hotel, or car rental agency and make your own arrangements. But few suppliers are satisfied with that level of business. Indeed, few could survive on just the business they generate through their own efforts.

Travel agencies, then, fill a valuable function for the suppliers by going out into the marketplace and promoting the suppliers' products to the general public. They also collect fares and other fees from the passengers they book. And they do all this for free! Free, that is, until they actually make a booking. Then they expect the supplier to pay them, ideally in the form of a commission.

What seems on the face of it to be a very simple relationship between the travel agency and the supplier is actually very complex. The suppliers, on the one hand, want the agent to deal honorably and professionally with the traveling public. They don't want their products and services misrepresented. They also want to make sure that the money collected by the agent on their behalf is actually received by them. The agents for their part want to make sure that their commissions are disbursed in a timely and accurate fashion.

As agencies grow, they seek to differentiate themselves from other agencies by negotiating better commission deals with certain suppliers, which then become "preferred suppliers." This adds another layer of complexity. Add to all this the sheer number of suppliers and travel agencies and you begin to see why it was imperative that some order be imposed on the industry.

Over the years, the industry — suppliers and agents, sometimes working together, sometimes working at odds — have created a system (or more accurately a network of systems) that regulate the way business is done. The result is that most suppliers will not deal with just anyone who tells them he or she is a "travel agent." They want some reassurance that this person really is a "travel agent" — as opposed to someone who only wants a 10 percent discount on his own travel! The ways in which you can "prove" that you are a travel agent are getting easier and more numerous these days, but most suppliers will ask that you jump through at least a few hoops before they will do business with you.

Of course, sometimes it's more difficult than others, especially when dealing with airlines. A number of organizations have been created to serve as buffers and conduits between the airlines and the travel agencies. They help assure the suppliers that the agents they deal through meet minimum standards of professionalism and fiscal responsibility. The agents, on the other hand, receive some assurance that they will get paid for their efforts and that their role as middlemen will be recognized and promoted.

And both parties are assured that there is a system in place to regulate their dealings with one another.

One result of this informal network of systems that has developed over the years is that the major suppliers (the airlines mostly) will not deal with any agency that doesn't have an "appointment" with or is not "accredited" by the proper industry entity. I use the word "entity" because these groups include industry associations, independent for-profit companies, and some that seem to fall in between. The ways in which these entities interact and overlap can be maddeningly confusing. The terms used to refer to them are equally confusing. I will try to unravel some of this confusion.

The Airlines Reporting Corporation (ARC)

The Airlines Reporting Corporation, or ARC, was created by the Air Transport Association, an industry group comprising the major domestic airlines, but it is now a separate entity. All airlines, domestic and international, can benefit from ARC's services. Very few opt out of the system.

That system is a highly complex and sophisticated financial clearinghouse operation called the Area Settlement Plan. It's a bank-like system that handles the flood of money going from the point of sale (travel agents) to the airlines. It also handles a trickle of money going in the opposite direction (service fees, refunds, and every great once in a while a commission payment). ARC acts as a sort of independent middleman charged with the fiduciary responsibility of making sure that everyone in the travel product distribution system gets what's owed them. ARC oversees the movement of the billions of dollars involved in buying and selling airline tickets for 135 carriers and about 23,000 agencies.

For all practical purposes, only travel agencies that participate in this system can sell airline tickets; there are a few exceptions (see *Chapter 12*), but they just prove the rule. To participate in this system and sell the vast majority of airlines, then, a travel agency must request an appointment from ARC and meet its stringent eligibility requirements. Among the most important are:

- ▪ *Bonding.* To make sure the airlines are protected from default by the agency, ARC requires the posting of a bond or letter of credit, which can range anywhere from $20,000 to $70,000.
- ▪ *Experience and certification.* ARC requires each agency location have at least one full-time employee with two years' of industry experience and standing as a "Certified ARC Specialist." In other words, no beginners (although a beginner who wanted to open an agency could hire someone with the proper credentials).

There are many other requirements, including stringent security requirements for handling and storing ticket stock, but those are the major ones for the purposes of our present discussion. One thing this course is *not* about is becoming an ARC-appointed agency.

When an agency has been appointed by ARC, it receives a unique eight-digit identification number drawn from the IATA database (see below), sometimes misleadingly called "the ARC number," which is attached to all its transactions with ARC and separates its bookings from the bookings of all other travel agencies.

By the way, ARC prefers to be referred to as "A-R-C" (three separate letters) and not "arc."

The International Air Transport Association (IATA)

The International Air Transport Association, or IATA, is another industry association of airlines, this time international ones. It is the international equivalent of the Air Transport Association (ATA).

Among the important things that IATA does is to administer the system of codes that are used to identify the world's airports and airlines. New airlines and new airports apply to ATA or IATA to be issued a code. (An airline doesn't have to be a member of ATA or IATA to get one.) These codes are used in every global distribution system (GDS) and make the easy, electronic booking of airline tickets possible. IATA also administers the system whereby travel agencies are identified via the unique, eight-digit code mentioned above. The number ARC uses is drawn from a database maintained by IATA. It is, therefore, an IATA number. Numbers drawn from this IATA database are also used to identify travel agencies in countries where ARC does not operate. That is why the terms "ARC number" and "IATA number" are often used interchangeably. And just as the Air Transport Association begat ARC, IATA begat IATAN.

The International Airlines Travel Agent Network (IATAN)

The International Airlines Travel Agent Network, or IATAN, was originally established as a wholly-owned, but technically and legally separate subsidiary of IATA. Or, to be more precise and even more confusing, it was the "operating name" of something called the Passenger Network Services Corporation, which was a wholly-owned subsidiary of IATA. It was created to manage IATA's relations with travel agents in the United States and operates only within the United States.

The arm's-length arrangement between IATA and IATAN was designed to avoid any possible conflict with U.S. anti-trust laws. In 2005, however, after IATA decided there really were no anti-trust concerns, this legal fiction was abolished and IATAN became what it always really had been — just another department of IATA.

Although the acronyms IATA and IATAN stand for very different things, there has long been a tendency within the industry to use them interchangeably. Only by careful examination of the context in which they are used (or by asking the person using them) can you know for sure which entity is being referred to. In fact, to many people in the industry, IATA and IATAN are the same thing. Now that IATAN is a department of IATA, you might think that, at long last, they really *are* one and the same thing. That's not quite how IATA sees it, however. Largely for marketing purposes, IATA prefers that people in the industry continue to think of IATA and IATAN as separate entities.

Like ARC, IATAN endorses or "appoints" travel agencies, but in a different sense and for different reasons. Like ARC, IATAN wants to maintain the financial integrity of the industry, so its appointed agencies must meet fairly strict financial standards (a $25,000 net worth and $20,000 in working capital). IATAN agencies must also operate commercial premises, like ARC agencies.

Unlike ARC, IATAN embodies a marketing component. Member agencies can display the IATAN logo on their stationery and in their windows. It's sort of a Good Housekeeping Seal of Approval for the travel agent industry. The idea is that IATAN membership serves as a sort of guarantee to the public that the agent is professional and reliable.

Another small but important function of IATAN, and one that has received a lot of industry attention in recent years, is that it issues ID cards to agents who work at or with IATAN agencies. The card is not issued automatically and there is no requirement that all agents in IATAN agencies have the ID card. The ID card has become important, however, because more and more suppliers are announcing that they will accept the IATAN card, and only the IATAN card, as proof that an individual is a travel agent. (See *Chapter 10: Straight Talk on Travel Industry Benefits*.)

IATAN has no system to parallel ARC's Area Settlement Plan. IATAN-appointed agencies in the United States simply avail themselves of ARC's services to settle accounts with the airlines.

Cruise Lines International Association (CLIA)

The cruise industry does not have a system that parallels the ARC Area Settlement Plan nor the ARC or the IATA system of appointments. Most cruise berths are booked and paid for well in advance. Fares and schedules don't change with anything like the frenzied pace seen in the airline industry, and cruise lines will have dozens of ships to an airline's hundreds of planes. So sorting out commissions is not such a problem. And if an agency is already appointed by ARC or IATAN, the cruise lines have a high level of assurance that it is reputable.

There are, however, a growing number of "cruise-only" and "cruise-oriented" agencies which, as their names imply, specialize in selling cruises and little or nothing else. Most cruise-only agencies have a relationship with an ARC agency to take care of the odd airline ticket. But for the most part, they deal exclusively with cruises and directly with the cruise lines. In theory, anyone can declare him or herself a cruise-only agent and start dealing directly with the cruise lines. Most, however, join CLIA.

CLIA is a marketing association of cruise lines. Through aggressive advertising, it sells the concept of cruising to the public at large. It also offers educational seminars for agents designed to teach the skills and techniques needed to sell the cruise experience effectively. By taking CLIA courses, you can become an "accredited" CLIA agent. The cost of membership is modest and the training you receive can make the difference between a successful cruise-only operation and an ignominious flop.

CLIA does not "appoint" travel agencies in the same sense that ARC appoints them, but it does issue CLIA numbers, which look and act a lot like IATA numbers, although they aren't.

By joining CLIA, you can display the CLIA logo on windows and stationery and call yourself "a CLIA agency." CLIA membership is increasingly required by cruise lines if you want to deal with them directly. Membership will also make it easy to deal directly with most tour operators, an increasing number of hotels, and even a few small airlines.

The ARC/IATA/IATAN/CLIA number

So to summarize, "ARC number" and "IATAN number" are really misnomers for the "IATA number." The CLIA number looks and acts like an IATA number, but isn't really. What all of these numbers do is serve as unique numerical identifiers that not only identify travel agencies as travel agencies but distinguish between travel agencies with the same or similar names in different locations.

When you hear people say that you need such-and-such a "number" before you can sell travel, this is what they are talking about. And they are wrong even if they believe in good faith that they are right.

Here's what is true. If a *travel agency* wants to sell airline tickets, it must have an ARC appointment (and, therefore, an ARC/IATA number). It is only in this very limited sense that a "number" is needed to sell travel. If *you* want to sell airline tickets, you do not need an ARC appointment or a number, just a relationship with an agency that does have these things.

These numbers then are primarily about identifying travel agencies rather than keeping people out of the travel business. The IATA number is the most widely recognized; next is a CLIA number. But you can still sell travel even if you don't have one of these numbers, as you will learn in the coming chapters.

Of course, there are times when having an IATA number makes a lot of sense for a one-person travel agency (which is what you will be when you've completed this course). If you really, really want your own IATA number, you can get one. And without paying the big bucks and making the major financial commitment of becoming an ARC-appointed storefront agency. That is an advanced concept I discuss in the Special Report, *How to Get Your Own IATA Number*. If you purchased this book as part of my home study course, you already have it. If not, you can order it at:

http://www.HomeTravelAgency.com/getiata.html

Other ways in which the travel industry is structured

So far I have tried to reassure you that there is no Big Brother out there trying to limit the number of people who can be travel agents or prevent you from becoming one. The entities I have discussed here are all perfectly rational and welcome attempts to impose some sort of order on the industry and are the only ones that in any way create barriers to selling travel. And as we have seen they are not really barriers at all, except to the uninformed. If you have any lingering doubts, they will evaporate as you proceed through the course.

Of course, there are other ways in which the travel industry is structured. There are professional associations that seek to bring various segments of the industry together for their mutual benefit. As a travel agent, you should have a basic familiarity with a few of them. The American Society of Travel Agents (ASTA) and the Association of Retail Travel Agents (ARTA) represent the world of full-service storefront agencies. The National Association of Cruise Oriented Agencies (NACOA) does the same for cruise-oriented agencies. The Outside Sales Support Network (OSSN) addresses the needs of home-based agents, both those working as outside reps for storefront agencies and those who are completely independent.

You do *not* have to be a member of any of these organizations to sell travel, although I recommend that you join OSSN for the considerable benefits and learning opportunities membership confers.

There are many, many other professional associations that represent various segments of the supplier community. They can be a valuable source of information.

You will find a complete list of travel industry associations in *The Travel Agent's Complete Desk Reference*. If you purchased this book as part of my home study course, you already have it. If not, you can order it at:

http://www.HomeTravelAgency.com/deskref.html

Summary

Travel is as old as the human race and helping travelers meet their needs has a long and proud history.

As big and as complicated as the travel industry is, there are remarkably few barriers to entry for those who wish to sell travel in the United States and Canada. There have been attempts to impose some order on the free for all that is the travel marketplace, but these efforts have had more to do with making sure things proceed smoothly than with keeping the travel distribution system closed to entrepreneurs like you.

It is extremely easy to participate and earn money in the travel distribution system. Those who tell you that you can do so only with difficulty and only with expensive "accreditation" and "licensing" may be well meaning, but they are wrong. You do not need a special "number" or expensive training to be a travel agent. All you need is an understanding of how the system really works and how to use that knowledge to your advantage.

Action steps

Here are some things you can do to put what you have learned in this chapter into action:

- To learn more about the history of the travel industry, read *Travel Agents: From Caravans and Clippers to the Concorde* by Eric Friedheim (New York: Universal Media, 1992). The

Home-Based
Travel Agent

book is out of print but may be available through your local library or on the Internet.

- Visit the following web sites to learn more about the organizations mentioned in this chapter:

The Airlines Reporting Corporation (ARC)
www.arccorp.com

International Air Transport Association (IATA)
www.iata.org

International Airlines Travel Agent Network (IATAN)
www.iatan.org

Cruise Lines International Association (CLIA)
www.cruising.org

Outside Sales Support Network (OSSN)
www.ossn.com

To join OSSN at a discount, download an application at:
www.HomeTravelAgency.com/ossnapp.pdf

Chapter Two:
Defining Yourself

What you will learn

After you have completed this chapter you will be able to:

- Name several distinct forms your travel business can take.
- Distinguish among referral agents, outside agents, independent agents, and independent agencies.
- Explain the crucial difference between storefront travel agencies and your new home-based business.
- Start the process of defining your new travel marketing business.

Key terms and concepts

This chapter involves the following key terms and concepts:

- There is no one "best" way to sell travel. You have a range of options in defining the form your travel selling business takes. Keep your options open.
- Referral agents do not actively book and sell travel. Their job is to steer customers to the inside agents at a travel agency who make the actual sale.
- Outside agents for a host agency are independent contractors who handle all the details of booking and selling travel. They are compensated by a share of the commission due the host agency.
- Unlike storefront agencies, home-based travel agents are free to decide what they are going to sell and to whom.
- Defining your business in terms of what you sell can be one of the most important decision you will make in your travel selling career.

PART I: *What Do You Sell?*

So far we have been talking about the mechanics of the travel business — how the travel industry works, how it is structured, the different ways in which you, as a home-based entrepreneur, can sell travel. We'll be talking more about that shortly. But before we do, I want to encourage you to start thinking about a decision I can't make for you, one that only you can make and one that is of crucial importance.

Just as important as *how* you sell — even more important to your success, perhaps — is *what* you sell. I urge you to read this section carefully and take its message to heart. Defining your business in terms of what you sell and to whom may be the most important decision you make. You don't have to make it right this minute and whatever decision you do make can be modified, adapted, or even changed completely later on. Even so, it's a good idea to start thinking about this important issue from the very beginning.

So just what is your home-based travel business all about? At first, you may think that you will be, indeed should be, just like any other travel agent in town. That's because you're familiar with the model of the "traditional" travel agency. Let's take a moment to examine that model and figure out why it is the way it is.

The "traditional" travel agency is a storefront operation. It's down there on Main Street, in a building made of bricks and mortar. (In today's travel industry, "bricks and mortar" is another way of referring to traditional storefront travel agencies.) There are maps and colorful posters in the windows and a few black-and white flyers taped to the glass touting "super" deals to special destinations. Without having to say so in any concrete way, the traditional travel agency sends out a very clear message to anyone who walks by: "Here I am, ready to take on all comers! No matter where you want to go, no matter how you want to get there, no matter what you want to do, no matter how long or short your journey, I'm the one to see!"

That's quite a responsibility! If someone walks into this agency and says "I want to fly upstate and back," the travel agent isn't going to say, "Sorry, there's not enough money in that ticket to make it worth my while." If someone walks in and says, "I want to go trekking in Bhutan," the travel agent isn't going to say, "Gee, I don't even know where Bhutan is." Oh, the storefront travel agent could turn away business; some no doubt do. But most simply can't.

Why? Because a traditional travel agency represents a large financial investment and involves considerable overhead. The agency needs to generate a lot of business every month before it can even begin to think about generating a profit. So there is tremendous financial and psychological pressure to snare every piece of business that walks in the door. Then, too, there is the matter of professional pride. By opening a storefront agency, the owner is saying that he or she is equally capable of serving the short-hop customer and the voyager to exotic locales. That's what being a full-service travel agent is all about!

While operating a traditional storefront agency has its rewards, it also has its problems and perils. Primary among them is, that by taking on all comers, the storefront agency inevitably winds up doing a major portion of its business in cheap airfares. There are a number of problems with this:

- Because the airlines no longer pay base commissions on airline tickets, travel agencies must charge service fees for making airline reservations — fees that often don't cover their costs.
- The fixed costs of processing tickets and reporting to ARC eat into those low fees, and the rent and utilities still have to be paid.
- Purchasers of cheap travel tend to shop around, cancel reservations, change dates, and so forth. Many agencies will absorb any reticketing costs rather than antagonize someone they hope will become a regular customer.
- Airline fare wars produce a flood of passengers who want their tickets rebooked at the new, lower fares. In a fare war, travel agencies can lose money on every single ticket they rebook, although most now charge fees to protect themselves.
- The amount of money earned for the amount of time invested is often negligible when selling cheap travel. By the time a customer hems and haws about dates, has the agent check ten different carriers searching for a cheaper fare, books, changes his mind and alters the dates, the travel agent's $25 service fee will seem paltry indeed. It can take the same amount of time to help a client select and book a cruise that will pay several hundred dollars in commissions.
- Many industry observers point to the problems associated with selling cheap travel as the primary reason for the high mortality rate among traditional storefront travel agencies.

Avoiding the cheap-travel trap

One of the best things about being a home-based travel agent is that you are not bound by the expectations and restrictions placed on a traditional travel agency. As an independent operator, you can avoid the cheap-travel trap by simply not selling airline tickets, except under certain very specific conditions.

In practice, that's easier said than done, especially by the beginner who doesn't yet have a following or a readily defined area of specialization. When you're just starting out, most of your first prospects will be family, friends, and neighbors who will have a need precisely for the kind of cheap air transportation I've just been talking about. You also may find that some of your customers will want to "try you out" with a simple plane booking or two before they trust you with putting together that African safari. Finally, you'll probably find that it's hard to turn down the chance to make your first booking, no matter what it is.

(Still, I urge you to just say "No") when friends ask you to sell them a cheap domestic airline ticket. If you can't bring yourself to do that, you can take the booking if you have a relationship with a host agency. Just don't expect to make any money.

There actually are some circumstances in which selling air can make financial sense, even for beginners. Also, as your business grows (and depending on your area of specialization), you may find that you have reached a volume of business where adding air into the mix makes sense. I will discuss all this in *Chapter 12: Booking Airlines*.

As you gain more firsthand experience with your new travel agent business, you will have to make your own decision about how much or how little air you will sell. Many very successful home-based agents never sell an airline ticket. Others make a decision to sell air sometimes, but they do not actively solicit air-only business and are very choosy about the requests to which they respond.

The important point to remember here, however, is that there is a fundamental difference between you and the storefront agency. While they pretty well have to accept any and all business that walks through the door, you have the choice of going out into the community and seeking only the kind of business that you want — business that will offer a high payback for the time and effort you invest.

The advantages of specialization

The more you adopt an "all things to all people" stance in the marketplace, the more likely you are to fall into the cheap-travel trap. And by trying to do *everything* you may never become truly good at *anything*. A storefront agency can assign different travel agents to become familiar with particular areas, but a home-based agent doesn't have that luxury. The best way to prevent problems like this from arising is to define yourself as a "specialist." By doing so, you do not necessarily cut yourself off from all other areas of the travel business, but you do provide a focus — both for yourself and your clients. By specializing, you make it easier for yourself, since it takes less time to gain an in-depth knowledge about one destination or mode of travel than about dozens. At the same time, you provide your potential customer with a convenient way to remember you — "Oh, yes, she's the one who books all those wonderful cruises!"

Businesses of all kinds specialize, and even businesses that seem very specific indeed have further specialized within their own market niches. It's called "positioning" by the MBA marketing types and it works like this: Cadillac and Harley-Davidson both sell something that will get you from point A to point B. But the similarity ends there. Harley-Davidson specializes in motorcycles. But saying that doesn't mean to imply that a chopped hog from Harley and a rice-burner from Kawasaki are one and the same vehicle. That's because Harley-Davidson has "positioned" itself very precisely in the marketplace. Their products appeal to a different kind of person and for different reasons than do Kawasaki's sleek racing models.

The fascinating thing about positioning is that, whether you are aware of it or not, you will "position" yourself in your travel business. Over time, the people who deal with you will develop a "picture" of your business in their minds, just as they have a picture in their minds about what Harley-Davidson represents to them. Since you're going to be positioned anyway, why not spend a little time thinking about it?

You may survey your available options and choose to specialize from the beginning of your travel selling career. Or you may begin to specialize gradually as you feel your way to your niche in the travel business. However you do it, the key to specialization is knowledge — you gain an in-depth familiarity with your area of specialization through a combination of study and experience. That means you become better equipped to advise your clients, offer them a wider range of options, alert them to great deals, or warn them of things to steer clear of. But specialization has another, equally important, benefit: You increase your earning power! That's because you work more efficiently. Someone who knows all the ins and outs of booking a scuba holiday will earn their $200 or $300 or $400 commission a lot faster than the person who is making this kind of booking for the first time.

Moreover, by specializing you increase the viability of charging fees for your services. When you are obviously knowledgeable it is easier for the customer to perceive value.

There are any number of ways in which you can specialize:

By destination

I know of a woman who specializes in Ireland. Even though she sometimes ventures to other destinations in Europe, it is her firsthand knowledge of the Emerald Isle that enables her to differentiate herself from the major tour operators by providing the kind of very special, off-the-beaten path experiences that the majors just can't match.

I know of an outside rep for a New England agency whose specialty is European FITs (that stands for "Foreign Independent Tours") with an accent on budget travel. If that sounds like she's limiting herself, think again. Europe is a huge market for the vacation traveler and the choices are so mind-boggling that keeping on top of all the changes is more than a full-time job. In exchange for her efforts, she has made herself an expert in one of America's favorite vacation destinations — Europe — a destination that is a natural for many people in her area. She is also building, I am sure, a steady referral business.

Or maybe you live somewhere special. One of my students lives in Hawaii and opened his own independent agency specializing in — you guessed it — Hawaii. Through the Internet, he reaches people around the U.S. and around the world. Because he's on the spot, he knows the resorts and beaches like the back of his hand. He does very well.

Do you have a favorite destination? One you'd like to get to know better? One you love so much that every time you describe it, your friends start thinking, "Gee, maybe I should go there"? Then you may have found a profitable area of specialization. It's a lot easier to sell a destination you

Defining Yourself

know and love than one you've only seen in travel brochures.

Of course, as a destination specialist you will have to make frequent trips to the area to check out the hotels, attractions, and tourist bureaus, to keep up-to-date on your market. It's a tough job, but someone has to do it.

By mode of travel

The most obvious example of this kind of specialization is the proliferation of cruise-only agencies. These are storefront operations that are just like any other travel agency office, except that all they sell are cruise vacations. There's no reason why you can't have the same kind of business, operating from your home.

Cruises have a lot going for them from the agent's point of view:

- They are a relatively high-ticket item (although they represent excellent value for the traveler). You should earn several hundred dollars on every cruise booking you make.
- They represent a well-defined, well-promoted market — you have those glitzy commercials on television selling for you!
- They generate repeat business. While a lot of people profess to hate cruises, the people who like them are very loyal. Eighty-five percent of people who take one cruise, take another, and that kind of repeat business is the key to a very profitable business.
- The cruise lines help you sell them. Cruise lines (at least the big ones) are very savvy marketers. They will provide you with all sorts of sales support, including video tapes to show to clients.

Cruises aren't the only way to specialize by mode of transportation. I know of a gentleman on Long Island who, as an outside rep and independent contractor, specializes in motorcoach tours, an extremely popular mode of leisure travel among seniors. Or you might be a person who just loves trains. Many train lovers will travel far and wide to re-create the kind of romantic journeys that are a thing of the past here in the States but can still be found in Europe (the Orient Express!), India, and Latin America.

By theme or activity

Another way to focus your travel marketing is by what your customers do when they get to wherever it is they are going. In this kind of specialization, the destination is almost secondary; it is the activity that takes priority. Here are some examples of specialization by activity:

- ***Skiing.*** Avid skiers get tired of skiing in the same old place. Once they get bored with Killington, they want to ski the Rockies and the Alps. If they're real fanatics, they'll head south of the equator so they can ski in the summer. There is a burgeoning industry of ski-oriented tour operators to serve this market.
- ***Golf.*** Golfers are an easily identified and targeted group that can be lured with the prospect of playing PGA-rated courses

in the Caribbean or the spectacular holes of Hawaii, or the legendary links of Scotland.

- **Scuba diving.** This is another activity that has spawned a mini-industry of specialty tours. Once people get hooked on diving in the Keys, they want to dive The Bahamas and explore the great reefs off Belize. Sooner or later they'll get a hankering to swim with the great whites of Australia's Great Barrier Reef.

- **"Alternative travel."** This is a catch-all phrase that is used to describe a grab-bag of vacation options that are outside the mainstream. That could mean a white-water rafting trip in Borneo, a three-week trek through the valleys of Nepal, or a month working on an archaeological dig in Israel. Environmentally sensitive "eco-travel," which focuses on indigenous cultures and nature treks, is also growing in popularity. This is a small but growing segment of the travel market and, despite its countercultural tinge, it is definitely not cheap travel. There are good commissions to be made here.

- **Pilgrimages.** There are a limited number of destinations throughout the world (Lourdes, Fatima, Israel, Mecca, and others less well-known) that attract a steady stream of religious travelers. The consumers for this type of travel are also easily reached through religious organizations.

And these are only a few of the options. It seems that, today, there is a tour for every interest — tennis players, opera buffs, nudists, whatever, you can find a place to send them. The key to succeeding with this type of specialization is a sincere interest in and knowledge of the activity or theme involved. I should also point out that some areas of specialization might prove to be limiting. If you live in rural, heavily Mormon Utah, for example, you may find the market for pilgrimages to Catholic shrines quite tiny, although with the Internet you might still be able to make a go of it.

By market segment

Some travel agents concentrate quite profitably on certain types of customers rather than on destinations or activities. Usually, this means serving the special needs and interests of specific (and easily identified) segments of the population. Catering to mature travelers or to families traveling together are just two obvious possibilities. Here are some additional examples of this type of specialization:

- **The disabled.** There is a growing market for travel and tours geared to the special needs of the disabled. As the options for leading a full and productive life have expanded for the disabled, so has their disposable income, and the disabled are just as keen to visit the great cities of Europe or ride on an elephant's back as anyone else. Many people are finding a profitable niche (and a lot of goodwill, too) by serving this market.

- *Recovering alcoholics.* These travelers also have special needs and tend to respond to the idea of traveling in groups. After all, it's easier to avoid temptation on a cruise if it's a "dry" cruise with other former tipplers. Many tours for this market include special support activities. Again, as with so many other special interest areas, there are a growing number of tour operators offering tours targeted to this market.
- *Religious groups.* This is another market with special, but often overlooked, needs. They may travel to Europe this year and Australia the next, but they will respond to the travel agent who appreciates that they are looking for an experience and an ambiance that resonates with their strongly held beliefs.
- *Sports buffs.* There is a tremendous market in sports-oriented travel. Golf and ski tours and dive travel are the most obvious examples, but sports travel is not just for active participants. People travel to see Spring Training in Florida or for the Super Bowl, too. You don't need to be a skier to specialize in ski tours, I suppose, but the closer you are in spirit to your customers the better able you will be to market to them.
- *Budget, or mid-range, or luxury travelers.* People are also defined by the amount of money they can afford to spend on their travel. Depending on where you are located and the kind of access or exposure you have in your market, you may find it most profitable to pursue the budget traveler. Or you might find a better fit selling mid-range tours and cruises. Or you could choose to address the luxury market and sell upscale vacations to the wealthy. By the way, don't make the mistake of thinking that you can't sell to the country-club set just because you are not one of them.

By payback

It may seem crass, but some agents like to go where the money is. We may be talking now more of a subspecialty than a specialty, or perhaps it's more accurately referred to as a marketing strategy. In either case, there are a number of ways in which the bottom line can determine where you focus your efforts.

If you become an outside agent, the host agency with which you affiliate will no doubt have a number of "preferred suppliers." These could be the members of a consortium to which the agency subscribes or suppliers with whom the agency has some sort of one-to-one relationship. If you decide to become an independent agency, you can still join some consortiums. The net result is the same: higher commissions.

It makes perfect economic sense to concentrate on selling the tour products of these preferred suppliers. For example, you can book an air and hotel package to a Caribbean resort through one of your host agency's preferred suppliers and earn 10.5% commission (assuming you receive 70%

of the 15% this supplier offers your host agency). Or you could book exactly the same package through another tour operator and earn only 7% (70% of 10%).

If you examine the offerings of a host agency's preferred suppliers, you may find that you will have a very nice "product line" to offer your customers. It will be rather like having a clothing store and choosing to carry only certain brands. The difference, of course, is that if your customer doesn't want what your preferred suppliers have to offer or if the preferred supplier offerings aren't right for your customer, you are free to sell them something more appropriate.

You may discover through experience that you can sell more of certain travel products — and sell them with greater ease — than others. That should tell you that you could increase your volume if you concentrated on those products. Higher volume, of course, means more money for you. Which products will turn out to be "winners" for you is impossible for me to predict. That will depend on a complex mix of your expertise and enthusiasm, the demographics of your market, and sheer luck. But once those winners emerge, you may want to consider the implications carefully to see if there's an opportunity you're missing.

Another way of letting the bottom line guide your business is to concentrate on the upper-income market segments. You could sell a wide variety of destinations and types of travel but specialize in luxury. Every doctor, lawyer, dentist, corporate VP, and stockbroker in your area takes vacations, and the vacations they take tend to be more glamorous than most. What's more, all the doctors, lawyers, dentists, and stockbrokers are listed in the Yellow Pages (the corporate types are harder to find), so they are an easily targeted audience.

By focusing on groups

No area of specialty offers a better promise of high payback than group travel. That means that instead of sending a couple on a trip, you send a dozen people, or 20, or 50. There are all sorts of groups that travel together — church groups, high-school reunion classes, college groups, fraternal organizations, the list goes on.

Here's where your commissions can be truly gratifying. If sending a couple to Europe nets you $400, imagine what sending 50 people there will pull in! It will likely be more than $400 times 25. Why? Because you'll undoubtedly get a bigger commission for bringing in a large group.

Sometimes you can find groups that remain pretty constant from year to year. For example, one part-timer I know services a group of students and faculty from Indiana that comes to New York once a year for a week of theater going. Then there's a women's club in New York that sponsors a trip to London just about every year. The faces change from year to year, but there's always a bunch of people traveling.

Groups like that can form a good base for your group business. But to really succeed, you'll have to beat the bushes for accounts. That can mean a slow and painstaking process of contacting potential groups, locating the right person to deal with, proposing some kind of group experience,

and working closely with your inside contact to promote and market the idea to the membership.

The other way of selling group travel is to select a travel experience (a cruise or tour, most likely), negotiate a "group rate" with the supplier based on the number of people you commit to selling, and then go out and promote the trip to everyone you can think of.

Selling to groups is fundamentally different from the onesy-twosy kind of travel bookings that most home-based agents do. For one thing, you won't find 20 people walking up to you and saying, "Oh, you're a travel agent? We'd like to go on a safari." No, you have to go and seek them out. That makes selling group travel a very specific type of sale.

By focusing on corporate travel

"Corporate travel agencies" are a special niche in the travel industry. These are agencies that operate out of modest offices in high-rise buildings rather than from storefronts. They don't deal with the general public (for the most part). Companies are their clients, not individuals. They make their money by serving all the travel needs of a business — booking air and hotels and rental cars for the client company's personnel when they travel on business. They usually offer their client companies lower fares, in effect rebating a portion of their commission, hoping to make their money on the increased volume. This type of business is heavy on domestic air travel, demands an encyclopedic knowledge of fare structures, requires its practitioners to play the GDS like Horowitz played the piano, and is fiercely competitive.

I don't think most of the people who will read this book have a prayer of competing in this marketplace as outside reps. That doesn't mean you have to turn your back on corporate marketing completely, however. If you stumble onto a chance to "sell" a corporate account, pursue it. In *Chapter 4: The Outside Sales Rep*, I describe how you can make money by bringing a corporate customer to an agency (perhaps your host agency) that specializes in handling that kind of business.

Creating a mix of specialties

If you specialize at all, you will most likely wind up mixing and matching among these various alternatives. You might focus on luxury travel to Latin America, thus specializing in both a destination and a market segment. Or if you specialize in activity-based travel, you may find yourself in the group business since birds of a feather, after all, flock together.

It is this tendency of people of like interests to flock together that produces another advantage of specializing — your customers are easier to reach. If you are selling luxury cruises, you can make some generalizations about your customer base — they are well-to-do, for example. It's relatively easy to figure out where the well-to-do live in your community. You also don't have to be a rocket scientist to figure out that doctors and lawyers tend to be more well-to-do than most. Or perhaps you may discover that your best customers are senior citizens. If so, you'll know that well-to-do seniors are people you want to contact.

Knowing all this, it is possible to get lists of these people's names and addresses. Doctors and lawyers are in the Yellow Pages, remember? And consumer mailing lists broken down by zip code are available as well, though often for a price. It is also a relatively easy matter to identify the upscale retirement communities within a 50-mile radius of your base of operation. Now you can begin a proactive campaign to drum up interest in your target market, instead of waiting for someone to come up to you at a cocktail party and say, "Gee, I'd sorta like to take a luxury cruise."

A final thought on specialization

There are some very sound financial and marketing reasons to specialize, but I would encourage you to think with your heart as well as your head. My experience has been that the people who succeed in their specialties have a certain affinity for what they are doing. Scuba divers book dive vacations, people who are seriously concerned about the needs of the disabled concentrate on that area, people who sell budget travel love to travel that way themselves.

You're probably reading these words because you love to travel. What are your favorite destinations? What do you like to do when you go on vacation? With which segments of your community do you have a particular connection or affinity? Consider these questions as you examine your options in the travel selling game. The answers may point you to a profitable and personally fulfilling definition of your travel business.

Of course, the chances are a lot of you won't specialize immediately or even anytime soon. And some of you may never get around to specializing at all. You might find that booking a cruise this week and then calling dozens of suppliers next week to nail down a specialty tour is part of the fun of the travel game. It's also generally true that the less travel you sell, the more difficult it is to specialize. That's because specializing implies marketing and if you're just going to book a few trips each month for close friends and family, then your business isn't developed enough to think much about marketing. What's more, you're probably relying on walk-up business for the few bookings that come in — just like a storefront agency!

Still, you may find it worth your while to consider some of the options available to you for defining your travel business and positioning yourself in your market. By having an idea of what has worked for others, you can get a better sense of what might work best for you.

PART II: How Do You Sell It?

Where do you fit in?

Your goal as a home-based travel agent is to find your place in the travel distribution system and make some money at it. Most obviously, you would be the "travel agent," as depicted in the diagrams in the previous chapter. For most people, that is the route they will choose to take. But it is also possible for you to be the "travel agency" or even the "supplier," often all at the same time. This course will guide you no matter which path you choose to take.

So let's look at the many ways in which you can find your niche within the travel distribution system.

The not-a-travel-agent

It is very possible to function in the travel distribution system without really being a travel agent, at least in the sense that most people understand the word. You don't have to call yourself a travel agent or make the commitment to be a full-fledged professional travel agent to sell travel and make money.

Often times, the "money" you make this way will take the form of free or discounted travel, but it can also involve earning commissions, even if they go by a different name.

Working at this level typically means forming a relationship, however formal or casual, with someone or some company that *is* part of the travel distribution system — a travel agent or supplier. If you regularly round up a bunch of friends to go on a cruise or take a tour, then you would fall into this category. If you are not earning free travel and perhaps a bit extra doing this, then change your approach.

Another category that belongs here is the "group travel leader." Sometimes these people work alone, calling themselves a "travel club." Sometimes they work for an institution, such as a bank. (Banks found a profitable niche and a good marketing strategy in offering attractively priced trips to depositors.)

You can be as casual or dedicated as you wish with this approach. However, if you are at all serious about making travel more of a business, then you will probably want to use other strategies taught in this course.

In *Chapter 3: Becoming a Tour Organizer*, I will discuss ways of being a travel agent without being a travel agent.

The referral agent

There are two broad categories of travel agent — referral agents and what I call "selling and booking agents." The main difference is that referral agents do very little work, while selling and booking agents do quite a bit of work. As you might suspect, another difference is that referral agents earn a little money, while selling and booking agents can earn a lot.

Referral agents have long been a part of the travel distribution system but they took on added prominence in the early 1990s when some travel agencies ("host agencies") began to aggressively market programs allowing people to become "travel agents" for a fee, typically $495. A big draw for these programs was the "travel agent ID card" they offered their agents. This card was said to open the door to many travel-agents-only discounts and other industry perks.

In *Chapter 5: The Referral Agent*, I will discuss this controversial niche in the travel distribution system.

The independent contractor / outside agent

The next step up in terms of formality is becoming an outside agent for an established travel agency, known in the business as a "host agency." These are the selling and booking agents I referred to earlier. Most home-based agents fall into this category, at least when they are getting started.

Outside agents are generally independent contractors, although they can also be employees. The distinction is important and will be discussed in detail later. This course focuses on independent contractors. Once you understand the principles involved, I think you will understand why it is infinitely preferable to be an independent contractor.

The outside sales agent takes all the responsibility of finding customers, assessing their needs, recommending travel products, closing the sale, making the actual booking, and handling ongoing customer service.

Outside agents are typically compensated by a share of the commission due to the host agency. That share can range anywhere from 20 percent all the way up to 100 percent, although if a host agency is offering 100 percent of the commission, it is also charging per-transaction fees that in most cases effectively lower the outside agent's share to the 70 to 75 percent range. Still, the compensation can be very attractive.

In *Chapter 4: The Outside Sales Rep*, I will discuss the role of the independent contractor as outside agent and the various ways of becoming one.

The independent travel agent

It is also possible to deal directly with suppliers, without going through a host agency. You can do this on a casual basis by establishing informal but mutually profitable relationships on a supplier by supplier basis. I will teach you how to do this and I think you will be surprised at how many suppliers will be willing to work with you on this basis.

Not every supplier will deal with home-based agents in this casual manner, however. They want more assurance that the agent is serious. It is quite easy, and surprisingly inexpensive, to provide suppliers with this assurance by getting your own unique identifying number that is universally recognized in the industry. Also, once you begin dealing with a good number of different suppliers, getting your own number will make establishing new relationships easier and cut down on your paperwork in the bargain.

Most home-based travel agents combine two approaches: working through a host agency when that makes the most sense and dealing directly with a particular supplier when that makes the most sense. However, it is conceivable that you could build a travel agent business from scratch without ever working through a host agency. What's more likely is that, as your business matures, you will find less and less use for your host agency and may decide to drop it altogether. The greater your degree of specialization and the smaller the number of products or suppliers you deal with, the more likely this could happen.

In *Chapter 6: The Independent Agent*, I will discuss the ins and outs of dealing directly with suppliers and help you decide when and when not to do it.

The independent travel agency

Once you get your own IATA number, or other unique industry identifier, you become, as far as the industry is concerned, a travel agency as well as a travel agent. That means you and your spouse can easily work together. It also means you can hire subagents or start your very own network of outside agents. In other words, you can be a host agency in your own right.

Going this route does not necessarily mean you will never funnel business through a host agency. Depending on how you choose to define your business, there may still be occasions on which dealing with a host agency will make a lot of sense.

This advanced strategy is covered in the Special Report, *How to Get Your Own IATA Number*. If you purchased this book as part of my home study course, you already have it. If not, you can order it at:

http://www.HomeTravelAgency.com/getiata.com

Being a supplier

Some home-based agents actually become suppliers, although some of them might not think that's what they are. If you provide travel planning services for which you charge an hourly fee, then you are a supplier. If you charge your vacationing clients to feed their pets, water their plants, and look after their house, then you are a supplier.

It is also possible to locate travel products for which you are the exclusive representative. For example, during your travels you may come across an overseas supplier who offers a specialized tour or who can put one together to your specifications. You can enter into an agreement to sell that product in your country on an exclusive or semi-exclusive basis. If you negotiate a net price for the tour and add sufficient margin (which you will know how to do after completing this course) then you can offer a fair commission to other travel agents. You have, in effect, become a tour operator, albeit on a small scale.

Ideas like this will be discussed in *Chapter 9: Getting Serious*.

Which is right for you?

Fortunately, you don't have to decide right now. In fact, you shouldn't even try. There's a lot more to absorb before you will be able to make an informed decision. For now, the important thing to remember is that you have a number of choices when it comes to defining the shape or form of your business. You can choose one or several of the choices listed above. It all depends on how you choose to define yourself.

So don't jump to any conclusions just yet. Keep your options open and keep reading.

Summary

You have two major choices to make in your travel business: What are you going to sell and how are you going to sell it?

You can feel your way to the answers to these questions by trial and error as your business develops. But you will be far ahead of the game if you make some decisions on these questions as you begin your career. Your decisions do not have to be "carved in stone." You can always change your mind and adapt as you gain more experience, but there's a lot to the old adage, "Plan your work, then work your plan."

In terms of assuring your future success, the most important decision you make about your travel business may be what you are going to sell.

Action steps

Here are some things you can do to put what you have learned in this chapter into action:

- This chapter lists different ways to sell travel (as a referral agent, as an outside agent, and so forth). Make a list of what appeals to you and what doesn't appeal to you about each of them. Try to write down both pros and cons for every one. It doesn't matter that at this point you do not know a lot about these varying modes of defining your business. Base your response on your initial, gut reaction to these methods *as you understand them now*. There are no right or wrong answers. The purpose of this exercise is to get you thinking about what will best suit you as you begin to develop your business.
- Make a written list of your favorite destinations, places you dream of visiting as well as places you have already visited.
- Make a written list of things you like to do in your leisure time; these do not necessarily have to be things you do only on vacation.
- Make a written list of things you know a lot about or are good at. Don't limit yourself to things that obviously have to do with travel (like a foreign language you speak or your knowledge of Mexican history), but include things that may seem to have zero relationship to travel (auto repair, child rearing, electrical engineering, singing in the church choir) just so long as they are things that you good at and, presumably, enjoy doing.
- Make a written list of all the groups you belong to or participate in on a regular basis. That could be everything from your bowling league to your church to the Parent-Teachers Association, to your little theater group.

- Now, put all these lists side by side and see if you can discover ways in which they go together. Do you like to play golf and do you dream of going to Hawaii? What about golfing in Hawaii? Do you love cruising? Maybe you can sell cruises to folks in your church.

- If you and your spouse are going into the travel business together, do these exercises separately and then compare notes. If you are flying solo, so to speak, share your thoughts with someone who knows you well and get their input; they may have some valuable insights to contribute.

- Finally, do some dreaming. Envision yourself as a successful home-based travel agent, no matter how you define success. What does success look like? How does it feel? Where are you traveling? How do people in your community feel about you? Don't be embarrassed to dream big. And make sure you write your dreams down with today's date at the top of the page. No one will see this but you. File it away and revisit it from time to time.

Chapter Three:
Becoming a Tour Organizer

What you will learn

After you have completed this chapter you will be able to:

- Name several ways to sell travel without becoming a travel agent.
- Distinguish between two types of student travel.
- Describe the pluses and minuses of promoting travel on a casual basis.

Key terms and concepts

This chapter involves the following key terms and concepts:

- Tour organizer. People responsible for putting together tours and finding enough people to take them function very much like a travel agent, even if they don't see it that way.
- Student travel. This subspecialty can mean a quick route to free travel for the tour organizer, but it has some special risks.
- People who put together tours and cruises on a casual basis are not realizing the full income potential of what they are doing.

Introduction

As I have already noted, there are people who will tell you that you cannot become a travel agent without specialized training, certifications, licensing, or whatever. Just to prove them wrong, I'd like to spend some time reviewing some activities that have been going on for decades without anyone in the travel industry complaining. The people engaged in these activities, as you will see, operate very much like travel agents. Perhaps the reason their activities have not attracted any great controversy within the travel industry is simply because no one has ever referred to them as travel agents. Many of these people don't think of themselves as travel agents either. Yet if you examine what they do in the context of those diagrams we created in *Chapter 1: A Brief Overview of the Travel Industry*, you will quickly realize that they are middlemen in the travel distribution system and as such they do pretty much what travel agents do — sell travel.

Touring with teens

Want to take a four-week, grand tour of Europe — absolutely free? All you have to do is take six paying teenagers with you.

I have found no quicker way to qualify for free travel than becoming an educational tour organizer. In this highly competitive market, tour operators are more than happy to give you a completely free trip just for signing up as few as six people to take a very moderately priced package tour. One even lets first-time organizers travel free with just five paying passengers. Sign up more than six and you can put money in your pocket. One of the best parts about getting into the travel game this way is that you don't have to be affiliated with a travel agency to do it.

Educational tours are designed for and marketed primarily to high school students, although as one executive of a large educational tour operator told me, "About thirty percent of the people who take these tours are adults who like to travel on programs that provide them with some learning activities or cultural enrichment activities." These aren't classroom tours, he was quick to point out, "but learning on the ground, as it were, in the course of travel."

Generally speaking, here's how the system works. Educational tour operators solicit high school teachers through direct mail campaigns to become recruiters for their tour programs. "Ask any high school teacher," says one educational tour insider, "and they'll tell you they have to shovel out their mail cubby, they get so much stuff from outfits like us."

These programs appeal primarily to teachers of languages or the humanities for whom foreign travel is a natural add-on or extension to their classroom activities. The teacher browses through the thick, glossy catalogs the tour operators send and selects an itinerary that appeals in terms of geography, emphasis, length, and cost. The teacher then contacts the tour organizer to discuss dates. If the teacher shows the potential to recruit a large enough group, the tour operator may tentatively block out a tour just for that school; otherwise, the tour operator may suggest putting two school groups together on the same tour. Generally, there is some negotiation over dates and the composition of the tour, but the tour operators try to do everything they can to accommodate the teacher's preferences.

"It's like putting together the pieces of a puzzle," says a spokesperson for a major educational tour operator. "We have an operations team working out of what we call a 'structure.' We'll have groups from all over the United States picking the same trip. Our London theater tour may have a group of 20 that wants to go on the 17th of April and 45 that want to go on the 18th of April and six that want to go on the 16th of April. That's when we begin to pull the puzzle together. At certain times of the year, where there are strict vacation breaks, we guarantee people that we will not move them more than a certain number of days. In general though, it's dependent on what the demand is, what the air is [i.e., the availability of space on the airlines], what the vacation schedules are; but we maintain high standards in terms of guaranteeing people that they will be able to leave pretty much when they want to."

Once dates have been agreed upon, the teacher, after clearing it with the school, begins to promote the tour to students and their parents, all with the help of marketing materials and how-to guidebooks provided by the tour operators.

To make the tours more attractive to the target audience, they are priced very reasonably. The tour operators can keep the costs down since teenagers can be lodged three to four in a hotel room — something the average adult tourist usually will not tolerate — and because youths qualify for lower admission charges to many sights and attractions. The tours can be made even more attractive to parents (who, naturally, will be footing the bill) by getting participating students to raise some of the money to cover their costs. Tour operators will even help out with fund raising suggestions.

Since teachers are the primary sales force for these tours, the tour operators have made a wise decision to support them with first-rate backup materials. They provide teachers with appropriate color posters to stick up on the school bulletin boards and there are plenty of brochures for the individual tours that teachers can pass along to parents. Most operators in the educational field also provide their teacher-recruiters with detailed instructions on how to market their tours in the school. One operator developed a "Ten-Day Plan" (see below) to guide participating teachers through the process in a structured fashion. Another published a "Teacher Enrollment Handbook." Some tour operators even provide toll-free help lines.

Once the teacher has signed up six kids to take the trip, he or she is qualified to go on the trip free, to serve as the "teacher-counselor." This 6 to 1 ratio is known in the business as the "prorate": one free berth for every six people signed on. After the six-person minimum has been met, the teacher-recruiter begins to earn a "cash stipend" for each additional person recruited. In effect, it's a commission on sales. The amount of the stipend depends on the price of the tour. For example, on a tour priced at $1,600, the teacher might receive a stipend of $150 for each additional person on the tour. If the teacher signs up ten people, the stipend is $600 (4 times $150). Once 12 students have been recruited, the teacher-recruiter becomes eligible for another free berth and many spouses go along on this basis. Or the teacher can elect to take the stipend instead. The teacher who is lucky (or ambitious) enough to sign up 20 participants gets a stipend of $2,100 — in addition to the free trip, of course.

All in all, this is one of the best deals going in the travel business. Consider what the teacher is getting on this $1,600 tour. First there's the free trip for signing up six paying customers. That's the equivalent of a 16.7% commission! After that, the $150 stipend for each additional trav-

eler is the equivalent of a commission of a little over 9%. Not too shabby for what can be a fairly easy sell to a captive audience.

Putting together a school tour

One of the things that makes putting together a school tour fairly easy is the assistance that the tour companies provide in abundance. First, there are the glossy brochures. Printed in full color on thick, shiny stock and professionally designed, they lend instant credibility to your marketing efforts. There are also beautiful posters for school bulletin boards and even videos of the countries to be visited. The last are almost guaranteed to whet the appetites of both students and parents. But perhaps most important of all, the educational tour companies are eager to help you become an accomplished salesperson.

Most tour operators provide short but savvy "manuals" to help would-be teacher-counselors map out an effective marketing program to make their recruiting efforts a success. The advice ranges from the fairly obvious ("Start early!") to the canny ("Do not raise this subject [medical emergencies] yourself as it may make the parents unnecessarily nervous.").

Despite the long lead time — getting the ball rolling in the first week of school is none too early for a Spring trip — the recruitment process can take remarkably little of the teacher's time, as one operator's "Ten-Day Plan" would seem to suggest. In outline, here's how it suggested a teacher proceed, step-by-step, over a period of about a month or two:

Day 1: Order all the material you'll need.

Day 2: Make a general announcement of both the trip and a student meeting in school. Discuss it in class, and hand out catalogs, itineraries, and other particulars.

Day 3: Continue to promote the student meeting. Put up posters, and spread the word among your fellow teachers.

Day 4: Keep up the promotion with more bulletin board announcements, classroom previews, and handouts. Make sure everything's set for the meeting.

Day 5: Hold the student meeting. Prime students to pitch the trip to their parents and get them to attend a parent-student meeting about the trip.

Day 6: Follow up with the kids about the parent-student meeting and mail out personal invitations to each parent.

Day 7: Continue to promote the parent-student meeting and get the meeting set up.

Day 8: Hold the parent-student meeting at which you attempt to gather as many signed applications as possible.

Day 9: Send in the applications you have gathered so far while continuing to push for new sign-ups. Review your progress and consult with the tour operator on next steps and additional tactics.

Day 10: Conduct another parent-student meeting and continue to request sign-ups.

There are even suggested agendas for both the student meeting and the parent-student meeting, sample letters to parents, and tips and pointers to guide you through each step of the process. Sounds simple, doesn't it?

Well, it is on the face of it. But the tour operators recognize that nothing is ever that simple. So there are alternate tactics and backup techniques. One operator suggests casting a wider net to include students from other schools, even adults. Another offers ten ideas for how the class can raise funds to underwrite its trip and yet another brochure lists a dozen outfits that you can turn to for fund-raising ideas and products. There are sample press releases, should you decide to spread the word through the local press. Other operators provide the prospective teacher-counselor with answers to the most commonly asked questions and suggestions for how to deal with parents' concerns. Most companies serving the educational tour market provide similar kinds of materials.

It is hard to imagine a teacher reading through this material and not becoming enthused both about the prospect of free travel on a fun-filled student tour and his or her ability to put together a group and make the fantasy a reality.

It's not just for teachers

High school teachers may be very familiar with the world of educational tour operators. But most people — teachers included — don't know that you don't have to be a teacher, or even a member of the high school's staff, to take advantage of the fabulous opportunities offered by these tour organizations. Anyone with the time, energy, and imagination to go after this very lucrative market can participate.

Of course, there will be some people who will have greater access to this market than others. The principal's secretary, school board members, even the school custodian have firsthand contact with their target market. Clergy and community workers who deal with youths are other likely candidates to become "teacher-counselors." If you are the parent of a high-school student, you have a natural entree to the school administration and may even have a copy of a school directory giving the names and addresses of every parent with a child in the school. But even if you have no "in" whatsoever with your local high school, there is nothing to prevent you from promoting tours to this market — as long as you have the permission of the school authorities.

There is also no rule that says you have to restrict your marketing efforts to one school. If there are three high schools within striking distance of your home, you can promote the tour in all three, thus significantly increasing the chances that you will qualify for the free teacher-counselor slot. Obviously, you would not want to mix apples and oranges in this case — mixing freshmen from School A with seniors from School B on the same tour could very well lead to friction and complaints. With a little common sense and a modicum of effort and imagination, however, there's no reason you can't earn one or two free vacations each year by serving the teen educational market.

These tours are conducted year-round, not just during school holidays. Of course, teachers have the inside track on leading tours during the school year since they are in a better position than you or me to negotiate with the administration to take the kids away from their regular classes for a week or two abroad. Fortunately, there's a way around this limitation because the tour operators are just as happy to arrange a tour for adults as they are for teens! In fact, as I noted earlier, fully 30% of those who take these tours are grown-ups. So if you feel more comfortable putting together a tour for your bridge club than for the local high school, go right ahead.

In principle, organizing an educational tour for adults is no different from organizing one for a school group. However, there are a number of points worth bearing in mind:

▪ Tours conducted for adults will be slightly more expensive than those for the kids. That's due mostly to a daily surcharge for putting the adults in double rooms rather than triples or quads. Typically the daily add-on is about $10 to $20, hardly a princely sum.

▪ These tours are designed for a younger audience, with an emphasis on learning. So if your adult group wants to tour the red light district of Amsterdam or the casinos of London, these tours will definitely not be for them. Still, there is a large adult audience for this kind of "cultural enrichment" experience.

▪ These are not luxury tours. Tour operators keep costs down by booking the less fancy hotels, often in outlying districts. So don't expect the decor of the rooms or the quality of the meals to be the same as those you might have had on your last European tour; that tour was specifically designed for an older, more affluent consumer. You can negotiate with the tour operator for a better class of hotel, at a higher rate, of course. Still, these tours offer great value. As long as the group knows what to expect, there should be few problems.

If you'd like to take things a step further, you can approach a tour operator that specializes in adult tours for the general consumer market. You may be surprised at how readily they will talk with you. The tour operator will work with you to design a custom tour to fit the needs and preferences of your group. You simply sketch out the sort of thing you have in mind and the tour operator will research and price the itinerary. They will also determine the prorate for the custom tour and then set you loose to promote it. Needless to say, you will have to persuade a tour operator that you have a reasonable chance of success in promoting such a customized tour before they will take your proposal seriously.

College tours

If the idea of touring Europe with a gaggle of high school students doesn't appeal, perhaps a week in the sun-drenched fleshpots of Florida or Cancun is more your cup of tea. Or maybe your tastes run more to a week on the slopes with the party-hearty crowd. If so you may be cut out for the college tour market.

This market operates in almost precisely the same fashion as the educational tour market just described. There are, however, some important differences: The target audience is a bit older, a bit rowdier. The prorate is higher, usually one for 15 or 20. The emphasis is on fun and not on (gasp, shudder) educational values. The destinations are almost exclusively resort-area hotels that do not mind being overrun by hordes of college students on Spring or Winter Break. In other words, these are not properties in the luxury or first-class categories. The tours are also not "tours" in the sense that the word is used in the high school market, but "packages," involving just the basics — airfare, transfers, and room. Meals are seldom included, although on ski trips, lift tickets are invariably part of the package.

My personal feeling (and I'm willing to admit that I might be wrong) is that this market offers far fewer crossover marketing possibilities than the educational tour market. Older travelers are far more likely to opt for a European tour of museums and historical sites than a week or two on a beer-can-strewn beach surrounded by collegians in full hormonal cry. Younger, but post-college vacationers can probably find much the same atmosphere in the better equipped singles resorts that cater to them.

In fact, this market is so specific that I would go so far as to say that it works best for college students — as both tour organizers and participants. Still, that's a huge market and this niche offers students an excellent way to get their feet wet and gain some experience and credibility in the travel industry. Collegians are a good market, too. "For one thing, college students like to travel in groups," one former college tour organizer explains. "They take their whole dorm floor, fraternity, club, or whatever, and they'll all go to the same place at the same time."

Standard operating procedure for this market goes something like this: The would-be campus tour organizer picks a specific trip he's interested in promoting. The supplier overprints a standard tour flyer with the organizer's name and phone number and gives him a supply (tour organizers are overwhelmingly male in the college market). The organizer distributes the flyers and promotes the trip on campus. The organizer is also responsible for collecting deposits and final payments. For every 15 trips sold, the supplier provides the organizer with one free trip. If the organizer decides he doesn't want to go on the trip, but would rather have a check, that can usually be arranged. If the organizer cannot sell enough slots to qualify for a free trip, he receives a 5% commission on what he has sold, which can be received in cash or applied to the cost of his trip.

Most college tour organizers opt for the trip rather than the cash. Indeed, it's the lure of earning their passage that draws them to the proposition in the first place.

Another way for college students to take advantage of the opportunities in this market is to serve as a tour liaison. After you've organized and taken a few trips, your experience becomes valuable to the tour company and you can propose yourself as a tour staffer. This means that you accompany the tour and serve as an on-location troubleshooter — track down lost luggage, deal with the hotel on behalf of the group, and so forth. Compensation varies but includes, at a minimum, free travel and lodging.

Becoming a
Tour Organizer

The risks of student travel

While putting together student tours can be a quick and easy entrée into the travel business for someone who is in the right position, student travel has its risks. Because kids sometimes behave like, well, children, they can get themselves in serious trouble. That in turn can lead to lawsuits. Because of this, some established travel agents simply steer clear of student travel.

If you decide to experiment in this area, make sure you come to an understanding with the tour operator involved about your legal liability. They should shield you and hold you blameless in the event of a suit, but make sure. You should also have the parents of any student involved sign a waiver that absolves you of liability if their kid does something dumb — like get drunk and try to jump from a hotel balcony into a swimming pool (it happens).

Most suits against agents are found to be baseless in the courts, but a waiver can go a long way toward protecting you.

Organize a cruise

Perhaps the idea of a museum-hopping tour of Europe or a hectic week on the ski slopes of the Rockies doesn't appeal to you. Perhaps your tastes incline more to leisure and luxury — long, lavish meals, high-rolling casino gambling, and a nightclub or two. Well look no further. The cruise industry has your ticket. Better yet, you can cruise the Seven Seas for free in much the same way you can tour Europe — just by convincing a few like-minded people that your idea of a great vacation is just what they're looking for.

Like their counterparts in the educational and college tour markets, cruise lines are more than happy to have people like you and me supplementing their own sales and marketing efforts. You can put your energy and imagination to work organizing a cruise group just as you would an educational tour. However, there are a number of factors that set the cruise industry's free travel apart from the opportunities we have been discussing thus far.

The price of admission is a bit higher, for one thing. That is, you have to recruit more people before you can sail for free. Captain Bill Miller, CTC (Certified Travel Counselor), is a travel agent and an expert in the cruise business. Bill explains it this way:

> *Most cruise lines give one free cruise fare for every 15 fares sold in group space. This free fare is referred to as a Tour Conductor Pass. The tour conductor fare provides free passage for the group's leader.*
>
> *If you have enough people, your mate will also sail for free. This is how the cruise lines usually figure a group's tour conductor policy:*
>
>> *1 for 15 means the 16th person sails for free.*
>> *2 for 30 means the 31st and 32nd passengers sail free.*

3 for 45 means the 46th, 47th, and 48th
passengers go free!
Note: 3rd and 4th passengers in a quad cabin are not
usually counted towards a tour conductor pass.
Port tax is not included. Everyone must pay this.

Roughly speaking, this is about two and a half times the number of spaces you have to sell to earn free travel with an educational tour. On the other hand, most cruise bookings are for couples, so you're making roughly the same number of sales.

Secondly, the fares you will be promoting to your friends and neighbors when you organize a cruise group are different from the ones you would be quoted if you called up the cruise lines or a travel agent to book passage for yourself and your spouse. You will be promoting "group fares." Group fares represent discounts granted in recognition of the work you are doing in bringing business to the cruise line. Group fares need to be "negotiated" with the cruise line and that is one reason for the third major difference in dealing with the cruise industry:

You must coordinate your cruise-group organizing with a recognized travel agency. Cruise lines depend heavily on travel agents to book their cruises and, while some lines have dabbled in selling directly to the consumer, most do not want to alienate an important constituency by letting you and me steal the travel agent's business. If you approach the cruise line directly, they will tell you to deal through an agent. They might even be able to direct you to an agent in your area. Usually, however, you will have to find one yourself.

Here are Bill Miller's suggestions:

If you're ambitious and ready to organize a group,
you'll need to find a good travel agent. You need an
agent who will teach you good skills. The agent must be
someone whom you will feel comfortable working with.
Visit the travel agencies in your area. Ask them how
they work with group leaders and outside salespeople.

Travel agents welcome potential group leaders, but
past experience has made them careful. Until you prove
yourself, they will probably have a 'show me what you
can do' attitude. New group leaders with limited experi-
ence are rewarded with a tour conductor pass.

It may be that, as a newcomer, you will have to settle for the tour conductor pass alone. (It is roughly equivalent to a 6.6% commission on the 15 fares you have to sell to qualify.) On the other hand, there may very well be a travel agency in your area willing to give you a piece of the commission as well. The travel agency is being rewarded by the cruise line with a commission of 10% or more for all the business you are bringing in. It never hurts to ask for a share of that income. Of course, once you prove your ability to bring in a group, you should demand a split of the commission for any future groups. (By the time you finish reading this book, you will know how to get not only the tour conductor pass but 50% or more of the commission as well, your first time out. But for now, let's assume that you're a complete beginner with no inside knowledge of how the travel business works and no desire to become a full-fledged travel agent.)

Some novice tour organizers see cruise groups as a way of making extra money, regardless of the deal they cut with the travel agent. It is theoretically possible for you, as the cruise organizer, to quote your potential customers a price that, while lower than the advertised individual fare, is higher than the group fare available through the travel agent. You would collect the higher sum from your customers, pay the travel agent the lower sum, and pocket the difference. That's in theory. As a practical matter, there are any number of problems with this approach. First, the travel agent almost certainly won't stand for it, and if you try to go behind the agent's back, you run the risk of alienating the agent, the cruise line, and your customers. Also, cruise passengers have a wonderful way of finding out how much other passengers paid for their berths. Once they figure out they've "been had," you can forget about any repeat business from them. And repeat business, as we shall see, is one of the major reasons for selling cruises. There are plenty of ways to prosper by organizing cruises without trying to get clever and make a few extra bucks in this fashion.

Another word of caution. Cruises may not be an option for college or high school groups. A number of cruise lines, reacting to damage caused on board and the complaints of other passengers, have banned high school and college groups from their ships. Teenagers on many lines will not be placed in a cabin without an adult chaperone. If you book such a group and the cruise line does not know high school or college kids are involved, your group may be denied boarding at the dock. This is not to say that you absolutely can't book youngsters on a cruise. Just make sure you are completely upfront about what you plan to do when you approach the cruise line. If there are any problems or special guidelines to follow, they'll tell you. If the cruise line says yes, get their agreement to accept your group in writing, just in case.

When you are organizing a cruise, the travel agent will (or should) provide the same backup and support functions that the educational tour operators do for their teacher-counselors. In other words, they should be able to provide you with brochures, even videotapes, about the cruise line and advise you on such matters as deadlines for deposits and the proper way to walk your prospective shipmates through the cruise line's brochures.

Now, of course, you have to get that group of people together so you can qualify for your free tour conductor pass. Here's how Bill Miller describes the process:

> *Organizing a group can be as simple as calling all your friends.*
>
> *Call your friend Marge:*
>
> *"Hello, Marge. You know how we had been talking about doing something special this year? Well, you won't believe what a terrific cruise deal I've come across. It's on that fabulous _____ , sailing from Miami, and we'll*

save tons of money off the regular rate!"

"You mean that cruise that's always on the TV advertisements?" says Marge.

"Yep, that's the one. A seven-night cruise to the Caribbean with everything included," you say.

"Just imagine all the food!" says Marge. "The midnight buffets and the impeccable service! I won't have to cook!"

"The guys can play golf on the islands. And with the twenty-seven percent that we'll save off the cruise price we can do some great duty-free shopping in St. Thomas," you remind her.

"WOW! Sounds terrific," says Marge.

"It really is a fabulous deal, but to get these great rates we'll have to get at least seven couples to go," you tell her. "Besides, it's more fun to cruise with a bunch of friends. Remember when we all went on that day trip together?"

"Yeah, we'll have to let everybody know," says Marge. "This is gonna be great."

You have just planted the seed. Next, tell everyone you know about the terrific deal on the cruise. Invite them to join you. Tell your butcher, hairdresser, minister, the insurance man, dry cleaners, the people at the library. Tell the society column writer at the local paper. TELL EVERYONE!

The important thing to remember is that selling through a network of friends and acquaintances can be a pleasurable and relatively easy experience — especially when the "product" is something as exciting and glamorous as a luxury cruise.

Organize a tour group

If sailing the high seas in style doesn't particularly appeal to you, there's no reason why you can't apply the cruise organizer strategy we just discussed to a land-based tour. Pick a tour you'd like to take, find a travel agent to deal through, and put together a group. The end result is the same: in exchange for putting the group together, you travel free on a tour conductor pass.

One tour conductor pass for every 15 paying customers may be standard in the cruise industry, but in the world of tour operators, where there are many, many more players, the arrangements vary somewhat. Some tour organizers may offer more generous terms while others look for a bigger group from their tour conductors. For example, one tour operator in New York runs fully escorted tours to Scandinavia and requires 20 paying customers before they issue a tour conductor pass, that applies only to the land portion of the tour. The airfare is your responsibility.

In a situation like this, you have an incentive to drive a somewhat harder bargain with the travel agent you book through. This particular operator suggests that you should be able to find an agency that will give you a decent share of the commission. Considering that the land portion of their tours can run from $1,600 to $3,000 per person and that they offer a sliding commission scale ranging from 10% to 17.5%, based on volume, this could be a very attractive proposition.

The major difference, then, between organizing a tour and organizing a cruise is that in the world of tours things are far less cut and dried. Be prepared to shop around for both the best tour conductor deal from the tour operators and the travel agent or agency who will offer you the best working relationship.

There is another important way in which tour companies differ from cruise lines: some of them may be willing to help you cut out the middleman — the travel agent.

Now the cruise industry sometimes does the same thing, but on the whole the cruise industry seems to have a more solid allegiance to the agent community. A small but apparently growing number of tour operators and travel wholesalers are willing to deal with private individuals on a one-time, ad hoc basis. Finding out which ones will deal with you on these terms can take a little detective work. As one tour operator told me, "We don't like to advertise the fact that we deal with the general public because, if that ever got back to the travel agents, they would complain that we were stealing business from them." And rightly so!

Still the phenomenon exists, and if you are interested you can seek out amenable tour operators. Some tour operators will actually advertise their willingness to deal with you this way. Usually this means small ads either in magazines that reach a highly specialized audience or in the travel trade press. For example, there are tour operators specializing in pilgrimages and other religious-oriented travel that will offer programs similar to those offered in the high-school and college travel markets. The parallel is obvious: Here is a specialized product, directed at a well-defined market with obvious "decision-influencers" already in place — in this case, members of the clergy. What better person to convince the flock to travel to the River Jordan than the minister who will baptize them when they get there?

If you are interested in the more straightforward mainstream tours, however, you will probably find that the tour operators who sponsor them are generally unwilling to deal with individuals in this fashion. But there are exceptions and, if you are determined to find them, my guess is that you can.

There are a number of reasons you might be interested in dealing directly with a tour operator and avoiding a travel agent. Some of them are better reasons then others, and you will have to decide for yourself if they warrant searching out a direct relationship with a tour company.

▪ *The hassle factor.* One reason people give me for going direct is that they don't want to go to the trouble or hassle of finding an agent to deal through. This could be because of embarrassment, temperament, lack of experience, or just plain orneriness. To these people I say that it may be easier than they think to ally themselves with a bona fide travel agency as an outside rep on a one-time basis. The tour operator may smooth the way for them, even refer the business to an agency in such a way that it's a "done deal." If it's still a problem for you, I will show you later how to form a relationship with an agency that will take you on as an outside rep sight unseen, so that you'll be able to deal with any tour operator you want in an open and aboveboard manner, and you'll have the widest variety of tours to choose from. Not incidentally, you'll also be able to deal with the best and most reliable tour operators — an important consideration, as we'll see later.

■ ***Commissions.*** Another reason to "deal direct" is the lure of larger commissions, or at least commissions that don't have to be shared with an agent. I have nothing against making more money, but I would counsel caution. Some (but not all) tour operators who are willing to let you "play travel agent" like this, may be on shaky financial footing. Before you enter into a direct relationship with a tour operator, make sure you are comfortable with whatever additional risks may be involved. (Later, I'll tell you how to protect yourself against this kind of thing when dealing with travel suppliers.)

■ ***Control.*** Of course, there are people who simply want to run their own show and would just as soon not involve a third party if it's not absolutely necessary. In my opinion, this will work best for those who choose a tight focus for their casual travel selling activities. For example, if you were specializing in travel to one country or region, you might be able to find a tour operator or two with a similar specialty whom you could deal with directly. You would, in effect, be dealing with them just as if you were a "regular" travel agent, which in many important respects you would be.

■ ***Your experience.*** Another factor that will (or should) influence your decision is your level of experience. Tour operators will be understandably reluctant to deal direct with an inexperienced tour conductor, especially if there is a risk of offending the agents who bring them the bulk of their business. So if you are new to the travel game and decide to go this route, make sure you are prepared to convince the tour operator that working with you will be to their benefit. Some tour operators are more sensitive to the possibility of angering travel agents than others, but any tour operator willing to take the risk of dealing with you directly will certainly take a very long and hard look at the likelihood of your actually producing a group before giving the green light to this kind of arrangement.

Of course, once you have established a bona fide home-based travel business (especially if you are concentrating your efforts in one particular area), then it makes a great deal of sense to seek out direct relationships. Moreover, tour operators will be more receptive to working with you once you can demonstrate a track record or a following. (A following is a group of people who book through you regularly.)

I mention all this for the sake of completeness. All things being equal, I recommend that beginners at tour organizing operate in the more traditional way — through a travel agency. As you gain some visibility in the industry, you will find more and more opportunities opening up for you. If you become active in a professional association like the Outside Sales Support Network (OSSN), you will probably be approached by tour organizers and wholesalers who are eager to deal with you directly. You can do this even if you are an independent contractor with a host agency.

Caution: Before we continue, let me just point out that there is nothing illegal or unethical in dealing directly with a tour operator, as opposed to going through a host agency. The decision is more a matter of practicalities. However, some states have so-called "travel promoter laws" or "sellers of travel laws" that regulate the sale of travel products. Be aware that your exposure to these laws may be different when you are working as an outside rep for a travel agency from when you are dealing directly with the tour operator. Many of the business and legal details of these relationships will be dealt with elsewhere in this course. For now, make a note in the margin to check with your lawyer on this before making your decision.

The freelance tour organizer

If you've ever been on a "package tour" then you've purchased the "product" of a "tour operator." These companies research a number of destinations and then assemble a number of separate elements into a single product (or "package") with a single price. The most common elements that are combined into a tour include airfare, arrival and departure taxes, transportation from airport to hotel, hotel rooms, tour buses, tour guides, restaurant meals, and admissions to museums and tourist attractions. Each of these elements will require separate negotiations with different companies or government entities and then separate payments to all of these separate companies. Putting together a tour also requires a lot of careful planning and coordination. It's not all that different from plotting a military campaign — and the process is often compared to just that. Once all the pieces are in place, the tour operator "costs out" the separate elements of the package, adds something to cover his or her overhead and time, adds something more to provide a reasonable profit, and then presents you, the consumer, with a single all-inclusive price.

What you may not know is that there are people who, on a smaller scale, do exactly the same thing. One woman who does this (let's call her Pat) lives in Colorado and puts together tours to Ireland, mostly, but she has taken people to Paris and Venice as well.

Pat's tours of Ireland are intimate, highly customized trips she leads herself. The intimacy is guaranteed by the ground rules under which she works. "So far, I've been restricting myself to the number of people I can fit in a mini-van," she says. "That's six people, including me." The customization comes about because of Pat's joy in travel and the special delight she takes in finding the out-of-the-way bed and breakfast or offering her guests the kind of special Irish experience that larger, more "professional" tours simply cannot match.

"I'll take people to the local Irish nights, or coelis as they're called,"

Pat explains. "Each community has one night a week where they have live music and dance. It's just for the local people and it's fun. It's great! But it's not a 'tourist' thing. To walk in with thirty or forty people off a big bus would be a little embarrassing."

Pat's method for putting together a tour involves both planning and promotion, but mostly planning. "I'll send out blurbs to people I think might be interested and I also get a lot of word of mouth. I even had one gal call me all the way from Houston, who wanted to be included! Then I start checking the airfares." She starts well in advance and keeps checking back, always looking for a better deal. "So I don't get myself in trouble, I estimate the airfare on the high side. Then, if I find a better deal, I take it. But I'm always sure I won't charge too little."

Pat arranges for the mini-bus rental and bed-and-breakfast (b&b) vouchers through an Irish supplier. The voucher system allows you to use coupons for a night's lodging at participating b&b's, and most b&b's participate. Pat takes it one step further. She writes ahead to the quaint little b&b's she knows to lock in reservations. She also writes ahead for listings of local activities, such as horse races, and plans her itinerary accordingly.

She hosts "Irish nights" to get people excited about joining her next trip. She has a collection of videos and books that she'll lend out to pique interest. "And I'm kind of a camera buff," she adds, "so I have a lot of really nice blowups of pictures I've taken."

One of the big drawing cards of her tours is their offbeat and eclectic mixture of experiences — from Dromoland Castle ("That's sort of a come-on, to spend one night in a castle. They like that idea.") to a stay in a thatched-roof cottage ("There's a peat fire and a girl brings a pie, or a tart as they call it, and fresh baked soda bread. It's totally different than what they would ordinarily get."). Because she deals with small groups, Pat is often able to accommodate requests and tailor the trip specifically to the interests of her guests.

All of this takes planning, organization, and more planning. Pat is the first to admit it's hard work. "I get a kick out of it though. I really enjoy doing it, otherwise I probably wouldn't be doing it. I love planning the itinerary and I love surprising them."

Finally, Pat takes out insurance to cover unforeseen eventualities ("It costs about $35."), adds up all the costs, divides by the number of guests, and then tacks on another $200 or so per person. She's careful to get a deposit ("about half") up front, just to make sure people are serious about taking the trip.

Has she made a lot of money? Pat laughs.

"It hasn't been a lot so far, just a little bit extra. But I get a kick out of going places and I love to see other people having a good time. It just tickles the daylights out of me. Basically, what I'm doing is taking a free vacation every year."

For many people that "free" vacation is lure enough. That is probably why there are so many Pats in this world, organizing travel, making a little on the side, and having a lot of fun.

Summary

In this chapter, I have described a number of ways in which people sell travel with out being "travel agents." In other words, they don't think of themselves as travel agents, they didn't have to go to travel agent school, they didn't have to get a certificate from some travel industry association telling the world that they are a travel agent. But guess what? They're all travel agents. In other words, they arrange trips, find people who want to take them, and receive some form of compensation for doing that. To my way of thinking, that's a pretty good definition of a travel agent. It certainly matches up with the criteria we discussed in *Chapter 1*.

Please understand that I am not suggesting that you implement any of the approaches or strategies outlined in this chapter. You can if you want, of course, but I have much higher aspirations for you. I merely wanted to illustrate in this chapter that selling travel is simple, that people like you have been doing it on a casual basis for a long time without "getting into trouble" or ruffling any feathers, and they've done it without any fancy credentials.

There's something else you should know, if you haven't figured it out already. All of the people I've been talking about in this chapter are "leaving money on the table," to use some business slang. They all could be making more money than they're making.

The teacher putting together a trip for the students in her class or school could be spending the same amount of time promoting a much higher paying tour.

The person rounding up a bunch of friends to go on a cruise and working through a travel agent, could be the travel agent herself, receive all the commissions, and get a free berth into the bargain.

The freelance tour organizer who puts together a lot of the elements herself could use wholesalers to do all that work. The result would be, in many cases, a lower cost for her customers and more money in her pocket.

Anyone who has done any of the things mentioned in this chapter has learned some valuable skills and garnered some great experience. They can build on that experience to start making some serious money, by putting into use the strategies I teach in this course.

Action steps

Here are some things you can do to put what you have learned in this chapter into action:

- Call some tour operators, especially those who specialize in student tours. Tell them you are thinking about organizing a tour for your school or group. Ask them how you can work with them to do that. (I am not suggesting that you actually go ahead and organize a tour, just that you sound out some tour operators on their policies.)

  You will find a list of tour operators in *The Travel Agent's Complete Desk Reference*. If you purchased this book as part of my home study course, you already have it. If not, you can order it at:

http://www.HomeTravelAgency.com/deskref.html

- Call some local travel agencies. Tell them you want to put together a cruise for about twelve or so couples. Ask them what they will do for you if you take the responsibility for rounding up the people. If they ask for specifics (like cruise line, dates, etc.) tell them you haven't gotten that far, that you're just trying to figure out if it will be worth your while to make the effort. Again, your goal here is to get an idea of what travel agencies are willing to offer.

78

*Home-Based
Travel Agent*

Chapter Four:
The Outside Sales Rep

What you will learn

After you have completed this chapter you will be able to:

- Name two distinct approaches to becoming an outside agent and list the pros and cons of each approach.
- Distinguish among several different types of host agencies.
- Begin the process of choosing the host agency that offers the best match for you.

Key terms and concepts

This chapter involves the following key terms and concepts:

- Outside agent. A person, working outside the travel agency itself, who brings business to the agency and is compensated for his or her efforts, typically by a share of the commissions generated by the bookings he or she makes. As used here, an outside agent is an independent contractor, a legally separate entity from the travel agency and not an employee of the travel agency.
- Host agency. Any travel agency through which an outside agent funnels bookings for travel products. Whenever a travel agency works with an outside agent who is an independent contractor, it is serving as that agent's "host." Some travel agencies do nothing but serve as the host for a network of independent contractors.
- Commission split. The financial formula by which commissions are shared between an outside agent and a host agency. Commission splits are a matter for negotiation and can vary widely from host agency to host agency.
- The relationship between a host travel agency and an outside agent must be a win/win relationship. Each brings to the table something the other wants and at a reasonable cost. Otherwise, the relationship makes no sense.

- The most important thing to remember as an outside agent is that you are completely independent, in every sense of the term, from your host agency.
- Choosing a host agency can be one of the most important decisions you will make in your travel marketing career.

In the last chapter, we talked about ways in which you can earn free travel and extra money without being a "travel agent" in any formal sense of the word. The strategies we discussed that involved working with a travel agency didn't require any formal relationship or long-term commitment. You could go on earning free vacations and a bit of extra money like that for many years. Many people do and are quite happy. If you are serious about selling travel and putting together groups as a regular part of your lifestyle, however, then sooner or later you will have to get a little more serious and a little more formal.

One way of doing that is to become what is known as an "outside agent." (Other terms you may see used are outside rep, outside sales rep, associate travel agent, independent travel consultant, and so forth. They all mean the same thing.) In fact, if you have successfully put together a few groups and booked them through a local travel agency, that agency may actively encourage you to become an outside agent without you asking about it.

In this chapter, then, we will discuss how to become an "official" outside sales representative of a bona fide travel agency.

What are outside agents?

Essentially, an outside sales representative (or "outside agent") for a travel agency is a person, working outside the travel agency itself, who brings business to the agency and is compensated for his or her efforts. That compensation might take the form of a straight salary, a salary plus commission, or a straight commission. Most of the readers of this book who become outside sales reps for a travel agency will be compensated solely on a commission basis. In this case the outside rep is an "independent contractor" and not an employee of the agency, an important distinction for a number of reasons, as we shall see.

Travel agencies and outside agents enter into this type of relationship for one simple reason: each has something the other wants.

The travel agency has an established relationship with the travel industry that includes things like an ARC appointment (allowing them to sell airline tickets), an IATA number (that confers instant credibility in the industry), a roster of preferred suppliers (who pay higher commissions), and a "back office" (a staff that handles things like tracking commissions). The outside agent wants those things. For the outside agent, becoming an outside sales rep for an established travel agency enables him or her to function much like a travel agency (remember, the outside agent, in this case, is an independent contractor with a legally separate business), without a lot of the expense and hassle. The outside agent looks on the share of the commission retained by the host agency as a form of "rent" for the use of the agency's ARC appointment, IATA number, and so forth.

The outside agent isn't tied to an office, but can roam throughout the community creating business. The outside agent may have contacts in the community that the travel agency doesn't. The outside agent can bring in new business at zero risk. (Why zero? Because the agency only has to "pay" the outside agent, in the form of a commission split, when the agent makes a sale.) The travel agency wants all these things. So the business calculation on the part of the travel agency is that giving away a portion (even a large portion) of the commission makes financial sense because they are getting additional business at little or no extra cost.

The prospective outside agent often has a burning desire to become a travel agent and is willing to pay money to make that happen. Many host agencies (not all, but many) charge a sign-up fee to those wanting to become an outside agent. So the question arises, is the agency in question seeking to make money from the additional business the outside agent will bring in, from the sign-up fee, or perhaps from both? I generally like to assume the best of people, but it's a question worth asking yourself as you weigh your options.

Not all outside reps are created equal. For one thing, some are compensated better than others. To some extent the amount of compensation an outside rep receives is determined by the marketplace. In other words, compensation is a matter of what the agency thinks is fair and what the outside rep can negotiate. When the agency and the rep reach an agreement on a commission split, that becomes the "market rate" in this particular situation. However, the "market rate," whatever it may be, is also affected to a very great extent by the amount of work the outside rep is expected to do in bringing in business. The extent of the outside rep's responsibilities enables us to make useful distinctions between types of outside reps.

For the sake of simplicity, we will concentrate on the two main categories: full-fledged outside reps and bird dogs or referrers.

Finders, steerers, bird dogs

A "bird dog," as the term implies, is a person who flushes out or brings in the game for the hunter, in this case the travel agency. Once the quarry is safely in hand, their job is over. Bird dogs can bring in small accounts (friends and neighbors, for example) or they can land major corporate accounts that will book a considerable volume with the agency each year for as long as the agency has the account.

If you are planning on letting the agency do most of the work, you will be in the bird dog category. For example, your Aunt Martha wants to take her granddaughter to Orlando to see Mickey Mouse, leaving on May 5th and coming back on May 15th. You relay this information to your agency, which researches the possibilities, finds the most attractive package, and so forth. You then get back to Aunt Martha to see if she's happy with what the agency suggests. Finally, you recontact the agency to firm things up and have them issue the tickets. Another, more likely, scenario is that you turn Aunt Martha over to an experienced inside sales rep, who then helps Aunt Martha make a decision. Since the agency is doing the lion's share of the work here, you can't expect to receive much more than a 2% to 5% commission. There are agencies that will give you a similar modest referral fee if all you do is bring Aunt Martha in to talk to one of their travel consultants. Bear this in mind if you are interested in bird-dogging.

You can ask around at local agencies to see how (or if) they work with outside people in cases like this. If you do, there are two basic rules of thumb: First, most agencies will be reluctant even to discuss the proposition. They will figure (all things being equal) that they have more to lose than gain by letting you go out and "play travel agent" in this fashion. You are an unknown quantity and they will be naturally concerned that you might damage their reputation in the community. Second, whatever compensation they offer will be a take-it-or-leave-it proposition. Don't expect to have much negotiating leeway in this kind of situation. And don't be too surprised to find that, while you may get a cut of the commission on Aunt Martha's first trip, you are cut out of the subsequent business she brings to the agency directly.

Bird dogs may be the "lowest" category of outside reps in terms of compensation but, make no mistake, they can play a valuable role in building an agency's business. Which is not always to say that a given agency will understand or appreciate that fact. It may be that serving as a bird dog for a local agency is just fine for you and there is nothing wrong with that. (By the way, keep bird dogs in mind as you build your business. You may wind up using them yourself!)

Strange as it may seem, you may find it more difficult to find a situation as a bird dog than as a full-fledged outside agent. If you do become a bird dog, your initial arrangement may be tentative and "unofficial." As you begin to build a track record, however, you will deserve a more formal understanding with the agency, preferably one that is in writing and spells out your mutual obligations. More on that issue later.

Bird-dogging major accounts

At the other end of the scale is the bird dog who brings in a corporate account that will book many thousands of dollars through the agency on an ongoing basis. Here the matter of compensation is more open to discussion and negotiation. Donald Davidoff, an industry expert who coordinated outside salespeople for an agency in Bowie, MD, considers two variables in setting compensation — how much work the rep will do after the account is landed and how big the account is.

At the first level is the outside rep who merely "refers" an account rather than actually "sells" it. In these situations, Davidoff feels an up-front "finder's fee" is appropriate. "The fee should relate to the expected volume of travel and be equal to about 10% of the expected commissions," he wrote in *Travel Trade* magazine. (Since then, the airlines have eliminated commissions, so the figures that follow should be adjusted downwards.)

If the outside rep takes a more active role and actually "sells" the account, Davidoff is willing to up the ante. "If we do not expect them to have anything else to do with the account once it is sold, then we usually pay 20%-25% of the commissions for the first year," Davidoff writes. "This applies to accounts under $500,000. For accounts between $500,000 and $1 million, the commission can be as low as 15%-20%. For accounts over $1 million, 10% is usually appropriate. These differences are not relevant to most agencies because 92% of agencies in the U.S. gross under $5 million in annual volume. It is not advisable for them to take on any account over $500,000." Be aware that the figures Davidoff is using here are gross figures. On a $500,000 account the agency commission would be approximately $50,000 (10%). So the bird dog's 15% commission would be $7,500.

Of course, you will not always simply walk away from an account you have brought to an agency. This would be especially true in the case of an account you were able to sell because of a close personal relationship with one of the principals. You might want to serve as the liaison with the account (the agency might even insist on it!). In this type of situation, you might handle the "macro" issues — Is the relationship working well? Are they happy with the service? Do they need any special travel-related computer reports? — while the agency handles the "micro" issues — sending the VP of Sales to Indianapolis for a two-day business trip, booking rooms at the local hotel for visiting executives, etc. "In these cases," Davidoff advises, "the salesperson should get 25% of the first year's commission and 10% of at least the second year's commission in consideration for the time and effort of staying in touch." Davidoff also recommends that agencies pay a smaller commission (5%) in the third year and following to encourage the outside rep to stay in touch with the account and to discourage him or her from taking the business to another agency in order to cash in on those bigger first- and second-year commission sharing arrangements.

Here's how the payout to you as an outside sales representative would work at such a travel agency for an account that brought in $100,000 in volume each year. If you referred the account, you would receive $1,000. If you sold the account but had no further client contact, you would receive $2,500. If you performed a liaison function with the account, you would receive $3,500 over the first two years and perhaps $500 for the third year and each year thereafter. Not a bad arrangement. By the way, Davidoff's article in *Travel Trade* was headlined "Outside Salespersons: Is Your Agency Paying Them Too Much?" That would seem to imply that some agencies pay their outside sales representatives more for bird-dogging than Davidoff recommends.

The arrangements at Davidoff's agency are only one way to go. Other agencies have other formulas. For example, I know of another agency that has a distinctly different approach to outside reps who bring in corporate accounts. For each corporate account an outside rep signs up, they pay one half of one percent (0.5%) of volume for the first three years, one third of one percent (0.33%) for the next two years, and one tenth of one percent (0.1%) for the next five years. This arrangement involves no further contact between the rep and the corporate client after the sale. For a $100,000

account, the payout over ten years would be $2,660.

One thing to note about referral arrangements like this is that they function like an annuity. Let's say, for the sake of discussion, that you are an outside rep for an agency that gives you 25% of commissions the first year, 10% the second year, and 5% the third, fourth and fifth years. Assuming a 10% commission rate, if you sign up just one $100,000 account each year, your income would look like this:

Year One	$2,500
Year Two	$3,500
Year Three	$4,000
Year Four	$4,500
Year Five	$5,000

I think it is unlikely that you will wind up following this route, at least as a full-time specialty. But who knows? If you do stumble upon an opportunity to land a big corporate account, at least now you'll have some guidelines.

Referral agencies

A new breed of travel agency has taken the concept of bird-dogging to a new level. They are called "referral agencies" by those who advocate their approach and "card mills" by those who don't.

Typically, a referral agency is designed solely to handle the bookings generated by a large force of outside agents; it does not accept off-the-street business or seek its own "in-house" accounts.

One way in which they recruit outside agents is with the attractive industry benefits the outside agent will supposedly receive once he or she has the referral agency's photo ID card. It is this marketing stance that has drawn the ire of many in the travel agency industry. They charge, with some justification, that most people who join these agencies do so only for the supposed benefits. Nonetheless, referral agencies do generate business.

Referral agencies take their name from the fact that their outside agents are generally not expected (or even able) to research fares and make bookings. Their job is to funnel business to the agency's 800 number where salaried inside agents take over the job of actually making the sale. In exchange for making this referral, the outside agent is paid anywhere from 25% to 50% of the commission, which is usually assumed to be 10%, even if the host agency is actually receiving a much higher commission.

Referral agencies generally offer some sort of bonus for recruiting new agents, making it possible (in theory at least) to make just as much (if not more) money by recruiting new agents as by referring travel business.

You will find more on referral agencies and the whole issue of travel industry benefits in *Chapter 5: The Referral Agent*.

The 'true' outside sales representative

Unlike the bird dog or the referral agent, the "true" outside sales representative functions in very much the same way as the travel agents working inside, as employees of the travel agency. That is to say, the outside rep is intimately involved in talking with customers, making suggestions, researching destinations and prices, planning itineraries, contacting suppliers, even in some cases entering booking information into a GDS (global distribution system, sometimes referred to as a computerized reservation system or CRS).

The major difference is that the outside agent tends to be proactive rather than reactive. Rather than sit and wait for business to come walking in the door (as inside salespeople often do), the outside agent is out in the community, beating the bushes, looking for new business. Most travel agencies recognize the importance of this kind of activity. Many encourage or require their inside people to generate a certain amount of new business. Some agencies even have outside sales reps on staff, with the specific responsibility to be out attracting new clients, corporate accounts, and groups.

The attraction the independent outside agent has for the agency is the same attraction the agency has for the supplier — it's a means to extend the agency's marketing reach and the agency only has to pay based on the agent's productivity.

Part-time, full-time

The amount of time an outside rep puts into the selling of travel can run the gamut from virtually no time at all to a full-time occupation. There are some people who form an outside sales relationship with an agency just to book their own personal and business travel. They are, in effect, their only customer. Some agencies, particularly the referral agencies, will welcome this kind of business, others will not. At the other extreme are individuals who are seeking to make their entire living, often a very good living, as outside reps. They do this by aggressively pursuing new business, especially upscale leisure travelers, group sales and corporate accounts, where truly impressive commissions are possible. Agents in this category will also, very likely, conduct a portion of their business directly with suppliers and not through their host.

How much time an outside agent puts in is up to the agent, not the host agency. Once again, you have to remember that the outside agent is an independent contractor. The agency cannot legally attempt to "control" the outside agent by setting minimum hours.

Another useful distinction that can be made among outside agents is the amount of work the agency must expend to service the outside agent's customers.

Most outside sales agents (as I am using the term here) do all the work up to and including making the booking with the supplier. That is why they can earn 70%, 80%, or more of the commission due.

There are some outside reps who have their own GDS in their home office. They can make airline, hotel, and car reservations directly on the system and tell the system to print out the required tickets and documents on the agency's printer when necessary, which is not often in this age of electronic ticketing. Typically, outside agents who fall into this category have many years experience as inside agents, know the GDS very

well, and have a "following" (a list of customers they've been dealing with for years). Because of the high volume they do, having an in-home GDS makes a lot of sense. It's not a strategy I would recommend to beginners, who can better direct their energies to building a high-margin business that doesn't require using a GDS.

On the other hand, there are agents who lean on their host agencies quite a bit — for advice, research, and so forth. Some agencies will "cover" for their outside agents when they are on vacation, dealing with their customers so the sale won't be lost. In all these cases, the host agency (quite rightly) expects to be compensated for its additional efforts and the compensation arrangements will be adjusted accordingly.

In theory, the amount of compensation you can expect as an outside agent should fluctuate according to how much work you're doing. If you've been getting 50% of the commission for phoning in leads, for example, you should attempt to renegotiate terms when and if you begin to handle more of the complete process.

Establishing an outside sales relationship

Let's say you've decided that you want to set yourself up as an outside sales representative and begin selling travel to your friends and family. What next? Your challenge now is to find a "host agency" — an agency that you will feel comfortable working with that will also feel comfortable working with you.

There are two basic ways to do that:

1. Find a travel agency in your community or, at least nearby, that will take you on as an outside agent, or
2. Turn to the growing number of agencies that are willing to let you become one of their outside reps regardless of your location, pretty much sight unseen, and usually for a fee. (If you find one of these agencies located nearby, don't assume that you will be able to "drop in" whenever you like; most of these agencies actively discourage that, although some may allow it.) These outfits are sometimes referred to, derisively, as "instant agencies" by people in the travel industry, but they occupy a valid niche in the travel distribution system.

All things being equal, finding a local agency you can work with is the preferable choice. Why? First of all, I am assuming that you have little or no travel industry experience. Although many of the instant agencies offer training, most of it is geared to mastering the GDS they use. (There are exceptions, of course.) Also, I don't think there is any real substitute for a caring mentor who will take you under his or her wing, show you the ropes, and be available to answer your questions on a timely basis. Local agencies also have the advantage of being close by. That means you can service the client who needs help now!

A little later, I'll tell you how to follow the "instant agent" route. For now, let's concentrate on selling your services to a local agency.

Finding a local 'host agency'

There are no hard and fast rules about finding a local agency with which to work but here are some suggestions:

- *Your own travel agent.* Why not consider approaching Susan, the owner of the travel agency you have been dealing with for the past several years? If Susan sees you are serious about adopting a new career as a home-based travel agent, she will realize immediately that, unless she signs you on, she will lose your business and perhaps that of some of your friends who also use her agency. She may be willing to accommodate you on that basis alone. Or maybe you know someone who is a travel agent, even though you don't book through him. My first foray into the travel trade was through an agency owner I met during a radio interview I was giving about one of my books. We struck up a conversation, one thing led to another, and I became an outside rep for her firm.

- *Referrals.* Ask your friends about the agencies they use. Do they like them? Why? How big are they? Do they have a lot of agents? Are they professional? Do they specialize in a certain type of travel? This could lead you to a very likely candidate.

- *The chains.* Chains of franchised travel agencies recognize the value of outside agents in the marketing mix of their franchisees and are willing to put interested agents together with local agencies. Some charge a fee, others do not. Many have structured inside support programs to assist their outside agents. They will be able to tell you what their policies are and refer you to agencies in your area that might be amenable to taking you on.

- *The Yellow Pages.* Don't overlook the trusty Yellow Pages. If nothing else, they will tell you how many agencies are out there competing for the travel dollar in your local area. Display ads will give you some clues as to which are the bigger agencies and what types of travel they specialize in.

- *Do your research.* Try to find out as much as you can about the agencies in your area before approaching any of them. Call the American Society of Travel Agents (ASTA) to verify their status. Check the Better Business Bureau to see if there have been complaints lodged against any of them. Drive by to see what they look like — sleek and inviting or grungy and sad. Drop in to check them out by posing as a would-be traveler. Or send in a family member if you are concerned you might be recognized later. Try to get an idea of how many people are on staff. Count the number of GDS's on the desks. Check the decals in the window to find out which trade organizations they are affiliated with. Buttonhole customers you see leaving the agency; ask them what they think about the service they receive there. Would they recommend the agency to their friends? Gradually, as you gather more and more in-

formation, some agencies will start looking better than others, and you can narrow your choices accordingly.

Selling yourself to an agency

The more you can offer an agency, the greater your self-confidence and the better your bargaining position. The less you can offer an agency, the lower your self-confidence and the poorer your bargaining position. Here are some of the things that an agency will (or should be) looking for in an outside rep. How many of them apply to you?

- *Travel industry experience.* If you've got it, great! If not, don't despair. And remember, if you were a secretary and had to make travel arrangements for your boss, you probably know more about the business than you think you do. Take careful stock of your past experience to determine just how much prior knowledge you do have. General computer and Internet skills (especially online fare research and booking) may offset your lack of GDS experience, for example.

- *Sales experience.* If you don't have a background in the travel agency business, the next best thing is sales experience. Sales, as I like to remind people, is the most transportable of skills. Any travel agency owner with half a brain should be able to recognize that having a proven track record as a salesperson gives you a tremendous leg up. So if you've been an outside sales representative for a distributor, a sales clerk at a department store, or a telemarketer, you have something to offer.

- *A following.* This means you have a client base you can bring with you to the agency. Unless you've been working in a travel agency and are looking for a career change, that probably doesn't mean a Rolodex full of people you've been selling travel to. (Besides, ethically and legally speaking, those clients would belong to your employer's agency, not you.) But it could mean the membership of a fraternal organization of which you are an officer. Or it could mean the local PTA in which you are active. Are there any groups to which you belong or in which you have some visibility? Have you ever arranged travel for them? The agency will want to know about that.

- *Market knowledge.* Do you know Italy like the back of your hand? Have you been taking three cruises a year for the past three decades? Are you an avid skier who has schussed down every major slope in the world? If so, you have knowledge that might prove useful to the agency and help convince them that you can build a following. In fact, you may already have a following of fellow enthusiasts and not know it!

- *Enthusiasm.* Make no mistake, enthusiasm alone will not win the day, but it's certainly a valuable quality to have — especially if it's tempered by realism. If you are inexperienced in selling travel, the agency may be willing to overlook that if you can show them that you have what it takes to learn what you need to learn and make a success of it.

Chances are that, as a beginner, you will be entering a buyers' market. That is, you will be far more interested in working with the agency than the agency will be in working with you. That, in turn, means you will have to work a little harder to convince the agency owner that working with you as an outside rep makes good business and economic sense.

Just because it may be a buyers' market, however, doesn't mean you should sell yourself short. After all, if you're not happy in the relationship, it's unlikely to work out well for either party. So don't feel you have to settle for the first thing that comes along. You have other options. As you will soon see.

Also, be aware that your beginner's status puts you in a relatively weak position as far as negotiating an attractive commission split. As I've said earlier, 50/50 is fairly standard in this type of arrangement with a local agency, but don't be too surprised if you are offered less. All things being equal, I would counsel not accepting anything less than 50/50. After all, if push comes to shove, you can always sign up with an out-of-town agency that will take you as you are. Then you can get the experience, build a following, and cut a better deal with the local agency later on, if that still appeals to you. In the end, of course, it's your call and working with an agency that's half a block from your house, with an owner who will really teach you the business, may be worth the tradeoff in terms of compensation.

Finally, after all this, I have to warn you that your chances of being successful in finding a local agency to work with are not that great, especially if you are a beginner. Those with past agency experience are in a slightly better position. Still, the anecdotal evidence is that this is a tough sell, unless you happen to be located near one of the growing number of agencies that specialize in dealing mainly or exclusively with home-based outside agents.

Paying to become an outside agent

If you're the impatient type, and don't want to spend the time to locate and negotiate with a local agency, or if the prospect of doing so just seems overwhelming, don't despair. There is another alternative. It is possible to become a travel agent for a multimillion-dollar travel agency virtually overnight, no questions asked.

As I mentioned before, a growing number of travel agencies are taking on outside sales representatives pretty much sight unseen. To the outside sales agent, these agencies are "host agencies," just like the local agencies discussed above. The difference is that most of the agencies we will discuss in this section charge a fee for allowing you to book travel through them and share the commission; for this reason, they are sometimes derisively referred to within the industry as "instant agencies." Let's simply call them host agencies, because that's what they are, regardless of what

you or industry cynics might think of the fees they charge. At this writing, there are still some host agencies that charge no sign-up fee, but they are getting harder to find. In my Special Report, *How to Choose a Host Agency*, I direct you to those that are still free. (See Action Steps, below.)

Why pay a fee?

You may be asking yourself, "Why should I pay a fee at all?" It's a question worth asking, although there are no hard and fast answers. Among the reasons a host agency might charge a sign-up fee are:

- ■ ***To deter people.*** This may seem counterintuitive, but many host agencies have learned the hard way that not all outside agents are worth having. I know of one host agency that had no sign-up fee for many years. They found they were having so many problems with non-productive agents that they instituted a fee of several hundred dollars, just to cut down on the number of new sign-ups. Eventually, they got out of the host agency business altogether.
- ■ ***To defray costs.*** Travel agencies incur costs when they take on a new agent. Many have chosen to pass these costs on to the agent.
- ■ ***To pay for products and services rendered.*** Sometimes a sign-up fee is justified by the training materials and other products and services the agency provides the agent.
- ■ ***To make money.*** While I wouldn't be able to prove it in a court of law, I suspect that at least some host agencies see their sign-up fees as another profit center for the agency.
- ■ ***Because other agencies charge fees.*** There could be a number of factors involved here. An agency may feel it's being foolish to not charge a fee when others are doing so. It may feel that charging a fee makes it look more attractive to prospective agents. Or it may just be a case of following the leader.

Whatever the reasons host agencies charge sign-up fees, the simple fact of the matter is that most now do. It has become something of an industry standard. Most outside agents either feel they are getting good value for their investment or accept it as just another cost of doing business. If paying a fee really bothers you, there are still agencies that charge no fee waiting for your business.

Once you pay your fee (if any) to an agency and get its materials in the mail, that agency becomes your host agency and you are ready to start booking trips and earning commissions. Assuming you have gone into this new relationship with your eyes open and without any unrealistic expectations, this can be a very good deal indeed.

In this section, I will give you a brief overview of the different types of host agencies and lay out some general guidelines about how they operate and how you will deal with them. What I can't do is provide a description of what every host agency is like or what your host agency will be like. That is the purpose of *How to Choose a Host Agency*.

Also, let me reiterate the importance of comparison shopping for a host agency. Take careful stock of your own goals and needs. Do your own research. Make your own decisions.

Types of host agencies

I have researched hundreds of host agencies over the years and no two offer precisely the same program. However, I have identified three broad categories of host agency that will, I believe, help you focus your search.

- *Bare-bones business partners.* These agencies charge relatively modest sign-up fees and offer little in the way of training, hand-holding, and support.
- *Quasi-franchises.* These agencies charge much higher fees but provide a great deal of training and support.
- *Referral agencies.* These agencies, as the name suggests, pay low commissions for referrals and are not a good choice for those who want to be hands-on travel agents. However, they have other features that might appeal to you.

Let's deal with each in turn.

Bare-bones business partners

I use this rather unwieldy term to distinguish host agencies that seem to regard the outside agent more or less as an equal. Their offers are structured in such a way that they make the most money from productive agents. In short, it's a win-win proposition. Among the characteristics that identify agencies in this category are:

- Low or moderate sign-up fees.
- Higher commission splits. Typically better than 50/50.
- A recognition, however grudging, of the outside agent's independence.
- A minimum of training and hand-holding.

Just because they may feature a low-low sign-up fee does not mean that agencies in this category are automatically your "best deal." One reason for the low cost is that these agencies offer few "bells and whistles."

These agencies will probably appeal most to those who have travel agency experience, especially if they are planning to specialize and create their own direct relationships with suppliers. They can then use their host agency to issue airline tickets and in other situations where it is difficult to collect commissions directly from the supplier.

They will also appeal to adventurous beginners who feel they can learn on-the-job. If that's you, read this course carefully and turn to it for the guidance you most certainly won't get from one of these agencies. Even then, be prepared to make some mistakes, perhaps some costly ones.

Most agencies in this category are not set up to guide you through the complexities of the travel business and they will not be sympathetic if an

error on your part costs you money. Few of them will be eager to explain to you how to construct a complicated FIT. Because many of them operate on wafer thin margins, there is always the possibility that bookings will "fall between the cracks." I have heard complaints about these and other problems from inexperienced agents affiliated with low-cost and no-cost host agencies. If you are not knowledgeable already or if you are not prepared to take a few hits as you learn "the hard way," I would advise you to think very carefully before affiliating with one of these agencies.

Even so, an agency in this category can be a good choice if you are uncertain about your commitment to a career as a home-based agent. It gives you a chance to test the waters without making a large financial investment.

Of course, I recommend careful investigation before jumping into any business relationship. However, in the case of most of these agencies, if you find you don't enjoy being a travel agent or have allied with an agency you don't like, little damage will have been done. At worst, you'll be out hundreds, rather than thousands of dollars. It's a simple matter to switch agencies. And with your hard-won experience, you will know what to look out for next time. (On the other hand, if the agency goes bankrupt or disappears while it still owes you commissions or travel documents for which your clients have already paid, the financial damage can be much more severe. But this is true regardless of which agency you affiliate with.)

Quasi-franchises

If you'd like a little more "hand holding" or feel that a little training is worth paying for, then you might very well decide to go with a type of host agency that I call a "quasi-franchise." Host agencies in this category offer in-depth training, a toll-free help line, marketing support, and all the rest — for a price, of course. These are agencies that share many features with full-fledged franchises. They tend to be identified by characteristics such as:

- High sign-up fees, often well over a thousand dollars.
- Extensive, in-house training programs.
- A requirement that outside agents be fully automated. Often they sell you the software and sometimes even the hardware.
- The assumption, spoken or unspoken, that outside agents will funnel all their bookings through them.

These agencies will appeal most to those who feel they need intensive training, who want to open a storefront operation, or who feel more secure dealing with a large organization that promises ongoing support.

These offers demand a great deal of careful investigation. There is a lot of money at stake, after all. If you're paying several thousand for training, you want to know it's first-rate. Virtually none of these agencies offer a refund if you are dissatisfied.

In theory, the travel agency makes its real money on the travel you book. The sign-up fee, or membership, or whatever they call it, is merely to cover the cost of setting you up in their system, providing you with materials, training, marketing support, and so forth. In practice, some agencies offering this opportunity charge such high start-up fees that you wonder whether signing up agents is a separate profit center. Of course, good training and solid support is worth something, but consider this: Assuming a 70/30 split with the agency and an average commission rate of 10%, you'd have to sell over $85,000 in travel just to recoup an initial $6,000 investment!

A number of these agencies present prospective outside agents with lengthy and scary-looking "disclosure documents." These are often required by state law for business opportunities charging a significant investment. They are designed to protect the consumer and shouldn't be a cause for concern. Your lawyer (you will consult with a lawyer before concluding any agreement, won't you?) will be able to explain it all to you. In fact, if an agency charging a substantial initial investment does *not* offer you substantial disclosure, you should ask why not.

Just as a low sign-up fee does not necessarily signal a great deal, a high sign-up fee does not necessarily guarantee superior quality. Examine carefully what you are getting for your investment. As one agency owner in this category put it, "People should look at the value as opposed to the cost." That's good advice.

Things like industry training, computer equipment, GDS software and training, marketing plans, marketing support, and ongoing toll-free support to answer questions and solve problems are all valuable and they all cost money. The question is, "Do you really need all this?" As you may have gathered by now, my bias is against GDS automation, certainly at the beginning of your career and perhaps forever. Of course, that's just one man's opinion. If you genuinely feel that you need or want any or all of these things, then a quasi-franchise may be a very good buy, despite any initial "sticker shock."

Many people who sign up with these agencies are very happy with their decision and enthusiastic boosters of their host agencies. However, there is no law that you have to do this at the very outset. You can learn the ropes on the cheap, as it were, and automate later, often at a fraction of the cost of joining a quasi-franchise.

The higher the initial investment, the longer it will take to earn it back through commission income. You will be well advised to calculate (using conservative estimates) how long it will take to recoup your initial investment with any host agency, but especially when that investment amounts to several thousands of dollars. Then you must make the very personal decision as to whether or not that makes sense for you.

Non-ARC host agencies

There is another category (perhaps *sub*-category is a better term) of host agency to consider — the non-ARC agency. As the term suggests, a non-ARC agency is one without an ARC appointment. For many years, CLIA agencies, which have traditionally been cruise-only agencies, were the only non-ARC agencies.

Things began to change when the airlines stopped paying base commissions to travel agencies. Many agencies (the ones that didn't simply close up shop, that is), dropped their ARC appointment because they stopped selling air, but they wanted to continue selling other types of travel. Now by definition, a non-ARC agency does not have an "ARC-IATA" number, the number that used to identify them in all those supplier databases. In response to the phenomenon of agencies shedding their ARC appointments, the industry responded by devising ways to let agencies continue in the business without having an ARC-IATA number. Some agencies switched to CLIA numbers. Others got one of the "new" IATA numbers, issued by various industry entities. Today, virtually anyone, including you, can become a non-ARC agency. I discuss this whole process in more depth in *Chapter 6: The Independent Agent* and in the Special Report, *How to Get Your Own IATA Number.*

For now, there are a few simple but important points to remember.

- Non-ARC agencies can take many forms. They can be either bare-bones business partners or quasi-franchises. A few are referral agencies or offer a referral program in addition to more traditional outside agent programs.
- While most non-ARC agencies are cruise-only agencies, more and more will allow you to book a wider array of travel products through them.
- Non-ARC agencies can run the gamut from well-established, highly professional operations to home-based operations run out of a bedroom by someone with not much more experience than you have right now.
- There is nothing "wrong" with non-ARC agencies in and of themselves. And if you are not selling air, then a non-ARC agency can make sense for you. Just understand that some non-ARC agencies are better than others. The same is true, of course, with ARC agencies, but in the case of ARC agencies the higher standards imposed by ARC imply (but do not guarantee) a higher standard of professionalism and expertise.
- Conversely, there is nothing "wrong" with using an ARC-appointed host even if you are not planning on ever selling an airline ticket.

Referral agencies

Also known derisively within the industry as "card mills," referral agencies promise lucrative benefits to outside agents who will steer business their way. Referral agencies tend to be characterized by:

- Relatively high sign-up fees. Some cynics have charged that these agencies typically choose $495 as their sign-up fee to avoid the higher level of regulatory scrutiny given to business opportunities charging more than $500.
- Agents who "refer" business to the agency rather than perform the research and booking tasks usually associated with being a travel agent.
- A strong emphasis in their marketing materials on the photo-

ID card they issue and the immediate access to hefty industry discounts and courtesies the card is said to provide. (Hence, the derogatory term "card mill.")
- A referral fee (typically $100 or more) for signing up new agents.
- Low commission splits (as low as 20% for some types of bookings) and/or a refusal to book or pay commission on certain products (such as hotels and car rentals).
- Special discount travel deals, sometimes positioned as "fam trips" for their agents only.

Clearly, referral agencies will not appeal to those who want to do all the things that travel agents normally do, because the referral agency's inside agents do all the research and booking. Nonetheless, such agencies do offer opportunities to market attractively priced mid-market packages to your friends, neighbors, and others. It is also conceivable that you might find it useful to join both a referral and a more traditional host agency.

Because referral agencies are such a fundamentally different type of host agency, I will discuss them separately and in greater detail in *Chapter 5: The Referral Agent*.

Sorting through your options

The information presented above should help get you started in your search for and negotiations with a host agency with which you can work on an independent, outside sales basis. As you can see, you have a lot of options; it's most definitely not a "one size fits all" kind of situation. Take your time and don't rush into anything. Above all, don't sign up with the first host agency that has a pretty web site and promises you the moon.

Selecting a host agency is such a crucial step in your home-based career that I have written a separate Special Report, *How to Choose a Host Agency*, devoted exclusively to the challenge of finding the right host agency for you. In that Report, I provide a detailed methodology for analyzing any host agency program. I also profile over 100 host agencies, with additional contact information on about 100 more. The point is not that there is one "best" host agency lurking out there. Not at all. There are many fine host agencies to choose from. But this is a very personal choice and the host agency that is right for you may not be right for the next fellow. Of course, if you sign up with a host agency and find you don't like it, it's easy enough to switch agencies. You'll probably have lost some time and money, but it's not the end of the world. However, if you'd like to maximize the chances of making the right decision the first time, I strongly urge you to consult *How to Choose a Host Agency* (See Action steps, below).

If you choose to do it on your own, research as many different host agencies as you can find. But whatever way you go, do not shortchange yourself on this crucial step in setting up your business.

Before moving on, let's summarize the pros and cons of the two, slightly different approaches we've just examined:

The 'Pros' of aligning yourself with a local agency

- It's convenient. The agency is close at hand and you can get tickets, brochures, and documents quickly if needed.
- It's cheap. It shouldn't cost you anything to become an outside rep for a local firm. If they do charge a fee, make sure of what you are getting in return.
- Help is close at hand. Hopefully, the agency will be willing to answer questions and teach you what you need to know. You may even be able to go into the agency and get training on its computers!
- An agency with which you have close personal ties may be more willing to work with you on getting perks like free or low-cost travel than one that is far away, for which you are just a number.

The 'Cons' of aligning yourself with a local agency

- Your commission split may be just 50/50 or less.
- You may be limited, by the agency's size, in terms of overrides (extra commissions) and other perks.
- It can be time-consuming to find an agency that is willing to work with you. It is also possible, in fact very likely, that you will spend a great deal of time and never find a local agency willing to take you on. I know of many would-be agents who were unsuccessful in their quest for a local agency.

The 'Pros' of paying to be an outside agent

- You can do it quickly, with little or no screening.
- You can often get better prices and commissions because these agencies have high volume.
- You can often get an excellent commission split, as high as 80%.
- You can get started right away.
- You can use your tenure with a distant host to build a track record you can later use to sell yourself to a local agency, if that still appeals to you.
- If you decide this career is not for you, it's easier to walk away from a distant host agency than a local one, where you may feel you're "letting the team down."

The 'Cons' of paying to be an outside agent

- It can be expensive (although it doesn't have to be).
- You'll be dealing by phone, mail, and email. That can be slow and inconvenient. You may have difficulty handling requests for last-minute bookings and you will probably have to pick up the costs for having tickets and other travel documents shipped to you.
- You may have to commit to an investment in computer software. It can take quite a while to earn enough in commissions to pay off that investment; so if you decide the travel

game isn't for you, you could wind up in the hole.

- If you have a serious problem with one of these agencies, seeking remedy can be difficult. It's hard to sue an outfit half a continent away.
- Sometimes it's hard to get personal assistance when you have a question or a problem.
- Finally, there is always the danger of being ripped off. You may be lured by "agencies" that aren't really travel agencies or by actual travel agencies that simply don't deliver on their promises.

Summary

There are two basic routes to becoming an outside agent, each with its own advantages and disadvantages. You can try to find a local agency to work with or you can choose from the growing number of host agencies, scattered across the country, that specialize in working with outside agents.

In the end, you'll have to make your own decision — a local agency or an "instant agency" like those described in this chapter. If you go the instant agency route, you'll have an additional decision to make — do you go with a low-investment, bare-bones host agency or pay more to join an agency that provides training and support? Do you choose an ARC or a non-ARC host? Or maybe a referral agency makes more sense for you.

Whatever your choice, you must understand that you are entering into a business to business (not a consumer to business) relationship and that no one is going to look out for you but you. You must understand that you are completely independent of your host agency and that your host agency has to suit you, not the other way around.

Action steps

Here are some things you can do to put what you have learned in this chapter into action:

- Write down the pluses and minuses, from your own very personal perspective, of being an outside sales rep for a host agency. You might want to create a "+" column and a "−" column. Then determine how important each plus and each minus is to you.
- Write down which path to becoming an outside agent appeals to you (local agency, paying a fee; joining a bare bones agency or a quasi franchise; etc.). Again, do this from your own very personal perspective. Next write down what you see as the pluses and minuses of the path you have chosen. Be honest with yourself, there are no right or wrong answers.
- Begin the process of researching host agencies, either travel agencies in your area or host agencies elsewhere that work specifically with outside agents. You can use *How to Choose a Host Agency* to assist you in this process. Don't make any

firm decisions just yet; at this point you are merely gathering information.

If you purchased this book as part of my home study course, you already have *How to Choose a Host Agency*. If not, you can order it by going to:

http://www.HomeTravelAgency.com/choosehost.html

Chapter Five:
The Referral Agent

What you will learn

After you have completed this chapter you will be able to:
- Define "referral agent."
- Discuss the pros and cons of being a referral agent.
- Make an informed decision as to whether or not you wish to join a referral agency.

Key terms and concepts

This chapter involves the following key terms and concepts:
- Referral agent. A person who introduces prospective customers to a travel agency, as opposed to researching, selling, and booking travel. Referral agents are compensated by a share of the commissions generated by travel sold to customers they introduce to the agency.
- Referral agency. A travel agency that focuses largely or entirely on business generated by a network of outside referral agents. The term "card mill" is a derogatory term for referral agency.
- Fam trips. "Familiarization trips" are a perk of the travel industry. They are reduced-rate (occasionally free) trips offered to travel agents by suppliers on the theory that the travel agent who is familiar with their product will sell it more effectively, or at least sell it more.

Introduction

Referral agencies have always been a controversial aspect of the travel distribution system and, even though at least a few of them have gained some grudging respect in the industry, they continue to generate controversy. My goal in this chapter is to provide you with the most complete information possible on referral agencies, how they work, and what they can and cannot do for you. I am sure that some of the things discussed in this chapter will infuriate some people in the travel agenting business. Don't shoot the messenger.

To fully understand referral agencies and the controversy they have stirred, you need to understand two intertwined threads in the history of travel agents. First, travel agencies have used finders and bird dogs (discussed in *Chapter 4: The Outside Sales Rep*) for nearly as long as there have been travel agencies. I strongly suspect that even today some travel agency owners who hate the very idea of referral agencies compensate bird dogs when they feel it appropriate. So "referral agents," whatever the term given them by different people at different times, have been around a long time.

Second, travel agents get some attractive benefits from the supplier community. Those benefits have always been one of the great attractions of a career as a travel agent, although in my opinion the benefits are often oversold, especially since they are not doled out as lavishly as they were ten or twenty years ago.

Many of the advertisements designed by host agencies and their promoters to attract home-based travel agent wannabes follow a predictable pattern: A picture of a lovely white sand beach, a beautiful young couple ("That could be me!") and lines like "As one of our travel consultants, you'll receive all the benefits given to other travel professionals; you'll be eligible for free and reduced-fare trips." Wow! Where do I sign up?

As with so much in the field of advertising, there is less here than meets the eye. Like the beer commercials that suggest that after a six pack or two you'll be surrounded by beautiful, bikini-clad babes, or the cereal ads that imply that after a few bowlfuls you'll look just like the gorgeous young model slithering into that slinky dress, the marketing materials touting host agent opportunities tend to, shall we say, exaggerate the benefits of their product.

Not that these outfits can't set you up to be a home-based outside agent — they can. It's just that sometimes their advertising makes you wonder if they're more interested in collecting your sign-up fee (which in some cases can be substantial) than in letting you make money, which is a necessary prerequisite to "free" travel. Even responsible observers and organizations tend to put on the rose-colored glasses when writing about the benefits that accrue to outside sales reps. My goal in this chapter is to give you the straight poop.

Don't get me wrong. There really are, in fact, a lot of nifty benefits that come with getting involved in this exciting career. It is actually possible (although rare) to travel free. It is far more common to get very attractive discounts on your travel. What a lot of the people pitching the "be-a-travel-agent-and-travel-free" pipe dreams won't tell you in plain English is that all these benefits must be earned by producing sales and many come with strings attached.

At any rate, these two threads — the bird dogging concept and travel agent benefits — came together some years ago to create a new type of travel agency.

The card mill controversy

In the early nineties, a few entrepreneurial companies, which were quickly labeled "card mills" for reasons that will become apparent, began offering a new type of business opportunity: You could become a travel agent — instantly and for a fee — by signing up to be an outside representative for a bona fide travel agency. As part of your sign-up package you received an "official travel agent photo ID card." This card was issued by the agency offering the opportunity but, perhaps not coincidentally, it bore more than a passing resemblance to the IATAN card, the universally recognized credential of the travel agent business. Many of these offers were accompanied by the kind of advertising hype I mentioned above. The marketing materials strongly implied (while not actually saying so) that the ID card provided would open the door to all sorts of wonderful travel bargains and professional courtesies.

This concept wasn't entirely new. Travel agencies had been using outside agents for decades, and a few unscrupulous agency owners had been listing their mothers-in-law, dentists, and others as "part-owners" and employees so they could gain access to industry discounts. What made this new phenomenon different was the open, excited, gung-ho way in which the opportunity was marketed and the emphasis on the instant access to free or substantially discounted travel. When the Internet emerged as a marketing powerhouse in the late nineties, the phenomenon really took off.

To a lot of people it looked like a great deal, and a perfectly legal one, too. The holders of these cards were travel agents, after all, outside agents for a real travel agency. And they were selling travel. Or were they? In the answer to that question lies the nub of a heated controversy that continues to this day and will probably last for years to come.

The fact of the matter is, a great many people who were attracted to these offers were genuinely interested in making an honest living — or at least a few extra bucks — selling travel. It is also hard to deny that many people were attracted to these offers for the promised benefits and had no real interest in selling travel at all.

To further complicate matters, not every home-based travel agent opportunity was created equal. Some outside agent opportunities were structured like quasi-franchises, with intensive training, full automation, extensive marketing support, and high fees to pay for it all. Others were straightforward, barebones operations that simply offered outside reps a convenient way to handle their ticketing needs. Still others seemed (to many observers) to skirt the boundaries of ethics and legality and came to be labeled as "card mills." Because of the controversy that erupted over the card mills, all home-based outside agents came to be looked on with deep suspicion by the traditional travel agent community.

What makes an agency a referral agency?

Although virtually every agency that openly announces its use of an outside sales force has been labeled a card mill at one time or another, true referral agencies share a number of distinguishing characteristics.

Referral agencies tend to be characterized by:

- A promise of lucrative benefits to outside agents who steer business their way. (In fairness, many host agencies in other categories make similar claims.)
- Agents who "refer" business to the agency's 800 number rather than perform the research and booking tasks usually associated with being a travel agent.
- Relatively high sign-up fees, usually $495. Some cynics have charged that these agencies choose $495 as their sign-up fee to avoid the higher level of regulatory scrutiny given by state attorneys general to business opportunities charging more than $500.
- A strong emphasis in their marketing materials on the photo ID card they issue and the access to industry discounts and courtesies it is said to provide. (Hence, the derogatory term "card mill.")
- A referral fee (typically $100 or more) for signing up new agents, sometimes with an override on the volume they produce. Some agencies touted elaborate multilevel marketing programs offering their "distributors" income through several "generations" by selling new-agent kits — a system that looked to some attorneys general suspiciously like a pyramid scheme. Most of these schemes have disappeared, but should you encounter one, approach it with extreme caution.
- Low commission splits and/or a refusal to book or pay commission on certain products (such as hotels and car rentals).
- A maximum commission split of 50% of a commission that is capped at 10%. In other words, the effective maximum commission is 5% of gross. If the agency gets an 8%, the agent's 50% share is 4%, but if the agency gets a 15% commission, the agent's "50%" share is still 5%.
- Some referral agencies can provide their outside agents with their own "branded" web site, at which members of the general public can book travel. Again, in fairness, other host agencies offer this feature as well.
- Special discount travel deals for their agents only.

As you can see, these agencies envision a substantially different type of "outside agent" than the one I described in the last chapter.

The vast majority of host agencies at least offer their outside reps the opportunity to do everything a "traditional" travel agent does. (Whether the agent actually does those things is another matter.) Most offer respectable commission splits (60/40 and up of the actual commission). Most "non-referral" host agencies make clear in their contracts (if not in their advertising) that agents are entitled to industry benefits only when they meet certain generally accepted industry standards, which I will discuss in more detail in *Chapter 10: Straight Talk on Travel Industry Benefits*. Some of them issue their own photo ID cards, others do not.

Referral agencies actually represent a small percentage of home-based travel agent opportunities. In fact, my thoroughly unscientific observation is that there are fewer referral agencies than there used to be.

How referral agencies work

Joining a referral agency is simple. Just pay your money and you're one of their "travel agents." You will be assigned a PIN (Personal Identification Number) that will identify you to their computer system and enable them to track any commissions due you. Send them a passport-sized photo of yourself and you'll get a "Travel Agent ID card" in the mail.

To book your own travel, you call their 800 number or log on to their web site and, using your PIN, make your bookings. To "sell" travel to others, you must get them to call or log on, using your PIN, to make their bookings. It is also possible to do it for them, assuming they will entrust you with their credit card information.

Some referral agencies will provide you with a "branded" web site. Essentially, it is a clone of their in-house booking engine that has a web site address unique to you. You can then direct traffic to that web site and earn a commission every time a commissionable booking is made there.

Some referral agencies also require you to submit a commission tracking form for some or all of the bookings you make. Failure to do so means no commission on that booking.

Do they make sense for selling travel?

As I noted earlier, many people join referral agencies because they sincerely want to sell travel and think this is a way to do it. However, actively selling travel as a referral agent presents some unique challenges:

- Once you get a customer to call the agency 800 number or log on to their web site, you effectively lose control of the sale and the customer's experience. You have no way of knowing, short of standing at the customer's shoulder, if they are getting good service from the inside salesperson or finding the online booking site easy to navigate and work with.
- For you to be credited with the sale, the customer must use your PIN (Personal Identification Number) at the time of booking. If the customer forgets your number or types it in incorrectly online, you lose your commission.
- One attractive element of the referral agency model is that once the customer is in the referral agency's records, they remain your customer forever. In theory, you can be earning commissions in perpetuity for making one referral. The problem is, how do you insure the customer calls that 800 number or logs on to that web site next time they need to book something?
- Commissions on some products are very low or nonexistent. For example, don't look to make much of anything on domes-

tic air or car rentals. Some referral agencies won't even take bookings in some product categories.

- There are two areas where the commissions paid by referral agencies begin to look attractive — cruises and tours. But the typical referral agency will only pay 5% of gross (50% of a commission capped at 10%), so even here your earning potential is somewhat restricted. Given the number of agents that the typical referral agency says it has and the high volume those agents must generate for it (even if many are booking only for themselves), it is hard to imagine that these agencies do not enjoy commissions of substantially more than 10% with most, if not all, cruise lines and tour operators.

   To be truly effective in selling cruises and tours you need to do more than hand out business cards. You need to generate excitement about specific cruises and specific itineraries or promote to groups (who by definition will be taking the same cruise or tour). If you are going to go to this amount of trouble, then there are ways to earn a considerably higher payback for the time and effort invested. And these ways can involve a much lower investment than the typical $495 entry fee for a referral agency.

- Your "branded" web site (if you have one) is only as good as the traffic it generates. But if you are computer savvy enough to drive traffic to the site, you are computer savvy enough to make better money on the Internet. Some referral agencies will sell you traffic generating services to drive traffic to your web site; these offers are of dubious value in my opinion.

- Conversion rates (the so-called "look to book ratio") on any travel booking web site (including the big ones) are notoriously low. The odds of making significant money on a web site provided by a referral agency are extremely long.

What referral agencies pay

Every referral agency will have its own commission schedule, but to give you an idea, here is what one referral agency was paying at press time. I suspect most referral agencies are in the same ballpark.

- *Air.* The vast majority of airline bookings result in no commission at all. In cases where there is a commission (up to 8%), the agent receives 10% of what the agency receives (up to 0.8%, or 80 cents on every $100).
- *Hotels.* 50% of commission (up to 10%). Of course, any hotel room booked at a travel agent rate is non-commissionable.
- *Cars.* 50% of commission (up to 10%). Some car rental companies only pay 5% commission and others offer this referral agency's agents a special non-commissionable rate.
- *Cruises/Tours.* 50% of commissions (up to 10%). There is no participation in overrides or commissions greater than 10%.

The major rule here is that anything booked using your card to get a discount and anything booked as a "fam trip" or as an agent-only special, is non-commissionable. As you can see, this is no get-rich-quick program.

Do they make sense for the benefits?

Although I have no way of knowing for sure, I suspect that most people join for the discounts (on their own travel) and the benefits they will get from flashing the card. I will discuss this issue in more detail in *Chapter 10: Straight Talk on Travel Industry Benefits*. For now, suffice it to say that referral agency ID cards are less attractive than they once were for two major reasons.

One, there are fewer commissions these days. When referral agencies burst on the scene in a big way, airlines were still paying 10% commissions. A businessperson who flew a lot could save a significant amount of money just on airfare. No more. Airlines have effectively eliminated commissions to travel agents. Other suppliers, like car rental companies have also lowered or eliminated commissions.

Second, the industry is getting savvier about travel agent ID cards. One result of all the controversy that referral agencies generated was a much wider awareness in the industry about what constitutes "valid" travel agent ID. More and more desk clerks can tell the difference between an IATAN card and an ID that looks like an IATAN card but isn't. More and more cruise lines and tour operators are asking for proof of an IATAN card before extending courtesies or fam trips to travel agents.

If you believe that having a travel agent ID card means you can travel for "next to nothing," you will be disappointed. If you have been traveling dirt cheap by staying in budget motels and hotels, traveling on low-fare airlines, and buying third-class rail tickets overseas, then you won't do any better with a referral agency's card. On the other hand, if you are used to paying top dollar at fancy hotels and resorts, then you may see some significant savings. A $200-a-night hotel room may look like a terrific deal if you're used to paying $350, but it won't look like much of a bargain if you're used to paying $60 a night for a hotel.

That's not to say that there are no benefits associated with these cards, just that the opportunities are more limited than they were, say, ten years ago. Referral agency membership does get you discounts, but in many cases they are comparable to the discounts you would get by joining a travel club for much less money. Still, there are ways to maximize the benefits of a referral agency ID card. I'll discuss them a little later.

Does a referral agency make sense for you?

Only you can answer that question. However, I can make some observations that will help you formulate an answer. In general, I feel that joining a referral agency makes the most sense for those who...

- *Are primarily interested in travel benefits.* My personal feeling is that while the benefits that come from holding an

ID card from a referral agency are overrated (see *Chapter 10*), there are benefits nonetheless. Many people find them worth the price of admission.

- ***Travel a great deal for pleasure.*** This could mean retirees or others with time on their hands and the disposable income to fill it. Referral agencies offer the best discounts (through their agent-only specials) and commission rebates on things like cruises and tours that appeal to the mid- to down-market leisure traveler. Now that airline commissions have effectively ended, business travelers will get far less benefit from a referral agency than they once did. However, there are certain circumstances in which a referral agency might work well for a business trip — if, for example, it is overseas or if you book air, hotel, and a rental car as a package.

- ***Want to have very few customers.*** If your main goal is to save money on your own travel, with a minor focus on booking trips for family and friends, then a referral agency makes a certain amount of sense.

- ***Focus on an easily identifiable market (like cruises).*** These folks should also be willing to "leave money on the table" in exchange for not having to concern themselves with details. As an example, if you can see yourself going on several cruises every year and convincing a bunch of friends to go on the same cruise and make their bookings through your agency, then this can be a good strategy for you. You won't make a great deal of money, but you will save some and you won't have to work too hard. In this case, you would be best advised to look for a referral agency that either specializes in cruises or has a good cruise program in place.

How to succeed as a referral agent

First of all, we need to define "success" in this context. The chances of making a large sum of money as a referral agent are slim. There are a few referral agents who earn what you might call a "living wage," but there aren't many. Even the owners of referral agencies will say, off the record at least, that their members aren't making a living at this. It's much more about the discounts and using whatever commissions are earned to offset out of pocket travel expenses.

So success for the referral agent probably means, on the high end, making enough money each year to cover their own travel expenses or, at the low end, enough to cover the cost of signing up and the annual renewal fees. With those parameters in mind, here are a few suggestions.

- ***Pay as little as possible to join.*** The "typical" fee for a referral agency is $495 to sign up and $149 to renew each year. But that's changing. Some charge less and at least one referral agency charges a $49 sign-up fee, plus $6 a month, a significant savings which puts it on a par with travel clubs. If your main interest is the ID card, and since any ID card is equally valuable (or worthless, depending on your perspective), why pay more than you have to?

- *Aggressively promote your agency's 800 number and/or web site.* My personal feeling is that a business card and your personal recommendation work better than the web sites. People who book online are notoriously fickle and will visit several sites to get the best price. Moreover, the vast majority of online bookers are booking cheap air, which pays you nothing.

- *Be a "pied piper."* This is what I was talking about earlier when I mentioned taking a cruise and convincing a bunch of friends to join you. You can steer people to your agency by touting the great pricing and pointing out that when they book with your agency, the group can be assured of having cabins near each other. A variation on the pied piper theme is to talk up trips you've taken and urge people who are interested to call your agency to get the same great deal you did.

- *Sign up new agents.* If this is the sort of thing you're good at (and some people are better at it than others) then you can probably easily cover at least your out of pocket costs for joining the agency.

- *Take advantage of the benefits.* This is a money-saving, rather than a money-making strategy. Most referral agencies offer "specials" for their agents only. Sometimes these non-commissionable trips offer excellent value; other times they are not much better than similar deals available to the general public. You need to be an informed consumer to get the most value out of this aspect of referral agencies. However, the more you "save," the less expensive your membership fee begins to seem.

- *Join a professional association.* Once you join a referral agency, you can then join an association such as the Outside Sales Support Network (OSSN), and become eligible for their ultra-low cost fam trips, mostly cruises. These trips are much less expensive than anything offered by the referral agencies and they often feature more upscale ships. If you are an avid cruiser, this strategy alone might make it worth your while to join a referral agency. You can download a discounted OSSN application at:

www.HomeTravelAgency.com/ossnapp.pdf

- *Focus on groups.* Sending 50 people on a tour obviously has a higher payback than sending yourself and a few friends. If you are in a position to "presell" your own groups (a minister organizing a pilgrimage, or the president of the ladies' club organizing a London theater tour), then this could work well for you. Be aware, however, that if you are in a position to develop significant group business, you can earn substantially more money, with not too much additional work, by using other approaches you will learn in this course.

Some additional thoughts

Referral agencies, as you now know, are a fundamentally different type of host agency than the host agencies discussed in the previous chapter. Most people will make a choice between these two types of agency and I suspect that most people reading this book will opt for the more traditional host agencies. However, it doesn't have to be an either-or proposition. Remember what I said earlier about being independent? There is nothing to prevent you from affiliating with both a traditional host agency *and* a referral agency.

Why would you want to do that? There are a number of reasons.

You might feel that joining a referral agency gives you immediate access to travel industry benefits that you can take advantage of while learning the ropes through your other host agency. Therefore, you might feel that the cost of joining is worth it. (Obviously, different people will come to different decisions on this.)

Even though you are actively booking and selling travel for a much better commission, you still might feel that the agent-only deals offered by a referral agency are easier to arrange and just as good as trying, perhaps unsuccessfully, to qualify for a regular fam trip.

You might see it as a form of insurance. Having that Travel Agent ID card in your wallet might come in handy when your flight is delayed and you need to book into that high-priced airport hotel.

Having access to a referral agency gives you more options in how to serve your customers. For example, there is a difference between telling a customer that you won't handle their Cincinnati to Seattle flight and saying, "You can book that online at www.My-Referral-Site.com!" You don't make money either way, but the customer has a different experience. In a similar way, you can refer people to a referral agency as a polite way of getting rid of customers you'd rather not have, typically those who ask a lot of questions but never book.

Summary

Referral agencies are controversial. In this chapter, I have attempted to provide as complete information as possible about how referral agencies work and how people are using them. Some aspects of referral agencies strike many in the industry as highly unethical. You might agree — or not. However, it appears that there is nothing illegal about referral agencies or their business model, at least as evidenced by the fact that after years of effort by some factions in the travel distribution system to shut them down, they are still very much in business.

Joining a referral agency will appeal most to those who want access to discounted travel and travel agent benefits. However, due to recent changes in the travel distribution system (the elimination of airline commissions preeminent among them) these offers are not as attractive as they used to be.

You can succeed as a referral agent, as long as you are clear on what "success" means in this context. Finally, joining a referral agency is not an either-or proposition; there are some perfectly valid reasons for having an affiliation with a referral agency even if you do most of your booking and selling elsewhere.

Action steps

Here are some things you can do to put what you have learned in this chapter into action:

- Start the process of researching your referral agency sources. Some are listed in *How to Choose a Host Agency*. Visit their web sites and examine them carefully, trying to "read between the lines" as it were. If you have any questions, or anything seems odd, send them an email or call for clarification.
- If you are seriously considering a referral agency as your main way of plugging into the travel distribution system, read *Chapter 10: Straight Talk on Travel Industry Benefits* before making a final decision.

If you purchased this book as part of my home study course, you already have *How to Choose a Host Agency*. If not, you can order it by going to:

http://www.HomeTravelAgency.com/choosehost.html

*Home-Based
Travel Agent*

Chapter Six:
The Independent Agent

What you will learn

After you have completed this chapter you will be able to:

- Discuss the pros and cons of dealing directly with suppliers.
- Make an informed decision as to when it makes sense for you to seek a direct relationship with a travel supplier.
- Make an informed decision as to whether or not you wish to form direct relationships and, if so, under what circumstances.

Key terms and concepts

This chapter involves the following key terms and concepts:

- Pseudo ARC number. An alphanumeric identifier used by a supplier to identify a travel agent with whom it deals directly on a relatively informal basis.
- Just because you *can* deal directly with suppliers, without using a host agency, does not mean that you *should*.
- As independent contractors, home-based agents are free to deal with host agencies when that makes the most business sense and directly with a supplier when that makes the most business sense.
- It is possible to obtain a unique industry identifier that will, in effect, allow you to become an independent *travel agency*, as opposed to an independent *travel agent*.

Introduction

So far, we have discussed two basic ways to function in the travel distribution system as a travel agent — becoming a referral agent (*Chapter 5*) or going the distance and becoming what I call (rather clumsily, I'll admit) a booking and selling agent (*Chapter 4*).

While these two approaches have some important and fundamental differences, they are alike in that they both involve becoming an "outside agent" for an accredited travel agency. You and the host agency will be two separate business entities (and you will most likely have your own, separate, business name), but when you book travel, you will do so in the name of your host agency. In other words, when you have dealings with a supplier you will present yourself and be seen as an "agent" of the "host agency" with which you are affiliated. When you make a booking with a supplier, the supplier's records will show the name of your host agency, not your separate business name. When it comes time to pay commissions, the supplier will pay them to your host agency, which will then share them with you according to whatever contractual agreement you have with your host.

The vast majority of bookings made by home-based travel agents (as I use the term in this book), are made in this fashion, by outside agents working through a host agency. This is the business model almost every home-based agent adopts when starting out. It's a very good business model, for any number of reasons, and most home-based agents stick to it throughout their careers.

However, it is actually possible to "disintermediate" (or eliminate) the host agency from the picture in some circumstances.

Dealing directly with suppliers

Of course, if you are a booking and selling agent, you will always be dealing directly with suppliers as you make bookings for your clients. What I mean by "dealing directly" in this context is establishing relationships in which the commission comes directly to you instead of passing through a host travel agency.

When you do this, you deal with the supplier not as an outside agent working for a host agency, but as a travel agency in your own right. You use your own business name, not that of your host agency. And when it comes time for the supplier to pay commissions, those commissions come to you, in your business name, and you don't have to share them with anyone.

Remember, the major reason for dealing through a host agency is because that is either the only way to sell something (domestic airline tickets are an example) or because it is a lot more convenient to do so (commissions from major hotel chains are a good example). As an independent contractor you have the right to do business where, with whom, and how you please. That means you have the right to deal direct when the circumstances and any relevant laws allow.

As more and more people in the travel industry wake up to the fact that home-based agents and home-based agencies are here to stay, more and more suppliers have shown themselves to be "IC-friendly," that is they are willing to work directly with you, the independent contractor, without a host agency serving as middleman.

Dealing directly with suppliers is not an either-or proposition. In other words, you can deal directly with some suppliers while dealing with others as an outside agent of your host agency. It is theoretically possible to deal directly with a given supplier for some bookings while channeling others through your host agency, although I wouldn't recommend it. The downside risk — of confusion, ill-feelings, and so forth — outweighs any benefits.

When home-based agents start forming direct relationships with suppliers, they do so in a relatively informal manner, a sort of gentlemen's agreement. And they do it occasionally, while still funneling most of their business through their host agency.

As their business grows, some home-based agents become more formal in their dealings with suppliers. I will discuss that phenomenon later. For now, let's concentrate on how home-based agents create informal, case-by-case arrangements to deal directly with suppliers.

When dealing directly might be possible

Here are some of the situations in which a home-based agent might collect commissions directly from suppliers.

- *Hotels.* Larger hotel chains identify travel agencies by IATA, ARC, or CLIA number and consolidate commission payments by computer. If you hope to get a commission from them, you'll have to get it through an appointed agency that has those numbers. Smaller hotels, b&b's, and many resorts, however, are individual properties or very small chains. They too pay commissions. (At least some of them do.) To them, your little operation, Mary Jane's Travel Boutique, looks pretty much the same as the Very Big Agency Network through which you do your airline ticketing. And the odds of them paying don't change according to whose name's supposed to be on the check. Moreover, suppliers in this category are most likely paying a flat ten percent in commissions. This is a no-brainer. Deal directly with the property or small chain.

- *Tour operators.* Smaller, newer, or more aggressive tour operators may offer an outside rep like you a full commission for any business you bring in. Of course, in doing so, they run the risk of alienating the agency through which you book. This has nothing to do with the legalities of your independent contractor relationship with the agency. It has everything to do with clout in the marketplace. The agency would maintain that it brings in a lot more business, as an agency, than any of its individual reps; that it has made a much higher commitment to the supplier in terms of its visibility in the marketplace and; therefore, should get some consideration. It certainly doesn't expect the supplier to give away business it would otherwise get to low-overhead upstarts like yourself. Most suppliers are in agreement with this line of thinking and are loath to offend larger agencies (like the one through which you book) by favoring smaller agencies (like you).

So you have to ask yourself, "Why would this tour operator

be willing to deal with me direct?" Often it's because they're hungry. They may figure your business (assuming they get some of it) is worth the rather small risk that your agency will get wind of it and complain. But their willingness to deal direct could mean they are on shaky financial footing. Exercise caution in a situation like this.

On the other hand, if you are bringing in a large group — especially if you are doing so on a regular basis — then you have a certain amount of bargaining power. In this kind of situation, even well-established operators will be interested in dealing with you on a discreet, direct basis.

- *Cruises.* As with tours, the likelihood of a cruise line showing a willingness to deal with you direct will be a function of volume and steady volume at that. If you are at the point where such a relationship makes sense, you are probably at a point where becoming a CLIA-member "cruise-only" agency makes sense (see below).

- *Airlines.* The most obvious example of dealing direct when it comes to airline tickets is getting a consolidator ticket for a client (discussed in detail in *Chapter 12: Booking Airlines*). You don't actually deal with the airline, but with a middleman. You buy it, mark it up, and pass it along. However, it's actually possible (if rare) for outside reps to form direct relationships with major airlines. When you get to that point, you and the airline will know it.

Reasons not to deal directly with suppliers

Just because you can deal directly with a given supplier does not necessarily mean that you should, especially if you are new to the travel industry. There are a number of possible reasons why dealing direct may not be such a good idea:

- *You don't know what you're doing.* I believe in taking things one step at a time. Using this course, the resources provided by your host agency, and the wide variety of continuing education resources (many of them free) offered by the industry, you can start to "learn the ropes" of the business. But don't fool yourself into thinking that you can bluff a supplier into thinking you're an old hand when you're not. Even if your host agency doesn't do a lot of hand holding, it at least functions as a buffer between you and the world of the suppliers and increases the likelihood that an error on your part will be caught before it does you or your client any grievous harm.

- *You run the risk of burning bridges.* If you reveal yourself to be an incompetent ninny to a supplier at the beginning of your career, you may find it hard to get them to take you seriously a few years later when you actually know what you are doing. Remember, the whole point of establishing a direct relationship with a supplier is to enhance your business and your bottom line. Trying to do that before you're ready can actually set you back.

- **You'll spoil it for others.** Home-based travel agents face enough prejudice in the industry without novices making everyone look bad. If you're intent on trying to run before you walk, this advice will probably cut no ice with you, but at least think about it.

- **You'll lose money on the deal.** If altruism can't deter you, this one should. Even if Supplier X is willing to deal directly with you, the odds are extremely good that they'll offer you the minimum commission, usually ten percent. But if Supplier X has a preferred supplier relationship with your host agency, paying 15 percent commission, and you enjoy a 70/30 split with that host agency, then you'll make more money putting the booking through the host agency. Don't believe me? Do the math. If you use *How to Choose a Host Agency* to guide you in making your choice, you will most likely end up having a very favorable commission split with your host.

- **You may want to get an IATAN card.** The most common way to get this widely recognized industry ID card (although not the only way) is to qualify for it by earning commissions as an outside agent for an IATAN-accredited travel agency. Any commissions you earn by dealing directly with a supplier will not be counted toward meeting the requirements for the IATAN card. For more on this issue, see *Chapter 10: Straight Talk on Travel Industry Benefits.*

Reasons to deal directly with suppliers

So if there are reasons not to deal directly with suppliers, when do you know the time has come to take the plunge and strike off on your own? That will depend on a variety of factors, but I believe that establishing a direct relationship with a supplier makes the most sense in the following circumstances:

- **You have specialized.** Let's say you have decided to concentrate on selling bicycle tours of Europe. Then it makes perfect sense to strike mutually satisfactory deals with tour operators running bicycle tours in Europe.

- **You are already well known to the supplier.** If you are, indeed, selling a lot of bike tours in Europe the chances are you already know the major suppliers pretty well. In a small niche like this, it might even be possible that you have become one of their major producers.

- **You will be doing a lot of business with the supplier.** If this is the case, then you are in an excellent position to bargain for a better commission. If you are already producing significant volume, the supplier may offer you a better deal. This also gets back to my earlier point about not spoiling it for others. If a supplier finds itself dealing with a lot of home-based agents who make one sale a year, it might very well decide that keeping track of so many agents doesn't make economic sense.

Host agencies and 'exclusivity'

You should also be aware that some host agencies will try to tell you that you and they have an "exclusive" relationship — that is, that you must book all your travel through them. This violates both the spirit and the letter of your independent contractor agreement, which you undoubtedly signed. The agency wants you to be an independent contractor so they don't have to carry you on their rolls as an employee, withhold taxes on the money they send you, and be liable for unemployment insurance and a lot of other inconveniences. But when they insist they are your "exclusive" agency they are attempting to control you as they would an employee. In other words they are trying to have it both ways and that is not fair. It's also probably not legal but, not being a lawyer, I won't try to call that one.

If your agency tries to claim "exclusivity," you have a number of options. You can refuse, perhaps even insist that the offending language in the agreement (if it is there) be changed. Or you can simply let them know that you disagree with their position and tell them that you reserve the right to make strategic alliances with whomever you choose, as befits your standing as a true independent contractor. Or you can say nothing, figuring (a) they'll never know of your other dealings anyway and (b), even if they do, there's nothing they can do about it.

Of course, you can choose to deal only with one agency, turning away offers from tour operators to deal direct or routing hotel reservations through your agency even when it's not absolutely necessary. You might do this just because it's easier or because you receive a great deal of support and training from the agency for which you feel they deserve your unswerving loyalty. You might also do it to increase your chances of qualifying for an IATAN card. However, you should know that you are not bound to do so. In most cases, the outside rep's relationship with the host agency is arm's length. The agency has little contact with the rep unless and until a booking is made and little direct knowledge of the rep's activities.

Most outside reps I've talked to don't make much of an issue of the matter of exclusivity. Rather they choose a line of least resistance. They go about their business, dealing as they wish, with whom they wish, figuring it's nobody's business but their own. I think they're right.

But let's say push comes to shove. Let's say your agency doesn't like the fact that you are maintaining direct relationships and makes an issue of it. I would recommend simply pointing out that, since you're an independent contractor, they cannot make such demands on you — unless they want to start paying your health benefits and withholding taxes like they do for their other employees. They are unlikely to want to do that, although who knows? If you have proven yourself a valuable asset, they may be willing to change the basis of the relationship. And you may be willing to entertain that possibility.

Of course, if the agency is really annoyed with you, they can always decide not to do your ticketing. Most agreements give them the right to terminate the arrangement for whatever reason they choose. Even if you had a basis for legal action in a case like this (and you'd have to review the individual facts with a lawyer to find out), it probably would cost you more to mount a suit than it's worth. It's far easier to simply move to another agency for the ticketing you need.

Pseudo ARC (or IATA) numbers

By and large, getting to the point of dealing directly with a supplier presupposes that you are doing a fair amount of business with them on a regular basis — or at least that the supplier believes that you will be. In other words, we're talking about an ongoing relationship rather than a series of one-shot deals.

As we've noted earlier, one of the major conveniences of having an ARC or an IATA number is that it makes it easy for suppliers to identify and track agencies in their computer systems, making the disbursing of commissions more efficient and more accurate. The suppliers with whom you deal directly are used to using that ARC number to track commissions, but you, the independent travel agent, don't have one. So what to do?

If you are going to be treated by the supplier like a "real" travel agency, they will probably set you up with a "pseudo ARC number" or a "pseudo IATA number." The number they issue to your agency is used solely to identify your agency and distinguish it from all others in the supplier's computer system. Sometimes they will simply use your phone number, which is unique; other times, they will create a number according to some system of their own devising. The pseudo ARC number will serve as a mechanism for identifying all bookings made by you and of assuring that you get your commission in due course. It means that the supplier intends to treat you exactly like all the other travel agencies with which it has relationships. What it does *not* mean is that you now have an ARC or IATA number. Your pseudo ARC number is just that — pseudo, or pretend.

Another thing to bear in mind is that you will not have one pseudo ARC number. Each supplier will issue you its own. Of course, since many suppliers use the agent's phone number, your pseudo ARC number may well be the same for several suppliers.

Obtaining a pseudo ARC number is becoming increasingly easy. Simply inform the supplier that you are an independent, non-ARC agency and that you would like to establish a direct relationship with them. Sometimes you can do it with a phone call, no (or very few) questions asked. More frequently, the process will be somewhat more formal. Among the things you may be asked to provide are:

- A letter of request on your own agency's letterhead telling them why you are seeking this direct relationship.
- Copies of your state or local business licenses (if any).
- Your federal employer ID number. Often you can supply your own social security number in a slightly different format. In other words, your social security number is 000-00-0000. If you write it as 00-0000000, it looks like a federal employer ID number. You can also request a federal employer ID number from the IRS, over the phone, even if you have no employees. For more information, visit the IRS web site at www.irs.gov and search for "employer ID."
- Proof of errors and omissions insurance. Suppliers do not always ask for this, but it's a good idea to have it if you plan to establish a number of direct relationships. The Outside Sales Support Network (OSSN) is a good source of guidance on getting affordable E&O insurance. You can join at a discount by downloading the application form at:
  www.HomeTravelAgency.com/ossnapp.pdf

Despite the increasing ease of obtaining pseudo ARC status, my advice is to avoid doing so unless and until you will be doing a considerable amount of business with the supplier. Remember that the 10% commission you are likely to get directly from the supplier is less than 70% of the 15% commission that you might obtain through a host agency that enjoys a preferred supplier relationship with the same supplier.

Putting it all together

So far, we have looked at a number of different ways to be a travel agent.

- In *Chapter 3*, we discussed ways to sell travel on a relatively informal basis.
- In *Chapters 4* and *5*, we discussed becoming an outside agent for an accredited, bonded travel agency.
- So far in this chapter, we have discussed forming ad-hoc, relatively informal direct relationships with suppliers when it makes sense to do so. In many ways, this strategy bears some similarities to what we discussed in *Chapter 3*, although now the "agent" is probably much better compensated.

For many, if not most home-based agents, these are the only strategies you need to have a long and rewarding career marketing and selling travel. Many agents will be quite happy as outside agents for a host agency, taking the responsibility to sell and book travel for their clients. Others may decide the part-time, low-payback model offered by referral agencies makes more sense for them. Still others might form relationships with both types of host agency.

As home-based agents become more knowledgeable and more serious about their business and the travel industry, especially if they begin to specialize to any great extent, they usually find themselves forming at least a few direct relationships with some suppliers (using pseudo ARC numbers), while continuing to book the bulk of their business through their host agency. Some agents, however, will want to take things a step further and become more truly independent.

Becoming truly independent

As independent contractors, home-based agents are completely free to design their businesses as they see fit. Each person's circumstance will be a little different, but if we look at the entire range of home-based travel agents, we can see certain broad patterns in their business models.

I don't know what the precise percentages are — statistics of any sort about the home-based travel agent industry are virtually impossible to come by — but I suspect we can divide the array of business models as follows:

- Functions solely as an outside agent for a host agency.
- Functions primarily as an outside agent but has some direct relationships with suppliers.
- Makes a majority of bookings directly with suppliers, but maintains a relationship with a host agency for certain categories of bookings.
- Is completely independent. That is, makes all bookings directly with suppliers and never uses a host agency.

Generally speaking, we can view this breakdown as reflecting increasing levels of complexity, sophistication, and business experience. We can also see it as a time line. In other words, most home-based agents start out by functioning solely as outside agents. Some of them — but by no means all — progress through the remaining stages, with only a very few winding up in the final category.

What you shouldn't see it as is a to-do list. Many agents remain in the first category for their entire careers; they make good money and are perfectly happy. I suspect that the majority of "mature" home-based agents, that is those who have been around for three to five years, find themselves in the second category and progress to the third category only when and if they specialize in a tightly defined niche. Of course, there is nothing to prevent someone from setting up their business to be completely independent from the very start. This will make the most sense for people with prior business experience and a very clear business plan that involves specializing in a very specific niche, with clearly identifiable suppliers. I don't recommend it, but it can be done.

But let's say you're the independent type. How do you get past the "pseudo ARC number" stage and make the transition to true independence? Well, if the pseudo ARC number is a "pretend" number that identifies you to a particular supplier, the next step is to get a "real" number that identifies you as a bona fide travel agent to the entire travel industry.

Getting your own IATA number

In *Chapter 1: A Brief Overview of the Travel Industry*, you learned how the travel industry is organized and the role of ARC, IATA, IATAN, and CLIA in structuring the industry and serving as gatekeepers to professionalism. One function these gatekeepers perform is to assign numbers to travel agencies, partially as a mark of "professionalism," but mainly to serve the humdrum purpose of keeping things organized, so Sue's Travel of Portland, Maine, never gets confused with Sue's Travel of Portland, Oregon, and suppliers can easily issue commissions to the agencies that have them coming.

Not so long ago, getting one of those numbers meant making a substantial financial commitment to a storefront operation, with all the bonding and high overhead that entailed. More recently, and especially after the airlines stopped paying commissions and travel agencies started giving up their ARC appointments (and with them their ARC-IATA numbers), a need was seen to make access to these unique industry identifiers somewhat less restrictive.

Today, it is a relatively straightforward matter to get your own IATA number (or its functional equivalent). It can be done for about $25,000, or it can be done for a few hundred dollars if you know how. In some respects, the IATA numbers you can get are just like the IATA numbers that storefront agencies have. They have the same number of digits and are issued by IATA; to the untutored eye they look exactly the same. In other respects, however, they are different. For one thing, they have prefixes that tell knowledgeable people in the travel industry (which is not to say *everyone* in the travel industry) that they identify a specific category of agency. For another, not every supplier will recognize them — that is, not every supplier will do business with agents or agencies that have one of these numbers — although the vast majority will.

Another reason to get your own IATA number is that it will expand the universe of suppliers willing to do business with you. Many suppliers will not work with agents on a pseudo ARC number basis, but will when the agent possesses a more widely recognized numerical industry identifier. There are even a few airlines (a very few) who will work with agents who have one of these numbers.

Once you have developed substantial gross sales volume through your direct relationships with suppliers, going this route begins to make more and more sense. Once your annual gross sales volume reaches $200,000 or so, it will be hard to resist. The danger is making the move before you are truly ready to do so.

It's easy to think of these numbers as a more convenient version of the pseudo ARC number concept. One number to remember instead of many. However, it goes beyond that. Getting your own IATA number (or other unique industry identifier) means making the major transition from travel agent to travel agency.

These numbers do not identify you, they identify your company. That's a big difference. To give you an idea of how big, once you have one of these numbers, you can hire other people to be agents for your travel agency.

You can also establish your own network of outside agents, becoming, in effect, a host agency. That's a *very* big difference.

Taking this step is a major commitment. It means you are a serious business seeking to make serious money selling travel full-time. It is not a strategy for people who want to book a few cruises for the garden club and save a bit of money on their own travel.

I cover this specialized and advanced strategy in a separate report entitled, surprisingly enough, *How to Get Your Own IATA Number (Or Other Unique Industry Identifier)*. If you purchased this book as part of my home study course, you already have it. If not you can order it by going to:

http://www.HomeTravelAgency.com/getiata.html

For now it's important to remember that it is quite possible to operate successfully for many years without progressing past the pseudo ARC number stage. Let's say you specialize in selling and leading art tours of Italy. If you have three suppliers you deal with regularly and exclusively and they are all willing to deal with you on a pseudo ARC number basis, why would you want to change?

Summary

As an independent contractor, the home-based agent is not bound to working solely with a single host agency. Home-based agents can and do work through several different host agencies, using different ones for different purposes. Home-based agents are also perfectly free to form direct relationships with suppliers when it makes sound business sense to do so. Many suppliers will work with home-based agents on an informal basis, paying them commissions directly, and using so-called pseudo ARC numbers for purposes of tracking the agent in their computer systems and paying commissions. Most home-based agents develop their businesses to the point where they are working through a host agency for some of their bookings and working directly with suppliers on other bookings. It is, however, possible to become truly independent and get a unique industry identifier that will allow you to operate pretty much like a storefront agency. This is an advanced strategy that should not be employed until you have a thorough knowledge of the industry and your business is making good money.

Action steps

Here are some things you can do to put what you have learned in this chapter into action:

- If you have chosen a specialty, research the suppliers that serve that specialty and make a list of the ones with which you feel it might make sense to have a direct relationship.
- If you have started researching host agencies, examine their

materials to see what they have to say about "exclusivity." Be wary of signing an independent contractor contract that does not specifically recognize your right to do business with anyone.

- Using the four categories listed under *Becoming truly independent*, above, write down how you see your business evolving over time and why. If you see yourself progressing from one category to another, try to be specific about when you think you will make each transition. Remember, there are no "correct" answers; be honest to yourself. You can always change your mind later.

- If you have *How to Get Your Own IATA Number (Or Other Unique Industry Identifier)*, skim through it to familiarize yourself with your options, but do not make any decisions at this point.

Chapter Seven: About Host Agencies

What you will learn

After you have completed this chapter you will be able to:

- Navigate the process of signing up with a host agency.
- Understand the basic components of a host agency-outside agent contract, and better appreciate the crucial importance of having every contract reviewed by a qualified attorney.
- Analyze and understand any host agency's compensation plan.
- Manage your relationship with a host agency with confidence, as an equal.

Key terms and concepts

This chapter involves the following key terms and concepts:

- The key element in an independent contractor relationship is that you are independent.
- When you work with a host agency, the only one responsible for looking out for your best interests is you.
- Both state and federal tax authorities have stringent standards for independent contractors. You must be certain that any contract you sign with a host agency protects your status as an independent contractor.
- A well-thought-out contract with your host agency is essential. It doesn't have to be overly complex, but it needs to cover the bases. The best way to assure yourself that it does that is to consult with a qualified attorney.
- You are in charge of your relationship with the host agency. It is your responsibility, not the host's, to make sure that your rights are being protected and that you get paid what is due you.

Introduction

Now that you have an understanding of the major ways in which you can function as a seller and marketer of travel products in today's travel industry, let's turn our attention to one of those approaches — working through a host. That is, becoming an outside sales representative for a host travel agency.

I don't know, but I strongly suspect that most of those who go through this course will take this route, at least at the beginning. Most, I suspect, will quite happily remain outside reps for their entire career in the travel industry, perhaps changing hosts as their business develops. Some will add a few direct relationships with specific suppliers as their business matures and when it makes financial sense. A few will become largely independent (as explained in *Chapter 6*), using a host agency only occasionally. A very few may sever all connections with a host.

Is it possible to build a business from scratch without ever dealing with a host agency? Yes, I suppose it is, but to be successful you will need a tightly focused niche, a solid business background, and a dynamite business plan. I don't recommend it, but if you decide to go this route I wish you good luck and Godspeed, and I'd love to hear about your success.

For most of us, however, dealing with a host agency makes a great deal of sense. So in this chapter, I will discuss the ins and outs of allying yourself with a host agency. This discussion will, of necessity, be general. As you'll hear me say many times, every host agency operates a little differently. Just locating host agencies and sorting through their varying offerings can be a daunting task.

The Special Report *How to Choose a Host Agency* will save you hundreds of hours and perhaps thousands of dollars as you seek a host agency with which to affiliate. If you purchased this book as part of my home study course, you already have it. If not, you can order it at:

http://www.HomeTravelAgency.com/choosehost.html

The Biggest Mistake Beginners Make

This is probably a good place to reiterate a very basic point about affiliating with a host agency as an outside sales representative. Whether you sign up for free with a travel agency down the street or pay a fee to an out-of-state host agency, you are an independent contractor. The key concept here is not that you work "outside" (although that is important). It's not that you represent other people's products (although that's important). It's not that you are a salesperson (although that's very important). It's not that you are not an employee (although that's extremely important).

The key concept here is that you are independent.

Think about that for a moment. It means that you are your own boss. No one can tell you what to do or how to do it. You control your own destiny. Your success (or failure) is entirely your responsibility.

And yet, I have noticed a peculiar psychological phenomenon that affects many home-based agents once they have affiliated with a host agency. Regardless of how it happens, once you've hooked up with a host agency, a commitment has been made. If money has changed hands then a certain "investment" has been made. Even though it is possible to work with more than one host agency at the same time, it is far more convenient to work with just one, so a certain sense of loyalty tends to develop. It can be a hassle to switch host agencies, so inertia sets in.

Perhaps for these reasons, many home-based travel agents start to think that they work for this host agency. They may know, intellectually, that this is not the case. But they behave as if it is. Because the host agency has a certain way of doing things, they start to think that this is the only way of doing things. Again, on an intellectual level, they may know this is not the case, but they behave as if it is.

They are thinking like employees. They gradually start thinking that their destiny, their success, is wrapped up with the destiny of the host agency. This is a mistake, but an easily corrected one. However, it is not the biggest mistake beginners make.

No, the biggest mistake newcomers to the home-based travel agent profession make — especially those who have had no prior experience running their own business — is that they think they are *customers* of the host agency. This is especially true if they paid a fee to get set up as an outside agent with that agency.

This kind of thinking is very dangerous.

Thanks to "consumer crusaders," *Consumer Reports* magazine, legions of product liability lawyers, and the growth of concepts like Total Quality Management and Total Customer Service, we live — for better or worse — in the Age of the Customer. Most of us have grown up hearing the phrase, "The Customer Is Always Right." In fact, some highly successful merchants have those words literally carved in stone at their entrances. If we order something from Land's End or Nordstrom's and don't like it, we can send it back, no questions asked. We don't even have to exercise plain old common sense. If we buy a cup of piping hot coffee from the McDonalds drive-thru and are stupid enough to stick it between our legs as we drive off, then McDonalds owes us a couple of million if we get burned. But the fact of the matter is, the host agency is not Land's End or Nordstrom's or McDonalds. And you are not your host agency's customer.

You and the host agency are two separate and independent business entities that have freely entered into a purely business relationship, because each party has independently decided that there's something in it for them. In the business-to-consumer model there is an unspoken assumption that the business is smarter and more powerful and that the customer is less knowledgeable and less powerful. Therefore, the reasoning goes, the customer's interests must be protected. In the business-to-business model there is an unspoken assumption that the parties involved are equally capable. On top of that, there is a general recognition that the interests of the two parties might be fundamentally different. In other words, what's best for you might not be best for the host agency and vice versa. Oh sure, if you have a problem with a host agency you can always sue. And maybe you'll prevail in court. But the court will apply very differ-

125

ent standards than it would if you were suing McDonalds because you spilled hot coffee on yourself.

Now don't get me wrong. I'm not saying that host agencies are crooks that are out to get you. And I'm not saying that they don't give two hoots about you or your best interests. Of course that's not true. But what is true is that every host agency is a business seeking to do business with another business. You, the independent contractor home-based travel agent, are that other business. Each of you has your own agenda and your own best interests at heart. Each of you is "in business."

Business is like a poker game. It can be fair and it can be honest and it can certainly be a lot of fun. But success in the game depends on keeping your cards to yourself and not giving away your secrets.

Do you think the people who want to set you up — working for them — in your own home-based travel business are going to say:

> *"Oh, by the way, I'm charging you $795, but you can
> get a better deal from someone else without paying
> anything."*

Of course not!

Are they going to tell you:

> *"I'll give you 50 percent of the commission, but other
> agencies will give you 60 percent or 70 percent."*

Of course not!

Are they going to say:

> *"I'd like you to give me all your business, but of
> course you can deal directly with many travel suppliers
> and keep the entire commission for yourself, without
> sharing it with me."*

Of course not!

The point is, they only tell you what they have to tell you. They don't have any obligation to take you by the hand and explain the facts of business life to you. They don't have to show you how the cards are stacked in their favor. They don't have to tell you that the only one who can lose money in this deal is you. They are not charitable institutions. And even though you may be paying a host agency several hundred (or several thousand) dollars, they still hold more power than you.

If you order a shirt from Land's End, wear it, and then decide you don't like it, they will most likely refund your money, no questions asked. If you join up with a for-fee host agency and then decide you don't like them or the business and ask for a refund, you will most likely be firmly refused — even if you paid many thousands of dollars and even if you've only been with them a few weeks. Odds are the contract is in their favor. The same is true of situations in which an error or oversight on your part causes you to lose money. Don't expect the host agency to shoulder the loss. Again, the contract is on their side.

So remember, when you contact a host agency about becoming one of its outside agents you are entering into a business negotiation with a great deal at stake. The more knowledgeable you are going into that negotiation, the better off you will be. So in this chapter and in the rest of this course my goal is to provide you with information that will put you on an even footing with the host agencies you contact.

Is this the agency for me?

I mentioned earlier that you should not sell yourself short. Let me repeat that advice. Don't allow yourself to get caught in the trap of thinking that you have to hook up with the first host agency you can find or the first one that says it will take you. This is true whether you decide to look for a local agency first or determine that it makes more sense for you to find a host elsewhere that will take you on pretty much sight unseen. The most important person to satisfy is yourself, not the host agency. So before you make any commitments, take some time to decide if working with this particular agency makes sense for you and what you want to accomplish in your new travel business. This is true no matter what type of agency you are considering or where it is located. Here are some things you might want to consider:

- *Is it big enough?* If the agency is too small or too new, it might not be able to give you the kind of support you need. You might even find that after a while you know more than the people on the inside. Also, the larger the agency's volume, the more attractive its commission structure will be with certain "preferred" suppliers. That, in turn, should mean more money in your pocket.

- *What kind of travel does it sell?* It may be that you want to concentrate on selling cruises. It might make sense, then, for you to hook up with a cruise-only agency, or one that does a lot of cruise business. On the other hand, an agency that does primarily corporate work may see your interest in cruising as a welcome addition to its business. The important thing is that both you and the agency feel comfortable with the fit.

- *Do they already deal with outside agents?* If so, you may find the relationship smoother than if they do not.

- *What about preferred suppliers?* Check to see what consortiums the agency belongs to. Membership in these co-ops, as they're called, means that the agency gets higher commissions when dealing with supplier-members of the consortium. That, in turn, should mean a higher payback for you. Some arrangements, particularly those involving cruise lines, mean not only better commissions but lower fares (guaranteed group rates or "GG fares") for your customers, making you more competitive in the marketplace. Just make sure the preferred supplier list reflects the types of travel you want to sell.

- *What kind of support can you expect?* The more willing the agency is to train you, the better the deal. At a minimum, you should expect that someone will be available and willing to answer your questions about the mechanics of making bookings and negotiating the best deals with suppliers.

The Outside Sales Support Network (OSSN), an organization that provides guidance and support to outside sales representatives in the travel industry, goes so far as to suggest that you interview the agency owner to find out if this relationship makes sense for you. Among the questions they suggest you ask are:

- Do you have, in writing, an "Outside Sales Agent Procedure Manual," outlining the commission splits and what is expected in the relationship?
- Do you have, in writing, a list of preferred vendors and their override commissions?
- Are you a member of a consortium or franchise?
- What industry organizations does your agency belong to?
- Will I have an inside contact to work with?
- Do you have a contract for me to sign as an Independent Contractor?

(By the way, OSSN is an excellent organization. You can download a discounted membership application form at
http://www.HomeTravelAgency.com/ossnapp.pdf)

That may seem a little daunting and don't feel too bad if you don't think you have the nerve to grill an agency owner on all those points. But it's a very important part of the process. That's why, in *How to Choose a Host Agency*, I provide a thorough checklist of questions to ask before signing on the dotted line.

Dealing with a host agency

Once again, it is impossible to describe precisely the operations of all host agencies because each operates in a somewhat different fashion. Of the scores of host agencies profiled in *How to Choose a Host Agency*, no two operate in exactly the same way. Nonetheless, there are many areas of similarity. The discussion that follows applies primarily to host agencies in the first two categories discussed in *Chapter 4: The Outside Sales Rep* (bare bones and quasi-franchises). I have kept it very general in nature, if only because it is impossible to account for every possible policy of hundreds of host agencies. The fact that you find a host agency that has a policy or procedure that differs from what's outlined below does not mean they are "doing something wrong." There are many ways to skin a cat.

The sign-up process

The first step in aligning yourself with a host agency is to request an application form. A few host agencies post application forms on their web sites. But before you go running off half-cocked, let me warn you: Many application forms take the form of a contract. As such, the application should be treated with care. Consult a competent legal professional before deciding that signing it and sending it in is in your best interests. That having been said, the form you receive will lay out the simple and straightforward business proposition the host agency has for you. Typically, it involves the following basic elements:

- They are a fully-appointed, industry-recognized travel agency. That could mean they have an ARC/IATAN appointment, necessary to sell airline tickets. It could mean they are CLIA members and specialize in tours and cruises. It could mean they have one of the "new" numbers issued to independent travel agents/agencies, which I discuss at some length in *How to Get Your Own IATA Number*. Obviously, you will want to make sure the agency has whichever appointment or appointments are important to you.

- You are an independent travel agent who would like access to their appointment. In exchange for your sign-up fee, you will be able to use their appointment when dealing with suppliers. In effect, when you call a supplier, it is just as if you were a full-time employee sitting in their office.

- They will give you 50%, 60%, 70%, or more of the commission on everything you book, subject to some exceptions and limitations, which will be explained in the contract.

- For this you agree to pay them their sign-up fee, usually payable at the time you submit the signed contract and usually nonrefundable. With many agencies there will also be an annual fee to renew the contract. Of course, some host agencies do not charge a sign-up fee.

And that, in a nutshell, is it! When they receive your application and your check or credit card number, they will send you a package of materials to get started. The package may be modest, containing nothing more than a slim "manual" outlining their policies and procedures and a few booking forms. Or it could be an elaborate kit filled with training manuals, video and audio cassettes, software, and so forth. Usually, the size of your start-up kit is in direct proportion to the size of the check you sent. Most host agencies will also assign you a "Member Number," "PIN Number," or some similar device, that identifies you to their computer system and which you will use in all your dealings with them. Some will also give you several days of training at their headquarters or some other location. Either way, once you have this material in hand, you are a "travel agent."

Before you sign up

While *in outline*, the sign-up process is pretty simple and straightforward, the actuality can be somewhat more complicated. That's because every host agency operates a little differently. While it's true that some host agencies will take you on "no questions asked," others are a lot pickier. As a very general rule of thumb, the lower the sign-up fee, the greater the likelihood that the agency will ask some pointed questions or ask for something in the way of "credentials." Here are some of things you might encounter.

- **A background check.** This will be (or should be!) at the agency's expense, but you might be asked to sign a release authorizing the agency to conduct such a check. The agency wants to be assured that you're not a crook and don't have financial problems that might cause it problems. You will actually find this requirement with many "quasi-franchises."

- **Proof of insurance.** Some agencies want you to carry your own errors and omissions insurance, which I discuss in more detail in *Chapter 9: Getting Serious.*

- **Proof of earnings.** Some agencies only want agents who are already producing significant volume. You may be asked to prove this in a number of ways including 1099 Forms.

- **Questionnaires of various sorts.** Some host agencies ask you to fill out questionnaires or surveys about your work experience, goals, income projections, and so forth. You may or may not feel comfortable with this.

- **Proof of some sort of industry certification.** This could be something like the Travel Agency proficiency test (TAP Test) given to recent travel school graduates, or certifications like the CTC (Certified Travel Counselor) designation, which is only granted to industry veterans who pass a stiff written test. By the way, you do not need any of this to become or succeed as a home-based travel agent. The agencies that ask for this sort of thing are simply trying to assure themselves that the people they accept have a certain level of experience in the business and are not rank beginners.

- **Business certificate.** They may ask for proof that you've registered your business with town hall, that is that you have a "fictitious name" certificate, sometimes known as a "DBA," which stands for "doing business as."

- **Experience.** Some agencies seek "experienced" agents, but are not terribly specific about what they mean by that. So in some cases you might have to make a case that you are "experienced." In a few cases, you might be able to site this course as evidence you know what you are doing.

Any host agency can set up whatever entry requirements it feels make sense. You have complete freedom to pick and choose among host agencies. So if, for example, you feel submitting to a background check is too intrusive, then you will have plenty of other hosts to choose from.

How much will it cost?

A word of warning about start-up costs. Many times the sign-up fee (if any) charged by a host agency is only part of the story. Here are some other things that can add to your start-up costs.

- **Mandatory errors and omissions insurance.** This is sometimes included in the sign up fee. Other agencies will add you to their contract for a moderate annual fee.

- **Monthly access fees.** These could be for a full-fledged GDS (global distribution system) or simply to get access to a private agents-only web site. Some hosts provide their agents with their own web site and charge a monthly fee for that.
- **Training.** Training may or may not be mandatory. Even if training is optional, you might feel you need or want it. If it is mandatory, some of the costs, including some travel costs, may be covered by the sign-up fee, but you will most likely incur additional travel expenses associated with the training.
- **Miscellaneous fees.** Some agencies charge per-transaction, per-booking, or per-invoice fees of anywhere from $5 to $15 or more.
- **Flat monthly fees.** Some agencies charge no sign-up fee per se but charge a flat monthly fee that covers all the services they provide. This fee can be hefty.
- **Additional fees for a spouse.** If you and your spouse plan to operate the business together (a fairly common phenomenon), some agencies will charge an additional fee at start-up.
- **ID card fees.** Some hosts will charge you a fee, usually modest, if you want them to issue an ID card. Note that this is not an IATAN card, but a private ID card issued by the host agency.
- **Annual or renewal fees.** While not precisely a start-up cost, be aware that many host agencies charge a fee to renew your contract

When comparing host agencies you are considering, it is a good idea to determine, as accurately as possible, what your total first year expenditures will be, plus the renewal fee. This will give you a good basis on which to make head to head cost comparisons among agencies.

A word about compensation

One of the first things you'll want to know about any prospective host agency is how and how much they'll pay you for the business you bring in. To the uninitiated, discussions about how outside travel agents are compensated can be confusing. Even worse, it can cost you money if you're not careful. So let's take a few minutes to explain the jargon.

Most often, an outside agent's compensation is expressed as a percentage of commissions. For example, an agency might tell you, "You'll get 50% of everything you book." That means that you'll receive 50% of the commission payable from the supplier to the agency. For example, if the commissionable fare is $1,000 and the commission is 10%, the agency gets $100, and passes $50 along to you. If the fare is $1,000 and the commission is 15%, the agency gets $150 and passes $75 along to you.

Sometimes, people will "simplify" things by saying, "You'll get 5% commission." That's because most of us have come to think of 10% as being the standard agency commission, and 50% of 10% is 5%. This works as a very rough rule of thumb, but it is misleading since 10% is not a universal commission rate. Some travel products, like most airline tickets, pay no commission at all, while other travel products, cruises for example, have commissions of 12%, 13%, 15%, or even higher. Some agencies have "preferred vendor" relationships with various suppliers that entitle them to special commissions that can be 20% or even higher. Some agencies double as wholesalers for a handful of travel products. In these cases, they may give the outside agent who books one of these products the entire commission. So if the commission is 12%, you get it all. The agency makes its money from its markup on the supplier's price. Some agencies will pay the rep a percentage of the base commission and all overrides. An override is an extra sum (usually expressed as a percentage) paid by the supplier as an incentive when certain volume conditions have been met. So if a cruise line offers a 12% commission and a 2% override and the rep gets 50% of the commission, he or she would get 7% on this booking (half of 14%, the total commission received by the host agency).

For the most accurate reckoning, figure your potential commissions on the actual percentage split rather than using a rule of thumb. If you are getting 70% of the commission, your cut on a 10% commission is 7%. It's 7.7% on an 11% commission, 8.4% on a 12% commission, 10.5% on a 15% commission, and so forth.

Of course, sometimes when an agency says "You'll get a 5% commission" they aren't simplifying things at all. They are saying that you will get 5% of the total sale no matter what the commission rate is. They will keep all overrides and anything over 10% for themselves. Other agencies will be even cagier and say "You get 50% of the commission" and then in the fine print let you know that the commission is always assumed to be 10%, unless it is less. In other words, if the agency is getting 20% commission because of a preferred suppler relationship, they will still only pay you 50% of 10%. This is fairly typical of referral agencies.

There is some other industry jargon that might be confusing. Some agencies might tell you, for example, "We offer a 60/40 split." That means one party gets 60% of the commission and the other party gets 40%. Usually, the agent's commission is listed first, meaning in this case the agent would receive 60% of the commission and the host agency 40%. But don't automatically assume anything. Always clarify who gets what.

Another thing to bear in mind when figuring your potential commissions is that they are paid on the "base fare" not on the total price the client pays. As an example, the port fees that cruise passengers pay are not commissionable. Taxes aren't commissionable either. And suppliers have started an annoying trend to add more and more non-commissionable "extras." So your client might pay $5,000 and you'll earn commissions based on $4,400.

The contract

Every outside agent-host agency relationship involves a contract, preferably a written contract that you can file away in a file folder for future reference. But even if you think you don't have a contract, you do. How can that be? Well there's something called an "implied contract" or a "verbal contract." Now many people maintain that "a verbal contract isn't worth the paper it's written on," but a verbal contract does has some force in law, although enforcing it might be difficult.

Also, you will find some host agencies that don't offer a contract per se (not one like the one that follows), but somewhere buried in the fine print in their brochures and web sites is a statement to the effect that by signing up you agree to abide by the "Terms and Conditions" spelled out somewhere else, perhaps in even finer print. In effect, your signature on the check is your signature on the contract that is those Terms and Conditions. I'm no lawyer, but it is my understanding that this type of "contract" is legally enforceable. So you should be sure you read those Terms and find them to your liking.

My personal opinion is that a more or less formal, signed (in ink on paper) contract is the best way to go, better than the kind of "click here to agree to our terms and conditions" contracts you'll find on the Internet. But let your own judgment and that of your lawyer be your guide.

Here is *one* contract used by *one* agency to formalize its relationship with its outside sales reps. It is provided only as an example, for the purposes of discussion. There are many, many variations on this theme and the contract placed in front of you by a local agency may be radically different in form and content. So don't think that just because a clause is in this contract that it must be in all contracts. All that being said, the following agreement covers most of the bases. Like I said, I provide it here for purely informational purposes and certainly not to provide anything remotely resembling legal counsel. You should consult with a lawyer before signing any host agency contract.

AGREEMENT

THIS AGREEMENT is made this _____ day of _____, 20__ by and between _____ hereinafter referred to as the "Independent Agent", and [name of agency], a [name of state] Corporation located at [address] hereinafter referred to as "The Agency."

Witnesseth

Whereas, "The Agency" desires to expand its sales of airline tickets, cruises, tours, and related services and

Whereas, "The Agency" has the potential to carry out this expansion and

Whereas, "The Agency" wishes to benefit from the experience and efforts of the "Independent Agent" in these fields.

Whereas, The "Independent Agent" has agreed to use her ability, knowledge, experience, and training to assist "The Agency" in the afore-mentioned expansion.

Now thereof [sic] the parties agree as follows:

I. "Independent Agent" shall grant to the agency her Full/Part time assistance and best effort by:

A. Attending once per week an organizational meeting at a time to be designated at which time a report will be submitted by the "Independent Agent" on sales calls and results.

B. Calling upon, telephoning or otherwise contacting prospective clients for travel services to be obtained through the agency.

C. Diligently carrying out sales endeavors for at least _____ hours per week.

D. Diligently following up any lead provided by the agency.

II. "The Agency" will use its best endeavors to assist in the training of the "Independent Agent" in the use of the reservation computer system and relevant travel information.

III. "The Agency" agrees to pay the "Independent Agent" the following fees:

_____ percent (___%) of the commission payable on sales derived from sales leads resulting in the purchase of travel services from the agency.

Fees are payable on a monthly basis.

Refunded tickets will automatically constitute a debit to commission of amount originally received.

IV. The "Independent Agent" shall not contact existing clients of "The Agency."

V. "Independent Agent" shall not represent any other travel company while associated with "The Agency."

VI. This agreement is valid for a term of 90 days from its execution at which time it may be renegotiated at the sole discretion of "The Agency." No travel concessions will be allowed to the "Independent Agent" under this agreement.

VII. Nothing in this agreement shall be deemed to grant any power to the "Independent Agent" to make any contract or commitment in the name of "The Agency" without the express prior written consent of "The Agency."

This agreement shall be construed in accordance with [state] Law and the venue for any disputes under this agreement would be in [county], [state].

This agreement has been signed in duplicate this ____ day of ____, 20___, in [county], [state].

[Signed by "Independent Agent" and "The Agency"]

Suppose this contract were placed in front of you. Let's analyze it to see what it can tell us about how this particular agency seeks to operate with you, its "Independent Agent." First of all the term "Independent Agent" itself is important. The agency envisions a relationship in which you are a separate and independent entity, not an employee. This is important for all the reasons we discussed above.

This agency uses (or intends to use) both full-time and part-time outside reps, as indicated in Paragraph I. That would seem to indicate that they are open to dealing with the home-based individual who is not going to make this (at least at the outset) a full-time job. Paragraph I-A asks that the outside rep have some accountability for his or her sales efforts. But this is actually a benefit for you as well as for the agency. With this clause, the agency is committing to sitting down with you once a week in a face-to-face setting. This will give you the opportunity to ask questions and get the guidance you need.

Subparagraph C once again indicates that not only is the agency willing to work with part-timers but with several categories of part-timers. The actual number of hours (5, 10, 12, or whatever) that goes into this blank space is, presumably, a matter of negotiation between you and the agency. Obviously each agency will have a minimum number of hours they expect you to put in each week, but that number will probably be slightly different from agency to agency.

Paragraph II commits the agency to train you, a good sign they are not going to let you sink before you can swim. If you were to sign this contract, you'd probably want to take the fullest possible advantage of this commitment.

Paragraph III illustrates another important point about the relationship between travel agencies and outside sales reps — the commission split is negotiable! If it weren't, the agency would have simply inserted its "standard" commission in this space. The number that goes into this space will be the percentage of a percentage. In other words if you are getting half of the agency commission, the number would be 50%, not 5%. Remember that the commission payable to the agency is not always 10%. This is a crucial point. Make sure you are absolutely clear on what the deal is. Consult with a lawyer before you sign.

So what should the number be? I know of outside reps who have worked full time for 35% of the commission. I myself have worked for 50% and 70% of the commission. I know of agencies that give 80% of the commission (one charges a "start-up fee" of several thousand dollars!). Fifty percent seems to be a rough industry standard, especially when you are dealing with a local agency like this. Like I say, it's negotiable. Obviously, the higher the number, the more attractive the contract will be to you. But just because the number is on the low side, doesn't necessarily mean you shouldn't accept. The training may be worth it. The experience may be worth it. If this is your only means of access to the travel game, it may be worth it. Remember that as you gain experience and prove your worth, you can always renegotiate or take your skills and abilities elsewhere.

The other items in Paragraph III create certain liabilities for you, the independent agent. Make sure you understand what they are before you sign. At a minimum you should expect to keep excellent records so you'll know what's due you at the end of the month. Will the agency provide an itemized accounting with your check? The contract doesn't say. It may well be worth clarifying this and getting the arrangement in writing. Again, a good reason to have a lawyer advising you.

The same can be said about the clause about "refunded tickets." It would seem that the agency reserves the right to determine what should be charged against your commissions and under what circumstances. Refunded tickets involve fees that can sometimes be larger than the commission you earned. I would say that this item requires further clarification. But I hasten to add that I am not a lawyer and you should seek competent legal advice on this one.

The agency wants an exclusive relationship with you (Paragraph V). This may be just fine with you, but then again it may not. For example, what if you found a cruise-only agency in your area that was willing to give you a better cut of the commission on cruises? If you'd signed this contract, you (presumably) wouldn't be free to work with them. Also, this provision would seem to violate one of the IRS's standards for determining independent contractor status; so this is probably an issue you would want to discuss with your lawyer.

In the real world, most outside reps feel most comfortable working with one agency. For one thing, it's just a lot more convenient. However, there are reps who deal with several agencies, placing each booking with the agency that gives them the best deal. You'll have to decide how you're most comfortable working. As a practical matter, however, the new outside rep will be well advised to establish and nurture a relationship with one agency.

Like any good contract, this one is stacked in favor of the party that drafted it — in this case the travel agency. Paragraph VI would seem to suggest that you are committed to them forever, while they can cut you loose after 90 days. "At the sole discretion of 'The Agency'" means they don't even have to give you a reason. "It's just not working out" will do just fine. Essentially, the agency is trying to protect itself here. If you turn out to be a pain in the neck who is a constant embarrassment to the agency because you alienate your customers, obviously the agency wants a quick and painless way out. Of course, the law and lawyers being what they are, nothing is ever cut and dried. The laws of the state will have something to say about how and under what conditions a contract can be terminated or enforced. This is something you'd want to talk over with your lawyer before signing the agreement.

Unlike some of the "instant agent" operations that will try to lure you with the promise of cut-rate and free travel, this agency makes it clear you can expect no such deals (Paragraph VI). Again, the agency is trying to protect itself here. It doesn't want you to get on the phone and start lining up fam trips before the ink on the contract is dry. This clause also helps assure the agency that you are serious about selling travel and not just looking for a free ride. On the other hand, travel benefits are something that an agent earns and, if you earn them, there's no reason why you shouldn't get them. This is probably another area you might want to discuss with both your lawyer and the agency. (There is a much fuller discussion of travel benefits in *Chapter 10*).

Paragraph VII seeks to protect the agency from lawsuits brought by angry customers. My guess is that the agency would seek to construe the term "contract" here as broadly as possible. In other words, if you say to the customer, "Don't worry, the weather in Cancun will be perfect," that might be construed as a "contract" on your part guaranteeing perfect weather. If the customer then sues because a hurricane hit Cancun during his stay, the agency wants to be covered. Again, talk to your lawyer and make sure that you understand what is at stake before signing.

Several items in this contract seem to be at odds with the IRS test for independent contractors. How much of a problem that represents is hard to say. Again, you'd have to get a ruling from your lawyer.

To summarize, this contract is presented here as an isolated example and to generate some interesting discussion. It is not meant to be a recommendation of what your contract should look like. Professional organizations such as the Outside Sales Support Network (OSSN) can provide you with other sample contracts, which differ from this one. So can any good lawyer, and I highly recommend that you seek one out. As always, you should rely on the advice of a competent legal professional when forging any important business relationship.

Your status as an independent contractor

To my way of thinking, your status as an independent contractor is the heart of any contract you negotiate and sign with a host agency. If the nature of that relationship is not spelled out clearly in any contract you get from a host agency, it should be.

OSSN urges its members to be sure they have a contractual agreement with the agency in which they are recognized as "independent contractors." In other words, they are self-employed persons and not employees of the agency. This is an important distinction come tax time because as a self-employed person you can deduct things that employees cannot. (See *Chapter 9: Getting Serious*.)

Because our elected representatives in Congress can neither write a decent tax code nor live within their means, the Internal Revenue Service is put under considerable pressure to extract every nickel possible under the confusing terms of the existing tax laws. They do this by "interpreting" the law in the narrowest possible way and challenging any business practice that they think is intended as a ploy to avoid taxation.

In recent years, the IRS has been particularly nasty about Independent Contractors. The IRS feels that many companies are transforming employees into independent contractors as a way of avoiding payroll and Social Security taxes. And to give the devil his due, many companies have done exactly that. But there are many other companies — travel agencies among them — that use legitimate independent contractors for legitimate business purposes. Unfortunately, given the IRS's penchant for attacking first and asking questions later, many legitimate companies and legitimate contractors have been forced to justify their business arrangements to a suspicious IRS. This is not only upsetting and time-consuming, it is expensive. And there's always the possibility that, because the i's haven't been dotted or the t's crossed in precisely the right way, well-meaning companies and individuals may suffer.

Consequently, before you enter into an outside agent relationship, take a few minutes to learn how to protect yourself. True to form, the IRS doesn't make it easy. The IRS, at least until recently, determined if an independent contractor really is an independent contractor by playing a game of twenty questions. In theory, the answers determined if you were, in fact, an employee in independent contractor's clothing. Here they are, as listed by Chicago CPA Richard S. Meyer in *Travel Weekly*:

1. Does the agency "supervise and control" you?
2. Can the agency "hire and fire" you?
3. Are you paid a straight salary (as opposed to a straight commission) and reimbursed for expenses?
4. Does the agency provide you with training?
5. Do you work continually with the agency and do the same kind of things that agency employees do?
6. Does the agency set your work hours?
7. Does the agency supply you with tools and other equipment for you to do your job?
8. Do you work on the agency's premises and have no significant investment in your own work space?
9. Do you have to perform your work in a certain order determined by the agency?
10. Does the operation of your business depend on the delivery of certain services?
11. Does the travel industry usually use employees to do the kind of work you do?
12. Does the agency have the right to bring in others to complete work you've begun?
13. Does the agency require that services be performed by a specific person?
14. Does the agency intend to treat you as an employee?
15. Do you have to submit regular written or oral reports to the agency?
16. Is there no way you can incur a loss?
17. Does the agency require that you provide it with your services on an exclusive basis?
18. Are you required to follow instruction from the agency on

when, where, and how to work?

19. Do you offer your services to others on a regular or consistent basis?
20. Can you quit without incurring any liability?

The IRS has been trying to get a little more rational about this. If you're truly interested in their latest thinking on the subject, which continues to hinge on the issue of how much control the agency has over the outside rep's behavior and business practices, you can obtain their 160-page document, *Independent Contractor or Employee?*, by calling the IRS Reading Room at (202) 622-5164. Or you can get more information, including downloadable publications, from the IRS via Internet at:

http://www.irs.ustreas.gov.

Even if the IRS decides your independent contractor status is kosher, your state's tax department might disagree. States have their own, albeit shorter, test for vetting independent contractors. Sometimes called the A-B-C test, it asks:

A. Is there sufficient lack of control over the worker?
B. Does the worker work outside the agency's place of business?
C. Does the worker have a separate, independent trade or profession? (Separate business cards and phone listings could meet this test.)

None of this is meant to scare you. After all, thousands of people have been operating as outside sales agents quite happily for many years and have never experienced any tax-related problems. However, the law is the law and we all have a responsibility to comply with both the letter and the spirit of the law. That is why having a carefully drafted agreement between yourself and the agency, spelling out the precise nature of your relationship, is so important.

Be forewarned, however, that just because you have signed a piece of paper calling you an independent contractor doesn't guarantee that the IRS will agree. Always consult with a qualified attorney and accountant before entering into any agreement that can have legal or tax consequences. And in business that means just about any agreement you can think of!

Due diligence

This is a legal term for doing your homework. In a business deal, businesspeople are supposed to make sure they know what they're getting into. In other words, they perform "due diligence." They examine the proposition and do whatever possible to assure themselves that the person on the other side of the table is being square with them.

When it comes to choosing a host agency, due diligence means, among many other things, not jumping into the first host agency relationship that comes along. You need to examine a lot of host agencies and then take a closer look at your "short list."

How to Choose a Host Agency will help you a great deal in this regard.

You should also take full advantage of the Checklist it contains to guide you in asking the "hard questions." You may want to take things a step further, by doing your own background check on agency principals or tracking down outside agents who work with or have worked with the agencies you are considering. It can take time, but it's time well spent.

This is an important business decision that might very well determine the success or failure of your fledgling travel selling enterprise. Don't rush into it.

After you've signed up

Whew! It took a while — at least it did if you did it right and conducted your due diligence — but you're now an official outside sales representative for a host agency. Now what?

Well, it's hard to say because (once again) every host agency is different. Most of them, however, will provide you with some sort of guidance in how they operate and how you can most efficiently work with them. That guidance can take the form of a few sheets of paper or an elaborate manual. It all depends on which host you hooked up with and to some extent on how much money you paid to sign up.

In this section, I will discuss a few things that will apply to most outside agent/host agency relationships.

Working with suppliers

Working with a host agency is almost like having your own travel agency — almost. First of all, you operate under a business name of your own choosing. Most host agencies want you to list a company name on your application, even if it is something like "Joe Smith Travel."

If you'd like, you can go down to Main Street, rent a storefront, and call it "Joe Smith Travel," just like a "real" travel agency. Some independent contractors do just that. Most of those who do, however, are experienced travel agents. Most newcomers operate out of their homes or out of existing business premises, their "travel agency" consisting just of a business card. Many host agencies ask that somewhere on your business card it says, "A Big Host Agency Affiliate" or something similar.

While you can call your new travel business anything you choose and present yourself to the world under that name, you typically must represent yourself to suppliers (airlines, cruise lines, tour operators, hotels, etc.) as an agent of your host agency. The reason is quite simple: you are using your host agency's IATA number. It is that identity that allows you to function as a travel agent and collect your commission. Without it, things get hopelessly muddled.

As an outside agent for your host agency, you quickly learn the answers to the following questions, when they are asked by a supplier:

- What's your agency? You give the name of your host agency.
- What's your IATA number? You give your host agency's IATA number.
- What's your address? You give your host agency's street ad-

dress.

What's your phone number? You give a specific telephone number at your host agency's office. (Some host agency policies may differ on this point.)

Most suppliers you deal with will already have your host agency and its IATA number in their computer databases. Some systems use the telephone number, since it is unique, to identify the agency. So if you give your own telephone number or a different number (most host agencies have several), the supplier will not be able to locate your host agency on its computer.

How you give your name to suppliers can also be an issue. Just about every supplier you talk to will have a field in its database to record your name. If a question arises later about a booking, the name in that field becomes important. Some host agencies insist that you use your last name only because they have so many outside agents. Trying to sort out first names and figure which Joe or Mary goes with a particular booking is nigh on impossible. This can feel a little awkward since most of the people you deal with on the suppliers' end will identify themselves only by their first names. However, other host agencies have different policies on this.

In theory, the supplier should never guess that you are an outside agent working from a phone on your dining room table in Peoria; they should think you are working at a desk in your host agency's offices. In practice, it really doesn't matter. The industry is getting very used to the idea of home-based agents working far from the headquarters of their host agencies. Some suppliers will come to know where you're really located. Usually this will mean tour operators or cruise lines that have to send brochures directly to you. That's fine, just so long as the all-important computer database has the correct information. When the question of where to send brochures comes up, you can simply say, "I'm an outside agent. Can you send them to my home without messing up the computer records?" Some suppliers can do this. Others have a policy of sending brochures only to the home office. Some host agencies have strict policies about this as well. In that case, you will most likely have to pay the postage to have your host agency forward them on to you.

Collecting payments

Part of your job is asking for the order and collecting payments from your customers. Fortunately, most of the bookings you make will be paid for by credit card. Many beginners think that means they will need to have "merchant status," that is be able to process credit card payments themselves. This is not the case. Your job as the outside rep is simply to collect the customer's credit card information and relay it to the supplier (or in some cases to the host agency). It is the supplier that processes the customer's card, not you, not the host agency. There are some legal technicalities and precautions involved with this process; I will discuss them in *Chapter 9: Getting Serious.*

There are cases in which you will have to collect payment by check.

For starters, some customers may simply prefer to pay that way. In that case, you will have to assure that the check is made out properly. Usually that means it will be made payable to the supplier, but you will have to check for the preferred wording. Do this before it becomes an issue. If you have a customer ready to give you a check for a deposit on a major cruise or tour purchase, you do not want to put things off while you find out exactly how the check should be made out. Buyer's remorse might set in!

There are other times when payment must be made by check regardless of the customer's preferences. A perfect example of this is consolidator tickets, which often must be paid for in cash or check. Some consolidators accept customer credit cards, but many do not. In this case, you will want to have the check made out to your business name (unless you are selling consolidator tickets with the assistance of your host agency). You may also have to ask for checks when selling certain tour products from smaller or foreign tour operators. Asking for payment by check can sometimes be awkward and may require a bit of "selling" on your part. You can point out that one of the reasons the price is so low is because the supplier in question does not have the high overhead of a merchant account. In the case of consolidator tickets this is quite true.

Coordinating bookings with a host agency

As an outside agent, your host agency typically expects you to do everything an inside agent would do, short of entering the booking into the computerized reservation system (GDS) and printing out the ticket — if in fact that's even necessary. If you're experienced enough or ambitious enough, using a GDS may be an option. And if you've signed up with a "quasi-franchise," it is probably required. For now, let's assume you are not using a GDS.

The last thing most host agencies want is for you to call them up and say, "Hi, my Aunt Martha wants to take a cruise sometime next month. Whatcha got?" No. That's for referral agents. You are expected to make all the contacts with the cruise line and make Aunt Martha's booking, gathering all the information your host agency will need to record and track the booking. (I will discuss the process of contacting various types of suppliers and making bookings in *Chapters 11* through *16*.)

Once you have made the booking, the next step is to send the information in to the home office. There are a number of ways to do this:

- ***Phone it in.*** Some host agencies still accept bookings by phone, but most have phased out this option. If you can phone in bookings, you probably will have to use the agency's local number, instead of an 800 number, which is meant to discourage the practice. If you do call in a booking, you are expected to have all the required information at your fingertips. Many agencies provide booking forms with their manual that make gathering and recording the necessary information a relatively foolproof process. Bear in mind that phone bookings may also earn lower commissions.

- *Fax it in.* This is the most-used option. It's fast, cheap (some host agencies have a toll-free fax number) and, thanks to those booking forms, less likely to generate errors.
- *Mail it in.* If there's enough time before the booking deadline, some agencies let you mail in your bookings.
- *Use the Internet.* This is the wave of the future. An increasing number of host agencies let you make bookings directly on their web sites or via a private agent-only intranet.

Most airline bookings these days are ticketless; in the rare instances when a ticket is required, the agency will print it out and send it to you, usually at your expense. Some bookings don't involve tickets or other types of documentation and don't need to be sent in immediately. These include:
- Hotel reservations, when the client will pay on checkout.
- Car rentals, when the client will pay upon return of the car. Many foreign car rentals, however, require prepayment.
- Travel insurance.

Bookings in these categories are handled in a variety of different ways by different host agencies. You may simply keep track of the bookings you make (hotel, client name, date of arrival, etc.). Then, every two weeks or so, depending on the kind of volume you are doing, send in a list of your recent bookings. Or you may be expected to keep detailed records on an agency-supplied form, submitting claims for commissions only in the month in which they are due for payment.

Keeping track of your bookings

Some host agencies keep track of your bookings for you, others do not. No matter how your host agency has things set, it is imperative that you keep track of your own bookings. Otherwise, you'll never know if you're being paid what you're owed.

Your host agency may supply you with a form or a format. Or, if they require that you "bill" them for your commissions, they will let you know the information they need and the form in which they prefer to receive it. Otherwise, it's not too difficult to set up a simple paper and pencil tracking system, using a series of columns to record information. Among the things you want to keep track of are:
- *Which booking is which.* You may want to give each booking a short "nickname" that will let you recall the booking in question. For example "Smith06/04" could refer to the Smiths' trip in April of 2006.
- *Supplier.* This is who owes you the commission. It will also be helpful to make note of a number to call regarding commissions. Many suppliers have separate departments for this. You could record this information on your tracking form or in a separate file.
- *Amount.* How much commission will the supplier pay?

- ■ **Date due.** When should you expect payment?
- ■ **Follow-ups.** You will want to record the dates on which you bugged the supplier for your payment and the results of those calls.
- ■ **Payment date.** By tracking when you were actually paid, you will begin to get a handle on who pays promptly and suppliers to be wary of in the future.
- ■ **Tickler file.** In addition to tracking the above information, you will want to have some system to remind you to check when commissions are due. Your computer probably has some built-in accessory program that will remind you to make a call on a specific date. If not, it's fairly easy to set up a tickler file using a simple printed desk calendar.

A simple system works best when your business is simple and that usually means when you are just starting out and have relatively few clients. As your business expands you will want to invest in one of the specialized software packages aimed at small travel agencies and home-based travel agents. These include Trams Back Office (www.trams.com) and TravelSales (www.wesmarc.com). They aren't precisely cheap, but when they start to make financial sense for your business, you will probably know it.

Getting your commission

The next step is receiving your share of the commission. The vast majority of host agencies pay out commissions once a month (a very few pay twice a month). Typically, you can expect to receive your commission in the month after your client has completed his travel, even if the agency has received it earlier. In no case can you expect to receive a commission before the host agency has received it from the supplier. That means that you may receive commissions months after the client's trip is over.

Most host agencies are honest and pay commissions when they are due. However, in any host agency-outside agent relationship, commissions should never be taken for granted. Nor should you simply "trust" that your host agency will pay you everything it owes you when it owes it. As a conscientious businessperson, it is your responsibility to look after your own interests. That means keeping detailed records of commissions due and questioning the host agency when there appears to be any discrepancy. Most outside agents have to do that from time to time. When you do this, payment is usually forthcoming or the reason for the discrepancy determined. Some host agencies force you to be conscientious by requiring you to submit a detailed report of commissions due before they will pay you. If it's not on the report, they don't have to give it to you.

Usually, when there is a discrepancy it is because a supplier has not come through with a commission. Some suppliers (hotels, especially) have a way of being "forgetful" when it comes to paying commissions. Typically, your host agency will expect you to hound the supplier in cases like these. They will take their cut when the payment comes in, but will not help you dun the supplier.

In some cases, you will collect your commission up front. When a client pays by check or cash for a product offered directly by the host agency (a tour or package, for example), you simply deduct your share of the commission and forward the resulting "net" payment to the host agency.

There are other issues that arise when it comes to commissions — overrides, bonuses offered by suppliers directly to agents, tour conductor passes, and so forth. You will have to deal with your host agency on these matters on a case by case basis.

How much can I make?

*"Selling is the only job where you can give
yourself a raise any time you want."*

Seasoned sales managers and sales motivators like to cite this old saying because it means that a salesperson's compensation is up to her (or him). They're paid on commission and, if they want to earn more, all they have to do is sell more and their incomes will go up in proportion. That's true as far as it goes and there are many outside reps in the travel business who make very handsome incomes.

I certainly don't want to discourage your dreams of making a princely sum as a home-based travel agent. Nonetheless, experience shows that what you can make will be determined, to a very large extent, by two variables — your commission structure and the dollar volume you can realistically expect to generate in the course of the year.

Outside reps will receive anywhere from 10% of commissions to 80% of commissions, depending on which agency they affiliate with and what they do. Again, the more work the outside rep does, the better the commission split. If all you are doing is steering clients to a particular agency, you can't expect to make much more than 10% or 20% of the commission. To earn high commissions, you will have to do most or all of the work associated with a booking. That means you will have to spend the time to find out what your client needs and wants; research the available products, fares, prices, and options; contact the suppliers to negotiate prices and terms; and make the actual bookings with the various suppliers involved, which could mean an airline or two, a car rental firm, and several different hotels. At this point, you may phone or fax in certain information to your host agency so the inside people there can generate the tickets or vouchers. Or you may create the bookings yourself by plugging into the agency's GDS. Do all this and you will likely earn 50%, 70%, or 80% of the commission. Some outside reps also charge their clients transaction fees, especially for airline tickets, and many host agencies will assist the outside agent in collecting those fees (by allowing the customer to charge the fee via the host agency's merchant account).

Everything is negotiable, of course, and the exact shape your outside rep career takes will depend on the deal you are offered (or negotiate) with an agency. In most cases, however, you will have to choose between being a "bird dog," referring business to an agency, or being a full outside rep with your own clients. A relationship that falls somewhere in between is possible, but agencies and outside people seem to prefer to keep things simple — either the rep does a little work for a small fee or does most of the work for a larger fee.

If you want that larger fee, expect to find a relationship in which you will do all the client contact and then phone or fax in the exact booking information, or book it yourself in the agency's GDS. The agency will expect you to do the work; they are looking for a situation in which their inside people will have to do nothing more than, at most, enter the information into the computer system to generate the ticket. In return, the agency will (or should) respect your client list. That is, they will not call your clients directly to solicit their business and cut you out of the loop.

Whatever your understanding, make sure it is in writing. (See the discussion of contracts, earlier in this Chapter.)

Why become an outside rep?

Now that we have discussed at some length the process of becoming an outside sales representative or outside agent for an accredited travel agency, let's pause to reconsider why you would to form such relationship in the first place.

- Depending on which host agency you choose, it can be the cheapest way of getting into the business, not to mention the fastest.
- Being an outside agent gives you instant credibility with suppliers. Many suppliers may take a lot of convincing before they'll deal directly with you as a "non-ARC" agency. Every supplier understands what an outside agent is and won't blink at taking your bookings.
- It takes some of the pressure off you as you learn the business. Suppliers will be tolerant of you as a new outside agent and (if you handle them correctly) help you through the booking process.
- You can often make more money by sharing your commission. How is this possible? Because your host agency might have a preferred supplier relationship with a cruise line or tour operator that gives them a much higher commission.
- It's not an all-or-nothing proposition. Remember, you're independent. You can put as much — or as little — business through your host agency as you want. Having an outside agent relationship with a host agency allows you to pick and choose, deciding on a case by case basis whether to use your host agency or deal directly with a supplier.
- You pretty much have to be an outside agent for an accredited travel agency if you want to be able to offer your customer domestic airline tickets. There are some exceptions to this "rule," but not many.
- Being an outside agent gives you a certain comfort zone. You

can learn the business and build your confidence while laying the groundwork for becoming a more independent agent later on.

- For some people, being an outside agent for 100% of their business is just the way to go. Many outside agents are perfectly happy with this arrangement and feel that its benefits (as they see and experience them) are worth whatever commissions they might be "losing" by not dealing directly with suppliers.

Everybody is different, of course, and you might very well be a smashing success by being totally independent from the start. However, I strongly urge you to consider the benefits of starting off as an outside agent. Gradually, you can start adding direct relationships with particular suppliers, when you've had some experience and when it makes sense to do so, as I discussed in *Chapter 6: The Independent Agent*. This topic is also discussed in more detail in the Special Report, *How to Get Your Own IATA Number*. If you purchased this book as part of my home study course, you already have it. If not, you can order it by going to:

http://www.HomeTravelAgency.com/getiata.html

Summary

You should always have a contract with your host agency. One of the things that a good contract will do is help assure your standing as an independent contractor, even though a contract is not an absolute guarantee. Always consult with a lawyer before signing any legal agreement.

Every host agency has different policies and procedures. Most of them are pretty straightforward and most of them make sense. However, if a policy does not make sense or seems to contradict your status as an independent contractor, then it should be questioned. It may even be a cause not to consider that host agency as a business partner.

Your use of a host agency is strictly a means to an end. You are not the "customer" of the host agency and the host agency is under no obligation to keep you "happy." It is your responsibility to look after your own interests and assure that you are getting everything that's due you.

Action steps

Here are some things you can do to put what you have learned in this chapter into action:

- Review the contracts of several host agencies. Many can be found on or downloaded from the web sites of host agencies listed in *How to Choose a Host Agency*. Compare them to one another, noting what's included and omitted in each one. Make notes of any questions you have. You may want to contact the host agency to clarify your questions. You will certainly want to discuss them with a lawyer when it comes time to actually sign a contract.

- Contact a few lawyers in your area. Ask them about their experience in general business practice and in the travel industry (specifically agency-outside agent relationships). Ask them about their fee structure.

- Review the Shopper's Checklist in *How to Choose a Host Agency*. (If you purchased this book as part of my home study course, you already have it.) It will help you focus your mind on the most crucial questions you will want answered as you investigate various host agency opportunities.

Chapter Eight:
Getting Started

What you will learn

After you have completed this chapter you will be able to:
- Choose a business name that accurately defines your travel business.
- Lay the groundwork for a professionally run business that will be able to grow along with your success.
- Shop wisely for the equipment and software you need.
- Begin the process of establishing professional connections for networking and continuing professional education.

Key terms and concepts

This chapter involves the following key terms and concepts:
- The best advice is to proceed slowly when making expenditures for your new business. Every penny you spend must be paid for by income that you probably don't have yet.
- Choose your business name with care; it will be with you for many years.
- Your first major business investment should be opening a business checking account in your new business name. This will go a long way to establishing your credibility as a "real" travel agent and allow you to purchase travel products such as consolidator tickets at a low, "net" price.
- A computer has become essential in today's travel business. If you don't have one, make getting one a priority.
- Joining a professional organization will return your investment many times over. The Outside Sales Support Network (OSSN) is the oldest such organization serving the needs of home-based travel agents and the one recommended by this course.

Introduction

One of the best things about getting into the travel business is that it's so easy to do. By now, you may have already hooked up with an agency in your home town or formed a relationship with a more distant agency to become an outside rep.

If you used *How to Choose a Host Agency* to locate a good host agency partner (and took the time to do your due diligence, of course), you may have been pleasantly surprised at how quick and easy it was to join up with a host agency once you had made your decision. It's equally easy to "set up shop" and actually start selling travel. When I made my first sale and booked my first ticket, I had literally nothing to show that I was, in effect, a travel agent. No storefront with posters in the window and brochures in wall racks. No desks. No computerized reservations system. No fancy letterhead and envelopes with the name of my agency on them. Not even a business card! And the amazing thing is, I could have gone on operating that way indefinitely.

Most of you will want to get a little more formal and organized than that, however. In fact, if you want to go to the other extreme, it's possible to become virtually indistinguishable from a "real" travel agent. That is, you can have your very own storefront and the whole nine yards. I don't recommend that you do that and my guess is that very few of you will want to go that far anyway — at least not immediately.

This chapter, then, is intended to show how easy it is to become a home-based, and profitable, travel agent with very few of the trappings and very little of the overhead of most businesses. The emphasis will be on a step-by-step process that holds your expenditures to a minimum. In the next chapter, *Getting Serious*, I'll show you how your fledgling travel agency can become more professional as your business and your ambitions grow.

Defining yourself

In *Chapter 2*, I spoke about the importance of defining yourself and your business and developing a specialty. I believe that this is so important that I'd like to revisit that discussion (briefly) here.

Traditional travel agencies pretty much have to be all things to all people. You don't. You have the freedom to sell exactly what you want to sell and nothing else. Don't get me wrong: I'm not suggesting that you "limit" yourself because you "can't compete" with the big guys. Specializing as a home-based agent is not a sign of weakness. It is, in fact, a source of tremendous power. This is something that you might not be able to appreciate right now but that will become increasingly obvious as your business, your experience, and your knowledge develop.

There is a tremendous pressure to "take on all comers" when you're just starting out. When friends and neighbors hear you're a travel agent, they may come to you with requests for advice and booking assistance for forms of travel and destinations that you know little about. There's nothing wrong with taking on these requests and muddling through. It will be a valuable learning experience.

If you haven't the foggiest idea of how you might specialize, that's okay, too. You can work your way towards it. And if you insist on "doing it all," that's fine, too. It's a noble calling and I wish you good luck and Godspeed. As I've said before, this is definitely not a one-size-fits-all proposition.

Still, my personal belief is that focusing your efforts on a well-defined travel niche is a very sound strategy. Sometimes doing this will mean limiting your income, but that may be perfectly all right with you. One gentleman I know of specializes in European tours for beekeepers. Talk about a niche market! He's not getting rich, but that's not his goal and he is performing a very valuable service for his core market. Another student sells nothing but vacations at a single all-inclusive resort chain. Not only that, but she sells them only to honeymooners! She is that chain's top producer and she does very well indeed.

So I urge you to pick a specialty as you start out. You don't have to stick to or limit yourself just to this one area as your business develops. But by choosing a focused niche, you will flatten out the learning curve as you make your first bookings as a travel agent. Instead of having to learn about five things all at once, you will be able to focus on just one area.

Let's say you live in or around New York City and you love to gamble. Then why not start out by serving the needs of your fellow gamers? You have Atlantic City to the south, the casinos of Connecticut to the northeast, and Las Vegas is a bargain-basement flight away. Plenty of suppliers offer convenient packages to all these destinations. This is plenty to get started with. Then you can apply the lessons learned to other niches and other specialties as your business grows. Or you might just find that this specialty will take up all your time and make you a very good income. It does for a lot of people!

The best advice for beginners

Slow down.

There is a tremendous temptation, I have observed, for people starting a new venture to go out and spend money on "things they will need." They will redo that spare bedroom and turn it into their home office, buying a new desk and an "executive" chair. They will hire a designer to create business cards, stationery, and envelopes, all with just the right "look." They will get a top-of-the line answering machine and fax and upgrade their computer system. When it's all done they've spent a lot of money and really feel like they're "in business," but they haven't generated a single nickel of income.

So slow down, take a deep breath, and take things one step at a time. First of all, I'm going to assume that, to begin with at least, you'll be running your travel business from your home, part-time. Most people do when they are starting out. The fact is you don't have to refinish the basement or clear out the attic to create an office for yourself. You really don't need a room for your office at all. In fact, you don't need a lot of things. Your "travel agency" can quite easily consist of a supply of business cards, an address book or Rolodex, and a telephone, preferably one with an answering machine attached. That's it!

Of course, as your business grows, you will start adding things. But you should do so slowly and only when it makes sound business sense. I am a big believer in keeping expenses to an absolute minimum.

Laying the groundwork

Since your home-based travel agency is a business, you'll probably want to conduct yourself in a businesslike manner. To my mind, the most important element of professionalism is behavior, rather than degrees, licenses, or certificates. Still, the world at large, not to mention the representatives of your city and state governments, tend to pay attention to these little details. While it's perfectly possible to conduct your business affairs with just a business card and a ready smile, sooner or later you will want to "get your act together" and start acting like the bona fide business that you are. You should also be aware that your failure to dot all the i's and cross all the t's might expose you to some unpleasant legal consequences.

So let's walk through the process of setting up your business in a more or less logical fashion, beginning with step one. We'll start with the paperwork and bureaucracy that goes into starting up your travel business, or virtually any business for that matter.

Choosing a business name

Remember, you are now not merely a person, you are a business. If you have formed a relationship with a host agency, it is tempting to think of yourself, perhaps unconsciously, as "working for" that agency. In some senses of the term, you do. But in a much more important sense, you work for no one but yourself. The essence of an independent contractor agreement, never forget, is that you are independent. You are a business, a separate business from the host agency.

So one of the first things you need to do, even before you start shopping for a host agency, is think about what you are going to call your business. This will have important implications for things as simple as your business card and as important as your checking account.

One option is just to use you own name. The commission checks you receive from your host agency will be made out to Jane Smith and can be deposited in your personal checking account. This option has any number of drawbacks, however, and will prove a problem as your business evolves. To cite just one example: One of the best ways to make money as a home-based agent is to sell so-called consolidator tickets. Most consolidators accept payment in the form of an "agency check." That means a check drawn on a "business" account; a personal check will not be accepted.

So most home-based agents choose a more formal "business name" for their new travel marketing venture. Selecting a name for your home-based travel business is one of your first and most important tasks. Unfortunately, many beginners don't realize the importance of the right name and choose one in haste or without thinking of the consequences. Devoting a little time and thought to this process can pay big dividends later on.

There are three main areas to consider when choosing a name for your business:

- Legal.
- Marketing.
- Personal.

Don't let the word "legal" scare you. Still, some common sense precautions need to be taken when choosing a name. Your first concern is at the local level. Once you've picked a name, you'll have to register it at town hall or the county court house so you can get a business checking account. If you live in Cleveland and decide to call your business "Tammy's Travel" the fact that there's a Tammy's Travel in Phoenix is most likely not a problem. But if there's one in Cleveland, you probably won't be able to register your chosen name at the county court house, where the clerks will check to make sure there is no duplication of business names. So you should check the "availability" of a name at the courthouse before you get too attached to it.

Another precaution you should take is making sure your name doesn't infringe on someone else's trademark. Let's say you decide that your travel business will specialize in American vacations only and you figure "American Express Travel" would be a great name. Wrong! This is a fairly obvious example, but you could accidentally infringe on a trademark without knowing it. A nationwide Yellow Pages search on the Internet should turn up companies with the name you're interested in (if any exist). If you have come up with what you think is a pretty nifty name, you may want to consider trademarking it. Consult a lawyer who specializes in trademarks and be prepared to pay well for your vanity.

While it's possible to have legal problems with your business name, the odds are that you will have no troubles whatsoever regardless of the name you pick. Marketing considerations, therefore, are far more important and deserve the lion's share of your attention.

You already know how I feel about specializing. Ideally, your business name should reflect your specialty. If you've decided to specialize in trips to Tunisia, "Tammy's Tunisian Tours and Travel" is a better choice than "Tammy's Travel." (By the way, I am making up all the names I use in this discussion, so any similarity to actual businesses is purely coincidental.)

In the best of all possible worlds, your business name will tell your best prospects, "This is the place to call." Names like "Italian Villa Holidays," "Ski Trips Unlimited," and "Japan With Jane" immediately tell people what you do. Even a name like "Hole In One Travel" hints at a golf specialty.

If you can't put your specialty in the name itself, plan to add a descriptive tag line on your business card (and anywhere else your business name appears). For example, if you have decided to call your business "Tammy's Travel," your business card could say "Tammy's Travel – The Tunisian Specialists."

That brings us to the last major consideration in selecting a name — personal preference. My guess is that this is the overriding consideration for most home-based agents when picking a name. Some of them are very creative, clever, or amusing. Certainly a memorable name like "I'm Outta Here!" (a real one, this time) has marketing value, but what exactly does the business do? Hopefully, they use a good descriptive subhead or tag line on their business card.

Of course, ultimately the name you choose, like your business itself, is an expression of your own personality. So if a name "speaks" to you, go for it, but keep your target customer in mind. If you've decided to call your travel business "Like Totally Travel, Dude" I won't say you nay. Just be sure that your prospective customers are on the same wavelength.

Registering your business name

So now you have a name for your business. The next step will be to register that name to "make it official." That means getting something called a "fictitious name certificate." It may be called something else where you live — a business certificate or a "d.b.a." (for "doing business as"). Whatever the name, the concept is simple: you, the real person, own a business, the fictitious name. A public record is created linking you to your business for all the world to see.

If you decide to do business under your own name (for example, "Joe Smith") and arrange to receive all checks under that name, you probably don't have to register. But if you decide to do business as "Joe's Wonderful World of Travel" you should register.

Registering your business name is a simple process. Exactly how you go about doing it, however, depends on where you live; each locality has a somewhat different way of doing it. In a small town, you can probably go to the town hall. Or you may have to go to the office of the County Clerk at your county court house, which may mean a trip to a different town.

If you have absolutely no idea of where you have to go, ask someone. Your best bets for guidance are your local town hall, the local chamber of commerce, or the office of one of your elected representatives at the local or state level. Any of these places should be able to clue you in on exactly what you have to do to register a business name.

Once you get to wherever you have to go, the people there will be able to tell you what to do. Generally, all that's involved is checking the town or county records to make sure no one already has the business name you want to use, filling out a form, and paying a fee. Hopefully, the fee will be modest. In my town it was just $7. However, when I was doing business in New York City the fee was an outrageous $120! In return for your money, you get a certificate saying that you are doing business under the name you've chosen for yourself. File this away in a safe place. You will need it later.

It is not absolutely necessary to register your business name immediately. You can wait until you *really* need to — like when you want to open a business checking account. However, doing it immediately protects you in the (admittedly unlikely) event that someone else in town wants to register the name you've chosen.

Do we need this?

Business cards

The next step is probably getting a supply of business cards.

Your business card doesn't have to be fancy. There are outfits that charge about $30.00 to print up 500 simple but classy business cards — the kind with raised printing. You might even be able to beat that price through a local printer. If you have the right software on your computer, you can even design them yourself and print them on your laser printer using special paper stock.

While your business card doesn't have to be fancy, a snazzy card can't hurt. In fact, it can go a long way toward establishing your credibility and enhancing your image. For the cost, a professionally designed and printed business card can be your most effective advertising. Potential clients and suppliers' reps you meet at industry functions, will form their first impression of you and your business when they glance at the business card you hand them. So if you want to "splurge," splurge on your business card.

Your host agency may have some say in your business card, so you may want to postpone getting business cards until you have finalized on a host agency or decided you definitely will not be using one (although I counsel against this for beginners). Many host agency contracts include a clause stating that your business card must carry a line that says something like "An Affiliate of Very Big Travel, Inc." Some hosts will supply you (for a fee) with business cards that feature their name prominently. My advice would be to have your own cards printed up. Feature your business name prominently and fulfill your contractual obligations to your host agency (if any) in small print.

Once again, my advice is to start small (and cheap). Just make sure your business card contains the basics: Your business name and tag line (if any) your own name, and the various ways of contacting you (including cell phone and email).

As your business grows, you can use some of the profit to get fancier business cards. There are full color cards, cards with clever cutouts, cards that fold in two, cards with your photo on them, even cards printed on little CD-ROMs that customers can pop into their computers to view your travel brochures. As you attend industry events, ask everyone you meet for their card; you'll pick up a lot of good ideas.

Opening a business checking account.

One of the most important reasons for registering your business name at town hall or the county court house is that you will not be able to open a business checking account without the proper certificate. And you'll need a business account if you want to cash a check made out to the name of your travel business and not to you personally. Bank regulations are strict and your bank will balk at accepting a check made out to "Jane Jones Travel," even if your name is Jane Jones. Another reason for having a separate business account is to manage your money and segregate funds, something that may be required under your state's laws.

To open a business checking account, retrieve your business certificate from its safe place and take it down to your bank along with your personal checkbook (so you can write a check for the initial deposit). A bank officer will take you through the simple process of opening your account. Once your printed checks arrive, bearing your business name, you will have gone a long way to establishing yourself as a bona fide travel agency in the eyes of à great many suppliers.

If you have a bank you already know and do business with, then you may be predisposed to open your new business account there. However, to be truly business-like, you will shop around for the best deal. Among the questions you might want to ask of banks are:

■ *What is your fee structure?* Service charges and per check fees can differ widely. Some banks will waive fees if the funds in "linked" accounts total a certain amount. This can be a good argument for opening your business account where you now have your personal account.

■ *How do you handle wire transfers?* If you start doing any significant business with overseas suppliers, wire transfers of funds will become important. Again, the fees charged by different banks can vary significantly. A $10 savings per transfer can amount to hundreds of dollars over the course of a year.

Once you have your new checks, you will be a "real" travel agent in the eyes of many suppliers in the travel industry. Most air consolidators, for example, will happily accept an "agency check," as it is known, as payment for the airline tickets they sell to bona-fide travel agents at rock-bottom prices.

Complying with local ordinances

Some local jurisdictions — cities, towns, counties — may have ordinances or laws that will affect you as a small businessperson operating within that jurisdiction. Some towns, for example, may require that you get a "license" to operate a home-based business.

Regulations like this are usually quite benign. They are not licenses in quite the same sense as a driver's license. In other words, the local government is not going to test you to see if you are competent to have a business. These regulations are really about making sure that no one is doing something truly dumb (like trying to operate a blast furnace in their garage) or doing something that might change the residential character of the neighborhood (operating a nightclub, or grocery store, or some other business that would create a lot of foot traffic and parking problems). Your home-based travel business will not have a problem in this regard.

The other main reason for these types of ordinances, of course, is to raise money for the town. So look on these regulations and the fees they might carry as inconveniences rather than hurdles. If there is a cost involved, it is minor. Ignoring these laws is not worth the small savings. Do your homework (ask the same people you asked about registering your business name) and be in compliance.

Complying with state laws

It seems that every year, somewhere in the state legislatures of the United States, some politician gets the bright idea that what his or her state needs is a law regulating, or should I say restricting, home-based travel agents.

These laws take a number of forms: simple registration (and payment to the state of a fee), bonding requirements, or the establishment of so-called "restitution funds."

To my way of thinking, these laws get passed for one of two reasons:

1. An effort by established, storefront agencies to raise "barriers to entry." In other words, they want the state to discourage new businesses so they can protect their own. They find a sympathetic pol and before you know it a new "seller of travel" law has been introduced.

2. A misguided effort by a politician to present him or herself as a consumer advocate. The problem is, none of these laws that I've seen actually prevent fraud. Instead, they may force honest travel agents to reimburse victims once the fraud has occurred, while the state authorities do precisely nothing to apprehend the bad guys. Of course, the politicos could care less. For them it's just as important to create the *illusion* of helping the consumer than to actually do something useful. Sometimes, it's a combination of the two.

Fortunately, most of these laws are minor nuisances. The additional costs will be negligible to anyone who is serious about their travel marketing business. Still, they do have a negative effect in that they discourage people from getting started or "testing the waters." This is a shame, especially since job creation should be a major goal of every state government.

But the law, as you know, is the law. If your state or province does have a travel promoter law, you may be bound by its provisions. On the other hand, you may be exempt as the outside sales rep for a travel agency — as long as you route all of your business through the host agency. State laws differ widely, so you should check to see what the ground rules are in your state and consult a lawyer.

The fact of the matter is many outside reps, through ignorance or choice, operate without regard to local and state regulations. Most of those who do are, I would guess, well-meaning people trying to make an honest buck. Most of them experience no problems. But if you are in violation of the law, even if out of ignorance or on a mere "technicality," the consequences can be irritating at best and financially devastating at worst. Why take the risk?

As of this writing, the following states have some sort of law that may affect home-based travel agents: California, Florida, Hawaii, Illinois, Iowa, Louisiana, Massachusetts, Michigan, Nevada, New York, Ohio, Oregon, Rhode Island, Texas, Virginia, and Washington. Puerto Rico, Ontario, Quebec, and British Columbia also have laws that might affect you.

You should always check the laws of your state or province regardless of whether you see it listed above. It is your responsibility to comply with all applicable laws, so check with your state attorney general's office to find out if there are any laws that apply to you. Again, you should also consult a lawyer.

Once you have complied with your state's laws, start working to change them. I think that once you have familiarized yourself with some of these laws, you will agree with me that they are regressive laws that unfairly hinder the creation of honest businesses. Now that you are a businessperson, it will be in your best interests to become politically active and work for the passage of good laws and the repeal of bad laws.

Lawyers

It used to be said that the only things that are certain are death and taxes. It's probably time to add lawyers' fees to the list. Even if it irks you to have to do it, consult with a competent professional early in your career as a home-based travel agent. If you're going to be signing a contract with an agency (and you should!), you'll probably want to have that vetted anyway. So while you're in the lawyer's office, ask her about the points raised here. The guidance you get will be worth the price in peace of mind.

Customer files

One of the most important things you can do to insure your success as a home-based travel agent is to keep excellent records of the people you meet who might become customers as well as the people who actually become customers ("prospects"). That list of prospects and customers can grow rapidly, so you'll need some mechanism for keeping track. For starters, a cheap address book or Rolodex will do just fine. As you get more serious or busy, or both, you can expand your record-keeping system and acquire more sophisticated tools. I'll give you some suggestions along those lines in due course.

For now, I want to impress upon you the crucial importance of recording at least basic information about everyone and anyone who might become one of your customers. That means name, address, phone numbers, and (increasingly important these days) email address. You can make additional notes, too, if you wish, but these basic facts are a must.

The sooner you acquire this discipline, the better off you and your business will be. So start today, before you do anything else, by making a list of everyone you know who might become a customer of your new travel business. If all you have is pencil and paper, do it that way. If you have a computer, do it electronically. If you know your way around a computer database or spreadsheet program, do it that way. The important thing is to start doing it now.

The next step: office machines

Now that you've taken care of the bureaucratic details and ordered up a batch of business cards, it's time to turn your attention to the hardware and software you will need to make your newly fledged business a going concern. As always, let me counsel you to take things one step at a time, spending as little out of pocket as possible. Many of the items I'll discuss below, you probably already have, which will make it a little easier. So if you already have some of these wonderful devices, great! You're ahead of the game. If not, you'll want to proceed carefully and keep a close eye on the cost-benefit ratio of any investment you make.

There is a bewildering array of choices out there, and so many variables to weigh in making a decision that the shopping process can quickly become a frustrating nightmare. One way to proceed is to pick up a "Buying Guide" type of publication. These are magazine-format publications that list, describe, and rate the numerous machines on the market. Another way is to talk to "experts." I find this to be an arduous task since the experts tend to be passionate about the machines they have chosen (especially computers) and equally passionate against all others.

Here is a selection methodology that, while not particularly elegant, makes a lot of sense to me. Find someone who has a computer, fax, or piece of software that they like. Get them to tell you about it, how it works, how they use it in their business. Ask them what you'll be able to do with it. Tell them the sort of things you'll need it to do and ask them if it can do those things. Then get them to show you how the machine or software program actually does those things. Most importantly, get a sense of whether or not you'll be able to call on them, once you have the machine, to ask for their help and suggestions. Shop around for the best price once you've settled on a brand and model.

This system probably works better with computers and software than with fax machines, but it can be used for virtually any important business-related purchase. My theory is that while you might not wind up with the cheapest of whatever it is you're looking for, the time you save shopping and dealing with problems and questions after the purchase will compensate for any extra cost. I will not try to cover all your options here. That would take another whole book! But I will make some observations that I hope will prove helpful as you set up your home travel agency.

Phones

Of course, you'll need a phone. It could be your existing home phone for now. The problem with your existing phone is that it is no doubt shared with your spouse and your kids. As you get more customers, you may want to consider adding a separate line just for your travel business. If you don't already have a cell phone, this could be a good opportunity to get one.

Your business phone should have call-waiting and some mechanism for taking messages, either an answering machine or a message-taking service offered by your phone company, so you don't miss any calls from would-be customers. If you have a dedicated line for your travel sideline, you'll probably want to have a "travel agency" message on it like, "Hi! You've reached Joe Smith, Travel Consultant." Your answering machine message can even do some advertising for you, alerting callers to special deals you may have found for tours or cruises.

Be aware that some host agencies require that you have a dedicated (that is, separate) business line and a dedicated fax line. *When will I need a fax??*

Computers

When I wrote the first edition of this book, back in the Dark Ages of 1994, it was very possible to function as a home-based agent without a computer. Today, it may be possible to do that although it is scarcely conceivable that anyone would want to try. The Internet-ready computer is quickly becoming as indispensable to the modern home as the telephone.

So there's an excellent chance that you already have a computer and Internet access. But just in case, let's talk a bit about the two main reasons you should have a computer. One has to do with running a business in general, the other is very specific to the travel business.

Computers not only allow you to take care of the annoying details of your business and personal life in an efficient, organized, and speedy way, they can actually impose order where none existed before. My personal finances were the usual jumble of receipts in a shoe box before I got a computer program to track them. Now I can account for nearly every penny I spend. Come tax time, I touch a few keys and I'm ready to head off to my tax advisor.

Here are just two of the most obvious ways you can put a computer to use in your new travel business (or any business, for that matter):

- *Tracking your customers.* At the simplest level this can mean having a computerized address book or Rolodex. In computer lingo, this is a "database." If you want to get more sophisticated, you can get programs that allow you to construct extensive and quite sophisticated databases. For example, later in this book I will give you a Client Profile Form that you can use to learn more about your clients' travel habits, patterns, likes, dislikes, and so forth. If you put the information from the profile form into a computer, you can have all this data at your fingertips instantly. If you find out about a great package for golfers, you can access your client database (there's that computer lingo again) and get a list of every customer you have who plays golf. You can easily update customer information as their lives and interests change — a couple becomes a family, the Smiths get interested in cruising, and so on.

- *Doing mailings.* I hardly ever did promotional mailings before I was computerized. It was just too much of a hassle. Now I can generate mailing labels in a few minutes. I can also churn out hundreds of form letters, each personalized to a different recipient ("Dear Joe,"... "Dear Martha,"... and so forth). And thanks to the Internet, I can often save the cost of printing and postage. I can quickly create "broadcast emails" that go to a carefully selected segment of my total customer base. It's a great advantage for the one-person business. When sending out these "mass" emailings, you need to be in compliance with the rules of your Internet service provider (ISP) and the sensitivities of your customers. But as long as you use email responsibly and take proper precautions, you should experience no problems.

The second main reason for getting a computer is that, once you've added a modem, you can gain access to a whole world of up-to-the-second travel information, either via the Internet or by dialing directly into another computer. The Internet is becoming increasingly important to home-based agents as a way to communicate with and make bookings through a host agency, as a means of making independent bookings, as a research tool, and as a communications and sales medium. There is no reason to believe these trends won't continue, become more pervasive, and even more crucial to doing business.

Which computer?

If you have a computer now, you may be able just to keep on using it. Even if you feel your computer is old and out of date, you should try to hang onto it for as long as possible. If you really want a "new" computer, get a used one; they're a lot cheaper. If you have tech-savvy friends, they may have last year's model gathering dust in a closet. They may even be willing to give it to you. Of course, if you want to buy new, I'm not going to try and stop you. Just remember that before you turn a profit, your future income will have to pay for the expenditures you make now.

The conventional wisdom is that your business PC should run Windows software from Microsoft. There's something to this, since more business-oriented software is written for Windows than for any other platform. You will find host agencies that won't be able to work with you if you don't have a Windows machine. Does this mean that if you have a Macintosh you should throw it out? Not at all. Most Mac users would rather fight than switch anyway and the Macintosh platform offers some advantages over Windows. If Windows compatibility becomes an issue, you can get "simulation software" that lets you run Windows programs on a Mac.

If you're in the market for a new computer and haven't already made a commitment to the Mac product line, then I must in good conscience recommend a Windows machine. There are problems with Windows and Microsoft. Windows has spent years trying to ape the ease of use of the Macintosh interface, but Windows is still frustratingly difficult to work with, at least until you get used to its quirks. Security has been an ongoing issue for Microsoft and because there are so many Windows machines, they are a prime target of hackers. Owning a Windows operating system and Microsoft software means dedicating yourself to constant vigilance against viruses, adware, spyware, malware, and any manner of other unpleasantness. Despite all this, Microsoft enjoys enormous market share which is the main reason I recommend it.

Some host agencies set minimum standards for the computers they want their independent contractors to have. Based on my survey of well over a hundred host agencies, here is about the lowest configuration that will work:

120 MHz Pentium processor or better
64 MB RAM
2.1 GB Hard Drive
CD-ROM drive
Windows 95 or newer
800 x 600 Screen Resolution (SVGA)
Internet Service Provider Netscape 3.0 or higher or Internet Explorer 4.0 or higher (not America Online or CompuServe)
Dedicated line (second phone line or voice-over-data line)

Another host agency wants you to have a 266 MHz processor and a 56K modem. One host agency suggests both a recommended and a minimum configuration:

Recommended Configuration:

450+ MHz Pentium Processor
128 MB RAM
10 GB Hard Drive
17" Color Monitor
CD-ROM drive
Color Ink-Jet Printer
Internet Service
eMail Service
High Speed Connection to Internet — Greater than 1.54 MBPS

Minimum Configuration:

166 MHz Pentium Processor
64 MB RAM
6 GB Hard Drive
15" Color Monitor—Screen Resolution minimum of 800 x 600
CD-ROM drive
Color Ink-Jet Printer
Internet Service
eMail Service
High Speed Connection to Internet — Average 512 K (DSL or Cable Connect)

This will give you an idea of what to look for. The processor is the "brains" of the computer and Pentium chips have become the de facto industry standard. In general, you want the fastest computer you can afford. Speed is measured in megahertz (MHz) or, increasingly, in gigahertz (GHz). The same is true of memory as measured by RAM (random access memory). Memory is not to be confused with storage on the hard drive, which these days is measured in gigabytes (GB). A 2.1 GB hard drive is considered pretty puny these days and if you are saving large files like photos and supplier brochures, you'll fill up space fast. Fortunately, storage is getting cheaper and cheaper and you can usually add an extra hard drive to most computers, either internally or externally.

These days a very peppy PC, with plenty of RAM and storage and a CD-ROM drive can be had for well under $1,000, some for under $500. Decent monitors are now under $500.

Printers

Printers, too, are getting cheaper and cheaper it seems, especially the ink jets (as opposed to the laser printers, whose output has more of a "printed" look). Color is nice, but not absolutely necessary, unless for some reason the host agency you choose to work with demands it. Give consideration to printers that can double as a fax machine and copier. These multi-function machines can come in handy. You should be able to pick up a decent ink jet printer for about $200 to $500. Laser printers are a bit more expensive. It's also worth giving some thought to a printer/scanner/copier/fax combination; some are very reasonably priced.

Software

To begin with, you will not need much in the way of specialized software. There are software packages designed specifically for travel agents, but they are relatively expensive and the functions they provide, such as accounting and contact management, can be accomplished (albeit to a more limited extent) with simpler, cheaper alternatives. When your business grows, you can upgrade to these "industrial-strength" programs.

For now stick with something like Microsoft Office, which combines a number of programs in one package. Word processing (Word) and a spreadsheet (Excel) will come in handy. Excel can even double as a database. You should also have some sort of financial program to track expenditures and income, Quicken is a good choice. You will need an email program, too. I advise against using Microsoft's Outlook, which probably came bundled with your computer. All email programs are vulnerable to infection, but Outlook is riddled with security holes and its popularity and widespread use make it a prime target for viruses. Eudora is a good alternative and a free version is available.

Internet access

There are several ways to connect your computer to the Internet:

- **Dial-up.** Dial-up uses a modem (usually installed inside the computer these days) and regular phone lines. It is slow but inexpensive ($10 to $25 a month). Using dial-up means subscribing to an Internet Service Provider (ISP). You dial up the ISP's computer to get connected to the Internet.
- **Cable modem.** This is a modem provided by your cable television provider. It is fast and moderately expensive (in the $50 per month range). In this case, the cable company becomes your ISP. Just because you have cable television, doesn't necessarily mean you can get a cable modem; it's not available everywhere. The speed of your connection can vary depending on how many of your neighbors have cable modems and are logged on at the same time you are.

- **DSL.** DSL stands for digital subscriber line and is provided by your local phone company. It too is fast and moderately expensive, about the same as a cable modem. Like cable modem, it is not available everywhere. The speed is about the same as with a cable modem.
- **T1 Line.** This is an ultra-fast connection offered by the phone company. It is very expensive and probably not a realistic option. It's nice to dream, though, and who knows, in a few years it may be affordable.
- **Satellite.** When no other option besides dial-up exists, you may be able to get a satellite connection to the Internet. This works much like those TV satellite dishes you see on the sides of houses. Speed is roughly comparable to DSL and cable modems. It is expensive.

Internet Service Providers (ISP)

There are two basic types of ISPs: Those that offer Internet access through one of the means listed above and those that host web sites on their servers. Let's consider simple Internet access first.

If you are currently using America Online or CompuServe as your ISP, my recommendation is that you switch providers as soon as possible. It will save you a lot of hassles in the long run. AOL, for example, restricts the email you receive, the amount and type of email you can send, and makes searching the Internet as difficult as possible. Why? Because AOL makes its money by keeping its subscribers a captive audience. It can be a highly useful and fun experience for consumers, but it is not friendly to businesses.

Another, slightly less important reason is that AOL addresses look amateurish to many in the business world. The same is true of those "free" email accounts at Yahoo and Hotmail.

So shop for an ISP that will allow you to present yourself professionally and that will not erect artificial barriers between you, the Internet, and your customers. Most ISPs charge anywhere from $15 to $25 a month to provide this service, but you can do better (see below).

If you want to take this line of reasoning to its logical end, you can get your own Internet domain name. This means your email address can read, for example, marj@travelwithmarjorie.com instead of marjorie@aol.com. This also means you will be dealing with the second type of ISP, one that is in the business of hosting web sites as opposed to giving people an "on ramp to the Information Superhighway." You do not need to have a web site to get your mail this way, but you'll have a domain name ready to go when (and if) you get to the point of having a presence on the Web. You can also send broadcast emails through the mail server at your domain, avoiding most, if not all, of the hassles of sending lots of email through a dial-up, cable, or DSL connection.

To shop for the best Internet connection and domain name services at the best prices, visit this web site:

http://ld.net/? intreptrav

Browsers

You will also need an "Internet browser," a software program that lets your computer display material from the Internet. Once you're "on the Web," you can read through reams of "pages" on that vast global network of computers, with its wealth of valuable and worthless information.

Any Windows computer will come with Microsoft Internet Explorer (IE) already installed. If you have IE 4.0 or earlier installed on your computer, you should get the latest version at:

www.microsoft.com/windows/ie/.

Like all Microsoft products, IE has its drawbacks, not least of which is it's vulnerability to adware, annoying rogue software programs that download themselves onto your hard drive and pepper your screen with pop-up ads. There are programs you can buy (some are free) that will help eliminate them or at least allow you to remove them when they get downloaded. Another option is to use an alternate browser like Firefox, Netscape, or Opera that is less vulnerable. Unfortunately, some web sites just won't work properly unless you are using IE — and a specific version of IE at that. Some host agencies require that you use IE to access their intranet (a private agent-only network).

Faxes

Fax (or "facsimile") machines translate images, such as a typed letter or an advertising flyer, into digital code that can be transmitted over telephone lines to another fax machine. The receiving machine decodes the message and creates a copy of the original image. There are a number of reasons you might find a fax machine useful in your business:

- **To communicate with your agency.** Even if your agency is just across town, you may find the convenience of a fax worth the investment. Bookings and other messages have a way of getting garbled when they are transmitted over the phone. A fax can prevent that. A faxed message also creates a record of what was "said." In many cases, it's essential to have this capability. Many host agencies prefer bookings to be faxed in, so you really may not have an option. Fortunately, they usually provide a toll-free fax number.

- **To communicate with suppliers.** When you're working on a booking with a short time fuse, it can be a tremendous help if the tour operator or other supplier can fax you information (price lists, terms and conditions, whole brochures). Getting brochures in the mail can take days, even weeks. A growing number of suppliers have "fax-back" service — you dial a toll-free number, punch in the code for the information you want (usually obtained from an advertisement), punch in your fax number, and the material is faxed to you immediately.

- **To communicate with customers.** Sometimes you will need to obtain some form of credit card authorization from a client. He or she can photocopy the credit card, write on the photocopy the travel being booked and the costs (e.g. "2 tickets to California from Joe's Travel, $842"), sign the photocopy, and fax the resulting document to you. You can then present (or fax!) the fax you receive to your agency or a supplier as proof that this person did indeed authorize you to charge the travel to their account. Obviously, not all customers will be able to do this, but you'll be surprised at how many can; faxes and copy machines are present in most places of business these days. You also may find it convenient to fax confirmations to clients on bookings they've phoned in. In effect, you are saying, "Here's what you told me you wanted. You'd better call if it's not right." It's an extra safeguard that can prevent problems and ill-feeling later.

- *To save time.* No matter with whom you are communicating, situations will arise where time is of the essence. The ability to fax something in a matter of minutes can sometimes mean the difference between snaring a $350 commission or losing it! A perfect example occurred while I was working on this section. Because of a glitch in a booking, my agency needed to get my signature on a form that I had to return to them, so they could send it to the supplier, so my client wouldn't lose the booking. It all had to be done by the afternoon of the same day!

- *To save money.* In spite of the initial cost of fax machines and the ongoing costs of phone lines and such, you may find that in some instances a fax will actually help you save money. One form of saving can be realized through increased efficiency. It takes less time to fax something than to find and address an envelope, put a stamp on it, and take it to the post office or mail box. That's time that can be better spent generating income for your travel business.

  Real savings start clicking in if you are doing a great deal of foreign business. Let's say you've become a destination specialist for France. Rather than telephone suppliers and run up gargantuan phone bills, you can fax them. Faxes seem to be ubiquitous in the French hospitality industry, with even the tiniest hotels and quaintest restaurants boasting their own fax machines. It can cost very little to send a terse fax requesting a reservation; that way you don't run up your long distance bill waiting for Jacques to come to the phone. The reservation will be confirmed by return fax.

Home fax machines cost anywhere from under $100 on sale to $300 or more. As a rough rule of thumb, figure you can get a fax machine that will please you most of the time for $250 or less. I say "most of the time" because it seems inevitable that once you've had a machine for a while you find yourself longing for a particular feature you could have had for a few dollars more. Here are a couple of the major variables involved in choosing a fax machine:

- ***Plain paper or thermal?*** Chances are, any fax you buy to-day will use plain paper. If someone tries to sell you a fax machine that uses thermal paper, run in the opposite direction. It's obsolete and a pain to work with.
- ***How many phone lines?*** The ideal situation is to have a separate, or "dedicated," phone line for your fax. However, if you want to save a few pennies, it's possible to have both a fax and a phone on the same line. Some faxes will automatically determine if an incoming call is a fax or voice communication and route the call accordingly; others require manual switching. Check out these features carefully to see how they work and how convenient their operation will be for you and the people who will be calling and faxing to you.

Other than the cost of the machine itself, the cost of an additional phone line is the biggest financial consideration in adding a fax to your office. There's no reason why, if you're working from home, this cannot be a residential (as opposed to business) line. You only need a business line if you absolutely must have a Yellow Pages listing and (in my humble opinion) that's inappropriate for most home-based travel agents. Another option is "distinctive ring" technology that lets you have two phone numbers sharing one phone line. Check to see if your phone company offers this option.

- ***When do you fax?*** Sometimes, you'll have to fax something right now, this very instant. But not all faxes are that crucial. Look for a fax machine that allows you to send a fax at a later time ("delayed transmission"). If you're using one phone line for voice and fax, you can schedule less important faxes for transmission after business hours, leaving your phone line free for business calls. Another money-saver is a feature available on some machines that allows you to fax half-pages for short messages, saving on transmission time.
- ***What about a fax/modem?*** A modem is a device that allows data to be transmitted between computers over phone lines. A fax/modem is a modem that also allows computers and fax machines to communicate. In effect, you can turn your computer (assuming you have one) into a fax.

  The main advantage is that letters, bookings, and so forth that you create directly on your computer can be faxed immediately. In other words, you don't have to print them out, go to the fax machine, and transmit them. There are, however, a number of disadvantages. You cannot fax existing printed matter that's not in your computer. For example, if you wanted to fill out a form and fax it, you couldn't, unless of course you have a scanner. The same goes for a magazine article or a flyer from a tour operator. Another problem is that, while you can receive faxes through the computer, printing them out is a slow process that prevents you from doing other work on the computer. You may want to consider using a fax/modem for outgoing, computer-generated communications and a separate fax machine for everything else.

- **What about a fax/copier/printer?** If you have a computer, the growing range (and declining prices) of single machines that combine the functions of a fax, a photocopier, and a printer may be worth investigating.

- **Virtual fax number.** As your business grows, I strongly urge you to consider getting a "virtual fax number" for incoming faxes. To the sender, it looks like any other fax number, but you collect your incoming faxes from an Internet site, not your office fax machine. You will thank me for this advice if you become a completely independent agent with your own IATA number. Getting your own IATA number makes your agency fax number "public" to virtually every supplier in the world and you will begin to receive an astonishing number of faxes about special offers and the like. This can be invaluable information, but dealing with the avalanche of paper can be a colossal pain, not to mention the cost of paper and ink cartridges. By collecting your faxes via the Internet, you can simply delete the faxes you don't want and print out or save electronically the ones you do.

As you can see, faxes and fax machines can be one of the trickiest strategic decisions you'll make in configuring your office. So spend some time thinking about how you want to proceed. You may want to start small and cheap with a bargain basement fax machine you can use on your existing phone line. Then, as you network with other home-based agents, ask the more experienced ones how they are handling their faxing. You'll get some good advice.

Help is at hand

This course will get you started in your new career as a home-based travel agent but it cannot answer all your questions and it certainly cannot provide all the reference material you will be needing in the months and years ahead. Sooner or later, you'll come across a question or encounter a problem that is beyond the scope of this course. So do yourself a favor; begin putting into place a support system that will fuel your professional growth. Here are some thoughts and suggestions:

Join a professional organization

All professions have organizations and associations that are dedicated to enhancing the professionalism of their members. The world of outside sales reps and part-time travel agents is no exception. The Outside Sales Support Network (OSSN) is the oldest and largest professional association devoted to the needs of outside agents and independent, home-based travel agencies.

I have been a member of OSSN for many years and have found it to be a consistently supportive and nurturing group, both for me and other home-based agents. It is the association I personally recommend, but I encourage you to make your own independent decision.

The newer, much smaller National Association of Commissioned Travel Agents (NACTA) is a subsidiary of ASTA, which also represents "traditional" storefront agencies, creating something of a conflict of interest to my way of thinking.

Both organizations offer a number of benefits to their members. Here is a sample:

- *A regular newsletter* filled with selling tips, news of interest to members of the outside sales confraternity, announcements of fam/seminars, and lists of agencies that actively support the concept of marketing through an outside sales force. If you've been having trouble finding an agency to hook up with (or are dissatisfied with the one you are hooked up with), this might be a good source of information.

- *Fam/seminars*, usually held aboard cruise ships, that provide ongoing training to members in sales skills and industry knowledge. Because the cruise lines benefit by having travel agents familiarize themselves with their ships, the cost of these seminars is very modest, and there's plenty of shipboard time for relaxing and just plain having fun. I have taken several such cruises with OSSN, serving as an instructor on some, and have found the experiences to be truly enriching.

- *Errors and omissions insurance.* Available to members at a modest cost, this is a specialized form of business insurance that protects you in case a client sues alleging that they suffered because you screwed up in performing your professional duties as a travel agent.

- *Reduced prices* on industry publications and reference works. Offers vary, but the savings can be substantial

- *Networking and learning opportunities.* Most important of all, from my point of view, is that OSSN and NACTA encourage members to get together at the local level for their mutual support. Typically, chapters meet once a month and there is a modest fee to cover the cost of renting the hall and/or providing dinner. The meetings usually feature a guest speaker from the industry — a representative from a hotel chain, a cruise line, or a travel insurance company, for example. Some meetings in the New York area have actually been held aboard cruise ships. The meetings are invariably interesting and filled with hints and tips that will make you more knowledgeable and help you to sell better. They are also a great way to get to know your fellow outside reps. The contacts and friendships that develop this way can be invaluable. With over 60 chapters scattered across the nation, OSSN is the clear leader in this category.

■   You can join OSSN at a discount by downloading the application form at:

http://www.HomeTravelAgency.com/ossnapp.pdf

Find a mentor

You may be able to find a mentor — someone who will take you under their wing and guide your professional development — at the agency with which you have affiliated as an outside rep. Or you may hit it off with a more experienced outside rep through an organization like OSSN and be able to turn to that person for advice. But no matter what the source, find a mentor if at all possible. Having a good mentor is a real gift, and most people will be flattered that you are seeking their expertise and will derive tremendous self-fulfillment by helping you up the ladder of success. But don't take advantage of their time or abuse their goodwill by asking them to do things you could do yourself. And whenever possible, find a way to pay them back for their kindness.

Learn about your product

It's not too soon to begin collecting a reference library about the products you want to sell. Some of this material you will have to go out and buy. If you are specializing in a destination, for example, you will want to have a good collection of current guidebooks to the area. But much of the material you will need (or at least find very helpful) can be obtained for free.

Destination information can be obtained from the tourist bureaus that represent nearly every U.S. state, Canadian province, and most foreign countries. Don't overlook foreign tourist bureaus that serve a particular province or region. There is also a veritable mountain of brochures and other support material that can be gathered from tour operators, packagers, and other suppliers.

Rather than try to get everything available (an impossible task which, if you could achieve it, would force you to move out of your house because it would be filled with brochures) let me suggest a plan of attack. First, check with your agency to see to which consortiums it belongs. A consortium is a group of suppliers, usually tour operators or cruise lines, offering higher commissions to agencies that commit to bringing them a certain volume of business. (I am making the assumption that the lion's share of your leisure travel will consist of tours or cruises and packages.) Your agency should be able to give you a list of the suppliers in the various consortiums, along with their toll-free telephone numbers. Call these suppliers and request their general brochures; once you have these in hand, you can then request more specific information as you need it. The idea is to build up your awareness of the products available to you at the best commissions.

Of course, the preferred suppliers don't have all the tours. So do some investigating to find out which other tour operators cover your area of interest, and request information from them as well. You'll find contact information for a wealth of industry suppliers, including tour operators, cruise lines, and consortiums, in *The Travel Agent's Complete Desk Reference*. If you purchased this book as part of my home study course, you already have it. If not, you can order it at:

http://www.HomeTravelAgency.com/deskref.html

Build a reference library

Any good professional has a reference library close at hand. No matter how good you are, you can't keep every little scrap of information in your head. In addition to materials about specific destinations and the offerings of specific suppliers, here are some suggestions for your collection based on my personal experience. You'll find a far more complete listing of reference materials in *The Travel Agent's Complete Desk Reference*.

- **References.** It's handy to have a one-stop reference that will provide you with definitions of industry terms and acronyms and guide you through the sometimes mysterious codes used to identify airports, airlines, car rental companies, and so forth. (*The Travel Agent's Complete Desk Reference* will certainly fill that bill.)

- **Atlas.** A really good atlas can be expensive, but it will make you feel like a pro. I know I urge you to be frugal, but if you spend $175 on a really spiffy atlas, I won't tell. If you don't want to go whole hog, at least start collecting maps of destinations that hold a special interest for you.

- **The trade press.** Subscribe to a few industry publications. If you can get some freebies through your agency, go for it. I get *Travel Weekly*, *Travel Agent*, and *Jax Fax*, as well as a few others. These publications not only will begin to give you a feel for the business but also contain a great deal of information that is immediately useful (commission deals, new tour products, etc.). You can often pick up half-off subscription offers to some of these trade magazines from friends in the business who already subscribe. A list of industry trade publications can be found in (*The Travel Agent's Complete Desk Reference.*)

- **Clippings.** Build a clipping file, designed according to your needs. The trade publications regularly include supplements devoted to a particular destination. Hang on to them. The specific information will go out of date, but if a client asks about The Bahamas or tours to the Holy Land, these back-issue supplements will let you talk knowledgeably and tell you whom to call.

- **Books.** Collect (and read!) books about any destinations in which you choose to specialize. If you sell France, have some good history books on hand. Many of your customers will want to see sights connected with Napoleon or World War II. Read famous travelogues. Fans of Peter Mayle's *A Year in Provence* will want to visit the places he mentions. Even novels can make you more of an expert in your customers' eyes. *The DaVinci Code*, to cite just one example, has created a legion of fans eager to visit places associated with the book.

Like I say, these are some suggestions. As your travel business develops, use your own investigative skills to determine which reference materials you want to have on your shelf.

Use Internet resources

The Internet is a treasure trove of information. The amount of travel-related information on "the 'Net" is immense and growing every day. In fact, there is so much information out there that there is a real danger of spending too much time at your computer simply "surfing" from one site to another.

Many tourist boards and convention and visitors bureaus have web sites. There are also many commercial, advertising-supported web sites dedicated to specific destinations. These can be an excellent source of information — if they are kept up to date.

The Internet is at its best when it is interactive. That is, when you can ask a question that is specific to your needs and get an answer. There are a number of ways to do that. Many web sites have mechanisms that allow you to request additional information.

Perhaps the best (and best known) source of answers on the Internet is Google.com. Google is a "search engine," a web site that helps you find other web sites. Simply type a "search term" into Google's search box and it will respond, at blistering speed, with a list of hundreds or thousands of sites that contain the word or words you typed in. With a little practice, you will learn that by varying what you type in, you can get very good at finding precisely the information you are looking for.

Another way to get answers to your questions is through "Usenet newsgroups," which are sort of public bulletin boards accessible by anyone with access to the Internet. Each newsgroup is devoted to a specific topic and many of them are tourism or destination related. So, if you are interested in b&b's in Nova Scotia, you can point your browser to "ns.general," a newsgroup devoted to that Canadian province, or to "rec.travel.usa-canada," and ask a question. There's a good chance someone will have an answer. Unfortunately, I have yet to find a newsgroup that specifically addresses the concerns of outside travel agents. Accessing Usenet will require a program called a "news reader." You may already have one installed on your computer. To learn more about news readers, visit:

http://www.newsreaders.com

For questions and insights specific to the world of home-based agents, OSSN's web site has a "chat room" for members only. If some procedure is puzzling you, or you need a recommendation for an eco-resort in Australia, you can post a message on this bulletin board and, hopefully, receive an answer from a fellow agent.

Similar resources can be found through online services like

CompuServe and America Online. Yes, I know I recommended against them earlier, but the fact of the matter is these online services do provide some valuable services. If you belong to one of these services, look around for a Forum that addresses the needs of home-based travel agents. Other sites of use to travel agents are listed in *The Travel Agent's Complete Desk Reference.*

Summary

While there is a great temptation to try to do everything at once when you are getting started, you will be well advised to slow down and start laying the groundwork for your new travel business in a logical and business-like manner. Start with the process of defining yourself, which will lead to a good business name, which will go on your business card, your fictitious name certificate, and on your business checking account.

It is your responsibility to familiarize yourself with and comply with local and state ordinances and laws. Most state travel laws are ill-advised attempts to discourage new businesses, but regardless of your personal feelings you should comply with the law. Fortunately, most of these laws are minor annoyances rather than true obstacles to your success.

A computer, meeting minimum configuration standards, is fast becoming as indispensable as the telephone. If you do not have one, make getting one a major priority. Getting the computer you need does not have to be expensive if you shop wisely, as you should for all office machines. However, you should proceed cautiously and only purchase something when you really need it.

You should start laying the groundwork for your continuing professional development as soon as possible. Much of this you can do on your own, using sources like industry publications and free supplier seminars. One of the best ways to plug into this cornucopia of free and low-cost continuing education is by joining a professional organization like the Outside Sales Support Network (OSSN).

Action steps

Here are some things you can do to put what you have learned in this chapter into action:

- Begin to brainstorm some names for your business. Test them out on friends and family. If you know someone with extensive business experience, get their opinion as well.
- Find out where you need to go in your area to register your business name. Find out how much it will cost and check to see if any of the names you are considering are "taken."
- Talk to your bank about opening a business account. Make sure you get a complete understanding of all fees they charge. Although you may not need the service for quite a while, ask what they charge for international wire transfers. Make sure your bank knows you will be looking into other banks; this

will (or should) keep them on their toes and encourage them to offer you some incentive to keep your business with them.

- If you don't have a computer, or have an inadequate one, start shopping. Don't forget to ask your computer savvy friends if they have an "obsolete" (but perfectly usable) PC they'd like to "get rid of."
- If you're not connected to the Internet, get hooked up and start exploring the resources available to you on the World Wide Web.
- Begin researching travel destinations and products you think you might specialize in. Start creating a reference library.
- Seriously consider joining a professional organization such as OSSN. Again, you can download a discounted application form at:

http://www.HomeTravelAgency.com/ossnapp.pdf

Chapter Nine:
Getting Serious

What you will learn

After you have completed this chapter you will be able to:

- Present yourself to the industry as a true professional.
- Get the most out of industry meetings and seminars.
- Begin the lifelong process of refining your product knowledge.
- Identify several ways in which you can maximize your income as a travel agent.
- Take legal and insurance precautions that make sense to you.

Key terms and concepts

This chapter involves the following key terms and concepts:

- Professionalism in any industry is a matter of conduct rather than credentials.
- Joining a professional organization such as OSSN is a key to developing both your professional standing and your product knowledge.
- Travel insurance can protect the traveler, the travel agent, or both, sometimes all at the same time.
- Errors and Omissions insurance is a special type of coverage that protects the travel agent against claims brought by customers alleging mistakes, incompetence, or negligence. Increasingly, host agencies demand that their independent contractors have this coverage.
- A travel agent is eligible for a broad range of perfectly legal tax deductions and should take advantage of them to the maximum extent allowed by law.
- As your business evolves, you will discover an increasing number of options available to you in terms of the form your business takes, the strategic alliances available to you, and the tools you can use. These are options not necessities and you must choose wisely.

Introduction

Once you get past the phase of experimenting with the travel business, the travel game is no longer a game; it is a career. Even if you pursue it only part-time, you should approach it with the same degree of seriousness and commitment that you would approach any other career. In this chapter, I will discuss some of the ways in which a part-time, "fun," avocation can grow into an important source of both income and personal and professional satisfaction. Along the way, I'll touch on some issues and pass along some tips that will be important to you regardless of how much or how little time you plan to invest.

Being professional

I am fond of the corny old joke about the two country rubes talking about the local boy who's planning on going off to college to get one of those new-fangled "eddycashuns." One of them has to explain the system to the other. "First, y'go off to some fancy pants college fer four years and they give you somethin' called a 'B.S.' An' y'know what that means, doncha?" he says. His friend allows as how he does, indeed, know the meaning of B.S. "But that's not enough," the first rube fumes. "Then they stay in school fer two, three years more and get an M.S. That stands fer More of the Same. Finally, they stay in school, studyin' they call it, fer four or six years more just to get somethin' called a P.H.D. — Piled Higher and Deeper!"

I think I like the joke because it speaks to my deep-seated prejudice that just because someone has a bunch of letters at the end of his name is no guarantee that he's either knowledgeable or competent. It's the same in all professions, travel included. Yes, there are travel schools and various certification courses that you can take. And they're all very good, I'm sure. In fact, I've collected some of those certifications myself and I'm proud of them.

But it has always seemed to me that the true hallmark of the professional is how he or she conducts his or her affairs. You can be a mere beginner and be professional. Or you can be an old hand and be an incompetent ninny — regardless of what your credentials say!

To me, being a professional home-based travel agent means dealing with people ethically and honestly, never promising more than you know you can deliver, and making a sincere effort to educate yourself about the business and your role in it. All in all, not a difficult code to live up to.

The American Society of Travel Agents (ASTA) has promulgated a code for its member agencies to live by. You can't go too far wrong by adopting it as your own.

Preamble

We live in a world in which travel has become both increasingly important and complex in its variety of modes and choices. Travelers are faced with a myriad of alternatives as to transportation, accommodations, and other travel services. They must depend on travel agencies and others in the industry to guide them honestly and competently. Similarly, carriers, hotels, and other suppliers must provide to the traveler the product as it was advertised. All ASTA members pledge themselves to observe this spirit in all their activities and to conduct their business in accordance with the following Principles of Professional Conduct and Ethics.

Responsibilities of All Members

1. All ASTA members shall be factual and accurate when providing information about their services and the services of any firm they represent. They will not use misleading or deceptive practices which could be damaging to the consumer or the travel industry.

2. All ASTA members shall remit any undisputed funds under their control within the specified time limit. Reasons for any delay in providing funds will be communicated to the claimant in a timely manner.

3. All ASTA members will provide complete details about terms and conditions of any travel service, including, but not limited to, cancellation and service fee policies, prior to nonrefundable payment being accepted for the booking.

4. All ASTA members will not make use of improperly obtained client lists or other confidential data obtained from agency personnel's former employers.

5. All ASTA members will cooperate with any inquiry conducted by ASTA to resolve any dispute involving consumers and/or another member.

6. All ASTA members will promptly respond to their clients' complaints. If the complaint cannot be resolved by the agency and/or client, it should be referred in writing to ASTA's Consumer Affairs Department.

7. All ASTA members shall consider every transaction for a client as a confidential matter and not disclose any information without permission of the client, unless such disclosure is required by law.

8. ASTA members operating tours shall provide all components as specified in their brochure or written confirmation, or provide alternate services of equal or greater value, or appropriate compensation.

9. ASTA members operating tours shall promptly advise the

agent or client who reserved the space of any change in itinerary, services, features, and/or price. If substantial changes are made that are within the control of the operator, the client shall be offered the opportunity to cancel without penalty.

10. ASTA members shall stand behind any program in which their names and/or logo are used with their permission for advertising or promoting travel.

11. ASTA members will not falsely represent a person's affiliation with their firm.

Conclusion

Adherence to these Principles of Professional Conduct and Ethics signifies competence, fair dealing, and high integrity. Failure to adhere to these Principles may subject a member to disciplinary action, as set forth in ASTA's Bylaws.

The naysayers

I think it only fair to warn you that not everyone in the travel industry will welcome you with open arms. Some people, primarily those with strong ties to or ownership positions in what I call "traditional" agencies, will resent your presence. They will call you a "pseudo agent." They will accuse you of being unprofessional, ignorant, and incapable of providing competent service to your clients. They will question your motives for getting involved in the industry, strongly suggesting that you're just trying to pass yourself off as a "real" travel agent in order to defraud travel suppliers out of discounted tickets and hotel rooms.

Some of this attitude can be attributed to well-intentioned concerns about the integrity of the profession and the best interests of the consumer. Most of it, I'm afraid, is born out of fear — fear of competition and fear of change. The good news is that this type of negativity is on the wane as home-based travel agents prove their professionalism and demonstrate their ability to move product. Still, you will encounter it from time to time, especially in Internet chat rooms where old line travel agents gather.

My advice to you, when confronted by this naysaying, is to ignore it. Go about your business and do your job. Allowing yourself to get sucked in to someone else's negativity will only drag you down to their level. And one of the keys to success in this business (or any sales-oriented business for that matter) is to maintain a positive attitude.

More on professional organizations

In the last chapter, I suggested joining a professional organization as a way of providing yourself with an instant support network and a place to turn for advice, answers, and continuing education. If you're truly serious about a career as an outside rep, part- or full-time, then joining a professional organization is a must. In this section, I will provide an overview of the major professional organizations with the caveat that the opinions presented here are just that — my personal opinions.

On the national level, there are two organizations that address themselves to home-based travel agents, The Outside Sales Support Network (OSSN) and the National Association of Commissioned Travel Agents (NACTA). There are also two organizations that seek to represent "traditional" storefront travel agencies, the American Society of Travel Agents (ASTA) and the Association of Retail Travel Agents (ARTA).

Not too long ago, there was a clear division between these two groups of associations. Not any more. In early 2000, ASTA purchased NACTA. In late 2000, ARTA formed a "relationship" with OSSN. On the one hand, these events demonstrate that home-based agents are at long last being taken seriously by the "big boys." On the other hand, as I have stated elsewhere, the interests of host agencies (which are, by definition, traditional "storefront" agencies) can be at odds with the interests of the independent home-based agent. So I have a certain concern that the legitimate and separate interests of home-based agents could get lost in the shuffle or at least muted. To my mind, the arm's length relationship between OSSN and ARTA tends to recognize this fact more than does ASTA's outright purchase of NACTA.

But these are philosophical quibbles. OSSN and NACTA are not your only choices. ARTA has welcomed outside agents for some time. Even crusty old ASTA has finally broken down and put out the welcome mat for home-based agents.

So which one to join? What should be foremost in your mind are the practical benefits of joining an association. Since NACTA and OSSN are very specifically targeted to outside reps, they are the logical first choices. And since the most important thing about joining a professional organization is the availability of regular, usually monthly, meetings, it makes sense to join the one that has a local chapter near you. That will most likely be OSSN, unless you live in one of the few places where there is an active NACTA chapter.

I have belonged to both OSSN and NACTA, but I find that most of my active involvement is with OSSN. It is the older and larger of the two associations, the one I joined first, and the one with the most active chapters (by a large margin). OSSN has also been generous enough to offer those taking this course a very attractive discount on membership. Of course, this is not to say that you should disregard NACTA. Although I have not been active in NACTA for many years, I have heard nothing but good reports from NACTA members.

I am a member of neither ASTA nor ARTA, but I suspect that their meetings are less oriented to the educational needs of beginning home-based travel agents than are those of OSSN. The impression I get from the trade press is that ASTA is the more staid, traditional association (it is the older), while ARTA is more the feisty upstart, more willing to go to the mat for travel agents' interests. ASTA's system of regional branches, each of which sets its own agendas and priorities, means that ASTA seldom speaks with a unified voice on major issues. Since politicians smell weakness like a shark smells blood, this tends to weaken ASTA's clout in the corridors of power. So if I ever felt a need to join one of these associations, I would probably choose ARTA. It might be instructive to inquire about membership in both of these fine organizations just to get a sense of how they present themselves.

There are also a number of local organizations formed by local travel agencies in their mutual interest. These may or may not provide a comfortable place for beginners; you'll have to sound them out to see if they are receptive to neophyte outside agents. You can find out if such an organization exists in your area by phoning local agencies and inquiring.

So again, which one to join? That I'll leave up to you, although I strongly suggest you join at least one. I further urge you to do your own independent investigation of these organizations before making a decision.

Getting the most out of meetings

These comments apply primarily to OSSN chapter meetings, but the principles are pretty universal and can be applied to virtually any industry get together, including free seminars put on by suppliers.

The primary goal of OSSN chapter meetings is "professional development." The OSSN meetings I have attended follow a predictable pattern. There will be refreshments (perhaps even a dinner), followed by a talk by a representative of one supplier or another, followed by a question and answer period. Usually there's a modest per-meeting fee to cover expenses, but it's money well spent. These are working meetings not social events, although socializing is an important part of the experience.

While these meetings are usually a great deal of fun, you should not lose sight of the very important role they play in educating you and helping you make more money. Plan to arrive early, come prepared, and pay attention. Here are some hints and tips that will make these meetings more productive for you:

- *Network, network, network.* Arrive early so as to maximize your opportunities to meet people. Bring your business cards and exchange cards with as many people as possible. Some people find it helps to set a goal — "I will come home with the cards of ten other people." There may not be an immediate payback on this activity but it will help you get a sense of the travel agent community in your area, since many of the people there will be outside agents with local agencies. Collecting cards will help you remember who people are; over the course of several meetings you will develop relationships, even friendships, with your fellow agents. In my experience, the people you are likely to meet are friendly and helpful and more than willing to share their expertise and experience, even if it is limited. It can be very comforting to know that there's someone to call on when you have a question or problem. You also may be surprised at how quickly you become "the expert" and are able to provide sage counsel to others.

Not all the people attending are agents. I have met representatives of locally based tour operators who attend these meetings as a way of increasing their visibility with local agents. You may also find people who specialize in certain types of travel and who have contacts and special deals you can use for your own clients.

- **Record the talk.** A small, hand-held tape recorder is inexpensive and a great learning tool. You can record the presentations of industry representatives at these meetings and then play the tapes back at home or in your car as a sort of "refresher course." If you can't use a tape recorder, take good notes and file them somewhere you can find them when you need them. Also, collect any handouts the speaker brings. Sometimes they underestimate the demand and bring too few, which is another good reason for arriving early.

- **Ask questions.** Don't bite your tongue for fear of looking stupid. If you have a question in your mind, it's a good bet several others have the same one. Participating in the group also raises your profile with your fellow agents. It's hard to quantify the benefit of that, but it is real. If nothing else, it will help increase your level of self-confidence.

- **Get to know the speakers.** Make sure you get the business cards of the speakers. Write them a thank you note after the meeting; you may be the only one who does. Find some reason to call them in the next week or so to clarify something mentioned in their talk or to request more information. Clarify their position within their company. Most of the people who speak at these meetings are sales reps themselves. Their job is to promote their products to the travel agent community and help travel agents sell more. If you need help booking a large group, they are the ones to call. If you're having a problem with the company, they may be able to straighten it out. They will also be able to tell you if it's possible to deal directly with their company, avoiding a commission split.

  Be aware that if you are an outside agent for a distant host agency, the sales reps you meet at these meetings may not be "your" sales reps. Reps usually cover a certain geographic territory. "Your" sales rep is the one who covers the territory in which your agency is located, even if that's across the country. That's another good reason for working with a local agency. Of course, you are perfectly free to deal with most suppliers directly, in which case the supplier rep you meet at a local OSSN meeting becomes "your" rep.

- **Volunteer.** Running these chapter meetings is a lot of work and a labor of love. The people who take on the responsibility never have enough hands. Getting involved and helping out in whatever way you can will earn you a lot of brownie points. Not only can getting involved be an enjoyable social experience, but you can also pick up useful leads, hot tips about special deals, and any number of other bits of inside information, all because you're in the right place at the right time.

Developing your product knowledge

Success in any selling endeavor depends on two things: product knowledge and selling skills. You have to know what you are selling and how to sell it. The category of selling skills can be further broken down into two additional categories: business skills and interpersonal skills. You have to know how your products are sold (business skills) and how to deal with the people who need those products in order to guide them to an appropriate buying decision (interpersonal skills).

In this section I will discuss ways in which to begin the ongoing, never-ending process of expanding your product knowledge. Many of the things you will do to increase your product knowledge will also increase your selling and business skills. In other words, as you read and carefully examine tour brochures and pore over the fine print, you will become clearer on the mechanics of dealing with tour operators. At the same time, you will learn what various tours have to offer your customers. Similarly, a seminar on selling cruises may offer many useful tips on dealing with customers, presenting the cruise, selling shore excursions and other add-ons, overcoming misunderstandings, and so on.

Getting to know your preferred suppliers

Since you have to start somewhere, I strongly suggest you start with your host agency's preferred suppliers. Make it a project: for the next month or so devote a certain amount of time each day to gathering material on these suppliers and familiarizing yourself with what they sell and how they operate. There are a number of reasons for this:

- *They're easily identified.* Your agency probably has already provided you with, at least, a list of who they are and how to contact them.
- *Detailed information may be close at hand.* If you're working with a local agency, they probably have a large library of brochures, videos, and other information on these suppliers. Load up and start reading and watching.
- *They are limited in number.* There are probably not too many preferred suppliers to handle, although you may be surprised at how many there are. If your host agency belongs to one consortium (see below), there will probably be about two dozen or so; if it belongs to more, the list will double or triple. In any event, if you research all of them thoroughly you will wind up with an awful lot of information (not to mention brochures to be filed). If the list of preferred suppliers available through your host agency seems overwhelming, I

would recommend researching the ones offering the highest commissions first.

- **_They will cover all the major destinations and modes of travel._** Expect the list of suppliers to be heavy on companies that offer cruises, European escorted tours, and packages to warm places like Hawaii, the Caribbean, and Mexico. The reason for this is that these are the places most American tourists want to go. Once you've gotten a good handle on what your preferred suppliers do and where they go, you will have a ready response to most leisure travel requests from your customers. You will also have a pretty good overview of leisure travel in general.

- **_They offer you higher commissions._** As long as you're studying suppliers, why not study the ones with the highest payback potential?

Essentially a preferred supplier is any provider of travel products that offers special inducements to a travel agency (usually in the form of higher commissions or "overrides") in recognition of the volume of business the travel agency brings them. But not all preferred suppliers are created equal. It will help your understanding of the business and your host agency's (and your) place in it if you draw distinctions among various categories of preferred suppliers.

- **_Consortiums._** Consortiums provide travel agencies with a ready-made list of preferred suppliers. By joining a consortium (for an annual fee), an agency gains access to better commissions from a group of suppliers the consortium has put together. The understanding is that, in return for the better commission deal and other inducements offered to consortium members, such as co-op advertising funds, the agency will "push" the consortium's suppliers.

- **_Direct relationships._** Many travel agencies develop direct relationships with certain suppliers. That's because they send a lot of people to certain destinations and/or via a certain supplier. For example, a travel agency in Minnesota may find itself selling a lot of travel to Scandinavia and form close relationships with tour operators serving that market and even with SAS, the Scandinavian airline. Remember the sales reps I mentioned in the previous section? Well, one of their jobs is to get to know the travel agencies in their area that are doing high volumes of business with their companies. It is through these contacts that direct relationships of the type we are discussing here are developed. In a case like this, the travel agency is being rewarded for past performance.

Another way a direct preferred supplier relationship can come about is when an entrepreneurial travel agency hooks up with, say, a specialty tour operator in Germany or a hotel association on a Caribbean island or some other supplier of travel products. The two entities enter into a mutually satisfactory agreement. The agency agrees to promote the product or products in exchange for a preferred commission rate. The supplier for its part hopes the association with the travel agency will help it sell more of its product.

- ***An agency's own wholesale products.*** An agency may take things a step further and become a wholesaler for certain travel products. It may even create its own tours and packages. It will then sell these not just to its retail customers but through other travel agents as well. Usually, although not always, it is products like this that offer you, the outside rep, the highest commissions of all.

Start educating yourself with brochures

If your agency can provide you with a supply of brochures and other information, so much the better. Otherwise, you will have to start calling the various preferred suppliers and gather your own collection of brochures. Some companies will not send materials directly to your home; they prefer to send brochures only to the agency. In that case you will have to make arrangements with your agency to hold them until you pick them up or have them forwarded to you. As soon as you begin to receive materials, start your research.

- ***Read the materials carefully.*** Allow yourself some daydreaming about how wonderful it would be to visit the places depicted so artfully in the color pictures. But keep your travel agent's hat on as well. You should analyze this material as well as read it. Ask yourself questions. Would I take this trip? Why or why not? Who do I know who would love this place? Who would hate it? What is the intended market for this product — singles, young couples, families, seniors? To what special interests (art lovers, scuba divers) does it appeal?

- ***Think about the offer.*** That is, what are they selling and how? Is there an all-inclusive price? What is there to do there? What amenities? What add-ons are available? What's the pricing like? Does the way the offer is structured and presented make it easy to present, explain, and sell?

- ***Pay particular attention to the fine print.*** Here is where the learning curve begins. Do you understand everything? Are there any unfamiliar terms or buzzwords? If so, write them down and find out their meaning. You can always ask someone at your agency. Or you can turn to reference works like *The Travel Agent's Complete Desk Reference*, which contains an extensive glossary of travel industry terms, abbreviations, and acronyms. If the brochure itself is unclear, don't hesitate to call the supplier to ask for clarification.

As I noted earlier, this little project will result in a largish collection of brochures. This is a good time to begin your filing system. Otherwise you will quickly be overwhelmed. The best way to file materials is by destination. That can be as specific as "Acapulco, Mexico" or as broad as "Latin America." Or do a bit of both. Using a battered old file cabinet with drawers divided by continents, you can keep general information about, say, "Europe" in the front, with more specific information filed first by country then by city or region.

It is also a good idea to start a "Special Interests" section where you can file brochures and other materials that focus on themes like honeymoons, golf, tennis, skiing, and so forth. It doesn't need to be elaborate, just useful. You'll want a way to put your hands on outdated brochures quickly and replace them with up-to-date information. You'll never be able to find anything if you let your brochures become hopelessly mixed together in random piles.

Your continuing search for product knowledge

If you follow my advice and make a project out of getting to know your preferred suppliers, you'll probably find yourself, a month or so later, with a pretty solid grounding in what is available out there in the way of travel products. But this is only the beginning. There is a great deal to learn, and expanding and refining your product knowledge will be an ongoing challenge and responsibility. Fortunately, there is also a lot of help out there if you'll just take advantage of it. Most of it is low-cost and a lot of it is free. Here are some suggestions:

- *The trade press.* Earlier, I suggested subscribing to a few industry trade papers and magazines. Now that you've done that, read them! They are a treasure trove of helpful information. What's more, many of them present product information in such a way that it's easy to clip and save the material. Each issue of *Travel Weekly*, for example, has a section on travel products divided by destination. A page — or two or more — is devoted to each destination and the top of each page is clearly flagged, "Selling Las Vegas," or "Selling Hawaii," or whatever. Many trade publications regularly publish separate magazine-sized supplements covering specific destinations or types of travel. Don't overlook the advertising either. It's filled with helpful information about new products, as well as special commission deals and fun contests for you to enter.

- *Supplier seminars.* One thing you'll find advertised in the trade press is traveling seminars sponsored by suppliers. These tour the major cities in the country and are designed to increase the knowledge of travel agents. They may be sponsored by a single supplier, such as a car rental company or a hotel chain, or they may focus on a destination and be sponsored by several tour operators, airlines, and cruise lines that serve that destination. They are a lot of fun and shouldn't be missed.

  These seminars are usually free (although some do charge a

nominal fee). Typically they last a little longer than half a day and offer a free continental breakfast and a lunch. The ones I have attended mix the learning with fun. There will be door prizes and contests in which the room is divided into teams, with prizes for the winners. I have left seminars loaded with upgrade coupons for myself and my clients.

The suggestions I gave earlier for getting the most out of meetings of your local professional association also apply to these events. Early in your career, I would suggest going to as many as possible, even if the subject matter doesn't seem immediately useful. For example, attend a seminar on Greece even though you have decided to specialize in the British Isles. Techniques used to sell Athens can be used to sell London as well. You also never know whom you'll meet; you might make a valuable contact at an unpromising seminar. Later, when you have a better feel for the industry and the volume of business you are doing leaves you less free time, you can pick and choose the seminars that interest you most.

- *OSSN seminars.* OSSN sponsors regular seminars, often on cruise ships, that are specifically targeted to the needs and interests of home-based agents. Seminars like this can be an excellent way to learn about a very profitable travel product (cruises), meet other outside reps from around the country, and have some fun. For a slightly higher fare you can even bring your spouse (who will, needless to say, be eternally grateful).

- *Books.* There is a small but growing library of books about the travel business. There is a much larger library of guidebooks and books about far off places and the adventure and excitement of travel. You will probably want to spend some time dipping into these books. The bibliography in *The Travel Agent's Complete Desk Reference* will get you started.

- *Videos.* Seeing is believing. Many suppliers will provide you with video cassettes about their products and destinations for a very moderate price. Some suppliers even offer sales training videos, designed to help you become a better salesperson for their products. For more information on using video to help you sell see *Chapter 21: Presenting the Wonder of Travel.*

- *Experience.* Experience, some wise person said, is the best teacher. As your home-based travel agent career progresses you will learn quite a bit on your own. My advice would be to write a brief note to yourself every time you learn a new process or technique. For example, the first time I had to book a ticket for a client using a frequent flyer award for a companion ticket, the reservationist had to walk me carefully through the steps of the process. I didn't write it down and regretted it a few months later when the same situation cropped up and I, of course, had forgotten the process.

Maximizing your income

One of the best ways to get serious about your home-based travel agent business is to cast a steely eye on the bottom line and get very clear about the things you can do to increase your income. One way of course is to sell more travel. But for now we will talk about squeezing more income out of the travel you sell.

In the simplest terms, this means paying less attention to low commission products (5% commissions on car rentals, for example) and paying more attention to higher commission products (city packages with a preferred supplier that carry a 12% commission and include a rental car). This is a matter of selling smarter rather than selling more.

The most obvious way to earn higher commissions is to book with your preferred suppliers whenever possible because preferred suppliers, by definition, pay higher commissions. More than that, book with the preferred suppliers that give you the best deal, since you may find that your agency's list of preferred suppliers contains a lot of overlap and duplication — different companies offering very similar products.

Be aware, too, that the commission structures offered by preferred suppliers can be confusing. The simplest possibility is that they will pay your agency a single (but enhanced) commission rate, say 11% or 12% on everything booked by that agency and its outside reps like you. So if you booked a tour and your split with the host agency is 50/50, you would receive half of 12%, or 6%. The other possibility is that the preferred supplier operates on an override basis. This is where things get confusing. (In the examples cited below, I will assume for the sake of simplicity that your split with your host agency is 50/50.)

An override is an additional payment, usually expressed as percentage points, which is added to a base commission. For example, the base commission may be 10% with a 2% override for your agency. That means the total commission is 12%. So far so good. What gets confusing is how overrides are applied. Here are the possibilities:

- **The override is based on volume.** In other words, the supplier pays a flat 10% commission until the agency books a certain, usually annual, dollar volume with the supplier. Let's say for the sake of discussion that the volume level is $50,000. You book a tour, the fifth booked by your agency this year. The dollar volume is still below $50,000, so you get half of 10%. But suppose you book the 215th tour and the dollar volume is well over $50,000. You get half of 12%, right? Well, maybe not. Read on.

- **The override may be retroactive.** If it is, all bookings made prior to reaching the $50,000 level will be eligible for an additional 2% commission once the $50,000 level is reached. If this is the case, how do you know whether you're in line for an extra 1%? Or for that matter how do you know that the 5% commission you receive really should be 6% because the $50,000 mark was crossed months ago? The honest answer is that, like Blanche duBois in *Streetcar Named Desire*, you are dependent on the kindness of strangers — in this case the person at your host agency who figures this sort of thing out.

- ■ ***The override may not be retroactive.*** Once again you must trust your host agency to do the right thing.
- ■ ***The override accrues to the agency and not to individual agents.*** So even if the dollar volume is well above $50,000 you may not receive the benefit. Or let's say the agency's volume goes over $50,000 and they receive a check for $1,000 (2% of the first $50,000). It's a lot easier to deposit that check in the agency bank account than it is to figure out how to divvy it up among the agents who booked with that supplier before the override kicked in.

This last situation can also arise when the override takes the form of a free trip or vouchers that can be exchanged for discounts. (Technically, these are not commission overrides but they are similar in that they are based on volume.) Let's say that among them, six agents at your host agency sell "x" number of cruise berths for a certain cruise line. The cruise line in a burst of gratitude writes the agency to say that a berth for two is theirs for the taking; the agency can sell it and pocket the entire sum or the owner and his wife (or someone else) can go for a cruise. Guess what happens?

Another word of warning: Remember that some agencies only share base commissions with their outside reps and keep all overrides for themselves regardless of the circumstances. This stipulation is usually buried in the fine print when you sign up or is not mentioned at all. Get very clear on this point before you sign on with a host agency — especially if they are asking you to part with a goodly chunk of change for the privilege of being one of their agents. If you discover this after the fact, you may want to consider switching to a host agency that offers you a better deal.

If you find you are receiving 5% of the cost of a tour when you were expecting 6%, it's time to have a heart-to-heart talk with your agency about its override policies. To be fair to the agency, figuring out who's entitled to what can be hellishly difficult and I suspect that most agencies that wind up shortchanging agents do so not so much because they are nasty and greedy people but simply because sorting everything out in an effort to be "fair" is not cost-effective.

Booking with preferred suppliers

Hopefully, things will not become this complicated in most cases. You will simply make the booking, the supplier will pay your agency the higher commission because of the preferred supplier relationship, and you will receive your fair share of that sum. However, for this to happen, the supplier must know you represent one of their preferred agencies. So make sure the point sinks in. When you call to make a booking, say something like:

"Hi, this is Mary Jones, with The Very Big Agency. We're an Consortium X member, and I'd like to make a reservation."

or

"This is Bill Smith with The Very Small Agency. I'd like to make a Consortium X booking, please."

The idea is to let them know that your agency belongs to a consortium that earns it a higher commission rate. It's a good idea to double-check later in the conversation and make sure they've recorded the booking as reflecting Consortium membership. You can also say something like:

"I'm showing that we receive a 15% commission because you're a preferred supplier. Is that correct?"

Sometimes the reservationist will have that information. Sometimes he or she will seem confused by the question. If so, ask to speak with a supervisor. You may feel a bit stupid doing this but if you're operating on erroneous information, it's better to find out now rather than when you receive a too-small commission check. Be aware that the relationships of suppliers with consortiums and the commission structures are constantly changing. If your agency handed you a list of consortiums, suppliers, and commission rates when you joined up, it may be out of date. The more time passes, the more incorrect information it will contain. So checking with the supplier at the time of booking is always a good idea.

Bonuses, spiffs and special promotions

Just like any other business, suppliers of travel products sometimes run sales. Some of these sales are directed at travelers and cost you money — you get a commission on a reduced fare. Others are directed at travel agents and can actually put money in your pocket if you're in a position to take advantage of them.

These sales take the form of bonuses (sometimes referred to as "spiffs") and special promotions. They are inducements to the travel agent community to take notice of particular suppliers and book their products. They take a variety of forms such as:

- Sharply higher commission rates for bookings made during a limited time period.
- A bonus payment of $10, $25, or more for every booking made within a specific period of time.
- Issuing vouchers or points for bookings. These can be redeemed later for free travel or cash payments.

Sometimes these promotions suffer from some of the same drawbacks as overrides. That is, they accrue to the agency and not the individual agent. Some suppliers, knowing that this fact can serve as a disincentive to the individual agent, design promotions that benefit both the individual agent and the agency owner.

Another possibility is to be a little pushy with your agency. Let's say there was a promotion for a resort that offered a free vacation for two for every 50 bookings. Let's further suppose that you made 18 bookings during the promotion period. When the promotion was over, you could call the agency and, if the requisite 50 bookings were made and if your 18 bookings made you the most productive agent, you might be able to make a case that you should go on the trip.

If the prize is not of any great value you don't have to bother to justify yourself at all. Call up and ask, "Did the agency get any upgrade vouchers out of last month's Hertz promotion? Could I have some?"

Of course, like so much else in the home-based travel agent business, you have to keep on top of what's owed you. If vouchers (or whatever) are sent to the agency rather than directly to you, make sure you follow up and have them forwarded.

Here are some random examples of promotions and bonuses taken from the trade press:

- A tour operator offered agents $10 vouchers for every booking to Mexico or Hawaii. The vouchers went to the agent, not the agency. Ten bookings earned the agent a roundtrip ticket to either destination. The vouchers could also be exchanged for $10 checks. The promotion ran for nine months, giving agents plenty of time to qualify for the free trip.
- A hotel in New York City offered agents a 20% commission on all bookings during a one-month period. With room rates of up to $275 a night, this was a very attractive deal.

Contests and sweepstakes

Another way suppliers try to create a little excitement, grab a little publicity, and (hopefully) sell more product is by running contests and sweepstakes aimed at the travel agent community. I cannot honestly justify this as a sensible, businesslike way of increasing your income, but contests are fun and, hey, the odds are better than in the state lottery.

Some contests and sweepstakes only require you to fill out a card or entry form and send it in. Often, this type of sweepstakes is to be found in the trade press and will require you to answer a few simple questions, the answers to which can be found in a brochure supplied along with the magazine. Other contests are open only to those who make bookings with the supplier sponsoring the game, and some actually require a fair amount of effort.

Here are a few of the contests and sweepstakes that were offered over the past few years:

- Agents booking more than $100 in car rentals during a one-month period were entered into a drawing for a $10,000 grand prize.
- A resort hotel in Bermuda sponsored a contest inviting travel agents to submit brief stories, with photos, about their clients' honeymoon experiences at the resort. Winning entries garnered a free trip for both the agent (and companion) and the clients.
- A major hotel chain offered a five-day vacation in Paris in one of its sweepstakes for agents who booked clients into the chain's all-suites properties during a one-month period.

Charging fees

Charging fees represents yet another way to increase an agency's income. But it is a special case and so deserves to be discussed separately.

Today, when travel agents charge a service fee to their clients it is most likely for booking airline tickets. In this case, the agency is not trying to increase its income, but to replace income lost when the airlines stopped paying commissions.

Still, many travel agents charge fees for a variety of services and those fees can represent a significant percentage of their income. Among the things for which agents may charge fees are:

- Planning services for FITs (foreign independent tours). Fees are particularly appropriate if you are making non-commissionable hotel bookings, restaurant reservations, and the like.
- VIP services such as arranging tee times for golfers or obtaining tickets from frequent flyer programs.
- Changes to existing plans. For example, some agents will charge an additional fee if a client wishes to change a tour date or if the client cancels a tour and a refund must be collected from the supplier.

Fees as gatekeepers

Service fees are sometimes intended to help the travel agent "lose" business. Or at least they can be used that way. Service fees for booking airline tickets, for example, will sometimes scare off a customer. In most cases, that's just fine with the travel agent, who realizes she can't work for free.

Another way travel agents use fees is to help them "qualify" their customers. Qualifying is a concept that gets its own chapter, later in this course. For now, think of qualifying as a way of deciding whether you want to do business with a prospective customer. The most conspicuous way travel agents use fees in this way is to charge a so-called "plan-to-go" fee.

A plan-to-go fee is, in essence, a *non-refundable* down payment on a trip the customer hasn't purchased yet. It is typically used when the customer is looking at a high-ticket item like a family cruise. The fee serves two functions: It is an indication that the customer is seriously considering booking with the agent and is not just a "tire kicker." The agent enters the research phase with a fair degree of assurance that a booking and a commission will be forthcoming. In this case, the fee is applied to the purchase price and can be looked on as a deposit. However, if the customer decides not to book, or finds a "better deal" elsewhere, the travel agent is protected. Her research time will have produced at least some economic benefit because she will keep the plan-to-go fee. In this case, the fee is just that, a fee.

Isn't there some danger that a policy like this will lose the travel agent some customers? Yes, of course, but many travel agents have decided, after many sad experiences, that there are some customers they want to lose. They wind up spending their time with customers who will benefit them financially, not with customers who will pick their brains and book elsewhere. The only customers who "lose" in this case are customers who do not recognize the value of the travel agent's time and expertise.

This can be a difficult concept for beginners to get their minds around. It can also be hard to summon up the courage to ask for an up-front deposit before agreeing to research a trip. It is, however, a technique that is used, to great success, in many professional selling situations outside the travel industry.

Collecting fees

Deciding to charge service fees is one thing; collecting them is another. In most cases, your customers will pay for their travel with a credit card, which is processed not by you, not by your host agency, but by the supplier providing the actual travel product. But the supplier has nothing to do with your service fees, so you must figure out how to collect. Here are your options:

- **Your host agency.** If you have an ARC-appointed host agency, it most likely has some mechanism for building in service fees when booking air. In this case, you will most likely be compensated with either a percentage split of the fee or the entire fee less a fixed service charge from the host agency. Some host agencies also provide mechanisms that will let you charge other fees to the client's credit card. Of course, none of this will help you when you are not working through a host agency.

- **Your own merchant account.** It is actually possible to get your own merchant account (a sort of "bank account" that lets you process credit cards), but it is expensive and difficult to get. Even if you qualify, it will most likely limit you to charging relatively small sums (which most fees are) and not high-end vacations and cruises. If you already have merchant status (for a business you already own, for example) be extremely careful about using it for *any* travel-related charges. It is conceivable that your processor may allow you to charge fees, but travel is a hot-button issue for credit card companies and they may just decide to close your account, no questions asked. So if you have merchant status and would like to charge some of your home-based travel agency fees to that account, call your processor and discuss it openly with them first. This is most definitely a case where honesty is the best policy. Merchant accounts really only make sense for agencies that are doing a considerable amount of business. If you get to that point and you're interested in going for merchant status, the best way to do that is to join the Outside Sales Support Network (OSSN), which can point you in the right direction. You can download a discounted membership application to OSSN at

  http://www.HomeTravelAgency.com/ossnapp.pdf

- **PayPal.** PayPal is an Internet-based service that allows you to collect payments from anyone with an email address. Like credit card processors, they deduct a small fee for each transaction. You will need to have a web site to take advantage of their services and your customers need to have their own PayPal accounts. To make a payment to a travel agent, the client would have to go to a specific page on the travel agent's site that has been set up with a form for such payments; the client would then have to enter his or her PayPal user name and password to make the payment. The client's actual credit card information is stored on PayPal's computers. In theory, a client could authorize the travel agent to make the payment on his behalf, by providing the travel agent with his PayPal login information. However, this strikes me as an unlikely scenario, except in the case of long-term customers with whom the agent has established a trusting relationship. So using PayPal to charge fees, while possible, poses some procedural challenges. Nonetheless, I have heard that at least some home-based agents are using this strategy. For more information, visit www.paypal.com.

PayPal is owned by eBay, which has an excellent reputation. Nonetheless, PayPal has its detractors, mostly on the consumer side. Be sure you do your due diligence and understand the pros and cons before deciding to use PayPal.

 Cash or check. Sometimes the old-fashioned way is easiest.

Making the decision

Is charging service fees a valid option for you? It's hard to say. Certainly, charging a fee for something that most people have long looked on as a "free" service will require some consumer education on your part. If you feel you are a good salesperson and can position yourself as a value-added service provider, you might give it a shot. Many agents who have started charging fees report that their customers were understanding and supportive.

My personal opinion is that you should not charge service fees unless you are really an ace at researching airfares and making bookings. After all, why should the customer pay you for the time it takes you to do a less than perfect job? But ultimately the choice to charge service fees or not is up to you.

Getting paid

Of course, taking steps to maximize your commissions won't do you much good unless you actually receive them. In most cases, getting your money is a two-step process: the supplier pays your agency, which deducts its share and passes the remainder on to you.

I will assume (as you should until you have reason to believe otherwise) that your host agency is honest and aboveboard and wants to do the right thing by you. That being said, the agency will also, quite naturally, want to do what's best for it. That's why most commission sharing systems that I've seen are tilted in favor of the agency. First they wait until they are sure the commission has been paid; don't expect them to advance you commission money on commissions they themselves haven't received.

Once the commissions have been paid and the checks have cleared, the next step is paying you and the other outside reps. Most agencies tend to hang onto commissions as long as possible before splitting them with you. This helps their cash flow; it also protects them against things like bounced checks from suppliers and other problems. What's more, it is more efficient and cost-effective to write checks once or twice a month instead of paying people off as commissions arrive. Most host agencies have arrangements whereby they will write you a check monthly on, say, the fifteenth of each month covering all commissions "of record" during the previous month; many will also provide you with a detailed breakdown of what the check covers.

So the first thing to get used to is that, even in the best-case scenario, your payoff is going to be down the road. Usually after your customer's travel has taken place. Sometimes well after your customer is back home. That means if you sell a trip that won't take place until nine months in the future (a not too uncommon occurrence), you may have to wait almost a year for your share of the commission. That also increases the possibility that, through negligence or poor management, you will lose track of what you are owed. It's bad enough to lose a commission. Losing one you forgot you were owed is even worse.

Then there's the problem of late, lost, and unpaid commissions. It happens. Hotels used to be notorious for not paying commissions, but they're getting better. Tour operators on shaky financial grounds also are tempted to "forget" payments. If your host agency will beat the bushes for missing commission checks, you're way ahead of the game. Most don't. Of course, if a commission well into three or even four figures is at issue, the agency may stir itself to go after it. If it's a $20 hotel commission, it's most likely your headache; you may find yourself hounding suppliers to cough up money that will go first to your host agency.

In defense of the host agency, it should be noted that most agencies operate on razor-thin profit margins. So there is a very strong incentive for them to hold onto money as long as possible and to weight the fiduciary relationship in their favor. That thought, however, will be of little comfort when you are steaming over a commission check that is long overdue.

Regardless of the specifics of your host agency's payment policies or the thoroughness of their accounting (or lack thereof), it is your responsibility to keep track of what you are owed and take steps to collect it if it is not forthcoming in a timely fashion.

Ideally, your host agency should provide you with a report that shows unpaid commissions, which you can review on a regular basis. At the very least, your host agency should provide some guidance on whom to call and how to proceed. The suppliers themselves may help in this regard. Most of the big hotel chains and car rental companies, for example, have special numbers for agents to call when tracking down disputed commissions.

Be systematic about tracking your commissions

All of this serves to make the point that you must have a reliable system in place for recording, tracking, and following up on your commissions. Every agency has its own system for tracking commissions and paying its outside agents; some systems are better than others. Some are faster. Some are easier to understand and monitor. I can't give you precise guidance on how to work with your host agency's system because each one is different, but I can offer some general guidance and suggestions on how to conduct this all-important aspect of your business, regardless of what the system is.

First of all, find out what your agency's system is and how it works. Familiarize yourself with its ins and outs, the rules and regulations. If there is anything you don't understand, ask about it. Ask to see the reporting forms you have to send to the agency (if any) and the reporting forms it sends to you with your payments (if any). Make sure you understand your responsibilities and carry them out. For example, one host agency asks its outside reps to provide, on a regular basis, information about the non-airline reservations they make — identifying the supplier, the dates of stay, the confirmation number, and any other information that will help the agency identify the payment when it eventually arrives. Also, find out what the procedures are for handling missing or disputed commission payments. If you can check into all of this before you select your host agency, so much the better. If not, make the best of the system that is in place.

Second, learn about how other agencies deal with their outside reps. The best way to gather this intelligence is by talking with other independent contractors you meet through professional organizations. If you find a host agency that has a better system or a better track record for timely and accurate payments, you might want to consider moving to that agency. Remember that you are an independent contractor. You have a right to deal with whichever host agency you feel best serves your needs.

Regardless of what system your host agency uses, you should have your own tracking system in place. This will serve to keep you up to date on what you are earning. It will also serve as a check and balance on the agency's accounting, so design it with that use in mind. If your agency pays you once a month, your ideal system will be one that enables you to quickly compare their accounting with your own and identify which commissions have been paid and which remain outstanding.

Among the things your system should record are:

- Booking date.
- Key booking information: supplier, client, dates, etc.
- Confirmation numbers.
- Due date. The approximate date on which you should expect payment (e.g., 30 days after the client's departure date from the hotel). This will alert you to start being on the lookout for payment.
- Payment date. The actual date you receive your check.
- Follow-up actions. If you are recording this information in table form (which is not a bad idea), create a column or two to

record the calls you make to suppliers trying to scare up over-due commissions.

Most agencies will not hound the supplier on your behalf when a commission is overdue. That's up to you. You should be able to reach customer service through the supplier's toll-free number. Needless to say, a supplier's record in paying you will affect your interest in recommending it to customers in the future. For example, many hotels, in response to persistent agent complaints, have instituted policies to respond promptly to queries about overdue commissions. It is also possible that a supplier will be able to show you that they paid your host agency; in that case, your beef is with the agency. Confronting them can be unpleasant but it must be done. Rather than assume the worst, assume that they simply overlooked or "lost" the payment (which may be perfectly true). Present the supplier's proof of payment and ask what went wrong.

Simply demonstrating to the agency that you will be persistent in tracking down payments due you will often be sufficient to encourage them to be scrupulous about paying you in the future. If, however, a pattern of late or missed payments develops over time, you have a real problem with your host agency. Since it takes time and effort on your part to extract these payments (which, individually, may be for quite small dollar amounts) you should give serious thought to switching hosts.

Protecting yourself

Why do bad things happen to good people?

Wiser men than I have been wrestling with that one since time immemorial. I don't have the answer but I have learned, through bitter experience, that bad things do indeed happen to good people. In fact, bad things have actually happened to one of the nicest people I know — me!

If you think bad things can't possibly happen to you in your home-based travel business, you're kidding yourself. Bad things probably will happen to you if you don't take some sensible precautions. In fact, they can happen even if you do take sensible precautions. But at least then you'll have the slender consolation of knowing you did everything you could to avoid them.

Getting 'street legal'

For those of you who never customized a car in your misspent youth, the term "street legal" refers to the minimum things you have to do to your automobile so those spoilsports, the local police, can't ticket you for violating silly rules about things like brakes and tail lights. Similar rules may apply to your home-based travel business. I say "may" because the rules vary from state to state. I touched on this topic briefly in *Chapter 8: Getting Started*. Let's revisit it here.

Several states, Florida and California prominent among them, have so-called "Travel Promoter Laws" that claim to protect citizens from various travel scams and rip-offs. Whether they will deter this type of crime is a subject of debate. What is less disputed is the fact that, for honest people in the business, they have the unfortunate result of adding another level of cost and complexity to what is already a low-margin business. Typically, these laws require registration, licensing, bonding, and whatnot for "travel promoters" in the state. My very personal bias is that these laws are being pushed by the "organized, traditional" travel agent community to hamper competition by raising the cost of entry to the profession. They also represent yet another abdication of responsibility by our elected officials. By making honest travel agents pick up the tab when criminals defraud travelers, the politicians can take credit for "protecting" the public when, in fact, they have done no such thing. Criminals won't register under these laws and the state won't pursue them aggressively when they strike again.

Are you affected by "travel promoter laws"? I don't know. Even the legislators who drafted these laws might have a hard time telling you how they affect you. Many of these statutes are new to the books and a great deal of uncertainty exists on how they will be implemented and enforced. Some people seem to think that as an outside agent, you are covered by the registration of your host agency. Others think that everybody must register, except perhaps outside reps for agencies headquartered out of state. I strongly suggest that you contact a lawyer. You'll probably want one to look over your contract with your agency anyway. Find out, first, if your state has a travel promoter law and, second, what your rights and responsibilities are under the terms of that law. Along the way, your lawyer should also be able to fill you in on what you need to do to become and stay "street legal." Some of the topics that might come up include:

- **Segregation of funds.** Essentially this means maintaining a separate bank account, or "escrow" account, so that money being held in trust will be separated from your general operating funds. In other words, if Jim gives you a check for $500 as a deposit on his honeymoon and you use it to pay the rent, with the thought that by the time the $500 is due the tour operator you will have received additional funds to cover that payment, you are courting disaster. Segregation of funds may be required by various state laws. Even if it's not, keeping your client's money separate from your own is a good idea.
- **Licenses.** Some states and/or localities require licensing for any type of business you may want to run, even if you're running it out of a file box at your home for two hours a week. You overlook these "petty" regulations at your peril.
- **Independent contractor status.** Since, if you follow my advice, you're going to be stuck with a legal bill anyway, why not make sure that you are doing everything you can to protect your status as an independent contractor? It can have important tax consequences, as we shall see.

I suspect that there are many outside reps who operate cheerfully oblivious to these and other state laws. Either they don't know about them or can't be bothered. I further suspect that most of these people are honest, well-meaning souls who operate in this fashion for years, providing good service, never getting into trouble with their clients or suppliers, and escaping the notice of the powers that be. Of course, one slip-up and their world can come crashing down around them.

If you want to operate in that fashion, that is your decision. Just don't go crying to Judge Judy that I didn't warn you.

Credit cards

In America, plastic is coin of the realm. If your customers are like mine, they'll want to pay with credit cards. While credit cards offer the customer a great deal of convenience and protection, they can create problems for you and your host agency. The following, made-up, story explains why.

Bill asks you to get him two consolidator tickets to London, which you do. He gives you his credit card number, which you phone into your agency, which accepts it. (Actually, it is highly unlikely that your agency would do that, but this is just a story after all.) Two days before flight time, Bill's mother dies and he flies, not to London, but to California, and doesn't use his London tickets. When the credit card bill arrives, Bill decides to handle the situation by telling the credit card company that he never bought tickets to London and they should remove this charge from his account.

The credit card company, thinking Bill is a perfect gentleman and not the cad and bounder he actually is, does as it is told and turns to your host agency and asks them to cough up for the London tickets. This is what is know in the business as a "chargeback." Your agency protests. The credit card company says, "Prove it!" Your agency is stuck. They have no way to prove that Bill actually authorized the charge, other than your word, which the credit card company won't accept. Credit card companies will always believe the customer's version of events until it is disproved at excruciating and indisputable length.

Because people like Bill exist, no travel agency in its right mind accepts credit card numbers over the phone in the fashion just described. Instead, they institute a policy, or series of policies, that will insulate them from chargebacks. One way they do that is to make you ultimately responsible for any and all bookings you make. For example, they may accept Bill's credit card number, but only if you "guarantee" it with your own credit card number. So if Bill stiffs them, they charge your card. They may even add teeth to this policy by asking you to give them written authorization to charge your card when the need arises. In fact, one host agency, as part of the sign-up process, asks you to authorize them to charge not one but two of your credit cards for unspecified "fees and charges" — a scary thought indeed.

Or your agency may insist that you document all credit card transactions in some fashion, creating a "paper trail" that can be used to prove, should the need arise, that the customer actually did authorize the charge. Now whenever you use your credit card in a store or restaurant, the merchant charges your purchase by running your card through a little countertop machine which makes an imprint of your card on a charge form (the Universal Credit Card form or UCC) which you then sign. You, of course, don't have that little gizmo.

There are several ways of getting around that problem, all of them rather cumbersome.

- **Photocopies.** Some agencies will ask for a photocopy of the customer's credit card and even his driver's license, accompanied by a signed statement that the customer authorizes the charge in question.

- **Signed statements.** Some agencies will accept the signed statement alone. It needn't be complex: "I authorize Joe's Travel to charge $400 to my Visa card, number 000000000, exp. 11/08, for airline tickets from Chicago to Memphis on Budget Airlines."

- **Power of attorney.** If you have clients with whom you regularly do business (and presumably you will), another possibility is to have them execute what is know as a "limited power of attorney" which authorizes your agency to make charges to their credit card for travel related purchases on an as-needed basis. Once this document is accepted and on file at your agency, you won't have to bother your client for photocopies or a signed statement every time you book a trip.

Here is one example of a Limited Power of Attorney. It is provided for the purpose of illustration only. Your agency may have a format it prefers or your lawyer may suggest a variation on the theme.

LIMITED POWER OF ATTORNEY

I am a client of [YOUR BUSINESS NAME] travel agency, which is affiliated with [THE AGENCY THROUGH WHICH YOU BOOK]. I hereby appoint the owner, manager, and all employees of [YOUR BUSINESS NAME] and [THE AGENCY THROUGH WHICH YOU BOOK], acting in their stead to be attorneys-in-fact for the purpose of signing all documents necessary to purchase and issue airline tickets and other travel documents as follows:

and to charge these purchases to my _____ credit card, account number _____, expiration date _____.

I agree I will pay for all such purchases and will not hold [THE AGENCY THROUGH WHICH YOU BOOK], or its affiliate [YOUR BUSINESS NAME], responsible for any of its actions pursuant to this power of attorney.

Signature

Printed name of client

Date

The blank space in the middle of the form can be filled out in any number of different ways. You (or your client) might feel most comfortable having the wording here cover only a single trip. However, the form will be most useful when it gives you the power to issue airline tickets and things such as tour vouchers and cruise documents on an "as needed basis."

You could also have the power of attorney authorize you to charge travel documents to one of several credit cards, at your client's direction. You can type up a power of attorney form on your letterhead and fill it out as circumstances warrant.

There's no point in pretending that these measures won't seem odd and more than a little off-putting to your customers, because they will. In the wrong hands, a limited power of attorney, like the one above, is a license to steal. Carefully explaining to the customer why these measures are necessary will help.

I know that some outside reps finesse the credit card issue by guaranteeing their client's charges with their own credit cards. That way, the outside rep never has to raise the matter with the customer. That's all well and good until something goes wrong. The result can be a credit card bill for several thousands of dollars for which the rep will be liable.

The other alternative is to deal only by check or in cash.

Other sensible precautions

The other major way in which you can get in trouble is when something goes wrong on a client's trip and, rightly or wrongly, the client blames you. In fact, in the worst-case scenario, the client sues you for damages. The remainder of this section deals with this, admittedly ghastly, possibility.

Perhaps we should begin the discussion by saying that worst-case scenarios are extremely rare. Also, the lawyers who bring these suits (and who make a handsome living doing so) are no dummies. Since (in my humble and uninformed opinion) they are after money rather than justice, they will tend to ignore you. They will sue the tour operator, or cruise line, which presumably has the "deep pockets." Unless, of course, they think (or know) you are insured and/or they can't get the money from someone else.

The threat of legal action aside, it just makes good sense to take some simple and sensible precautions to lessen the odds of something going awry for you or your clients. Here are some rules of thumb. They are not applicable in all situations and some travel agents ignore some of them with no ill effect. Still you might want to reflect on how you might apply them.

- *Do your job and do it well.* This is one rule that should never be broken. It means paying attention to details and making sure every aspect of a booking is A-OK. Less obviously, it also means keeping on top of things and being reasonably well-informed about what is going on in the travel industry (Who's going bankrupt?) and the world (Who went to war this week?).

- **Avoid suppliers in trouble.** Some travel agents will never, never, never book a client on an airline in bankruptcy. There's always the danger that the airline will fail in its attempts to salvage itself and go belly-up at the worst possible time, stranding its clients in some far off airport. Very, very few airlines that go into Chapter 11, as it is called, emerge whole again. The same is true of tour operators. Courts have held travel agents liable for damages because they "should have known" about an operator's precarious financial position which had been widely reported in the trade press.

- **Stick with suppliers you know.** This is a variation on the previous rule. One reason some agents stick with their preferred suppliers is that, in addition to the higher commissions, they have a reasonable level of assurance — although not an absolute guarantee — that these firms are stable and in no immediate danger of going under.

- **Stick with suppliers who are insured.** Both the United States Tour Operators Association (USTOA) and the American Society of Travel Agents (ASTA) have programs which insure tour operators against default. We'll discuss insurance in more detail a bit later.

- **Avoid trouble spots.** It was no accident that tourism (American tourism, at least) to the Middle East dried up after the September 11th attacks of several years ago. It is also true that many travel agents booked some great trips and offered some stunning bargains during that period. You will have to decide where your (and your clients') best interests lie. Many agents decide that, with so many fascinating places to see, it makes little sense to send clients to countries where fanatics are murdering tourists to make a point.

Disclaimers, disclosures, and waivers

We live in strange times. Two juvenile delinquents, trying to break into their school in the middle of the night, fall through a skylight and sue the school for damages. (True story.) A woman goes on a cruise, slips on a wet rock during a shore excursion, and sues her travel agent. (True story.) It's no wonder that some travel agents are starting to get a little twitchy about protecting themselves from the litigation-prone and their ever-eager attorneys.

The legal justification (such as it is) for suits against travel agents seeking recompense for injuries suffered while traveling usually revolves around the assertion on the part of the client that the travel agent somehow "guaranteed" or "insured" their well-being by sending them on this trip. Or that the travel agent breached some putative professional duty by not fully informing them of the dangers involved. "He didn't tell me that wet, slimy rocks are slippery!"

One way travel agencies seek to protect themselves from this sort of nonsense is getting travelers to sign "disclaimers" or "waivers" saying that the travel agent is off the hook if something goes wrong. Tour companies, cruise lines, and airlines do something similar. If you read the fine print in their brochures or the tariffs filed with the government, you will see that these carriers say something to the effect that by accepting a ticket you (the passenger) acknowledge that you are traveling at your own risk and will hold them blameless if something awful happens.

One of the interesting things I've noticed about disclaimers is that they don't prevent lawsuits. All they really seem to do is give the sued party some basis on which to mount a defense — "I told 'em so." Sometimes, the defense, whatever its logical justification, doesn't work. Judges and juries tend to be sympathetic to plaintiffs in full-body casts. The good news is that the vast majority of suits against travel agents are dismissed. (The woman who slipped on that wet rock lost her case.)

So why bother? Good question and I don't have an answer other than, perhaps, to suggest that it is better to light a single candle than to curse the darkness. At the very least, a disclaimer creates a paper trail showing that you weren't misrepresenting your role in any way to the client. Here is one example of a disclaimer that I picked up at a professional meeting. It was printed on an agency's letterhead and was included with the tickets and other travel documents the agency gave its clients.

DISCLAIMER

[NAME OF AGENCY] and its agents, in providing consultation, making reservations, and issuing airline tickets or any other documents relating to travel or transportation is acting solely in its capacity as agent for the carrier(s). [NAME OF AGENCY] and its agents, neither guarantees nor insures the service to be provided by any carrier and shall assume no responsibility or liability for actions beyond its own control in connection with the service to be provided. [NAME OF AGENCY] and its agents, are not responsible or liable for any act, error, omission, injury, or any consequences resulting therefrom, which may be occasioned through the neglect, default, or any other action of the company, carrier, or person engaged in carrying out the purpose for which tickets have been issued. We highly recommend the purchase of trip cancellation insurance.

The above disclaimer doesn't ask the client to agree with the agency's position. Of course there's nothing to prevent you (or a lawyer acting in your behalf) from drafting a disclaimer that will ask the client to acknowledge with his or her signature that he or she understands and agrees with your position.

Another way of trying to avoid some of the same problems is with an insurance waiver. This is a document that says, "We offered the client insurance and she declined." The inference, of course, being that when she finds herself laid up after slipping on that rock, she has only herself to blame. Waivers, for some reason, seem to be less aggressive than flat out disclaimer statements, perhaps because most people are used to signing them when they pick up a rental car. Here is an example of what such a waiver might look like.

[NAME OF AGENCY] INSURANCE WAIVER

Date of departure: _____ Date: _____

I have been offered the following travel insurance and I have declined the purchase of:

___ Trip cancellation & emergency evacuation.
___ Baggage.
___ Travel accident/limited sickness.
___ Flight insurance.
___ All of the above.

I, the undersigned, will not hold this travel agency and/or its agents responsible for any expenses incurred by me resulting from cancellation of my trip, accident, sickness, stolen or damaged baggage.

Agent's signature _____

Client's signature _____

Insurance for the client

One of the reasons that people sue travel agents (aside from the fact that a caring lawyer talked them into it) is that they find themselves in some sort of financial difficulty due to an injury or loss of baggage or whatever. On the theory that it's better to have someone else pay your bills than pay them yourself, they engage an attorney and sue.

That's one reason travel insurance makes a lot of sense for both travel agents and clients alike. From the traveler's perspective, if they are insured against whatever disaster has occurred, then presumably their financial worries are taken care of. For the travel agent, there are a number of nice things about travel insurance:

- Even if the client decides not to take any, the travel agent has at least gone on record as having advised the client of the possibility that something might go wrong. The travel agent may even be protected in some small measure from retribution.

- If the client takes out insurance and something goes wrong, the client will be looked after. And if the client is unhappy, his or her wrath will be directed at the insurance company, not the travel agent.

Travel insurance is commissionable, often up to 35%! Selling travel insurance to your clients can be a highly profitable add-on to your travel business. In fact, I've written a Special Report on the subject, entitled (appropriately enough) *Selling Travel Insurance* (see below).

As the waiver above suggests, there are different kinds of travel insurance. Among the things your clients can insure themselves for are:

- Trip cancellation/interruption.
- Travel delay.
- Medical emergencies.
- Baggage delay, loss, or damage.
- Emergency medical transportation.
- Legal help related to travel.
- Death, dismemberment, and similar misfortunes.

Many policies allow the insured to pick and choose among the things covered and the amounts of coverage, while others are sharply limited in what they cover and for how much. For example, many tour operators and cruise operators offer optional insurance products, usually covering cancellation, trip interruption, and similar eventualities. Most of these policies are quite limited in what they cover and under what circumstances. Coverage is also available from outside vendors specializing in travel insurance. Their policies may provide somewhat more coverage for more eventualities (like medical evacuation) than those provided by the travel suppliers themselves.

Check with your host agency to see with which travel insurer they have a relationship and what your share of the commission will be. Take the time to familiarize yourself thoroughly with the coverage offered. Read the fine print with a critical eye. Note the deductibles and the exclusions carefully. Travel insurance can seem expensive to the consumer and it can be a tricky sell for the agent. But it makes a lot of sense. As I get older, I have become increasingly aware of the advisability of taking out insurance that will lay on an air ambulance should I come a cropper in some far corner of the globe. But you don't have to be older for insurance to make sense. For example, one of my clients had to cancel an expensive cruise when their child became ill the day before they were scheduled to depart. Fortunately, they were covered.

The real trick with selling travel insurance is getting credit for having sold it. Most companies provide brochures containing sign-up forms that are coded in such a way that your host agency can be identified when the form arrives at the insurance company. You can simply hand these forms to your customers and hope they see the wisdom of taking out insurance and send them in. That doesn't always mean that you, specifically, will get the credit, however. You may have to work that out with your host agency. Another problem is that the brochures usually include an 800 number for the client's convenience. If they wait until the last minute to take out insurance — and many people do — they will call the toll-free number, use a credit card for payment, and there will be no record that you handed them the brochure — unless the company asks them for the code on their brochure, which in my experience they don't always do. If at all possible, sell the insurance face-to-face and get a check. You can also take the client's credit card number and forward it to the insurer. Position this as another service you provide the client, which in fact it is.

Another possibility is to create a direct relationship with a provider of travel insurance, thus avoiding the necessity of sharing your commission with your host agency. That is relatively easy to do in some states, much harder in others. In some states, you may expose yourself to various regulatory laws by the mere fact that you make travel insurance available to your clients. I'm sure you are an honest, well-meaning, and decent individual. Unfortunately, the regulatory agencies of your state may not be willing to grant you the same benefit of the doubt. Your host agency may be able to tell you what the relevant laws and rules are; a representative of a travel insurance provider is another excellent source of guidance.

The various providers of travel insurance have sales representatives whose job it is to serve the travel agent community. They often speak at the meetings of organizations like OSSN. You might also call a provider, get the name of the sales rep covering your territory, and get some one-on-one advice. Whether you are certain you'd like to add travel insurance to your product line or are merely curious, I would urge you to attend a seminar on the subject when one is presented in your area.

Travel insurance is such an important topic — not to mention a great profit center for the home-based agent — that I have written a Special Report titled *Selling Travel Insurance*. If you don't already have it, you can order it at:

> http://www.HomeTravelAgency.com/insurance.html

Insurance for the travel agent

Travel insurance for the customer may solve some problems for the travel agent. But for the truly paranoid there is yet another alternative — errors and omissions (E&O) insurance. This is a type of professional coverage whereby the insurer accepts the fact that, as a human being, you are fallible and might neglect to do something you should have done (like tell a customer that Whoopee Tours was in Chapter 11 bankruptcy and might go under before their tour took place). What's more, they'll agree to cover your assets in the unlikely event that should happen and the customer sues.

Insurance of this kind can be expensive unless you go in on it with a large number of others. Most (but by no means all) host agencies will allow (or require) you to get coverage on their E&O policy for a modest annual fee of a few hundred dollars. Some host agencies include E&O insurance in their sign-up fee.

If you get E&O coverage through your host agency, you will only be covered for transactions you make through the host agency. In other words, if you send a client on a tour and deal directly with the supplier, bypassing the host, and the client then sues you, you're on your own. If you plan to do a significant portion of your business as a completely independent agent, then purchasing your own E&O insurance makes a great deal of sense. Once you have it, you can inform your host agency (if you have one) that you no longer wish to be covered under their policy, as your own policy will cover you when operating on the host's behalf. The host agency will most likely ask that you prove to them that you have the coverage, which is a perfectly reasonable request. OSSN assists their members in getting E&O coverage at a moderate cost. Otherwise, you can contact the major underwriter of E&O insurance directly:

> Berkley Agency Ltd.
> P.O. Box 9366
> 100 Garden City Plaza, 5th floor
> Garden City, NY 11530
> (800) 645-2424
> (516) 294-1821

Another form of business insurance, <u>general liability</u> insurance, covers you for such things as the client who comes to your home office and slips on your icy front stairs. It is available, usually at a modest cost, from any independent insurance agent.

Incorporation

Another strategy designed to protect the businessperson against unforeseen legal actions is incorporation. Instead of being Joe's Travel, you become Joe's Travel, Inc. Incorporating your business can cost anywhere from several hundred dollars to several thousand.

The idea behind incorporating as a means of protection from lawsuits is that the assets of a corporation are separate, legally speaking, from the personal assets of the person who owns or runs the corporation. Thus, the theory goes, if you were sued they could get the value of your corporation (a box of business cards and a bank account with $100 in it, presumably) but <u>not your house and</u> car. The problem is, more and more clever lawyers are figuring out ways to "pierce the corporate veil" and go after personal assets.

Incorporation also brings with it certain tax consequences which don't make a lot of sense for many very small businesses. So-called "Chapter S" corporations offer many of the benefits of incorporating, while retaining much of the tax simplicity of a sole proprietorship. Consequently, they are attractive to many small businesspeople. Another option is forming a so-called "limited liability company" or LLC.

Corporations, no matter what form they take, also add considerably to your paperwork load. Whether or not incorporation makes sense for you is a matter for you, your conscience, and (of course) your lawyer.

Precaution or paranoia?

Having gone on at some length about the awful things that can go wrong and the often uncertain ways you can seek to protect yourself, we must now ask whether we're talking about sensible business precautions or raving paranoia. As with most things in life, there are two schools of thought on the subject.

I happened to be privy to a conversation between two travel agents, a lady who was an outside sales representative and a gentleman who was a travel agency owner in addition to being a lawyer. The subject was whether or not she should spend $523 to take out errors and omissions insurance. She feared that the advice she rendered clients left her open to lawsuits. He countered that there was nothing she could possibly say that would leave her open to a valid suit. He did admit that the possibility of an invalid suit was always present. After much back and forth, the travel agent-lawyer said, "My advice, as an attorney, is to put the $523 in a bank and watch it grow. In ten years you'll have seven or eight thousand." She replied, "I like to sleep at night, and to me $523 is cheap for a good night's sleep."

That's where they left it, and so shall I. Just be aware that if you decide you don't need insurance, you will have to shop for a host agency that does not require that you have it, and that might limit your options, since more and more hosts are realizing the value of having all their outside agents insured.

The tax man cometh

You will be pleased to hear that there is actually good news to report on the tax front. But first, let's take care of some minor points that, while not exactly bad news, must be mentioned in the interest of completeness.

First, you have to pay taxes on any income you make as a home-based travel agent. That really shouldn't be news to you but I just thought I should remind you. Among other things, that means that you will have to keep complete and accurate records so that you can (a) report your income and expenses accurately and (b) defend yourself if and when you are audited by the IRS.

Most host agencies issue their outside agents 1099 Forms at the end of the year, assuming their income was high enough. The threshold is $600, but many agencies will issue a 1099 regardless of the sum. These forms are a mechanism whereby the IRS seeks to track significant payments made by companies to people other than employees. Taxes are withheld from the wages of employees but not from payments made to consultants and other "independent contractors" such as yourself. If you receive a 1099 from your host agency, the odds are close to 100% that the IRS received a copy of the same form. The IRS, naturally, will want to make sure that your tax return and the 1099 match up. Or perhaps to be more accurate, the IRS will want to see that you are reporting at least as much self-employment income as is reflected on any 1099s you may have received.

Some host agencies take the position that their outside agents are not independent contractors at all but "customers" and that the commissions the outside rep receives are, in fact, "overpayments" which the agency is simply refunding to the outside rep. These agencies do not issue 1099s. I'm not sure what the government's take on this distinction is. What I do know is that, just because you don't get a 1099 from your agency, you can't pretend that the income you received through that agency doesn't exist. If you do pretend that income doesn't exist, you are cruisin' for the proverbial bruisin' from Uncle Sam.

Finally, the slim possibility exists that you may receive a W-2 Form at the end of the year. If you do, take immediate action because something has gone very wrong. A W-2 Form is used to report the annual income of employees. If your agency gives you one of these, it is probably an error; they are using the wrong form to report your commission income. The problem is, the IRS will think you are an employee and treat you as an employee, which is a terrible thing, as we shall see.

The tax benefits (yes, benefits)

If you've never been in business for yourself, becoming a home-based travel agent will open up a whole new world of possibilities for you when it comes to settling accounts with the tax man. Congress, in its infinite wisdom, has decided that businesses should not have to pay taxes on money they spend to stay in operation. Consequently, small businesses, even teeny-tiny sole-proprietorships such as you, can deduct a whole laundry list of expenses from their gross income, paying taxes only on the net income that remains.

Here are just some of things you can deduct from your income as a bona fide home-based travel agent:

- *A home office.* If you have a room in your home that is set aside for conducting your travel agency business, especially if you meet clients there, then a portion of your total home expenses can be deducted. That includes a portion of your rent or mortgage and utilities. Note, however, that the rules require that the room be used exclusively for business purposes.

- *Family employees.* Transform your layabout teenager into a valuable asset. You can hire your kids to work for you (filing, cleaning the office, etc.), pay them a reasonable wage, and deduct the expense from your taxes.

- *Your car or van.* You can deduct the cost of using your family car in your business. Trips made for business purposes — picking up office supplies, going to your agency to get brochures or tickets, taking clients to the airport, driving to a nearby city to attend a seminar, etc. — are deductible. The simplest way to keep track is with a mileage log. At the end of the year, you can determine what percentage of miles driven were for business purposes and then deduct that percentage of your expenses for automotive insurance, repairs, maintenance, gas, and so forth.

- *Business-related educational expenses.* The government wants your business to be a success. So they let you deduct the cost of learning how to do a better job at your business. That means that the cost of attending a fam/seminar given aboard a luxury cruise liner is a tax-deductible expense. In many cases, so are the books you read to learn the business — including this one!

- *Business-related travel.* Not only can you deduct the cost of a seminar, you can deduct the cost of getting there and back. If you are on a fam trip as a travel agent, you can deduct any expenses you incur. If you have specialized in Hawaiian vacations, you can even make a case to the tax man that going there twice a year to check up on resorts is a legitimate business expense. There are limits to what you can deduct when traveling on business, but they are reasonable and relatively easy to track.

- *Entertainment.* If you treat a client to lunch while pitching that luxury cruise, or if you throw a "cruise night" party at your home, those expenses are at least partly deductible. Again, certain limits exist and your record keeping must be impeccable, but staying within the letter of the law is far from impossible.

- *Business loans.* If you'd like to invest in some equipment for your business but can't quite afford it, remember that you can deduct any interest you pay on a loan taken out for business purposes. If you borrow money from your kids' college account, you get a double benefit — deductibility for the interest that raises the principal in their account. (Check with a lawyer to make sure any such loans are structured legally.)

- *A retirement fund.* As a self-employed individual you will have a new opportunity to set aside a portion of your income each year in a tax-deferred retirement account where it will grow, untaxed, until you are ready to retire. With company pension plans dropping left and right, looking out for number one in this manner is an increasingly wise course of action.

- *And on and on and on.* Every aspect of running your business is tax-deductible — things like phone calls, business cards, postage, books, subscriptions, computer fees, and so forth. Just make sure you keep good records and retain all your receipts.

And speaking of retaining things, retain a good accountant, one who is knowledgeable about and sympathetic towards small businesses. He or she will be able to educate you further on this intriguing subject. If you can't afford an accountant, use the bibliography in *The Travel Agent's Complete Desk Reference* and begin to educate yourself about your rights and responsibilities as a taxpaying small businessperson.

Of course, you can't simply spend and spend and spend without any heed to the amount of money coming in. Only the government can do that. Once you start declaring a loss on your Schedule C (the IRS form used to report profit or loss from a business) you start raising eyebrows at the

IRS. Of course, that doesn't mean you can't declare a loss. Businesses do it all the time. I am constantly amazed at the number of businesses, big businesses, that have been around for years and have never shown a profit. Still, the IRS tends to treat folks like you and me a little differently from major corporations.

Be prepared to prove to the IRS that you are serious about making a profit, even if you haven't managed to do so just yet. Otherwise, the IRS may rule that your business is merely a "hobby" and deny your deductions. Of course, showing a profit every now and again doesn't hurt — either your self-esteem or the government's view of your business.

Presumably, you will be showing a profit right from the start of your home-based travel agent career. I did. The important thing is to conduct yourself like a bona fide business and not pay a penny more in taxes than is your legal duty.

As your business evolves

There is a very good possibility that your business will start simple and stay simple. That is, you will be dealing through one host agency for all your ticketing needs, funneling all your business through them. One advantage of that, aside from the simplicity, is that it increases the likelihood of reaching an earnings level that will qualify you for travel benefits (see *Chapter 10: Straight Talk on Travel Industry Benefits*). However, as you already know, your home-based travel business doesn't have to be that simple, even at the beginning. And as you grow — in experience, in clients, in income, in ambition — it may become increasingly difficult or unwise to keep it simple. In this section, I will deal with some issues that might arise as your travel agent business evolves.

Getting your own IATA number

I discussed this in *Chapter 6: The Independent Agent*. I go into much greater detail on the various ways to get your own IATA number in *How to Get Your Own IATA Number (Or Other Unique Industry Identifier)*. If you purchased this book as part of my home study course, you already have it. If not, you can order it at

http://www.HomeTravelAgency.com/getiata.html

Taking this step is the one of the most common "next steps" that home-based agents make as their business expands. Just remember that it doesn't have to be an all or nothing decision. Just because you have your own IATA number doesn't mean that you won't continue to do some business, perhaps the majority of your business, though a host agency. Having your own IATA number simply increases your options; it even allows you to have your very own network of outside agents!

Specializing

It may seem ironic that, in a section discussing ways in which your business might become less straightforward, I start off with the possibility of simplification through specialization. It's not as odd as you think.

You can specialize and still have many of the permutations and combinations mentioned below.

Just be aware that, as your business expands and you gain more experience and knowledge in the travel industry, the advantages of specialization may become more apparent. Whether you wind up specializing and, if so, in what area, is up to you. Still, the fact of the matter is specializing makes an awful lot of sense, especially from a sales and marketing standpoint.

Whatever you do, don't make the mistake of thinking that just because you started out being a general-service agency you have to continue being one. It's true that you may lose some clients and some business by specializing. They might be clients and it might be business you don't mind losing anyway. And you can always make exceptions to any rule to accommodate special customers. For more on specializing, review *Chapter 2: Defining Yourself.*

Automation

Another issue that will arise as your business grows is whether or not you should automate. Elsewhere, I made known my opinion that beginners should steer clear of host agencies that require them to automate from the outset. It's expensive and there's no guarantee you'll like it — and no getting your money back if you don't.

Once you are in the industry for a while and have gotten a sense of what kind of travel you will be booking and how much, you can begin to make some informed decisions about whether getting "automated" in the travel industry's sense of the word makes sense for you. This means buying the software of one of the industry's several proprietary global distribution systems (GDS), formerly called computerized reservations systems (CRS). The cost of the software can be as much as $400 or so, while "access fees" to the system will cost $35 to $75 a month. You may have to dial into a distant computer or you may use one of the newer web-based products, which enable you to use the Internet to connect. Training, which you will almost certainly need, is another matter. It can cost anywhere from nothing to several thousand dollars. Typically you will make arrangements for automation through your host agency, which can usually arrange for training. In fact, the training may be mandatory.

There are four major GDS vendors — Amadeus, Galileo (often known by its old brand name, Apollo), Sabre, and Worldspan. Which system you get depends on which agency you are booking with. Obviously you will need to be speaking the same electronic language, as it were. Some agencies use more than one system; others have made a choice and stuck to it. For what it's worth, Sabre has the largest market share among travel agencies.

Another reason for holding off on automating for a while is that new Internet technologies are coming online every day, or at least so it seems. In a year or two, you might have a whole new set of low-cost options to choose from. In the meantime, monitor the trade press to keep abreast of what's happening in this exciting and rapidly changing area.

While the most logical reason for having a dedicated GDS is to book airline tickets, proponents of automation are fond of pointing out that there is a lot of other information on these systems and the amount and variety are growing daily. In addition to sending your Aunt Matilda to Dayton, you can receive the latest industry news and explore the availability of fam trips — an exciting wrinkle to the travel industry that we will discuss in the next chapter.

If you decide that the time has come to automate, you should be open to the idea of switching hosts or even becoming completely independent. There are a number of reasons for this. For one thing, you may be able to get a much better deal on automation from a different agency. Also, some hosts are very specifically designed to serve agents and non-ARC agencies that want to have full automation; these agencies typically operate on a "100% commission less fees" basis. Since becoming automated represents a major change in the way you do business, switching agencies at the same time will not seem like that big a deal. If you do decide to switch agencies in the process of automating, you will find a great deal of information to assist you in *How to Choose a Host Agency*.

Automation alternatives

I have been using the word "automation" in the sense of using one of the major GDSs to make bookings. But there are other, less elaborate ways to do much the same thing, at least for some bookings. They are sometimes free and they are getting more numerous as time goes on.

Some host agencies have their own private computer networks, called intranets, that you can either dial into or access via the Internet. These password-protected sites allow the outside agent to book many products. Moreover, many of these systems employ user-friendly interfaces that make the booking process a lot easier than it is on the major GDSs.

A growing number of suppliers are now allowing travel agents to book their products on their web sites and earn a commission by doing so. Even some airlines let you do this. Typically, you will need your own IATA number. In fact, some host agencies will direct you to supplier web sites to book that supplier's products. You should understand, in these cases, that you could be doing this directly and keeping the entire commission.

It is becoming increasingly possible to build a viable business just by using supplier web sites in this fashion. For example, several all-inclusive resort chains offer this capability. Be sure to crunch the numbers before making a decision to deal directly with any supplier, however. It may be that you can earn a higher commission through a host agency, thanks to their preferred suppler relationship, than you could by booking directly on the supplier web site.

Specialized software

As your travel business becomes larger (the number of customers you have) and more complex (the range of products and services you provide), you may decide that you need more than the basic software tools that most home computers users have. In addition to GDS software, there are a growing number of products that are designed especially for travel agents and travel agencies. They fall into two main categories and some combine both. These categories are (accounting and customer relationship management (CRM).)

These programs are versions of accounting and contact management software that have been tailored to the specific needs of travel agencies. They range in price from several hundred to several thousands of dollars. Some of them are offered by host agencies as part of their package of services to their independent contractors; others are stand-alone programs designed for small independent agencies, even sole proprietorships.

Here are some of the more prominent packages on the market as we go to press. All of them operate in a Windows environment, except as noted.

TRAMS. Offers a number of products including TRAMS Back Office, which automates management, marketing, and accounting.

(www.trams.com)

ClientBase. A TRAMS product, this is an elaborate CRM program.

TRACC. An accounting program for travel agencies.

(www.wbabin.net)

TravelSales. An all-in-one package designed for smaller independent agencies.

(www.wesmarc.com)

ClientEase. Combines CRM and accounting, but instead of installing the software on your computer you access it via the Internet. There is a monthly fee for access.

(www.itams.com)

TravCom CS and **ClientMajic** are two interlinked products that combine back office accounting and CRM.

(www.travcom.com)

It is unlikely you need any of these products now. You may never need them, but be aware they exist. You may want to visit their web sites. Then, as you meet agents who use them or come across these vendors at industry trade shows, learn more about them.

Switching or combining agencies

As I mentioned earlier, you may find it advisable to switch or combine agencies at some point. There are any number of reasons why you might want to do this:

- **Getting a better deal.** You may decide the grass, or at least the commission, is greener elsewhere.
- **Convenience.** You may have joined an agency out of state as a way to get started quickly. Once you have some experience under your belt and a growing client list, you may want to market your services to a local agency.
- **Better service.** If your agency is slow in paying, or not paying at all, you may want to seek out one that is more fiscally responsible.
- **Getting the best of both worlds.** It's possible to have relationships with more than one host agency to serve different

needs. For example, you may use one agency with its better commission cut for virtually all your bookings, but join a referral agency so you can have a "branded" booking engine on your web site.

One thing I sincerely hope this course will give you is the confidence and know-how to be able to face the possibility of switching agencies with confidence. It can be done, it can be done easily, and you owe it to yourself to give yourself the best deal possible. Loyalty is a wonderful thing, but if "dumping" your host makes financial sense, then you should do it. I strongly suspect your host would "dump" you if it felt that was in its best interest.

Joining a consortium

As home-based travel agents have become established in the travel distribution system, the industry has adapted. One of the most intriguing developments is that home-based and independent agents and agencies now have their own consortiums. It used to be that only traditional, storefront agencies — the "big guys" — could join consortiums. Now you have the option of doing that yourself.

Joining a consortium is definitely not a strategy for beginners. For example, one consortium open to home-based and independent agents requires five years of industry experience and $850,000 in sales to consortium suppliers each year. But make no mistake, there are home-based agents who produce that kind of volume. If you are getting close to reaching that threshold, joining a consortium could put you over the top, thanks to the higher commissions they offer. In the meantime you can get much the same benefit by selling the suppliers of a consortium to which your host agency belongs.

You will find a list of consortiums open to home-based agents in *The Travel Agent's Complete Desk Reference*. OSSN is another good source of information on newly formed consortiums.

Your own web site

It is now fairly easy (if not always inexpensive) for home-based travel agents to have a web site showcasing their travel marketing business. Because of the relative ease of setting up a web site, many beginning home-based travel agents feel they will be at a competitive disadvantage if they don't have one. That's simply not true, if only because travel agent web sites are merely a tool and not a solution. Still, a web site is worth considering at some point in your career.

There are essentially three ways to get your own web site:

- *Through a host agency.* The most obvious example of this is the "branded," self-replicating web sites offered by many referral agencies (see *Chapter 5: The Referral Agent*), but other host agencies have similar programs for their independent contractors.
- *From a web developer.* A number of companies, such as OnlineAgency.com specialize in creating and, if needed, host-

ing web sites designed especially for travel agents. They provide the bulk of the content but allow the site owner to customize the site with his or her own content.

- **_Do it yourself._** You can always create your own site if you have the necessary skills or hire someone, usually at considerable expense, to create it for you.

Branded or replicated web sites have limited value as a money-making strategy, although they can be useful for getting rid of customers you don't want to serve personally. They offer minimal customization. The web sites created by web developers can offer a wide array of travel products and can be customized to your special offerings. The trouble is the many thousands of these web sites owned by other travel agents are offering pretty much the same thing. My feeling is that these sites represent overkill for the beginner; however, as your business and your client list expands these sites can become useful and justify the ongoing expense.

Creating your own site from scratch has a number of advantages. You have total control and your site doesn't look exactly like thousands of others clamoring for attention on the Internet. If done right, your own site can be extremely successful in attracting potential customers for your particular travel specialty (see _Chapter 2: Defining Yourself_). Of course, there are disadvantages as well, including the time and expense needed to develop such a site. If you are not already knowledgeable about web development, the learning curve can be steep. Once the site is up and running, you have the responsibility of being the "webmaster," the person who maintains the site and keeps it up to date. In today's Internet-savvy world, being a webmaster is a highly specialized career in and of itself.

It is well beyond the scope of this course to teach you how to create your own web site. For those who want to pursue this option, I provide more information on my web site. There are a number of reasonably priced tools available that make the process very doable even for the novice. For more information, visit:

http://www.HomeTravelAgency.com/websites.html

Summary

I've thrown a lot at you in this chapter but I hope it has served to make the point: While becoming a home-based travel agent is easy, truly mastering the travel agent's profession takes diligent effort. It will also take considerable time. A few major points, however, should be more or less self-evident:

- **_Be a professional._** You can behave in a professional manner from the moment you decide this is the job for you. If you do, you will be treated as a professional, by suppliers, your clients, and your host agency. A professional doesn't have to know it all; in fact, one of the hallmarks of professionalism is to know what you don't know and know how to get the information you need. Professionals never try to "fake it" in front of clients. Instead, they promise to do the necessary research and get back to the client with an answer.

- *Keep your eye on the bottom line.* Although you can have a lot of fun as a home-based travel agent and I sincerely hope you do, this is a business after all. And in business, we keep score in dollars — gross and net. So you should constantly strive to increase your income by selling more and selling smarter. At the same time, you should seek to decrease your outgo by keeping an eagle eye on expenses and mastering your rights under the tax code.
- *Protect yourself.* We do not live in a perfect or necessarily just world. Bad things do happen to good people. So take appropriate steps to avoid mistakes and your exposure to the slings and arrows of outrageous fortune.
- *Take it one step at a time.* There are a lot of permutations and combinations in the travel business and this chapter has just scratched the surface. As you discover all the wonderful things you can do and the fabulous places you can go as a travel agent, and all the nifty strategies you can put to use, there will be a tendency to do it all. My advice is resist the temptation and build your business, your expertise, and your confidence level gradually but deliberately. That way, when you start to branch out you will be doing so from a firm basis of knowledge and experience.

Action steps

Here are some things you can do to put what you have learned in this chapter into action:

- Attend a few industry events. If you are a member of OSSN, attend a chapter meeting and begin the networking process. Attend a supplier seminar in your area. You can find out about them in the travel trade press. Put the networking tips you learned in this chapter to work.
- If you are actively considering a number of host agencies, ask them to provide you with a copy of their E&O policy. If you are a member of OSSN, submit a request for a quote for your own policy. This is especially important if you plan on doing any business apart from a host agency.
- Collect a number of independent contractor contracts and review them carefully. Make a list of what is included (and omitted) in the various contracts. Write down any questions you have. When you have narrowed your search for a host agency to a few possibilities, consult a lawyer to review the contract(s).

Chapter Ten:

Straight Talk on Travel Industry Benefits

What you will learn

After you have completed this chapter you will be able to:

- Describe various ways in which travel agents identify themselves to others in the industry, especially to suppliers. You will also be able to begin formulating a plan for how you will establish your own professional credentials as your career develops.
- Distinguish between good deals and bad deals for travel agents.
- Take immediate advantage of the benefits available to industry beginners.
- Make the most of any fam trip you take.

Key terms and concepts

This chapter involves the following key terms and concepts:

- Travel agents are identified in a variety of ways, some of which carry more weight in the industry than others.
- The phrase "the benefits" is used in the travel industry to refer to any discount, courtesy, complimentary upgrade, consideration, or other perk extended to a travel agent by a supplier.
- Perks, discounts, and other industry benefits are extended to travel agents for a variety of reasons and always at the discretion of the supplier.
- Just because something looks like a benefit or a discount doesn't mean it really is.
- A fam or familiarization trip is designed to teach travel agents about the features and benefits of a supplier's products.
- Fams are hard work. Fams may be offered during the low season when the weather is less than ideal.

Introduction

As we have seen, one of the most fundamental and controversial differences among home-based, independent travel agents is the divide between referral agents and so-called booking and selling agents. There are any number of distinctions that can be drawn between these two broad groups, but rather than repeat myself here, I refer you back to *Chapters 4 and 5* for a refresher.

The most important difference for the purposes of this chapter revolves around identity and benefits. Are referral agents "real" travel agents? And, if so, are they eligible for all those wonderful travel industry perks that their host agency touted in its marketing materials?

The answer to the first question is "Yes," even though I know there are those in the industry who disagree. It's hard to dispute the fact that referral agents can sell travel, even if some of them sell it only to themselves. It's also true that referral agents have gained widespread acceptance within the industry, even if some of it is grudging. The fact that there are still vocal elements within the travel distribution system that are vehemently anti-referral agent doesn't alter these facts.

The second question asks "Are the ID cards carried by referral agents valid industry identification and should they be accepted as proof of the bearer's eligibility for benefits?" This is a little harder to answer. At the risk of sounding Clinton-esque, the answer depends a lot on how you define your terms. A whole slew of subsidiary questions come to mind. Here are a few of them.

- What benefits are we talking about?
- What's to prevent any business from issuing ID cards to its independent contractors?
- Is there any intent to deceive in issuing these cards?
- Who is offering the benefits and why?
- If offering a perk is discretionary on the part of the supplier, who has the right to second-guess the supplier's decision about those to whom it grants benefits?
- Is it possible in some cases that it's the travel agent with the ID card who's getting hoodwinked and not the supplier?
- Do these cards open all doors or just a few?

In this chapter, I will try to unravel the very tangled ball of yarn that is the travel industry controversy on ID card and travel agent benefits.

What is travel agent ID?

Since the discussion of benefits hinges so often on how the travel agent "proves" his or her eligibility, let's take a moment to review the ways in which a travel agent can be identified. I will list them in relative order of "importance," a ranking which is entirely subjective on my part.

- *The IATAN card.* No doubt about it. This is the "gold standard" within the industry. To get it, the agent must meet minimum earnings requirements (see below). It is a photo ID card.

- **The CLIA card.** Issued by CLIA to all who join, this card has the advantage of being an "industry" card, but because of CLIA's focus on cruises, it is seen as somewhat limited. Still, it is accepted by many suppliers for fam trips. It, too, is a photo ID card.
- **An agency-issued ID card.** These are the ID cards produced by those so-called "card mills." Interestingly enough, they tend to look an awful lot like an IATAN card, but without the IATAN logo. It is usually, but not inevitably, a photo ID card.
- **A business card.** If it says you're a travel agent, you must be one, right?

There is another way in which travel agents are recognized that I haven't included in this list because it is not a card and it is difficult to rank in terms of importance, although I think it probably ranks pretty high. That is, the personal relationships a travel agent might have with suppliers. If you are known to a particular supplier as a travel agent, it doesn't matter if you have any of the cards listed above; you are a travel agent in the eyes of that supplier. Almost inevitably, a travel agent will have this kind of personal relationship with a supplier because that travel agent has brought the supplier business, usually a significant amount of business. As we will see, this is the most valuable form of identification a travel agent can have.

What are the benefits?

Apparently there are a great many people walking around with some form of travel agent ID in their pockets. Some of them are "real" travel agents, but some are non-travel agents who have paid $495 (or more!) to obtain access to travel industry discounts. What are these great deals? Can you get them just by waving a card? And are they as hot as they're cracked up to be? Here is a brief survey:

AD75 fares

Also called "quarter fares," this refers to the airline policy of allowing travel agents to fly at a 75% discount. Pretty impressive, right? Except that this is 75% off a fare few people ever pay — the full, unrestricted coach (or "Y") fare. Most "super-saver" fares represent a 55% discount off full coach. So the discounts, while real, are not as huge as they first seem. Still, they're a pretty good deal — except for the blackout periods. The airlines aren't about to let agents travel cheap during peak travel periods — like Thanksgiving, Christmas, Spring Break, and most of the summer. Then there's the paperwork. Most airlines don't let an agent walk up and buy a ticket. A request has to be made, in writing, in advance, and approved.

For the airlines this is a good deal. First, they generate a certain amount of goodwill with travel agencies. They reward travel agents who have sent them business in the past and stroke agents who might send them more in the future. Second, they make money on the deal. That's because no travel agent ever sits in a seat that could be occupied by a customer who would pay a higher fare. While the airlines book these fares as "positive space," they reserve the right to bump the agent (without any "denied-boarding" compensation) if the flight is overbooked. "Positive space" simply means that the agent can book ahead and get a seat assignment, as opposed to being put on a standby list. So every time an agent (even a phony one) flies, the airline is getting a few hundred dollars it might not otherwise have gotten.

First-class upgrades

Some airlines will, on a space-available basis, let travel agents fly first class on a coach ticket. I have had numerous referral agents tell me of their success in getting this perk. I know that it can happen because I've seen it done. Of all the deals available to "phony" travel agents, this one strikes me as the juiciest.

Actual statistics about this type of upgrade are impossible to come by. However, the anecdotal evidence is that getting an upgrade is far easier on smaller, lesser-known foreign carriers than on U.S. domestic or major international flights. My guess (and it's just a guess) is that the U.S. and major international airlines have become much more savvy about the travel agent ID issue since the turn of the century.

Hotel discounts

Card mill type agencies will often tell you that hotels offer travel agents a 50% discount. But that is 50% off the rack rate, which is the outrageous rate they charge when the big convention's in town and you don't have any other choice. Real travel agent rates at hotels are much more attractive. When you ask for a hotel's "agent rate," the reservationist may simply pick a number out of the air. Remember, they have considerable bargaining leeway. Often a little smart shopping or use of half-price hotel programs will get you as good a rate as a travel agent ID from a referral agency.

One agent told me of being quoted an "agent rate" at a hotel only to discover a promotional rate that was not only $10 cheaper but was commissionable as well.

Car rentals

Car rental firms vary widely in their use of agent discounts. Sometimes they will offer no more than 5% and sometimes you can get real bargains, like a flat rate of $10 a day with unlimited mileage. Again, since rates vary so widely from company to company, the agent rate at one may be more than a special promotional rate at another.

Tours and cruises

While tour operators and cruise lines will sometimes extend straight discounts to travel agents, most reduced-rate travel for travel agents in these areas takes the form of "fam trips," which are discussed a little later.

Special in-house deals

Some host agencies will tout their special deals and discounts, "available to our agents only." Often, these bargains are presented as fam trips. Are these real? And how can they offer them?

One agency that has drawn a great deal of fire as a card mill claims 40,000 outside agents and was at one time listed by *Travel Weekly* as one of the 50 largest agencies in the United States (as measured by sales volume). An agency this size can get hotel chains to offer its members special rates. However, you should realize that these 50%-off deals are <u>usually no better than a corporate rate that anyone can negotiate for on the phone.</u> The same is true of many of the tour and cruise deals these agencies offer their own agents. These could come from a number of sources:

- Discounts and freebies given by suppliers in recognition of the agency's booking volume.
- Deals offered by suppliers to agencies (and even the general public) to fill in tour and cruise dates that haven't sold well. In these cases, the supplier may not be too fussy about how "real" the travel agents are.
- Plain old bargains of the sort you might find advertised in the Sunday travel section.
- Genuine fams offered by suppliers who feel that this particular agency represents a good source of business for them.

Most referral agencies make a point of saying in their marketing materials, "We are not a travel club." Yet, when it comes to travel benefits, they function very much like one. You pay your money and you get the travel discounts that come from sources like the ones just listed or from suppliers who are not too fussy about which ID cards they accept.

What's wrong with this picture?

From what I have been able to determine, it actually is possible to gain some benefits by flashing a photo ID card of dubious provenance. In some cases, first class upgrades for example, the benefits are very nice. In most cases, however, you are merely getting a discount that is not that special. In many cases, a good travel agent or a smart shopper could have found you a better deal — and one that would not have required you to purchase a $495 ID card.

But is there anything wrong with all this? Is any of this illegal or unethical? Good question. I will try to answer as best I can. First, there is a simple answer to the abuses of card mills. Since every card mill requires an ARC/IATAN appointed agency to do its ticketing, ARC and IATAN could simply pull the accreditation of offending agencies. Problem solved. Why haven't ARC and IATAN done this? I have no idea, although I suspect the reason is they have no legal basis on which to do so. Many so-called card mills are represented by distinguished and respected travel attorneys who forcefully argue the rectitude and legality of their business methods.

The "pyramid scheme" aspect of some card mills is another matter.

Not too long ago, the Federal Trade Commission took action against a California-based operation and shut it down. Most, if not all, of the referral agencies and so-called "card mills" operating today do not use a true multilevel marketing model. They may provide substantial referral fees for signing up new agents, but that's about it. There simply isn't enough margin in a travel agent's commission to support an elaborate multilevel "downline."

The question of ethics is more complicated. Since time immemorial, suppliers have been extending courtesies to travel agents. The supplier does this to either reward past or current business or to encourage new business in the future. Some people take the position that, if a supplier grants a discount or other perk to someone with an official looking ID card, that is the supplier's prerogative. After all, they can always refuse. (In fact, many agencies that fit the "card mill" definition now counsel their "agents" that industry courtesies and discounts are discretionary and that agents shouldn't complain if they do not receive the perks they request.)

My personal feeling is that a travel agent deserves every benefit to which he or she is honestly entitled. How do you know if you are "honestly entitled" to a given benefit? I believe that if you look into your heart, you will know.

The industry strikes back

Thanks to some national publicity about "phony travel agents" on one of the network news magazine programs, and a steady stream of coverage and commentary in the trade press, the question of "who is a travel agent?" became a burning issue in the travel agent community in the early 1990s. Over a decade later, it still is.

One of the saddest things about the whole controversy, to my mind, was the way it pitted travel agent against travel agent. Spurred by the national publicity, the travel agent community went in for some internecine bloodletting. For a while, it was the "haves" against the "have-nots," with the haves being the larger ARC- and IATAN-appointed agencies and the have-nots being outside agents and cruise-only agencies. My personal opinion is that many "traditional" travel agents seized on the "abuse" issue to fight the rising tide of competition from home-based independent agents and cruise-only agencies; both of these groups operated without the high overhead of the traditional ARC- and IATAN-appointed agencies. There were calls for more government regulation of travel agents (a self-defeating initiative that was, unfortunately, successful in some states), an industry-standard "test" of travel agent competence (still being discussed), and increasing calls for an industry-standard ID card — the IATAN card — that would be universally recognized (and, not incidentally, be unavailable to certain categories of travel agents).

Non-traditional agents fought back, however, with the result that there is today a growing awareness in the industry that not every home-based agent is a fraud, that in fact most home-based agents are committed professionals. Still, the call for making the IATAN card the sole mark of the "true" travel agent continued and continues as you read this.

For the suppliers, especially the airlines, the ID card flap was more of a public relations problem — they were understandably concerned that their loyal full-fare-paying customers might get upset. For them, saying that henceforth they would demand the IATAN card as identification represented a quick and easy fix. Nonetheless, the suppliers, too, are wrestling with the thorny question of who is a travel agent and how do I tell the "real" ones from the "phony" ones.

Towards the IATAN card

The IATAN card existed before the whole card mill, phony agent flap erupted. It is (and always was) simply an optional photo ID card available, for a modest fee, to inside and outside agents associated with IATAN-appointed agencies (who meet certain requirements.) When the controversy broke out, there were many agents eligible for the card who had never bothered to pay the extra fee to obtain one. In fact, I met agents who turned their backs on the IATAN card as a matter of personal pride, figuring they could get all the industry perks they needed or wanted without it, thank you very much.

That changed with the controversy and the steady stream of announcements from suppliers that they would henceforth be demanding it of agents seeking discounts and fam trips. Suddenly the IATAN card was "hot." Applications for the card flooded in at the rate of 15,000 a month. One industry insider estimated that IATAN would make $10 million a year off its card's newfound prominence. Needless to say, IATAN cheerfully embraced this heaven-sent opportunity. For one thing, ARC-only agents would be forced to join IATAN to get the card. (Since most international carriers process payments through ARC's Area Settlement Program, there was no crying reason for an agency to belong to both ARC and IATAN — until then, of course.)

So, has moving to the IATAN card put an end to the abuse of agent privileges once and for all? Not on your life. The final arbiter of who is eligible for an IATAN card is still — guess who? — the agency owner, the same guy who was putting his mother-in-law and dentist on the list of employees. What probably will change is that the cost of becoming a pretend travel agent will go up a bit. But the "part owners" and the others will still have their IATAN cards. Many already do.

IATAN, to its credit, has been policing this type of abuse. In one year, IATAN struck 4,633 people off its lists, 3,188 of them involuntarily. In addition, more and more suppliers have not only been announcing their intention to crack down on the abuse of industry courtesies, but have actually started to do something about it. This will no doubt continue. What will also undoubtedly continue to happen is that at least some travel agencies will issue phony IATAN credentials and at least some suppliers will extend courtesy discounts to members of the travel agent profession, on a discretionary basis, whether they have "proper" identification or not.

Qualifying for travel benefits — really

In spite of all the brouhaha over "phony" IDs and "instant agents," there are lots of people out there who have a perfectly legitimate claim to industry discounts and other privileges. You can be one of them; it's not as difficult as you may be thinking. It does involve work selling travel; but that, after all, is what you want to do anyway.

There are two main ways part-timers and full-time outside agents can join the "pros" when it comes to travel benefits — get the IATAN card and establish direct relationships with suppliers.

Getting the IATAN card

First, let's talk about qualifying for the IATAN card. Assuming you are not going to con, cajole, or pay a travel agency owner to put you up for the card (none of which I recommend), you will have to earn your way to the card. You do that by selling travel to your friends and family, even to yourself.

To get in the running for an IATAN card you must first be affiliated with an IATAN-endorsed agency. If you are a cruise-only agency, or an independent contractor for such an agency, it is also possible to obtain an IATAN card. There are even procedures whereby ARC-only agents can get one. However, for the discussion that follows, I will assume you are affiliated with a host agency that is a member of IATAN.

First, your host agency must register you with IATAN via IATAN's Personnel Registration Form. Next, you must have an annual income (from commissions) of $5,000 or more. (IATAN based the $5,000 floor on the federal hourly minimum wage of $5.15, times 20 hours, times 48 weeks a year.) That means that if you are splitting your commission 50/50 with the agency you will have to sell $100,000 worth of travel product during the course of a year (assuming a uniform 10% commission rate). If you get 60% of the commission, the figure would be about $83,333. At 70%, it would be $71,428. All of which serves to underline the importance of shopping for and negotiating the best split possible.

Perhaps because of this, an increasing number of host agencies are using a system that pays the outside agent "100% of commissions." The agency then charges the outside rep either a flat monthly fee or a per-transaction fee to cover its costs. This arrangement has the advantage of making it possible to meet the IATAN earnings requirements much more quickly. Assuming once again a uniform 10% commission rate, it would take only $50,000 in gross sales to meet the requirement. OSSN provides its members with a model contract that uses this formula. Of course, the travel agent would actually receive less than $5,000 in this scenario, since the host agency's fees would be taken off the top. As far as IATAN is concerned, however, the agent has received $5,000 out of which he or she has compensated the host agency for its fees.

In addition to the earnings requirement, the employee or independent contractor must have been "registered" with IATAN by the host agency for at least six months, work at least 20 hours per week (a requirement that strikes me as hard to police in the case of independent contractors), and be at least 18 years of age.

The agency owner must "certify" that you earn and work the minimum amounts to qualify. My experience has been that an agency will back up your application for the card as long as you meet the requirements. You should also expect the agency to pass through to you any costs associated with applying for the card, which are extremely modest. You can learn about the current requirements and costs for the card at www.iatan.org.

IATAN says it will "verify each registration." They do that "by correspondence, interview and/or inspection of all documents, records and reports," including 1099 forms. Of course, if you receive commission payments directly from suppliers, the host agency will not have those payments on its records and, presumably, won't be willing to count that money towards your quest for the card. This can be a thorny issue for truly independent contractors. However, if you are receiving substantial income directly from suppliers, there is another way to qualify for the IATAN card, which I detail in *How to Get Your Own IATA Number*. If you have deep pockets, you can get it even before you produce the income. It's expensive to do it this way, but if you have the right business plan it might make sense for you.

Finally, it should be noted that while the IATAN card may be "king of the hill" for now when it comes to travel agent ID, that could change. There is some pressure growing in the industry to increase the number of ways in which bona fide travel agents can prove that they are just that. The day may come when, just as restaurants accept Visa, MasterCard, Diner's Club, American Express, and so on, suppliers will accept a number of different IDs as proof that you are, indeed, a travel agent.

Direct relationships with suppliers

When someone in a position of authority with a travel industry supplier (airline, hotel chain, or cruise line) knows that you are a travel agent worthy of a discount or other special treatment, that is the best form of ID you can have. Many outside reps have just this kind of relationship with one or more suppliers.

I know of an outside rep in the Midwest who specializes in travel to Europe. She does most of her ticketing through an IATAN-endorsed agency but she tickets directly with one of Europe's major airlines. They have issued her a "pseudo ARC number" and send tickets directly to her just as if she were a "regular" travel agency. Why? It probably has to do with the fact that she sends over $350,000 worth of business their way every year. You can also best believe that when she needs to go to Europe, this airline will accommodate her, perhaps even let her fly for free.

This example serves to illustrate the central point of these relationships — it's very definitely a quid pro quo arrangement: You bring us the business, we'll reward you. It also depends on volume, although you don't always have to be up into six figures before you see a payback. Fairly typical is the story I heard from one fledgling outside rep who booked his first big group with a Caribbean tour operator. The tour operator called him up a short time later and offered him an all-expenses-paid fam trip to the destination — which he promptly took, of course.

Sometimes, you don't even have to demonstrate that you can produce sales for the supplier. Every agent who showed up at an educational seminar hosted by one car rental company left with an ID card that entitled him or her to agent rates at all the company's locations.

Most of these relationships develop naturally, almost by accident, but there's no reason you can't help the process along. If you are specializing in a destination — and most of these direct relationships develop out of agent specialties — get to know your sales rep. As mentioned earlier, most suppliers of any size have salespeople who service the travel agent community. Your host agency may be able to tell you who they are, or you can simply call the supplier to find out. Bear in mind that the sales reps' territories are determined by where the agency is located, not where you are. So if you live in Illinois but book through an agency in Florida, your supplier sales reps will all be based down there. That doesn't mean you can't deal with them; it just means that it will be a long-distance relationship. When and if you develop a direct relationship, such as the one the Midwest agent has with the European airlines, you will deal with the supplier's local rep.

There are any number of ways to get to know your suppliers' sales reps:

- **Industry association meetings.** I have met many sales reps just by attending local chapter meetings.
- **Sponsored seminars.** Many suppliers organize touring "dog and pony shows" to tout their wares and increase agent proficiency in selling them. When they come to your local area they are usually put on by local sales reps.
- **Trade shows.** Again, if the trade show is held near you, at least some of the people staffing the booths will be local sales reps.
- **Calling them up.** Like everyone else with a nine-to-five job, supplier sales reps have to justify their existence. If you call them up for general information or to help you solve a booking problem, that counts as a sales call for them. So don't hesitate to call. That's what they're there for.

Of course, most supplier sales reps are doing an awful lot more than just trying to look busy. They are genuinely committed to growing the sales of their employers' products, and you are a very good vehicle through which to do that. If you show any likelihood of bringing in more business, they will do whatever they can to help you out. In the process, they will get to know you; you will get to know them; and notice will be taken of your success. It also goes without saying that these folks are savvy enough to separate the productive agents from the rest of the herd. If you're just wasting their time, they'll catch on real quick.

Finally, and at the risk of seeming repetitious, the benefits of the kind of direct relationships we're talking about here are yet another good reason to specialize in your travel business.

Benefits for the beginner

There are a lot of you who won't get an IATAN card, or who won't develop the kind of direct relationship that comes with selling $350,000 worth of airline tickets. At least not to begin with. That doesn't mean you are out of the running for free travel or other nifty benefits of the travel agent business. You just have to be realistic about what you can and cannot expect. It may help to redefine your terms a bit, as we shall see.

Here, then, is a summary of some things I've already mentioned and some new thoughts on how to maximize the benefits of your newfound, home-based travel agent career:

- **Tour conductor passes.** All in all, the fastest way to free travel for the beginner is the tour conductor pass, or teacher-counselor slot if you're doing educational tours. This was discussed in some depth in *Chapter 3: Becoming a Tour Organizer*.

- **Seminar benefits.** There are all sorts of nifty things you can pick up (besides knowledge and skills) by attending the many seminars that are sponsored by suppliers for agents. These can range from an agent ID card entitling you to special treatment by that supplier, to dollars-off or upgrade coupons, to free trips given as door prizes. Add that to the bedrock educational benefits, and there is no reason you shouldn't try to attend as many of these enlightening and entertaining events as possible.

- **"Fam/seminars."** Some seminars, such as those sponsored aboard cruise ships by OSSN are, in effect, discounted travel packages. The discounts are sometimes spectacular, but at the very least they offer good value compared to "the going rate." Then, too, don't overlook the value of the seminars themselves and the value of the tax deduction to which you will be entitled.

- **Earn "free" travel with commissions.** One way to view the commissions you earn as a part-time or fledgling full-time travel agent is as earned credits towards a "free" vacation at the end of the year. I think this is a very healthy mindset for the beginning home-based travel agent. In other words, you may not earn the amount that would qualify you for the IATAN card, but the $3,000 you do earn (money you wouldn't have had otherwise) will pay for a very nice holiday, especially if you can get a free airline ticket using the next suggestion.

- **Earn frequent flyer miles on other people's travel.** This is a very risky strategy. Every time I use it myself, I wonder if this is the time I'm going to get soaked. It works like this: When a customer books, say, a consolidator ticket, you accept payment from them by cash or check. You then put the cost of the ticket on your own credit card when you book with the consolidator (assuming the consolidator allows this, not all do). Of course, it has to be a credit card that gives you a mile of frequent flyer credit for every dollar you charge. The client's check covers the cost of the tickets you charged and everything's hunky-dory — unless, of course, the check bounces. That's why the strategy is risky and I can't say I wholeheartedly recommend it for everyone. I certainly don't use it with every client. Still, I figure I qualify for one free ticket each year that I might not otherwise have been eligible for without using this ploy.

■ **Tax-deductible travel.** In the last chapter, I mentioned any number of ways in which your home-based travel agenting will affect your tax situation. Much of the travel that used to be "just a vacation" will take on a whole new importance as an integral part of your new business. As such, you are entitled to tax deductions to the maximum extent allowed by law. Check with your accountant, or other competent professional, to make sure you are getting every deduction to which you are legally entitled.

■ **Asking for a discount.** Finally, if discounts are important to you, and you feel you are entitled to them, then show your ID (whatever it is) and ask for them. The worst they can say is "no." (If they do, ask why. You'll gather some valuable information for future reference.) The second worst thing they can say is "You can get the discount if you do such-and-such" — which may not be too hard to do. Sometimes, of course, you will get the discount with no problem at all.

Much of the relatively little that gets written about the quick and easy ways of becoming a travel agent focuses on "free" travel and "fabulous" benefits. Far too much, in my opinion. In the final analysis, there's no such thing as a free lunch. All the benefits that accrue to folks in the travel industry are earned. And that goes for the full-time "old pros" just as much as it does for the part-time beginners. Keep that in mind and you will have a profitable and enjoyable experience as a home-based travel agent.

Fam trips

"Fam trip" is short for "familiarization trip." As the name implies, these are trips sponsored by suppliers to familiarize travel agents with the destinations they serve and the products they offer. Fam trips take a number of different forms. Most typical is the fam trip sponsored by a tour operator. A fam of this type will include airfare, transfers, hotels, a number of sightseeing excursions, and at least some meals. There are also "land-only" fams that require the travel agent to pay his or her own way to the destination. These are generally offered by tourist boards and "receptive tour operators," that is, tour operators and wholesalers who handle arrangements at the destination but don't get involved in getting the tourists there. Finally, there are special deals offered by individual hotels, resorts, attractions, or even carriers (air or rail). These are sometimes called fams but probably belong in a different category.

Very few fam trips are free. Your actual out-of-pocket costs will depend on which type of fam trip you take. While the industry itself does not tend to discriminate among types of fam trips, I group them into three general categories:

- **_Run-of-the-mill fams._** Pricewise, these fam trips aren't big bargains. You could get approximately the same trip for yourself or a client for about the same amount and be free of fam obligations (see below). These fams are almost always announced in the trade press. They, too, require some proof of agent status, although I suspect that the standards of proof are not as high in this category as in others. Tour operators, after all, are under a certain obligation to prove to airlines, hotel owners, and motorcoach companies at their foreign destinations that they are actively promoting their wares. Sending a busload of travel agents through every once in a while is one way of doing that. You may even find yourself being solicited by tour operators when it starts to look like a fam trip won't attract enough warm bodies to make it economically viable.

- **_Good-deal fams._** This is a term of my own devising which I use to distinguish fam trips that are offered at truly steep discounts. For example, I was once offered a seven-day fam trip to Chile that included air, transfers, hotels, visits to three cities, sightseeing, and almost all meals for $449. The airfare alone at the time was running about $1,000 roundtrip. My rule of thumb is that, once the per-day cost for an air-inclusive fam drops below $100, the deal becomes attractive. Fam trips in this category may or may not be announced in the trade press. The best way to learn about them is to be in contact with tour operators and booking your clients with them (that's how I happened to be offered the Chile fam). Fams in this category are generally open to serious agents only. If you approach the tour operator, expect to be asked to justify your status as a bona fide travel agent.

- **_By invitation only._** These are the cream of the crop and the most likely to be completely free. These fam trips are seldom, if ever, announced in the trade press. To get on one of them, the tour operator must ask you, not the other way around. Being asked is usually a function of the amount of business you have brought the supplier. It is possible, however, that a supplier might approach a largish agency with an offer of a fam trip in the hopes that the agency would begin sending business its way. But in that case, it would be unlikely that you, as an outside rep, would be given the slot.

One final point: Fam trips are often scheduled during the off-season or the shoulder-season. There is a good reason for this. These are the tour operator's or the cruise line's slower seasons when their tours and cruises are seldom full. Consequently, they have room for a bunch of travel agents. Also, the reduced fees they charge agents for the fam is money they wouldn't have otherwise. (Remember the point I made about fixed costs in *Chapter 1*.) This means that you might encounter less-than-ideal weather on your fam. It might be blisteringly hot or uncomfortably cool. On one soft-adventure fam I took, the seas were incredibly rough, although I was assured that during the high season the sea was as calm as glass.

Getting on a fam

As noted, the best way to get on a fam is to be asked. Failing that, you will have to approach the organizer of the fam and ask to be included. Most likely, you will learn about fams through the trade press. *Travel Weekly* and *Jax Fax* have regular features listing upcoming fams. There are also a number of specialized publications claiming to offer up-to-the-minute inside information on fams. They are listed in *The Travel Agent's Complete Desk Reference* (If you are a member of OSSN, you will be eligible for a dozen or more "fam/seminars" each year.) Another possible source of information about fams is your host agency. They may receive faxes or other notices from operators and suppliers about trips in the offing.

The best way to start the applications process is to phone the operator sponsoring the fam trip and ask for details to be faxed to you. I have yet to encounter one that couldn't or wouldn't fax complete information. In most cases, an application form will be included with the information they send.

Fams are seldom free. There are three cost categories that you will need to become familiar with:

- **Agent fare.** This is the price you pay.
- **Single supplement.** All fams are priced on a per person, double occupancy basis. That means that you will be paired with another agent with whom you will share a hotel room or cruise ship cabin. If you prefer to travel solo, you will have to pay the single supplement. This can range anywhere from a few hundred dollars ($250 on a base fare of $1,095 on one fam) to the complete agent price (in other words, a single room costs twice as much as sharing).

  Of course, there's always the possibility that you'll be the odd person out and get a single room at no extra charge. Also, tour operators will try to accommodate cases of obvious incompatibility (your roommate smokes cigars, for example).
- **Spouse/companion fare.** Tour operators try to make fam trips more attractive for agents by allowing them to bring along a spouse or "significant other." Their fare is typically a few hundred dollars more than the agent fare. For example, one 8-day fam trip to Bulgaria charged agents $690 and

spouses just $130 more. A 12-day fam to China sported an agent fare of $1,390 and a companion fare of $1,590.

Once you have decided on a fam you want to take, the next step is to apply. Typically, the application form that accompanies the information you have faxed to you will ask you for two things: a down payment and proof of agent status. The down payment is usually in the $200 to $250 range. Payment in full is required anywhere from 15 to 45 days prior to departure. Most fams have cancellation policies similar to those of regular tours.

As to proving your status as an agent, the operators will phrase it in a number of ways. "A copy of IATAN/ARC list," "a current IATAN list," "CLIA or IATAN card," and "business card and IATAN list" are all common phrases. In addition, some fam operators may require that the request come through your agency rather than directly from you. They may also specify payment via an "agency check" that corresponds to the agency whose IATA number is being recorded as the agency of record.

In other words, you may (in fact, probably will) have your own separate business identity with a business checking account and checks with your business name on them. But if you seek to qualify for the fam trip as an outside agent for Acme Travel and give Acme's IATA number, the fam operator may want the check to come from Acme rather than from you. Many fam operators, however, are quite familiar with the way outside agents operate; so this will not always be a problem.

In addition to satisfying the policies and procedures of the tour operator, there's your host agency to consider. You will have to sound out your agency about their policy on fam trips. Some agencies won't want to hear anything about fam trips from outside reps who don't qualify for the IATAN list. Even if you meet the most stringent requirements, your agency may be less than overjoyed at the extra work involved.

My philosophy is that, if you honestly feel you are qualified to take a fam trip, you should apply anyway. Act as if your acceptance on the fam is a sure thing and see what happens. For one thing, what the fam operator says it wants on its application form and what it will actually accept may be two different things. You have no way of knowing just how strict or loose their policies are or how desperate they may be to fill slots for the dates you requested. Remember, too, that you are sending a check with your application. A bird in the hand being worth two in the bush, the operator may simply cash your check and not ask any further questions. If they do ask for more information, you can respond appropriately.

If you are not on the IATAN list, or haven't quite qualified for it, or are in the process of applying for it, and the operator questions your eligibility, simply explain your situation and send along what you do have. That might include your business card, a photocopy of any ID card issued by your agency or just a letter on your letterhead stating that you are an outside sales representative for such and such an agency, with IATA number such and such. You might want to explain why you want to take the trip and why you think it would be mutually beneficial if you did. You could even provide additional information about how much business your agency does, but that's probably overkill.

The point is this: Ask and you may or may not receive. Don't ask and you definitely won't receive.

Fam trips are hard work

One thing that is important for any travel agent to understand is that fam trips are business trips. They are *not* vacations. The tour operator wants to sell its wares, and it fully expects you to sit up and take notice. Many fam trips shuttle agents about on exhaustive — and exhausting — visits to several resort and hotel properties in a single location. At every turn you may be expected to sit through yet another "orientation" session, in which all the wonderful features of the hotel, cruise ship, resort, tourist region, or whatever are extolled at great length and in great detail.

Far from being a penance, this is precisely what you have come on the fam trip for. At least this is what you should have come on the fam trip for. From your perspective, the fam trip offers you an unparalleled opportunity to gain the product knowledge and the first-hand experience to be able to go home and sell the dickens out of the location you just visited. (Indeed, some tour operators have deals whereby they will rebate a portion of the cost of the fam trip based on how much business you send their way during the next year.)

Go on the fam trip prepared to learn and to ask a lot of questions. Gather as much descriptive literature as possible. Gather in-depth information about the places you visit.

- How many rooms in the hotel? What configurations?
- How are rooms priced? Are suites worth the extra charge?
- Which amenities are provided? Which are extra?
- Is the hotel in a quiet part of town or is it noisy? Are interior rooms a better bet?
- How does it stack up against an American hotel? Some people find the "foreign-ness" of a hotel part of its charm. Others want a hotel room just like the ones at Holiday Inn back home.
- What are the hours of popular tourist attractions? How often do the guided city tours run?
- What restaurants can you wholeheartedly recommend to clients?

Remember that in addition to gathering all the basic information about the places you go on the fam trip, you are serving as the eyes and ears of your customers — both the ones you already have and ones you might have in the future. View every attraction, every hotel, every town and resort through the eyes of these customers.

- What's the clientele like? Young and hip or middle-aged and stuffy? Middle-aged and hip or young and stuffy?
- Are there lots of stairs to climb or is everything easily accessible?

- Does the hotel have a disco? Is that good or bad?
- How will your clients take to the guides and tour escorts?
- What about crime? What tips should you pass along?
- Is the water good for snorkeling? Or better for sailing?
- Is there golf nearby? Tennis? Opera? Theater?
- Is Paris really for lovers?

Personally, I find this kind of touring to be a lot of fun. I find I enjoy myself just as much being shown around a five-star French hotel by the owner as I do wandering through a chateau or museum. It also provides a unique opportunity to share ideas and experiences with other travel agents. If, on the other hand, you think that a fam trip offers a great opportunity to get away from the regular grind and relax for a week, you're in for a rude awakening. You'll also, not incidentally, make some life-long enemies along the way — not just the tour operators, but your fellow agents as well, most of whom take their profession very seriously indeed.

So if you prefer to investigate destinations in a less pressured, less hectic fashion, avoid fam trips. Do it on your own time and pay the going rate. With your newfound skills and knowledge, you should be able to find some good deals and negotiate some attractive rates — and you'll probably be able to write it off as well.

Summary

Yes, there are benefits associated with being a travel agent, home-based or otherwise. And, yes, they can be quite wonderful. Some of them are available to beginners; you will have to pay your dues to earn others. The very best benefits are earned, although the work required to earn them doesn't have to be all that difficult, in fact it can be a lot of fun.

On the other hand, some "benefits" are not really benefits at all. The person who has purchased a $495 ID card and uses it to get a "travel agent rate" at a hotel, may be getting no better a deal than they could have received by showing their AAA card. It is only with experience and knowledge that you will be able to distinguish the really good deals from the rest.

Suppliers extend discounts and courtesies to travel agents for a variety of reasons, but there is usually a quid pro quo involved. That is, the supplier expects to profit from the deal in some way, usually in the form of increased business, which is ideally received before the discount is extended.

Fam trips benefit both parties and you should never hesitate to apply for a fam trip when you sincerely believe it will benefit both you and the supplier. Just be prepared to work when you go, because the primary purpose of a fam trip is to help you better service your clients due to the superior first-hand knowledge of the destinations you have gathered by taking the fam trip in the first place.

Action steps

Here are some things you can do to put what you have learned in this chapter into action:

- Visit the IATAN web site (www.iatan.org) and learn the steps necessary to qualify for the IATAN card. There are plenty of explanatory documents and forms that you can download from that site. File them away for future reference. Make a note of the date and then see how long it takes you to qualify for the card, if that is one of your goals.

- Call a hotel and ask what their "travel agent rate" is for a specific date (avoid weekends). Ask if there are any specific requirements (you are trying to see if they'll ask for a specific form of ID). Then, have a spouse or friend call the same hotel and ask what the AAA and AARP rates are for the same night. (Or do it yourself a few hours later; you'll usually wind up speaking with a different reservationist.) Then bargain a little; ask if they have a corporate rate or any special promotions going on for that date. Try to get the reservationist to lower the rate as much as possible. Research prices actually paid for hotels at various discount web sites, such as Priceline. Do this with a few hotels and you'll learn a lot about how flexible hotels can be with their rates.

- Join OSSN and sign up for one of their fam/seminars. You'll learn a great deal and be energized by sampling the benefits that accrue to the productive home-based agent.

- Ask any host agency you are considering about their policy on travel agent benefits and fams. Ask what kind of assistance they will give you with fams and under what circumstances.

The Craft
of Booking
Travel

Chapter Eleven: The Basics of Booking

What you will learn

After you have completed this chapter you will be able to:

- Distinguish between the various products and product lines you will be selling.
- Approach every booking in an organized and systematic fashion.
- Use "the magic words" to smooth the learning curve.

Key terms and concepts

This chapter involves the following key terms and concepts:

- A travel product is a discreet, separate item you can sell to a customer. A cabin in Category G on a cruise ship is a travel product. A travel product line is a group of similar products. Cruises, for example, represent a product line.
- The product your customer wants will determine any number of things, including the supplier(s) you will use, the jargon you will use, the commission you will make, and the profit you will realize.
- Every booking, no matter what the product, requires a systematic step-by-step approach. Ignore the steps at your peril.
- Common courtesy will draw out the best in the reservationists with whom you work when making bookings, especially at the beginning of your career.

Introduction

Let's assume that you have now, through one means or another, become an outside sales representative for a travel agency. You are now, if not a full-fledged travel agent, at least a partly-fledged one. You can sell travel to your friends, family, and neighbors. You are part of the huge and ever-growing travel industry.

First of all, congratulations! You're probably all fired up and rarin' to go. That's great. Your enthusiasm will stand you in good stead.

Second, be careful! You may have taken to heart my sage advice about defining yourself. I certainly hope you did. But it is in the nature of things that, to begin with at least, you will wind up taking on all comers and fielding some requests that may puzzle you. Once you start spreading the word that you're in the travel business, your next door neighbor may say, "Gee, I have to go to Denver next week. Can you get me a ticket?" Your uncle might say, "Your Aunt and I want to take a cruise this winter. Which one should we take?" A co-worker might say, "I'd like to take that cross-country sleeper train I heard about. How much does that cost?"

You'll probably find it hard to say, "Oh, I don't want to handle that sort of thing," or "Gosh, I don't know anything about cruises yet." No, chances are you'll say "Sure, I'll check that out for you." But how?

You're pretty much on your own. And that can be a bit scary. I know because I've been there. I can't make you an expert in the next few pages, nor can I cover all the possible permutations and combinations. But I can pass along the basics and offer a few tips. This chapter and the ones that follow, then, are designed to help you make your first bookings with a modicum of self-confidence and a minimum of errors.

Travel products

Conveniently, perhaps inevitably, the travel industry can be divvied up into a fairly small number of "products." Airline tickets are one product, cruises are another. Taking things a step further, it can be helpful to distinguish between "product lines" (airline tickets, for example) and the individual products available in each line. In other words, a coach seat on Continental and a first-class seat on British Airways are two different products, although they belong to the same product line. So, looked at from this perspective, knowing that your client wants an airline ticket does not immediately tell you which specific product will be right for her.

Generally speaking, though, once you know what the customer wants, you'll know immediately where to go to get it. As you gain more experience in and exposure to the travel business, you will become more and more comfortable dealing with these products, just as if they were nuts and bolts or cans of soup. You will also learn that, just as a steel bolt differs from a can of minestrone soup, each travel product is a separate entity, with its own jargon, booking procedures, and folkways.

Your clients will have a need for different travel products at different times. Often they will have a need for more than one travel product during a single trip. Which products they need will determine a number of things:

- **The supplier.** Different suppliers sell different things. You can't book a cruise from Avis. That may seem crushingly obvious, but it is an important distinction because it can determine . . .
- **Your access to the product.** There are some products you

simply cannot sell unless you meet the right qualifications. For example, unless you are presently an accredited travel agency, an employee of such an agency, or an independent contractor for such an agency, you cannot sell Aunt Matilda a no-commission American Airlines ticket from New York to London. On the other hand, you might be able to find a consolidator who would sell you a ticket to London at a "net fare," which you could then sell to Aunt Matilda for whatever you thought she'd be willing to pay.

- **Your profit.** Some products pay higher commissions than others. Most domestic airline tickets pay nothing, international air can sometimes pay 10%, cruises and tours anywhere from 10% to 15%, and some car rentals just 5%.

- **Your profitability.** It is a truism in the business that it takes just as much time to book a $5,000 tour as it does to book a $200 airline ticket. Obviously, the tour will make you more money than the ticket. On the other hand, it probably will take you longer to sell the tour. The point to be made here is that, as a businessperson, you will be concerned not just with how much money you make in a given transaction, but how much time and effort you have to expend to make it. You may charge a $25 fee on a domestic airline ticket that takes you 10 minutes to book. But you may have to spend several hours to research rates, book, and confirm a luxury hotel room in Helsinki that nets you a $40 commission. It doesn't take long to figure out which one is more profitable.

- **The ease of booking.** A three-day cruise aboard the Disney Magic is a pretty straightforward proposition. Once you know what you are doing, you should be able to research the possible fares pretty quickly. A tour of Japan, on the other hand, could mean days of research — checking your library, contacting many suppliers, and reviewing dozens of brochures and itineraries — before finding the right fit for your client. The ease of booking will also be determined by your familiarity with the product. If the bulk of your business is selling cruises, it will be correspondingly more difficult to fly a client to the middle of the Amazon jungle and help him hire a boat and a trusty Indian guide.

- **The language you speak.** By this I mean the special jargon that all industries use as a kind of shorthand to speed the flow of business or exclude outsiders or sometimes both. If cruises represent only 5% of your bookings, you will feel the same uncertainty every time you book one that you feel when you resurrect your high school Spanish on your occasional trips to South America.

Note: The jargon I'm talking about here is the jargon used between you and the reservationist. Never use jargon when discussing travel with your clients. You'll just confuse them and damage your chances of making the sale and building an ongoing relationship.

Some general notes on bookings

Before we look at the individual travel products in detail, let's take a moment to review some general considerations that are common to booking all travel products. Every booking you make for a client can be seen as having several steps or stages:

Step One: Gathering information

Your first task is to gather complete information about what the client wants. This may seem obvious, but inexperienced travel agents often go off half-cocked.

For example, your good buddy Harold wants to fly to San Francisco on the 15th and return on the 28th. Terrific. Off you go to make the booking. But wait. Does Harold want to leave in the morning or the afternoon? Is he more concerned with schedule or price? Does he want to use a specific airline so he can boost his frequent flyer credits? Does he prefer a window or an aisle seat? And what's he going to do in San Francisco? Does he need a hotel reservation? A rental car? These are all things you need to know before you start the booking process.

Of course, the client might not have all the answers. That's why people use travel agents — to help them make choices. When the client doesn't know exactly what he or she wants, ask what the parameters are. In other words, how much leeway do you have to make decisions on the client's behalf without checking back with the client for permission?

The goal of this stage is to avoid having to call the client back to request more specific information. Not only is this not a very efficient use of your time, it doesn't do much to reassure your customers about your competence.

A word of warning, however: Never let your embarrassment stop you from calling the client when you have forgotten to get some crucial bit of information. Hopefully, the tips and techniques that I discuss below will help you avoid this unpleasantness, but mistakes do happen. Chalk it up to experience. Ultimately, the client will be more annoyed by a faulty booking than by your calling back for more information.

Step Two: Research

Your next job is to go out and see what's available and at what price. In some cases (like Harold's trip to San Francisco) this will be a pretty straightforward proposition. But what if Harold had asked you to look around for a vacation destination for him and his wife, "somewhere warm." Fulfilling that request will take a bit longer.

Again, your goal here is to get complete information to present to your client. If you present your findings and the client asks three questions that require you to say, "Gee, I'll have to check and get back to you," you probably haven't done your research properly. Obviously, you can't anticipate every question the client might ask, but you should be able to research the most obvious options. This requires doing a good job of gathering information about the client's parameters. ("What's your absolute upper limit on the cost?") It also means asking logical questions when doing your research. ("What's included in the honeymoon package and what's extra?")

Don't worry too much if you report your findings to the client and then find you have to go back and do more research. From a purely business standpoint, you might prefer not to have to do this, since the more time it takes to make a booking the less profitable it becomes. But often your research will open new possibilities the client hadn't considered before. And that's part of the service you provide.

Step Three: Making the sale

In all but the most straightforward of situations, you will have to get back to your client either to make sure that the arrangements you have made are satisfactory or to discuss the several options available and guide the client to a decision. This is what's meant by "making the sale." Of course, in many — even most — cases, you will have made reservations to lock in a fare or guarantee a berth, as long as you know that those reservations can be changed or canceled within a certain time frame.

We will discuss techniques you can use in making the sale in *Part III*. For now, just be aware that until the customer has agreed to your recommendations and given you the green light to proceed, the booking is not official (the "sale" has not been made). At a minimum, review verbally with the customer all the key elements of the booking (time, date, supplier, fares, etc., etc.). Make sure you have it right and the customer agrees that you have it right. You may also provide this information in written form, but if you do, be sure you get the customer's agreement to it.

Step Four: Making the booking

As we just saw, this step may have preceded Step Three or you may be carrying out these steps in tandem. However it plays out, you have to actually make the booking with the supplier to make the client's trip happen. Again, as a general note, your goal here is to have complete information to give the supplier. The specific information you need will depend on the product you're booking and the supplier with whom you are dealing. Here are some of the more frequently overlooked bits of information that can slow down the booking process for beginners:

- Credit card expiration dates and security codes (those three digits on the back).
- The name "as it appears" on the card. You may know a Ken Smith but his credit card might say John Kenneth Smith.
- The billing address for the card.
- The client's daytime (or other) phone number.
- Frequent flyer numbers. Also, client identification numbers for any number of "affinity programs" for hotels, car rentals, etc.

Passport numbers.

Special requests. For example, does your client require a special meal on the flight, or a wheelchair?

Your host agency's IATA number. This number identifies your agency and separates it from all other agencies. You probably won't make this mistake more than once. Stick the IATA number on your phone until you have it memorized.

Your host agency's "official" phone number. Some suppliers identify agencies by their phone numbers, since they are unique. Some agencies have more then one phone number; make sure you know which one to give to suppliers. Again, this is one of those mistakes you probably won't make twice.

Think/oo

The specific steps you take to make bookings for different travel products will be discussed in *Chapters 12* through *16*.

Step Five: Confirming the booking with the client

Finally, you have to get back to the client and confirm the booking. To "confirm" the booking you have to verbally review with the client the key elements of the booking (date, time, supplier, cost, etc., etc.). You may also provide this information in written form. If this sounds familiar, you did much the same thing in Step Three.

This is partly a matter of professionalism and courtesy. It is also a safeguard. If you have made an error in the booking, better to find it out now than when the customer gets to the airport Tuesday and discovers the ticket is for a Wednesday flight.

The magic words

I know that some of you reading this will have a great deal of trepidation about presenting yourself as a travel agent for the first time. So before you pick up that phone to make your first booking, let me share with you some "magic words" I discovered. They will go a long way to helping overcome any nervousness or uncertainty you may have. The magic words can vary from situation to situation, but they go something like this:

> *"I'm kinda new at this; so if you could sorta guide me through the process, I'd really appreciate it."*

Another variation might sound like this:

> *"I just started as an outside rep and I've never made one of these bookings; so forgive me if I sound a little hesitant."*

I suppose there are some sourpusses out there who won't respond to these magic words, but I have found the reservationists who work for the various suppliers to be a pretty nice bunch of people. For example, when I was just getting started, back in the days of airline commissions, an airline reservationist helped me get a commission that I otherwise would have missed out on by patiently explaining the booking procedure for frequent flyer awards. Also, these people are very well trained by their companies. Most suppliers realize that the quality of service they provide to you, the travel agent, can mean the difference between getting a steady stream of business from you or having you cross them off your list.

So if you ever get the feeling that you have to "pretend" to be a travel agent, my advice to you is "just don't do it." 'Fess up that you're still learning and place yourself in the capable hands of the reservationists. Most likely, they will respond in a very positive and friendly way. Remember that these people get far more than their fair share of abuse from "know-it-all" travel agents. You can be the exception. My experience has been that if you are polite and friendly to them, reservationists will bend over backwards to help you out.

Summary

The number of travel products is truly mind-boggling. That is why it is comforting to know that virtually all bookings follow a certain structure or pattern, which recurs over and over. Until you get into the rhythm of it, you may want to check back to this chapter from time to time and review the general notes on bookings.

Yet in spite of the similarities among the booking processes for the various travel products, there are also some very important differences. In the following chapters, I will walk you through the specifics of making bookings for each of the major travel products:

- Airline tickets (*Chapter 12*).
- Hotels (*Chapter 13*).
- Rental cars (*Chapter 14*).
- Tours and packages (*Chapter 15*).
- Cruises (*Chapter 16*).

Action steps

Here are some things you can do to put what you have learned in this chapter into action:

- Choose a product line (cruises, for example) and then make a list of as many products as you can think of that fall within that product line. You'll probably get tired and run out of paper before you complete the list. Don't worry. The purpose of the exercise is to help you realize how many different products there are.

  Hint: If you choose cruises, shore excursions, on-board spa treatments, and post-cruise resort stays are all products of this product line.

- Close this book and write down the five steps of making a booking. If you can't remember, review this chapter and keep trying until you can.

■ As you make your first bookings, make notes to yourself about how you used the five steps in each transaction. This process will be made easier by the material in the following chapters.

 As you make your first bookings, try to develop your own "magic words" to use when you have to throw yourself on the mercy of the reservationist. Write down what you said, then try to refine it.

Chapter Twelve:
Booking Airlines

What you will learn

After you have completed this chapter you will be able to:

- Decide whether you want to include airline tickets in your product mix and, if so, under what circumstances.
- Make an informed decision as to whether or not you will want to automate your business, either at the beginning of your career or later.
- Understand the major issues confronting home-based agents when they automate.
- Name several different ways to sell airline tickets without a GDS.
- Deal confidently with consolidators.

Key terms and concepts

This chapter involves the following key terms and concepts:

- GDS. This is an abbreviation for global distribution system. It is a relatively new term for the computerized reservations systems (CRS) used by travel agents to book airline tickets and other travel products. Many agents still refer to these systems as CRSs.
- Automation, as it is used in this chapter, refers primarily to the use of a GDS, although the term can also be used to refer to any use of computer technology in business.
- It is not necessary to have or use a GDS to participate in the travel distribution system and earn good money.
- A consolidator is an individual or a company that enters into a contract with an airline to sell large blocks of seats for that airline. In exchange, the consolidator gets a discount on the tickets enabling him to pass considerable savings on to travel agents. Consolidators represent one of the best ways for home-based agents to make decent money selling air.

Can we deal with These Guys?

Introduction

I'm starting off with airlines for two main reasons. First, booking airlines is the most complex and daunting issue facing the brand-new home-based travel agent. And, second, my very strong hunch is that the very first request you are likely to get as a newly minted travel agent will be for a domestic airline ticket. Whether you want to accept that booking is another matter. It is my equally strong hunch that, after finishing this chapter, you will decide to book airline tickets only under very specific situations, if at all. On the other hand, some of you will feel you're not really a travel agent unless you have GDS access and book every puddle-jumping flight you can, so let's forge ahead. *SABRE*

No, wait! Let me add a word of caution first. This is a maddeningly complex area. Policies and procedures change from airline to airline, from GDS to GDS, from host agency to host agency. Consequently, it is virtually impossible to establish any "universal" rules. On top of that, things are changing constantly; what might be true as I write could change before you get a chance to read it. So be sure to "test" everything I say for accuracy as it applies to your particular situation, based on which host agency you use, which GDS (if any) you use, and so forth. Okay, *now* we can forge ahead.

Airline tickets are the throbbing heart of the traditional storefront travel agency business. It's no accident that one of the main things that distinguishes a "real" travel agency from all others is a global distribution system (GDS). And a GDS is all about booking and printing airline tickets. Oh sure, you can book many hotels, some tours, and most rent-a-cars with a GDS, but its primary function is to serve the airlines. It is the airlines, after all, that created the majority of today's GDS systems.

As I explained elsewhere, the selling of airline tickets involves huge amounts of money changing hands. It requires a large, expensive, and complex bureaucracy to make sure that all that money flows smoothly from one place to another and winds up in the right hands. This is the primary reason that the cost of entry into the world of the "traditional" travel agency is so high.

Booking airline tickets is one of a travel agent's most challenging jobs. It requires detailed and sometimes arcane knowledge, extreme attention to detail, and an ability to keep calm when your client is going ballistic. There are a number of reasons for this:

- The number of choices (of airlines, fares, routings, schedules, and so forth) is huge. It can take a long time to sort through your available options.
- Doing it right requires access to one of the GDS systems. That requires an investment of money (for the software and/or the access) and time (to learn how to make that software sing).
- There is virtually no way around the electronic infrastructure of the GDS systems. Sooner or later, the booking information has to be entered into a computer to generate the ticket.
- Because computer systems are completely unforgiving, the

information you provide must be precise, accurate, and in the required format. So booking airline tickets requires a high degree of attention to detail.

- The airline industry itself is in turmoil, making airlines extremely unstable travel "partners."
- No airline booking is ever completely finished until the traveler returns home. Passengers often change their plans several times before departing. Even after they've left home, their plans can be disrupted by air traffic delays, the weather, and other unforeseen events.

Given all that, the first question you must ask yourself is, "Is this really something I want to do?" Good question.

Is it worth it?

I was tempted to make this a very short chapter — "How To Book Airlines: Don't!" After all, a lot of home-based travel agents make very nice livings and never deal with air-only (as it is referred to in the trade). If these agents do sell airline tickets, it is always as part of a "package" such as a tour or cruise. That way, they avoid the considerable hassles of dealing with airline tickets, leaving the air details to the tour operator or cruise line.

Selling airline tickets — never a big money-maker in the first place — has become a far less attractive proposition for the home-based agent in recent years. Here are some of the reasons why:

Airline tickets pay no commission

Yes, you heard right. In 1995, the airlines announced that they were paying travel agents too much to book tickets, so they instituted "caps" — a maximum commission that would be paid regardless of the face value of the ticket. The highest commission paid became $50 per ticket. For many storefront agencies that made issuing a ticket a money-losing proposition. Many instituted per-ticket fees to cover their costs.

For a while, commission caps gave home-based agents something of a competitive edge, since their overhead was lower. On the other hand, commission caps made all airfares cheap fares and were yet another reason for home-based agents to specialize in more lucrative forms of travel.

As if caps weren't bad enough, starting in 1997 the major U.S. airlines began to cut commissions from the then industry standard 10% to 8%, then to 5%. Only a very few airlines paid more than 5%, most of them foreign carriers. The handwriting was most definitely on the wall and many observers began predicting the imminent demise of commission on air. Many travel agents simply refused to believe it could happen.

But the airlines had become obsessed with squeezing every nickel and dime out of the distribution system. Eventually, the axe fell. On May 15, 2002, the airlines ended commissions once and for all, forcing virtually every storefront agency to implement transaction fees. In fact, a great many storefront agencies went out of business altogether, while some just stopped selling air and reinvented themselves. Interestingly, a great many of the travel agents thrown out of work at this time became home-based agents!

A few airlines, mostly low-fare airlines with a limited number of routes and a few foreign airlines that you may never have occasion to book, still pay modest commissions, a phenomenon I will discuss a little later.

Airfare is a commodity

A commodity is any product that is so generic that the major consideration in the buying decision is price. Think about the way you buy gas. Given your druthers, my guess is you choose to fill up at the cheapest pump. Sugar and salt are other examples of the same phenomenon.

In air travel, people have decided that there is so little difference between one cramped coach seat and another that they buy tickets almost exclusively on the basis of price. Even if they are shelling out big bucks to fly in business or first class, they still want the cheapest business or first class ticket they can get. Just about the only consideration that can persuade people to pay more for a ticket is frequent flyer miles and in that instance, more often than not, they are not paying for the ticket themselves.

On top of this, many people have become almost pathological about hunting down the best deal on an airline ticket. I personally know professionals who bill hundreds of dollars an hour for their time who will spend hours on the Internet and calling around to travel agents trying to save ten bucks on an airline ticket. Crazy, but it happens.

NOTE!

Airline tickets are complicated

Even if you have no travel industry experience, you've probably noticed that just about every seat on an airline flight seems to have been sold at a different fare. This is due to the fine art of "yield management," and the airlines have gotten so good at it that airfares and the codes, rules, and regulations associated with them have become bizarrely complex. It takes a special talent and years of experience to get really good at playing the airfare game.

Another complicating factor in dealing with airline tickets is the maddening habit people have of changing their minds. If you sell a honeymoon trip or a summer vacation, chances are the people you sold it to will go where they said they would when they said they would. But air-only customers, especially if they're business travelers, will change, alter, and cancel trips with gusto. They'll decide they can't leave early in the morning after all or that they absolutely have to fly into Newark instead of New York's La Guardia airport. On and on it goes. Of course, all these changes can be accommodated and it's the travel agent's job to do so, which would be all right if you got paid for it. But it is actually very easy to lose money every time a customer asks for a change, for reasons that will become clearer as you read on.

Airline tickets are unforgiving

In this era of e-tickets, booking occurs instantly. And once that ticket is booked, there's no turning back. Changed your mind? Want a refund? As they say in New York, fuhgeddaboutit! Only the most expensive, "unrestricted" fares are refundable, and few people buy those. Most tickets can be changed to different dates — at a substantial penalty. A $92 ticket can have a $100 change fee! To add insult to injury (from the traveler's perspective), most travel agencies will charge them another fee to handle the change. It's no wonder many travel agents are turning their back on air.

The good news, as I've already mentioned, is that you can make a very good living while avoiding air-only entirely. As you read the succeeding chapters, I think you'll be pleased to see that other travel products offer few of the hassles and pitfalls associated with air-only. But this chapter is about booking airline tickets, so let us continue.

Airline tickets can be dangerous to your wealth

Airline tickets have a way of attracting con artists. Here's a sad tale that was reported in the trade press. A relatively new home-based agent got a call from a gentleman out of state. He wanted to buy a bunch of first-class tickets for flights leaving in a day or so. "My web site's really working," thought the excited novice agent. She booked the tickets on the GDS, the credit card was approved, and them — BAM! — the host agency was hit with a debit memo from the airline. Seems the credit card wasn't so good after all.

Many people think an approval code means everything's a-okay and that, should things prove otherwise, they are protected. Not so. An approval code merely tells you that at the time the sale is processed the card hasn't been reported stolen and that there is sufficient credit in the account to cover the purchase.

The host agency was stuck with a $24,000 bill, which was most likely passed along to the agent. I don't mean to scare you with this story. (Oh, all right, maybe just a little.) The point is, airline tickets require a heightened level of vigilance. Be very wary of calls like the one this agent received. Think about it: why would a high roller from out of state be calling a brand-new home-based agent he'd never laid eyes on for very expensive first-class tickets?

To automate or not

Although it is still possible to book and sell at least some airline tickets without using a global distribution system, or GDS, it is becoming increasingly difficult, especially when it comes to the garden-variety, cheapest-fare-possible, short-haul, domestic airline ticket. Most host agencies will require that you book your airline tickets through a GDS or not at all. To add another layer of complexity for the novice, you will hear the "old" term CRS (for computerized reservation system) used to refer to the GDS.

On the other hand, automating is not the hassle that it once was for agents operating outside the confines of a storefront agency. All of the

← NOTE

Think! But What To Say??

MAKE SURE The Card Belongs To That Person!

major GDS providers — Sabre, Galileo (Apollo), Worldspan, Amadeus — offer an easy-to-install program of some sort that can be used by a home-based agent in conjunction with his or her host agency. From the home computer, the home-based agent either dials directly into a mainframe computer or logs onto a web site on the Internet to access the GDS.

Dial-up systems are fast giving way to web-based interfaces and may be entirely obsolete by the time you read this. I recommend getting a web-based system because of the flexibility it provides. If you can access the GDS over the Internet, you can make a booking while sitting with your client in Starbucks, sipping a latte, and using its wireless access; you can't do that with a dial-up. In the case of Internet interfaces, the agent may not need special software on his or her home computer. Any tickets the agent generates in this fashion are handled just as if the agent were working at the host agency's storefront location.

Typically, the home-based agent shoulders the cost of these systems. There will be a charge for the software (if any), usually several hundred dollars; $395 is a fairly typical figure. Then there will be hourly or monthly access fees. Hourly fees tend to be in the $6 to $7 range; monthly fees range from $35 to $75. Even host agencies that use a strictly web interface will likely charge their agents for using it, although some may not. Sometimes access fees are bundled into a flat monthly fee of up to several hundred dollars that covers all the services provided by the host agency. There are many variations on this theme, as you can see, so if you are intent on automating be prepared to shop carefully and at some length for the right deal. Be especially alert for host agencies that lower or eliminate access fees as the number of bookings increases. If you are an experienced agent with a following, this can be a very attractive deal.

The decision to automate or not will inevitably be influenced by your level of experience. Those who have mastered a GDS will be less intimidated than those who are beginners to the industry. Unfortunately, many beginners believe that having a GDS is an absolute "must." That's probably because so many host agencies selling this type of home-based business opportunity require that their outside agents purchase GDS software. So if you're new to the industry, please understand that you do not need to have a GDS to participate in the travel distribution system. That bears repeating, so let me say it again.

You do not need to have a GDS to participate in the travel distribution system.

Even so, beginners may want to consider the possibility of automating — at least at some point. The GDSs are not simply for booking airlines. They can be used to book an ever-increasing variety of other travel products. After an initial investment of time and effort to learn how they work, they can make your life a lot easier.

The GDSs are also a vast and expanding source of general travel industry information. Looked at simply as an informational resource, a GDS system becomes a very reasonable investment for the full-time professional. Still, an expense is an expense, and it will take some time and a certain number of bookings each month to make a GDS pay its own way. If you pay $400 for the software and $50 a month for access, that adds up to a first-year investment of $1,000. Not bad for a system that puts you on an even footing (at least in theory) with every other travel agent in the country. But are you likely to book enough commissionable product on a GDS to pay off that investment? If you're a beginner, the chances are no, at least not the first year. If you are considering automation, do the businesslike thing and figure out what you'll have to do to break even. Some of the data you need will come from your potential host agency. Other things, like how many tickets you'll sell each month, must be estimated. Be conservative and run the numbers. It will prove an interesting exercise.

Another consideration is the cost of learning the system. GDS systems are a bit like a foreign language, some people pick them up faster than others. If you are considering automation and you are new to the business, shop carefully for a host agency that provides good training at a fair price. (It won't be "free" even if it looks that way; the cost is always built in somehow.) Otherwise, consider taking formal training classes at a travel school.

If you do decide to automate, you will find *The Travel Agent's Complete Desk Reference* an extremely helpful companion. It contains cross-referenced sections on airline and airport locator codes, as well as other codes used by the GDSs. If you purchased this book as part of my home study course, you already have it. If not, you can order it at:
http://www.HomeTravelAgency.com/deskref.html

Which GDS?

Another point to consider is that your choice of a host agency will limit your choice of a GDS. Some hosts offer more than one option, but most use just one solution. Likewise, your choice of a GDS will limit your choice of hosts. If you are an experienced Sabre agent or have learned Apollo (a Galileo product) in travel school, then you will most likely want to affiliate with a Sabre or Apollo agency as the case may be.

Again, there are four major GDS systems — Amadeus, Galileo, Sabre, and Worldspan. All of them offer at least one dial-up or Internet option that can be used by home-based agents. All of them operate pretty much the same. And once you learn one of them, you should be able to pick up another without too much difficulty. Some agents swear that one system is the best and other agents are equally enthusiastic about another system. Although I'm sure that the marketing folks with the various GDS companies would disagree, it probably doesn't make much difference which one you wind up using, as long as you are using it in conjunction with a host agency that you enjoy working with and that gives you a good deal on the commission split. Sabre enjoys about 43% market share, so if you are conversant in Sabre, you have more host agencies from which to choose.

Automation alternatives

An increasing number of travel suppliers, including a few airlines, are creating free, web-based booking tools that allow travel agents to book online. Some allow the agent to earn a commission, typically five percent.

Others allow booking but do not pay commission, which means the agent would have to charge the customer a fee to make any money on the deal. The airlines that provide this functionality seem to have three things in common:

- They are low-fare, regional airlines that presumably recognize the value of using travel agents to drive market share.
- They do not participate in any of the GDSs.
- They require participating agents to have a valid industry identifier. Not every airline will accept every industry identifier; some are quite choosy in fact.

The need for an industry identifier leaves you with two basic options: Use your host agency's IATA number or get your own unique industry identifying number as explained in *How to Get Your Own IATA Number*. It may be that your host agency will not permit you to use their number in this fashion or, if they do, you may never see a commission on the theory that the host agency simply does not have the time or the resources to track bookings made this way. Of course, there is nothing to stop you from working with a host agency and also having your own number.

Since these airlines have limited route systems and low fares, the earning potential is limited. Still, it is possible that an agent in the right location, with the right specialty, could use one of these booking engines and enjoy a steady, if small, additional stream of income. Among the U.S. airlines that offer this capability are Spirit, AirTran, Frontier (no commission), and USA3000. Canadian airlines with online travel agent booking include CanJet, CMA, and WestJet. This list may — in fact, probably will — change. A number of European low-fare airlines also allow travel agent bookings on their sites.

Another alternative to a GDS is to use the branded booking engine provided by various host agencies, most notably the referral agencies. There is typically no commission to be earned by booking air on these systems, although you may be able to pick up the odd buck. However, if you have a mechanism for collecting fees, it would at least allow you to service your customers. Just be aware that low fare searches on these systems may not be as robust as on a full-fledged GDS.

A final word on automating

As you can see, there are a great many variables and many pros and cons to automating. The automation decision is a very personal one and I cannot make it for you. It is also well outside the scope of this course to teach you how to use a GDS. But I can give you some advice. Just remember that it reflects my personal opinions and biases and so should be taken with a grain of salt.

- *If you have no prior experience.* Wait. Try the alternate strategies for booking air (outlined in this chapter) to avoid getting a GDS until you know, first, that the travel business is for you and, second, that the investment in a GDS makes financial sense.
- *If you have experience* (i.e. you have worked in an agency

and know a GDS language or have been trained in a travel school). You still might want to wait. In fact, many experienced agents go the home-based route to avoid air-only and concentrate on high-margin business that can be handled without using a GDS.

Booking airlines with a GDS

If you use a GDS, you can book a lot of airlines, although by no means all. Many low-fare airlines popular with your customers have opted out of the GDS systems altogether. If you are not using a GDS, your booking options are considerably reduced. Because of this essential difference, I have divided the discussion of booking airlines into two sections.

In the first section I will review booking airlines via a GDS, using the five-step process outlined in *Chapter 11: The Basics of Booking.* Then I will discuss the ways in which non-automated home-based agents can still sell (and profit from) airline tickets. Regardless of your situation, I encourage you to read both sections, because each will have something of interest to you. The first section, lays out some basic principles of dealing with your customers that have universal relevance. The second section, lays out strategies that all home-based agents can use, automated or not. Finally, by reading both sections you will be in a better position to decide what place selling airline tickets will have in *your* travel business — if any.

Gathering information

Automated or not, the process of gathering information from your customer about a potential airline booking is pretty much the same. The key things you need to know at this time are:

- *The passengers' names.* Don't laugh. You may know who the client is, but do you know the names of his wife and two kids who will also be going on the trip? The airline will want to know. And, because of increased security at all airports, it's important that the name on the ticket exactly matches the name on the passenger's passport, driver's license, or other form of photo ID. People have been denied boarding when the name on the ticket didn't tally with the name on the ID they produced at check-in. This can be an especially thorny problem for women who have a ticket in their married name and a passport in their maiden name.
- *Destination.* This is pretty self-explanatory. Just make sure you don't confuse Portland, Oregon, with Portland, Maine.
- *Dates and times.* This is not so self-explanatory. You not only need to know that the client wants to fly on the fifth, but you also need to know at what time she wants to go. She may want to get there for lunch or she may not want to leave until after work. Don't automatically assume that people will vol-

(Text continues on page 256.)

Notes on the Client Request Form

The *Client Request Form* is designed to be used when you are first talking with a client and gathering basic information about his travel needs. It is designed primarily for air travel, but can be used to gather information about any form of travel.

Most of this form is self-explanatory. Here are some notes on items that may need clarification:

- *Date & Time.* Don't forget to find out *what time* the client wants to fly. Will he leave first thing in the morning or after work? Does she need to be at her destination by a certain time?
- *Special Instructions.* Note any special requests the client may have. Also, record any parameters the client has given you in making the booking. For example, "Schedule more important than price," or "Will fly Delta if American is not available."
- *Age.* A passenger's age is important only when a child, youth, or senior fare is involved.
- *FF#s.* Frequent flyer numbers are useful to have because you can enter them into the record when making a booking with the airline.
- *Hotels/Rental Cars.* Don't forget to ask the client about hotels and rental cars. These are easy add-on sales.
- *Other Information.* Use this space for passport numbers of those traveling overseas, notes on tours or cruises — or anything else that doesn't fit elsewhere. A discussion on the kind of information you will need to gather from tour and cruise customers will be found in *Chapters 15* and *16*.
- *Credit Card.* It's not always absolutely necessary to have this information now, but it can be helpful. For example, you will only be able to hold a hotel room for a client's late arrival by giving the reservationist a credit card number.

Some of this information can also be entered into the *Client Profile Form* (see *Chapter 20*) for future reference.

Client Request Form

Client: _____   Phone: _____
Address: _____
Fax: _____   Email: _____

Booking Information

Destination(s): _____   Preferred Airline(s): _____

Departure Date & Time: _____   Return Date & Time: _____

Preferences: ❑ Window   ❑ Aisle   ❑ Smoking   ❑ Spec. Meals _____
❑ First   ❑ Business   ❑ Coach   ❑ Other _____

Special Instructions:

Passengers

Last Name	First Name	Age	FF#s

Hotels? Rental Cars?

Other Information

Payment Information

Credit Card #: _____   Exp.: _____
Name on Card: _____
Billing Address & Phone: _____

unteer this information. Frequently, when they ask you to look into getting them a ticket to, say, San Francisco, leaving on the fifth and returning on the fourteenth, they are just shopping for fares. So it never occurs to them to mention that if they do go, they'll want the evening flight. (Remember that when a flight leaves can affect the fare.)

- **Client preferences.** Does the client have a preferred airline? Is he willing to trade convenience for a lower fare? How flexible are the dates? If business class is full, will she fly coach?
- **Which airlines serve your local airport.** Again, please hold the laughter. There may be airlines flying out of your area that you've never heard of or low-cost or charter airlines that won't show up on a GDS. Next time you're at the airport, stroll around and check out all the airlines. If you can get hold of a printed schedule (increasingly rare these days) do so. At a minimum, try to get hold of a route map, which is often available in the airline's in-flight magazine or on its web site.

While it's not always necessary to have the following information, it's nice to know:

- **Frequent flyer numbers.** At this early stage, you may not need to know this information. Once you have settled on a particular itinerary, however, it's nice to be able to include the client's frequent flyer number with the booking. If the customer isn't a member of the airline's frequent flyer program, you can usually enroll them at the time of the booking.
- **Seating preference.** Window or aisle, front of the cabin or rear. It can make a difference to many clients.
- **Meal preference.** Another thoughtful touch that can win you brownie points with clients, if they are flying on one of the dwindling number of flights that offer food.

Your goal in gathering this initial information is to have enough data to be able to research available flights and fares and make an actual reservation (to lock in specific flights, seats, and fares). This will not always be possible but it is the ideal.

Note: In *Chapter 20: Qualifying*, you will find a *Client Profile Form* on which you can begin to compile dossiers on your customers. You can use the form to record some of the information mentioned here. So for the next booking you won't have to ask again. This will not only make you more efficient but will enhance the client's opinion of your professionalism.

Misteaks can kill you (how to avoid them)

Because they involve so many different elements, airline bookings are prone to errors. Making a mistake in a booking is not only embarrassing, it can cost you money. The best insurance against making costly errors is to have a system that lets you gather and transmit information completely and accurately. A good system will have checkpoints built into it to insure that information is checked and double-checked for accuracy.

Your campaign for accuracy begins the minute you get a request from a client. All too often, the beginner will gather incomplete information, discover the gaps when researching the booking, and have to get back to the client to fill in the holes. (This kind of embarrassment is easy to avoid.)

The *Client Request Form* on page 255 lets you capture the key information you need from your client to do your job quickly and efficiently. It is designed to be used with the client's initial request for any travel product — airline ticket, cruise, or tour. You can use it as is or adapt it to suit your preferences.

Researching available flights Talk To Ann

Your next step is to find out what flights go where the customer wants to go, when the customer wants to go there, at the price the customer wants to pay, which in most cases will be the lowest possible fare. This is where the automated and non-automated home-based agent part company.

The agent with a GDS types in a few cryptic commands (every GDS does it a little differently) and a theoretically complete list of available flights, listed in ascending order of price, appears on the screen. I say theoretically because, as I mentioned earlier, not all airlines play ball with the GDSs. Then again, some airlines reserve their very best fares for bookings made directly on their web sites, although there is an increasing trend to make these fares available to GDS users. The point is, if you want to perform a truly comprehensive search, you will have to look beyond the GDS. Here are some options, some of which will prove useful even if you are booking on your GDS.

Airline web sites

Low-fare and other non-participating airlines can be researched via the Internet. In the process, you might find that one of your local low-fare airlines offers online booking capability for travel agents. Your host agency may already have an account, but there's nothing unethical (to my way of thinking, at least) about establishing your own direct relationship if you qualify. You could also check the web sites of major airlines for web specials, but this can be time-consuming. As a practical matter, travel agents must limit their research time because the income they receive from service fees does not justify lengthy searches.

Destinations Unlimited

This site, located at http://www.air-fare.com, has quickly become one of my favorites. It monitors fares to and from 50 large United States markets on a daily basis and calls out fare cuts of more than 20%, so if you log on regularly you can keep on top of good deals from your market.

Click on the city that interests you and you will find up-to-date information on the fares to all the other cities covered. For each destination, the system displays up to eight major fare options, from the lowest standard excursion (the most restricted fare), to the lowest refundable fare (the kind business travelers most often use), to the lowest regular first class. For each fare, you learn the airlines offering it and the class in which you must book, along with the most important restrictions associated with the fare. With this information, it will be easy to find the fare in a GDS.

The system is not ideal (oddly Orlando, Florida, the most popular leisure destination in the country, is not listed), but if you are located in or near one of the 50 markets Destinations Unlimited covers, you will find the site invaluable.

ITA Software's QPX

ITA Software is a tremendous innovator in the arcane field of searching airline schedules and fares. To show off their expertise, they have made their QPX product available free of charge to all comers on the Internet at www.itasoftware.com. It has no booking capabilities, but it is a terrific research tool.

QPX lets you research one-way, roundtrip, and multi-segment fares. There's even an option that lets you search a 30-day period for the lowest fare. The results are broken out in a number of ways: by price, by the number of stops (none, one, or two), by flight time, and by airport, if there is more than one serving the area. This is a great way of zeroing in on the right combination of price and convenience. The system also provides helpful "Warnings" such as whether a given option involves using prop planes or requires an overnight stay between flights. You can find the exact fare codes for each flight segment, although not a complete explanation of the fare rules themselves.

The real beauty of the ITA system, in my opinion, is that it can search for alternative flights at other airports, up to 300 miles distant from the ones you specify. This feature can save lots of time if you want to check fares from various airports; many agents with GDS capability use ITA for precisely this time-saving feature. Once they locate the right itinerary, they switch to their GDS to pull it up and book it.

Consolidators

Don't overlook consolidators when you are researching long-haul flights. If your client can live with the restrictions that often come with consolidator tickets, this can be a very attractive option. Some consolidators have online search and booking capabilities, making the process even easier. I discuss consolidators in some detail a little later.

Making the sale

At this point in the sales process, you should be sitting in front of your GDS. You can log on earlier, of course, but if you haven't done so already you should now. Ideally, you will be talking with your client, either in person or on the phone, as you make the sale. Time was when you could make a "passive booking," that is *reserve* a ticket now and *ticket* it later, usually within 24 hours, giving you a certain amount of leeway to check back with an absent client. That's not quite as true now. With some airlines reserving and ticketing are one and the same thing, that is they happen instantaneously and that fare is nonrefundable; other airlines give you some wiggle room, usually on the same calendar day. Keeping track of which airline has which policy adds a level of complexity that can drive you nuts; it's far better to avoid it altogether by having the client in front of you and making the reservation, in its final form, in "real time," as it were.

So, with both the client and the GDS in front of you, begin constructing a PNR (passenger name record) in the GDS. Whatever information you haven't already gathered from the client you will gather now.

Before reaching any final decisions, you need to review the following points with your client:

- **The dates and times of flights.** If you have researched more than one possibility, you may want to include details like whether dinner is served. That may help the client choose among alternatives.

- **The fare.** If several people are going on the same trip, quote the fares individually and for the entire group. If there are several fares, explain the tradeoffs. For example, a cheaper fare might mean an earlier departure, more stops en route, or a change of plane.

- **If the fare is nonrefundable** (most are), make sure you impress this fact upon the client. It is also a good idea to make a note to the effect that you informed the client of this fact.

- **If any charges or fees will result** from changes to the ticket once booked, this, too, should be impressed upon the client.

What's the best flight for the client?

The exact flight you eventually book for each individual client will depend on a number of interrelated variables. Some will be more important than others, depending on circumstances. It is your job as the client's agent to weigh the variables and guide the client to the best choice.

In the vast majority of cases, the price of the ticket will be the number one criterion when it comes to choosing straight air travel, especially when an international flight is involved. If you can find a ticket that's $5 less than anything a rival travel agent is quoting, you'll be a hero. This tendency towards penny-pinching holds true even among high rollers. Who wants to pay $6,000 for a first-class ticket when it can be had for $5,899? However, other factors sometimes are as important as — even more important than — price.

- **The airline.** Many people have been seduced by frequent flyer programs into putting all their travel eggs into one airborne basket. Other people have found the service and reliability of one airline to be superior to all others and will go out of their way to use it when at all possible. Some customers I've had have insisted on flying with a US carrier on their overseas flights.

- **The schedule.** Flight times can sometimes be an overriding factor. If the client can save three hours or avoid a layover by paying a bit more or flying a different airline, he might opt to do just that.

Making the booking and confirming with the client

Once you have constructed the itinerary in the GDS and the client has agreed that everything is to his or her liking and understanding, you have two choices. You can type the letter "e" and "Enter" to make the booking or type the letter "i" (for ignore) and "Enter" to cancel the booking. (At this writing, this is standard across all major GDSs.) If you cancel at this point, the airline inventory that was being held for you while you were building the PNR will be released for sale to someone else. If you and the client decide to cancel, you probably should print out the PNR before you do; that way, you and your client will have a record of the booking that might have been. Make sure that the client understands that the same fare might not be available if you try to book later; in fact, the flight might be sold out. No fare is guaranteed until the ticket has been paid for.

If you do it this way (that is, in the presence of the client and with the client's full approval), once you have entered the client's payment details and you hit "e" and "Enter," the booking will be "done deal" in the eyes of the client. Everyone's happy and you've made your life considerably easier.

Today, virtually all bookings are electronic, that is to say there will be no paper tickets. If, for some reason, your client wants or needs a paper ticket, consult with your host agency on the appropriate procedure. At a minimum, you will need to print out a basic itinerary for your client, something he or she can take to the airport with flight number and times on it. This is especially true in a case where you have not used a GDS, for example, when making a booking on your client's behalf on an airline web site. Many GDS systems and/or add-on software products have the ability to generate nice looking itineraries with your letterhead and logo. If you have these capabilities, by all means use them.

Getting paid

I've already said that airlines don't pay commissions. Allow me to amend that slightly. Airlines don't pay "base commissions." That is, they don't pay out commissions on a per ticket basis. Airlines will, however, pay travel agencies a commission based on volume; sell enough tickets in a year, get some money. It is possible that your host agency may qualify for these backend commissions from at least some airlines. If so, it's also possible that your host might cut you in, although that's doubtful.

To make up for the lack of commissions, just about every travel agency charges "transaction fees" of anywhere from $10 to $35 (or more!) to clients purchasing airline tickets. Some agents charge fees regardless of the circumstances. Others will waive the fee if the client books other things at the same time, on the theory that the commissions from these "add-ons" will compensate them for the hassle of generating the airline ticket. If your host agency does air, I would be very surprised if it does not add on a fee.

(If you charge a transaction or service fee, you have the problem of collecting it.) Most people will want to pay for their airline ticket with a credit card. That's not a problem because the credit card information is passed on to the airline, which does the actual charging. But the airline will not include your fee in their charge. Your host agency will probably allow (or require) you to charge a fee through their merchant account. In this case, your host agency will charge you something for providing this service or split the fee with you in some predetermined fashion.

If you are not funneling the booking through a host agency, collecting a fee becomes something of a problem. There are a number of options, which I discussed in *Chapter 9: Getting Serious*. As you can see by reviewing that discussion, charging fees creates a number of problems, since none of these alternatives is ideal.

There are a number of other ways to make money selling airline tickets that don't involve using a host agency and/or a GDS. Some of them involve collecting fees, some do not. (Some allow you to effectively set your own commission and collect it upfront from the client at the time of the sale.) These strategies are discussed in the next section and will be of interest to all travel agents, including those working with a GDS and a host agency.

Booking airlines without a GDS

Now let's turn our attention to the options available to home-based agents who do not work with an ARC-accredited host agency but who want to sell at least some airline tickets, at least under certain conditions. The strategies described in this section, by the way, can also be used by agents who do work with an ARC host, even those who use a GDS for most of their airline bookings. None of them will work in all situations; in fact, some of them are very specific. Think of them as a tool kit that you can dip into as the need arises. Feel free to use them when the spirit moves you or the situation dictates.

- **Don't.** Option one is simply to swear off dealing with airline tickets. Perhaps that admonishment doesn't belong in a section called "Booking airlines without a GDS," but I couldn't resist reminding you one more time that you do, in fact, have this option.

- **Book air with packages.** Another option is to sell an airline ticket only when you can sell something else along with it, such as a hotel booking, a rental car, or both. This is what is known in the business as a "package. Tours and packages are discussed in greater detail in *Chapter 15*. For now, just be aware that many airlines have separate wholesale operations that will deal with home-based agents, either directly or as outside sales reps for a host agency, when the agent is booking one of their air-hotel-rental car combos. The same thing goes for air that is booked through a cruise line as part of its package. So in other words, the airline that says it doesn't sell airline tickets to non-ARC agents actually does in this roundabout fashion. Go figure.

This option creates some practical problems, since packages will not be available to all destinations from all airlines. However, if you regularly sell vacation trips to popular destinations like Las Vegas, Orlando, the Colorado Rockies, Hawaii, and so forth, this option should work quite well for you.

- ■ ***Book online and get a commission, Part I.*** You might also decide to sell airlines that let you book on their web sites and earn a commission. Often these sites will let you book vacation packages as well as straight air. As I mentioned earlier, the few sites that offer this capability are typically low-fare airlines with limited route structures.

- ■ ***Book online and get a commission, Part II.*** There are actually web sites owned by wholesalers that allow you, as a non-ARC agency, to book air and earn a modest commission. One such site is Oneminutebooking.com, which at press time was paying a 3% commission for airline tickets (15% on tours) booked on its site. Not every airline is available, but the selection is fairly decent. To sign up, you will need to get an IATA number as described in *How to Get Your Own IATA Number*. Sites like this are popping up all the time. Unfortunately, locating them is difficult. The best solution is to monitor the trade press and network through a professional organization such as the Outside Sales Support Network (OSSN).

- ■ ***Become an affiliate.*** Another possible strategy is to become an affiliate of one (or all!) of the popular online booking sites and then refer your airline shoppers to them. Affiliate programs work through coded hyperlinks. When someone visits a site via a link that has your code embedded in it, the site makes a note of that fact and when the visitor makes a purchase (usually within a defined period of time), you are credited with a modest commission. It is conceivable that you could prepare a form email letter that says something to the effect of "I don't book airline tickets, but the following online sites offer excellent prices and I suggest you check them out." Then provide a list of sites along with hyperlinks containing your affiliate ID code. It's unlikely you will see significant income from this strategy, but once again, you have provided a service and avoided wasting time on low-payback, high-hassle business.

- ■ ***Book online and charge a fee.*** Another option is to use your superior knowledge of airline fares and the Internet to do your customers' fare shopping for them. This is providing a service and as such demands that you charge a service fee.

- *Find a partner.* Be on the lookout for wholesalers that are offering innovative solutions for travel agents. One such is Leisure Resource (www.LeisureResource.com; 800-729-9051), which has made a specialty of helping agents book the many low-fare airlines that are popping up like mushrooms in the deregulated European airline environment. Leisure Resource makes the booking, adds a $45 fee, processes the client's credit card, and pays the agent a 12% commission. If you are involved in selling independent travel in Europe, this could be a terrific resource for you.

- *Refer it elsewhere.* You may also want to consider the benefits of referring queries for airline tickets to your host agency, where an inside agent can handle the request and make the booking directly on the GDS. It's extremely unlikely you will realize any income from this approach, but your investment of time is minimal and you have provided a service to a client from whom you are presumably earning money on other bookings. If your host agency does not want you to refer business like this, you still have some options. You could find another agency, a local one perhaps, that would like to get your airline referrals. Who knows, maybe they'd pay you a modest bird-dogging fee (although I doubt it). One possible problem in an arrangement like this is that the local agency would be tempted to "poach" your customers, selling them cruises and tours as well as cheap airfare.

- *Become a referral agent.* Another possibility would be to pay $149 to $495 to join one of the so-called "referral agencies" just so you could pass out business cards with a PIN number to cheap airfare shoppers. Again, there's no money involved (at least not very often), but you've avoided wasting your time. With the referral agencies, there is less chance of your customers being poached because, as far as I've been able to tell, the referral agencies don't actively market to consumers, preferring to rely on their network of outside agents to drive business to the inside sales staff. Of course, your customer is free to call the 800 number the next time she wants to take a cruise. In this case, you would most likely receive a 5% commission; you might find this fair enough considering you did none of the work.

If you do decide to join a referral agency, I would recommend choosing one that provides you with a branded web site at no additional cost. That way, you can have customers book their air online by themselves — something that a lot of people actually appear to enjoy doing! If you have some means of driving traffic to this site (your own web site, for example), this can become a small but steady income stream.

The downside of joining a referral agency is that it will take a good long while to earn back your investment on the commissions you'll earn;

in fact, that may never happen! It's really more a matter of convenience than anything else; you are politely avoiding spending time with low-level prospects. Of course you can also recruit other agents for the referral agency, in which case you can actually make some money. It may seem counterintuitive to do this but the people who are most likely to consider becoming referral agents are the least likely to become your best customers anyway. As far as them competing with you, I wouldn't worry, since most referral agents sell travel only to themselves and use their referral agent ID card in the hope of receiving discounts. If you discover you have a friend or acquaintance who is constantly asking for price quotes but never buying, you may have a prospect for a referral agency.

Finally, as I've noted elsewhere, referral agencies are controversial and you may very well decide against this option on principle. Even if you don't dismiss the possibility of becoming a referral agent out of hand, I would still advise you think about it long and hard before taking the plunge. Carefully weigh the pros and cons before making your decision. You'll probably want to have at least several months of travel marketing experience under your belt before you even consider this option.

Consolidators

One of the best ways to make a decent commission selling airline tickets is to deal in consolidator tickets. This option will be attractive to all home-based agents, but especially to those who are not automated, because you don't need a GDS and there aren't any cumbersome workarounds to deal with. However, consolidator tickets have their own drawbacks and you must take care to protect both yourself and your client when dealing in this lucrative market.

In simple terms, a consolidator is someone who buys wholesale and sells below retail. In this case, the commodity being purchased is airplane seats. Consolidators "buy" large blocks of seats from the airlines at steep discounts. Then they turn around and sell those seats at a price that is well below the "face value" of a ticket but still high enough to earn them a profit. Most specialize to some extent; in other words, there are very few consolidators that can get you a ticket to every possible destination.

We are seeing more consolidation on domestic flights, but this is still primarily an international phenomenon. Competition is stiffer on international runs and some of the smaller foreign carriers are willing to be quite aggressive in their discount pricing to consolidators. When consolidator tickets are available on domestic flights, it is usually on long haul routes (especially to Hawaii).

Not all consolidator tickets are created equal. Some will be on regular, scheduled airlines, and the consolidator should be able to tell you which one before you make a commitment. Others will be on charter flights. Some "consolidators" are actually tour operators and wholesalers who are selling excess inventory of planes they have chartered to accommodate their tour customers. This may be okay by your customer or not. Remember that when the chartered plane has a mechanical malfunction, the passenger may be stuck until it's fixed. If they are flying on a regularly scheduled airline, there is usually a backup plane available somewhere. It could mean the difference of a delay of several hours and several days.

The basic attraction of a consolidator is price: Consolidator fares are (or should be!) lower than anything you can get directly from the airlines. I say "should be" because some surveys have revealed consolidators selling "discount" tickets at a higher price than the cheapest excursion fare. The old warning, "Buyer beware," applies in this area as much as it does in others — and maybe more so. Some consolidators deal only with travel agents, while others sell only to the public, and still others sell to both. It might be reasonable to assume that consolidators that sell just to agents will have better prices than those that sell to the public; but you should comparison shop anyway. Even if a consolidator sells directly to the public, you may be able to buy a ticket from that consolidator and resell it to your client at a higher price, while still offering your client a good deal.

Another, less frequent, reason for using consolidators is availability. It may be that a consolidator has the only tickets left for a particular destination during a particular time frame. It is also unfortunately true that a consolidator cannot always get you tickets to where your customer wants to go, when she wants to go there.

Dealing with consolidators

Before you start shopping for consolidator fares, you must know what the going rate is for the destination under consideration. Using one of the online booking engines will give you a good idea. You can also call a few of the airlines that fly there to inquire about fares.

Consolidators will quote fares in one of two ways, and it's important to be very clear on which method is being used before you make an embarrassing mistake. Some consolidators quote "net" fares only. In this case you would mark up the cost of the ticket to your client. If the ticket cost, say, $700, you would write out a check for $700 to the consolidator, collect a check for, say, $800 from the client and bank the difference. The client, by the way, will not know what you paid for the ticket. On the ticket, the space for the fare will either contain the full "retail" fare or contain only the notation, "Bulk," meaning the consolidator paid a bulk (i.e. discounted) rate for the ticket.

With net fares, you are free to charge your client whatever you feel is a fair price for both the ticket and your services in obtaining it. As a practical matter, however, you will probably not want to charge more than the lowest fare available directly from the airlines. That's just smart business. On the other hand, you might want to pass the ticket along at cost or at a very modest markup to a friend or family member.

Some consolidators, on the other hand, quote commissionable fares. That means that the quoted fare includes a commission for the agent and you will receive a check from the consolidator for your commission. Imagine that, a commission for selling an airline ticket! Typical commissions are 10%. But commissions of 12% and 15% are not uncommon, and some consolidators advertise commissions of "up to 27%." Obviously, in these cases, the markup is fixed, unless you choose to rebate a portion of your commission to the client. You will also have to wait (in most cases) for your check and may have to remind "forgetful" consolidators that they owe you money. I would advise working exclusively with net fares unless there is no alternative.

Most consolidators prefer to operate on a "cash and carry" basis. They will probably accept your check but will not be too happy about credit cards. All things being equal, cash is probably the easiest way to deal with consolidators. As long as the consolidator is on the up and up, it's quick, it's clean, and it gets your money into the bank quickly.

Many clients, however, prefer to use credit cards. They are more convenient, and many people have learned that they can stop payment on a charge if they feel ripped off in any way. Many consolidators who quote net fares will work with you if your client wants to use plastic. You decide the price you want to charge for the ticket, then add a "service charge," typically 3% or 4%, to cover the consolidator's costs in processing the charge. Let's say the consolidator's net fare is $900. You decide to charge your client $1,000. With a 3% service charge, the total cost to the client would be $1,030, which would be the amount charged to his credit card. The consolidator would then give you a check for $100. Remember, too, that credit cards give your client some protection in case of default on the part of the consolidator. If, on the other hand, the consolidator won't accept plastic and the customer demands it, you may not be able to provide a consolidator ticket.

Consolidators are located all over the country. Generally speaking, the location of a consolidator is not an impediment to doing business. You can live in New York and get tickets from a consolidator in Los Angeles. It's all handled on the phone and through the mail. For my part, I prefer to deal with consolidators whose offices I can get to in person. That way, at least, if something goes wrong, I have a desk I can pound on and demand satisfaction. Of course, I live near New York and many consolidators are close at hand. If you live in a smaller city you may have no choice but to deal with consolidators on a long-distance basis. Eventually, you will find one or two consolidators with whom you feel comfortable and whatever concerns you have at the outset will subside.

Most consolidator tickets are sold on a nonrefundable, nonchangeable basis; that's certainly true of the cheapest ones. In fact, most consolidator tickets lack many of the "extras" associated with "regular" airline tickets. Some tickets, for example, will not earn the customer frequent flyer miles. On the other hand, some consolidators will supply you with tickets that have all the usual bells and whistles. The tradeoff, naturally, is money. The more options, the higher the price. It is important for you to understand exactly what you are buying and for the client to understand what she is getting and giving up in this cut-rate ticket.

Locating consolidators

Finding consolidators, especially the right consolidators, can be tricky. Some consolidators advertise in the travel trade press; an Internet search can turn up some web sites; and there is a listing of consolidators in *The Travel Agent's Complete Desk Reference*.

If you will be dealing in consolidator fares on a regular basis, you will want to get a subscription to *Jax Fax*, an oddly named monthly magazine whose primary purpose is to list current offerings from consolidators to the travel trade. The listings are conveniently arranged by continent and then by country so you can get a sense of what the lowest consolidator fares are. A word of caution: the lowest fare listed in *Jax Fax* may not be available on the dates your client wants to fly, but at least the listed fares give you a "ballpark" range. *Jax Fax* is cheap, too. Contact *Jax Fax* at (800) 952-9329, or write 48 Wellington Road, Milford, CT 06460.

'Air Piracy': another way of charging fees

Service fees are, by definition, fixed. You can't charge this customer $10 a ticket and the next customer $25. There's another way to charge fees and set them on a case by case basis. That is to sell your superior ability to save the customer money.

Bruce Reichert of Leisure Resource in Naples, FL, a good friend and something of a mentor to me in the travel agent game, calls it "Air Piracy" — with a wink and a nod, of course. Behind the wry humor is the very serious business of beating the airlines at their own game, for fun and profit. It goes without saying that if you are going to do this, you really have to know your stuff. Here are some examples of how an experienced and extremely knowledgeable agent can charge premium prices and still have happy customers.

- An agent had a client who needed a one-way fare between San Diego, California, and Fort Walton Beach, Florida. The lowest published fare the client could find was $800. The agent knew there was a roundtrip fare of $198 between San Diego and Orlando and a one-way fare from Orlando to Fort Walton of $121, for a total fare of $319. He offered to charge the client $125 to find a fare under $350. In other words, the maximum the client would have to pay would be $474.99. Since he actually paid just $444 ($319 plus the $125 fee), the client was delighted, and the agent pocketed $125 for a few minutes work.

- Not so long ago the major airlines were all charging $598 for a roundtrip ticket from Miami to Los Angeles. But Bruce knew that United Airlines was offering a $498 fare for bookings made on its web site. A $100 savings right off the bat. But Bruce knew an even better deal. A low-fare upstart, had a fare of $398; now the savings are up to $200. But as a good air pirate, Bruce also knew that just 30 minutes up Interstate 95 is easy-to reach, less congested Fort Lauderdale Airport. Low-fare giant Southwest flies out of Fort Lauderdale, creating the kind of competition the major airlines hate. As a result, roundtrip fares to LA from Fort Lauderdale were just

$298. How much is Bruce's client willing to pay for a $298 fare when it's easy to demonstrate to him that the "going rate" is $598?

- I was once able to help someone find a last-minute trip from New York to Rome. Since he only wanted to stay three days, the fare was an astronomical $1,500. Through my knowledge of the air courier business, I was able to find a ticket for just $250. What do you think this service was worth? (Alas, the air courier business has pretty much dried up and, with it, deals like this.)

- Another service a savvy agent can provide harried business clients is assistance in booking so-called back-to-back tickets that get around the high prices airlines charge to business travelers who aren't staying over a Saturday night at their destinations. Here's how it works: A traveler needs to go from Boston to Minneapolis on Monday and return Thursday. Book two roundtrip tickets, both with a Saturday night stay. One ticket departs Boston on Monday, the other departs Minneapolis on Thursday. The traveler uses only the first half of each ticket. On coast to coast routes it is possible to save clients as much as $1,200 using this ploy. Great care must be taken in booking these cost-savers to avoid retaliation against you or your client by the airlines, but the savvy air pirate knows how to do that.

These examples illustrate a growing trend in the travel distribution system. Those who will survive and prosper selling air in the new marketing environment of commission caps and cuts will be those who find creative ways to market what they have to sell — their knowledge.

Obviously, working this way requires dealing with clients who appreciate the value of their time (and yours) and who respect your right to profit from your know-how. Unfortunately, not all customers are that sophisticated.

Bruce offers a number of guidelines for would-be "air pirates." First, and most obviously, determine the going rate and prove it to your client. This is easily done by using the features of a web site such as Expedia. You can print out Expedia's list of fares and show them to your client. Second, your client has to be aware that she is engaging you for your research expertise and that you expect to be paid for your services just as if you were a lawyer or auto mechanic. Tell her you will quote a price that includes the fare and your fee and that the fee may be charged separately to her credit card. (If you don't have credit card capability, you may have to ask for your fee by check or in cash.) When you have the lower fare in hand, quote your price to the client and do not proceed until you have a firm commitment and the money in hand. Then, and only then, reveal which part of the price represents your fee.

Finally, Bruce cautions against bragging to the client about how you did it. Obviously, the client will be able to figure it out to a greater or lesser extent, but part of what you are marketing is your wizardry, and a little bit of mystery will go a long way to enhance your reputation as the person to see for great airline deals.

All of the ticketing ploys used by air pirates, including several ways to handle the delicate issue of back-to-back tickets, are detailed in my Special Report *Ticketing Ploys: How to Beat the Airlines at Their Own Game.* If you don't already have a copy, you can get one at:

http://www.HomeTravelAgency.com/ploys.html

Summary

We've covered a lot of ground, so let's briefly recap the various ways of booking and selling airline tickets:

- *The "traditional" way with a GDS.* This option gives you all the capabilities of a storefront agency. On the downside, you have to be generating pretty decent volume to pay for the carrying costs of the system and turn a profit. And as we've seen, cheap airfare is not the best way to make a lot of money. Of course, you can book other, more straightforward travel products on the GDS, so you might eventually generate the volume you need to justify the investment.

- *GDS alternatives.* There are a few ways to book at least some airlines electronically, on the Internet, without a GDS. Although such sites represent a tiny minority, their numbers are growing and I suspect that we will see more and more such opportunities springing up in the future.

- *Consolidators.* Selling consolidator tickets solves a lot of problems for the home-based agent. You can make decent money and avoid the hassles of a GDS. On the downside, consolidator tickets are heavily restricted, which may not appeal to your client. Also, consolidator tickets are typically for overseas flights (although more and more consolidators are offering long-haul domestic tickets, too); that could limit the number of opportunities you will have to offer consolidator tickets.

- *"Air Piracy."* This is an excellent option for the experienced agent making a transition from storefront agency employee to home-based entrepreneur. It is less of an option for beginners, at least until they learn the ins and outs of airline ticketing ploys.

- *Referring airline business elsewhere.* This will be a very individual decision. It has its pluses and minuses. On the plus side, the travel opportunities offered exclusively to "agents" by some referral agencies can be very attractive. One recently offered a whole laundry list of cruises for the next best thing to free — agents paid only the port charges. Low-cost travel like this can substitute for "fam" trips until you build your business and can qualify for travel agent rates. (See *Chapter 10: Straight Talk on Travel Industry Benefits* for more on this issue.)

As lengthy as this discussion has been, it has only scratched the considerable surface of the subject of airline ticketing. If you keep booking air travel you will eventually have to deal with "open jaw" tickets, circle trips, round-the-world fares, one-way fares, frequent flyer awards, ticket redemptions, and many other niceties that drive travel agents to distraction. Gradually, you will begin to understand why I spent so much time in this chapter making the case against booking airlines.

The good news is that, compared with booking airline tickets, booking the other travel products we will be discussing is a piece of cake!

Action steps

Here are some things you can do to put what you have learned in this chapter into action:

- If you are seriously considering automating, contact some host agencies and begin the lengthy process of doing your due diligence. Compare several agencies on such matters as training, toll-free help desks, and ongoing software and access fees.

- Find out what airlines fly from your nearest airport. Then visit their web sites to see if any of them have a mechanism that lets travel agents book on their sites. (If you find any, they will most likely be low-fare airlines.) Research the qualifications. If you have decided to specialize in a particular area of the world, research airlines there and see if any of them offer agent booking capability. Europe is a good place to start.

- Begin researching consolidators. Call several and ask how you can establish a working relationship with them.

- If you have decided you want to automate, write down all the things that might go wrong and, for each one, sketch out a plan for how you would deal with it.

- If you have decided you want to automate, begin networking with other agents through OSSN or another professional organization. Ask automated agents which GDS they use and why. Ask them what obstacles they faced when getting started and how they overcame them.

Chapter Thirteen: Booking Hotels

What you will learn

After you have completed this chapter you will be able to:

- Gather the information you need from your client to make a hotel booking.
- Use a variety of research tools to find the right hotel for your client.
- Get the best rate at a variety of different types of properties, using a variety of techniques.
- Book hotels with confidence using a variety of channels.

Key terms and concepts

This chapter involves the following key terms and concepts:

- Hotels can represent a significant profit center for travel agents, this despite a sometime troubled history of hotel-travel agent relations.
- Hotel pricing is elastic, that is the same room can be sold at many different price points. At the same time, clients are less price-resistant when it comes to hotels than they are with airline fares.
- A hotel consolidator has much in common with an airline consolidator. Each hotel consolidator has different policies when it comes to travel agents, ranging from pure net pricing to 12% commissions.
- Condominium rentals (sometimes called villa or holiday home rentals) offer especially good commissions and represent an excellent opportunity for both travel agents and their clients.

Introduction

Hotels and travel agents have a troubled history of working together. Unlike airlines, hotels were slow to appreciate the position of the agent in the travel industry. Many of them saw little point in offering a commission. Even those that did were haphazard about actually paying up. Some hotels had a habit of offering commissions only on their higher rates, then informing the arriving guest that a lower rate was available, thus finessing the agent out of the commission. As a result, many agents have looked on hotel bookings as a value-added service to their customers rather than as a source of income.

This has started to change. More and more hotels, independents as well as chains, are courting agents. Even the budget motel chains pay commissions on bookings. And collecting a commission has become a better bet. According to a survey by *Travel Weekly*, 79% of all hotel commissions owed to travel agencies are now being paid. Not a great record, perhaps, but a decided improvement.

In fact, hotels can be a very nice source of income, especially when your customers are heading for a resort, a romantic bed & breakfast mansion, or to a downtown hotel in a major city; in these situations, the per-night charge can be as high as $300 or $400. A five-day stay in one of these high-ticket establishments can be worth a hefty commission to the agent who books it.

Gathering information

While misteaks... I mean mistakes... are not as lethal in booking hotels as they are in booking airline tickets, they are still embarrassing at best. In the worst cases, they can lose you a good customer. So it is in everyone's best interests that you take the time to collect the right information from your client when the subject of booking a hotel comes up.

Usually, a hotel booking will be a model of simplicity. A single business traveler or a couple on vacation need a room for a night or two. Often they will even know precisely where they want to stay. Nothing could be simpler. But sometimes it gets more complex. Here is a checklist of the key information that can go into a hotel booking:

- *The dates of arrival and departure.* This is pretty self-explanatory.
- *The location of the hotel.* Don't laugh. The customer may be flying into New York City but need a hotel in Rye, or Stamford, or Montclair, or any of hundreds of other locations in the New York metropolitan area. Even in a smaller city, location can be an important factor. Always ask where the client will be in the city being visited and what she is going to be doing. This will help you pinpoint the hotel that will be most convenient for the client.
- *The number of rooms.* If there will be more than one, you will also want to know who's going to be in which room and who's going to be paying for each room. Don't automatically assume your client is picking up the entire tab for a multi-room booking.
- *The ages of any minor children.* "Kids-stay-free" is pretty

standard these days, but you can shop for other kid-friendly amenities.

- **_Room configurations._** First of all, will it be a double or a single? Hotels charge different rates for the same room depending on the number of people in it. So ask your client if a spouse or companion will be along. (If you are also booking airline tickets, you may already have this information.) Beyond that, there are many possibilities in hotel rooms: double rooms with two queen beds, double rooms with one king-sized bed, double rooms with an extra bed, and so forth. The makeup of the traveling party may dictate the room configuration needed. If your client likes a specific room configuration, note this as a client preference (see below).

- **_Price range._** In general, people are not as price-sensitive when it comes to hotels as they are about airline fares. A businessperson may be meeting clients at her hotel or need a hotel within walking distance of his ultimate destination. Beyond that, marketing campaigns by the major hotel chains have educated people to expect a "comfortable night's stay" when they travel. Indeed, many travelers have come to look on their hotel as a way to pamper themselves on the road, perhaps to compensate for the sacrifice of being away from home and family or suffering through the hassles of air travel. Of course, if you offer a client a choice of three hotels, at three different prices, she may choose the least expensive. But when she finds that the hall carpets are old and shabby, the room smells faintly of mildew, the mattress is soft and lumpy, and the bathroom faucet drip-drip-drips through the night, she won't blame herself for being cheap. No, she will blame you! So, you are better off finding out what general price range a client will accept. (You may have to educate people on this point; most people are horrified when told the cost of even a modest hotel room in places like New York City, for example.) Once you've determined the range, you will have some leeway in recommending an appropriate property.

- **_Credit card information._** Typically, the client will pay for the hotel room with a credit card on departure. Hotel reservationists will frequently ask for a credit card number to "hold" the reservation. Be aware that this means that they will charge the room to the client's credit card even if the client doesn't show up! If you (and the client) want to book the room on this basis, you will need to know the client's name as it appears on the credit card, the number, expiration date, and (perhaps) the billing address and a telephone contact.

These points cover the basics. There are additional bits of information that you might need when making a specific reservation for a specific client. They will be discussed a bit later.

Research

Sometimes, clients will know exactly where they want to stay. In that case, your job is easy. Sometimes they will request a specific chain. Sometimes they will know generally where they need a hotel ("Near the airport"). Sometimes the customer will have no idea where the hotel should be, except, of course, that it should be somewhere in the metropolitan area to which they are traveling. In most cases, you will have to do at least some research to find an appropriate property for your client.

Here are some of the major sources of information:

- **Hotel & Travel Index (HTI).** I loved *Hotel & Travel Index.* This massive reference, once published quarterly, contained very complete information on a wide range of hotel properties around the globe, including tidbits not readily available elsewhere, such as commission rates and the names of the computerized reservations systems through which a hotel's rooms can be booked. It also told you the hotel's age, an important bit of information that can warn you that one property may be less desirable than a brand-new property down the street. With its imposing bulk, just having *HTI* around the office was enough to make you feel like a pro.

  HTI is still around, but not in printed form. It is now an online service, at www.hotelandtravelindex.com, that performs much the same function as the printed version. Although the information available is not as extensive, it is a convenient way to get information fast. Still, I miss the old *HTI*.

- **Hotel chain directories.** Every chain of hotels publishes a free directory of its properties. You can pick these up at the reservation desks of hotels in your area or as you travel. You can also request copies from the good folks at the hotels' toll-free reservations numbers. Be warned, however, that it can take as long as two months for a requested copy to show up in the mail.

  The chains' directories contain a wealth of useful information, including (in many cases) thumbnail maps of cities and the neighborhoods around specific properties. Listings of individual properties invariably tell you what points of interest (tourist attractions, colleges, corporate headquarters, military bases, etc.) are close by and how far away they are. All of this can help you pinpoint the best hotels for your clients.

  The directories also provide a wealth of information about the chain's special programs for frequent lodgers, senior and weekend discounts, and so forth — information which may be of interest to you and your clients. While they seldom tell you how old a property is, they will point out the newer properties or ones that meet special standards of excellence. Building a reference library of hotel directories is a good idea, even if you have no immediate use for the information they contain.

- **AAA Tour Books.** Members of the American Automobile Association (AAA) can obtain free copies of Tour Books covering various regions of the country. These books have the advantage of giving you AAA's independent ratings of properties.
- **The Internet.** The World Wide Web is a vast and growing repository of information about hotels. The problem is finding it. One place to start is the "search engines" that let you search the 'Net by typing in key words. For example, typing in "hotel Atlanta" might get you to sites listing hotels in Atlanta, Georgia, many of which will be of little use. The Internet is now awash in sites listing hotels, each hoping to earn a few pennies if you click on a link. The same search also might find the home page of the Hotel Atlanta in Antwerp. Eventually, you will find the search engine and the search strategy that works best for you. When you find a site that has good information, remember to "bookmark" it.
  Taking the time can be worth it. Many hotel sites on the 'Net allow travel agents to book online and earn a commission. *The Travel Agent's Complete Desk Reference* contains an extensive list of hotel web sites; it's worth exploring.
- **The trade press.** The magazines that cover the travel industry offer a constant flow of new information about hotels. New properties, mergers and acquisitions, special programs or offers for travelers, special commission rates and incentive deals for travel agents, and so forth. You may want to glance through recent issues when researching a hotel for a client, just in case something pops out at you.
- **Hotel toll-free numbers.** If worse comes to worst, you can call the toll-free number of a hotel chain you know the client likes and ask what's available where the client is going. This is a last-ditch ploy, however, because it won't necessarily be the most convenient for the client or offer the most amenities for the price paid.

Keeping your hotel research collection up to date will be an ongoing chore. All guides to hotels go out of date, perhaps sooner than you imagine. That's one reason *Hotel and Travel Index* gave up publishing a huge directory every quarter and moved to the Web. The chains may update their directories several times a year. The *AAA Tour Books* tell you when the information in them becomes obsolete.

What to look for

Once you have your reference materials, it's time to pick the right hotel or a suitable selection from which your client can choose. First you want to cover the basics: location, price, preference. In other words, you want a hotel that is convenient for the customer, is in a price range with which the customer is comfortable, and meets the customer's criteria (brand name, style, or whatever). There are some other things you will want to be looking for:

- **What's included?** Extra touches like complimentary cocktails or free breakfasts are not only nice to know about, they may help make up the customer's mind.
- **Special offers.** If you are calling the hotels, ask about any special offers they might have going at the time the client will be visiting. For example, hotels sometimes offer the third or fourth night free during special promotions.
- **Amenities.** What does the hotel have to offer besides a comfortable room? Extras like tennis courts or proximity to a shopping mall might be important to your client. You will want to be able to provide as much information as possible.
- **What's in it for you?** It's also appropriate to find out if the chain offers a competitive commission and, if so, if there are any special deals for you, the agent, available.

Factors influencing your choice

Unless the client makes a specific request, you have a fair amount of leeway in recommending hotel accommodations. This gives you more of a chance to make a choice and then "sell" it to your client than you have when booking airline tickets. You can make a case for a property that's slightly more expensive or one that provides you with some special payback, in the form of a higher commission or entry in a sweepstakes for example. It's the travel industry equivalent of the suit salesman selling the $800 wool suit with two pairs of pants. The important thing is that the client feels happy with the choice and doesn't feel he has been arm-twisted into paying too much money.

Client preferences

Never forget that your first duty is to the client, so client preferences are the most important factors in choosing a hotel. Among the things that may be important to your client are:

- **The hotel chain.** Travelers develop brand loyalties, and you should know those of your customers. Many hotels have "frequent lodger" programs which mimic the frequent flyer promotions of the airlines. It's a good idea to know to which programs your clients belong and make a note of their membership numbers on the Client Profile Form (see *Chapter 20: Qualifying*).
- **Frequent flyer programs.** Even if the client is not a member of a frequent lodger program, he or she is probably in one or more frequent flyer plans, the vast majority of which have tie-ins with hotels. Try to pick a hotel that will earn the client maximum mileage. This can be a powerful selling point.
- **Type of room.** This means configuration. Some clients prefer a king-sized bed and a non-smoking room. Others will

insist they stay on the "concierge level" of a hotel, where they receive an extra level of service and amenities. A relatively new wrinkle in hotel marketing is the "green room." These are specially designated rooms that are "environmentally friendly" and feature special air filters, biodegradable soap, recycled paper products, and so forth. These may be attractive to some of your clients; they also are priced higher than other rooms, resulting in a slightly better payback for you!

- **Extras.** Today, many hotel properties come with a long list of amenities. Some of these may be important to your client. If your client wants or needs things like an on-premises health club, a pool, meeting rooms, high-speed Internet access, a 24-hour restaurant on the premises, or any of the dozens of other things hotels are providing to lure guests, you, the travel agent, should know this.
- **Location.** This can sometimes be an overriding factor. And don't forget that a more expensive room in the right location can actually be less expensive if it saves the client the need to rent a car.

As I mentioned earlier, price tends to be less of an issue in choosing a hotel. That is not to say it can be completely overlooked. The cost of a hotel room tends to become important in relationship to the purpose of the trip. Someone traveling on business may want or need a flashy hotel in a good location. The same person traveling to visit family may only require the simplest motel room. This goes back to the most basic rule of booking travel: find out why your client is going.

Also, I don't want to convey the impression that you should attempt to book the client into the most expensive hotel room you think you can talk him into. Far from it. Within the price parameters the client has given you, or which you feel are appropriate, you should always strive to get the best deal possible. (See "Getting the best rate," below.)

Again, what's in it for you?

Hotel properties are constantly trying to attract your attention with special commission deals, spiffs, and contests. Sometimes making the "right" hotel booking can put an extra $50 in your pocket or give you a chance of winning a free vacation. There are two problems with this:

- First, if you are a small operation — and outside sales reps almost invariably are — you may find that a hotel's promotion never seems to coincide with your customers' travel plans, and
- Second, there's always the temptation that you will spend more time chasing a $50 bonus than doing the more important job of looking out for your clients' best interests.

Chances are, you will find the first more of a problem than the second. Still, as I've said before, you are a businessperson. It's only smart business to keep your eyes peeled for any opportunity to legally contribute to the bottom line. You will find a more complete discussion of commission deals, contests, and the issues they raise in *Chapter 9: Getting Serious.*

You should also bear in mind that, as your client list grows, these special hotel deals and offers will become more attractive. That's because you can market them proactively. For example, an all-inclusive Caribbean resort may offer a $100 bonus for every booking made during a certain three-month period. If you have a large and growing list of customers, you may be able to put together a special promotion, complete with brochures from the resort in question, and find several takers.

Otherwise, it's a matter of luck whether a client's trip to Seattle will coincide with a special commission deal being offered by a hotel there. It's not a bad idea when calling around to research hotels for a customer, to ask the reservationist if there are any special deals for agents being promoted at the moment. The reservationist should have this information.

Getting the best rate

Just as you want to get the best deal for your client, the reservationist wants to get the best deal for the hotel. Hotel rates are a bit more open to discussion than airline fares. Within broad limits, reservationists have the discretion to settle for any of a number of different rates for the same room. Typically, they will first quote the highest price for a given category of room, the so-called "rack rate." With a little prodding, you can often do better.

Let's say, for example, that your client wants to stay on the concierge level of a certain upscale hotel, a fairly expensive room. You notice in the chain's directory that this property is a mile away from a major corporation. You can ask for a corporate rate, mentioning the major company's name, and save your client $40. Whatever you "lose" in commission will be more than made up in goodwill and customer loyalty.

Here are some suggestions on bargaining for a better rate:

- *Membership rates.* Groups like the American Association of Retired Persons (AARP) and the American Automobile Association (AAA) have negotiated attractive rates for their members at many hotels. Of course, it helps if your client is actually a member of one of these groups; often they will be asked to show a membership card at check-in to qualify for one of these rates.

- *Corporate rates.* Sometimes just asking, "Do you have a corporate rate?" will garner a lower rate. Other times you will have to pick a corporation. For example, you might say, as in the example above, "My client is with AT&T," if you knew there was an AT&T office nearby. These aren't policed as thoroughly as membership rates; the reservationist just needs some justification for offering the lower corporate rate.

- *Promotional rates.* If the rate is still too high ask if there are any "special promotional rates" available for the dates your client will be staying. Sometimes, the reservationist will "discover" a rate that she had overlooked before.

- ***Quote a price.*** Sometimes you can succeed by begging for a lower rate. You might try saying something like, "Gee, my client doesn't want to spend more than $99 a night but I'd like to put him into your hotel. Could you accommodate him at that rate?"

Be aware that some lower rates are not commissionable. The reservationist will sometimes use that as a subtle bargaining chip by saying something like, "We have a lower rate but there's no commission on that." So be careful about bargaining too hard, unless you are willing to forego a commission. Working on the theory that honesty is the best policy, you might try asking, "What's the lowest rate I can get and still get a commission?"

Of course, if you are going to bargain aggressively for the lowest rate and (most likely) lose a commission, you should consider charging your customer a per-booking service fee. Many customers will understand the logic of this, although some will not. The very best customers, of course, are those who have high standards and don't mind paying for them.

Making the sale

Ideally, the customer will leave the choice of hotel up to you. The customer knows you understand her needs and preferences, including the price range with which she's comfortable; so she trusts you to make the best decision. Arriving at this point usually requires developing a track record with the customer such that she will trust your judgment.

Sometimes a client's willingness to give you free reign will vary with circumstances. In many cases, however, customers will feel most comfortable when you offer a range of choices and let them make the final decision. Part of your job in researching the alternatives is to narrow the choice to those properties that best meet the customer's needs. You definitely don't want to get back to a customer and say, "I've come up with seventeen hotels in Centreville; let's go over them."

So as not to overwhelm the customer, be prepared to present just three choices, with two major contenders and a fallback. Of these, one should be your choice and should be presented first ("I would recommend..."). Be prepared to justify your choice with specifics. Always give the customer the option of choosing your primary recommendation before presenting the other choices.

Your second choice should be presented as an alternative. You can use phrases like, "A bit farther away, but slightly less expensive," or "If you'd like something a bit more luxurious," to highlight the tradeoffs you are presenting. A good travel agent will be able to discuss the pros and cons of the properties intelligently. Your recommendation will be more persuasive if you can point to your own experience of the hotel or that of another, satisfied, customer.

A much fuller discussion of the techniques of making the sale will be found in *Part III*. For now, the important things to remember are that you must get a clear go-ahead from the customer and you must make sure the customer understands all the key elements of the booking — price, frequent flyer or lodger points, the fact that the room will be held with his credit card, and so on.

If none of the choices tickles the customer's fancy, you may have additional properties to recommend, or you may have to do a little more research.

Making the booking

You may actually make the booking before you make the sale; you would do this to hold the room. Whenever you make the booking, do so in a methodical and professional manner. You want to make sure that nothing is left out that will inconvenience the client, embarrass you, or cost either of you money.

If you have opted for a host agency that requires GDS connectivity, then you will be following whatever procedures apply to the GDS you are using. Once you get the hang of it, booking a hotel via a GDS becomes a quick and painless process. But there are other situations and other options:

Booking on the Internet

As I mentioned earlier, some hotel chains allow travel agents to book on their web sites, a phenomenon that seems to be more prevalent in Europe and elsewhere than in the United States. In addition to hotel chain sites, there are a number of wholesalers that allow online booking for travel agents. To make this happen, you will need to have an IATA number or another unique industry identifier. If you don't have one, you can always try to set up a "pseudo ARC number" with the hotel or wholesaler in question, which can be a long, frustrating, and very often futile process. For guidance on how to get one, read *How to Get Your Own IATA Number*. If you purchased this book as part of my home study course, you already have it. If not, you can order it at:

http://www.HomeTravelAgency.com/getiata.html

If you are working through a host agency and plan to use their IATA number, check with them to make sure your booking will be trackable when you book on a hotel site. Your host may have special pages set up on its own web site to facilitate bookings at some hotels. It may also have special arrangements with a consortium or with preferred suppliers. Whatever, the situation, your host will be able to guide you — at least, it should.

Finding sites that allow travel agent bookings is a matter of patient research. Here are a few wholesalers/consolidators that were active at the time this book went to press: www.Hotels.com, www.LeisureLink.com, and www.WorldRes.com. Here are some foreign sites: RelaisChateaux.com, Atel-Hotels.com, Resapro.com, Minotel.com, and Riu.com. And one in Canada: SandmanHotels.com. American hotel chains that offer online booking for travel agents include Hilton, Holiday Inn, Loews, and the Starwood Hotels family of brands.)

This is just a random selection and the policies at these sites may change at any moment and without notice. To find others, you can monitor the trade press or ask for suggestions from fellow agents. You can also search through the hotel sites listed in *The Travel Agent's Complete Desk Reference* to locate ones that might be of interest. The travel agents' link is usually in teensy print in some out of the way location on the home page. Just because you find a special travel agents' section, doesn't always mean the site offers online booking capability.

In many cases, if you have an IATA number, you just plug it in at the appropriate time in the booking process. However, you may want to contact the hotel just to double check proper procedure (for example, do they require pre-registration?) before making your first booking.

Booking on the phone

Most hotels will let travel agents book on the phone. If the reservationist tries to steer you to the GDS (which for the sake of this discussion I am assuming you don't have), try saying, "The GDS is down." You'll seldom get an argument to that one. Here's how this scenario will most likely play out.

First, identify yourself as a travel agent. You might say:

"Hello, this is Martha with Anytown Travel
Agency. I'd like to make reservations for a
client, please."

This is the only way you will be able to collect your commission. At some point during the booking process, the reservationist should ask for your agency's IATA number, address, or some other identifier. Don't conclude the booking until you have given this information!

Information to give

You will want to provide the reservationist with the following:

- *Dates.* The date of arrival and the number of nights the party will stay. Hotel reservationists seem to prefer a number of nights rather than a date of departure.
- *Configuration.* The number and configuration of room(s). For example, two doubles with king-sized beds.
- *Name.* The name in which the reservation will be held. It is seldom necessary to provide the names of others in the party. If it is, the reservationist will tell you. The exception of course, would be if different people are paying for different rooms.
- *Any client preferences.* This would include things like "non-smoking room," "on the ground floor," "near the pool."
- *Loyalty programs.* The client's frequent lodger number or frequent flyer number, as appropriate.
- *Approximate time of arrival.* If you know the client's ap-

proximate time of arrival, give it. If it will be a late arrival, you will have to provide a credit card number to guarantee the reservation.

- **Credit card information.** If the booking is to be guaranteed, you will need this information.
- **IATA number.** Be sure to provide your host agency's IATA number, along with any personal identifier your host agency uses to track your commissions. Of course, if you have your own IATA number, you will give that. This all-important step will help assure you receive your proper commission.

Information to get

There is also some very important information you will want for your client and for your records on each booking you make:

- **Confirmation number.** Like the record locator number in an airline booking, this is a unique identifier for this booking. You will want to give this number to the client, just in case there is any misunderstanding at check-in.
- **The name of the reservationist.** It's also a good idea to ask for the name of the reservationist. If a problem arises later, it's good information to have. Usually, the reservationist gives his or her name when answering the call. If you forget, just ask again before the call ends. You can do it like this:

"And your name is... ?"

"Jim."

*"Well, thanks, Jim. You've been very helpful
and I appreciate that."*

- **The rules of the booking.** Usually this means the time until which the reservation will be held without a credit card to guarantee it. Some hotels now assess a penalty if the guest stays fewer nights than originally booked. There may be other conditions that you and your client should know about. Make sure you relay the important information.
- **The hotel's local phone number.** This can come in handy in case the client is delayed.
- **Commission information.** Again, make sure that the reservationist has your IATA number. If he or she doesn't seem to know what you're talking about, ask about their commission structure and policies. If they don't seem to have one, you may want to think twice about steering business their way. You also might want to ask if there is any special commission incentive available. Sometimes, special commissions will only be given if you ask for them. If there is one, make a note of it and remember to tell your host agency.

If you booked online or via a GDS, you will have much of this information in electronic form, often with the capability of printing it out in a form that can be provided to the client.

Relaying the booking

Your final task is to get back to your client, confirm that the reservation has been made, and provide the client with all the information about the booking he or she will need. That could include:

- The quoted rate.
- The confirmation number.
- Rules of the booking.
- Hotel phone number.
- Directions to the hotel or instructions on how to request airport pickup service.

Getting paid

Getting paid your hotel commissions is not always a sure a bet. There is some evidence that the situation is not as bad as it once was, but some sources claim that 35% to 40% of hotel commissions remain unpaid 60 days after they were due. This doesn't mean that they'll *never* be paid, just that a lot of travel agents have to work a little harder for what's coming to them. In other words, collecting hotel commissions will require attention and vigilance on your part. Bookings made on the GDS or online at least have the benefit of creating an electronic trail that (in theory, at least) will be instantly available on the hotel's system should a dispute arise. Most problems arise, perhaps not surprisingly, when trying to collect commissions from smaller and foreign hotels.

Also, hotels typically don't begin to think about paying your commission until after the client leaves, sometimes 30 days after the client leaves. Since many trips are booked well in advance, this means not just a long wait for your commission but the possibility that commissions may be forgotten (by you, the hotel, or your agency) or otherwise fall through the cracks. A complete discussion on making sure you get your commissions will be found in *Chapter 9: Getting Serious.*

Hotel consolidators

Just like airline consolidators, hotel consolidators buy in bulk and sell at a discount to retail. They are a growing force in the hotel distribution system. Like airline consolidators, they have differing policies on working with travel agents. Most hotel consolidators sell directly to the public, often via a web site. They are happy to take travel agent bookings but it is up to the agent to negotiate and collect a fee from the client. Typically, that will take the form of an upfront service fee. You may be able to find hotel consolidator web sites that allow commissionable travel agent bookings, although policies in this regard change with some frequency. In any event, the commission may be modest.

Dealing with hotel consolidators can be tricky and you need to know how each one works or risk some misunderstandings with your clients. For example, some consolidators require prepayment, but the client will be hit by unexpected taxes and "fees" by the hotel. Or a reservation will be made with payment due on checkout, when the quoted rate will mysteriously expand. Those taxes and fees again. This is not to say that using a hotel consolidator cannot be a good deal; you just need to be precise.

A hotel consolidator with a more personal touch is Hotel Reps (HotelReps.com, 800-729-9051), which offers a particularly generous 12% commission on a worldwide array of properties, and they will process the client's credit card for you. All of their bookings are prepaid and all-inclusive, including taxes, fees, and (in most cases) breakfast in overseas hotels. You can make your bookings online or call their 800 number for personal service. What's more, HotelReps doesn't require an IATA number from agents. If you don't have one, you can use your phone number, including country code, as your unique ID.

Mondo condo

Another profitable area of opportunity for the savvy travel agent is condominium and "villa" rentals. They are similar to hotels (they are lodging, after all), but offer some distinct advantages:

■ They often come with extremely attractive commission rates — as much as 20% or more.

■ Despite the high commissions offered to travel agents, a condominium vacation can be a real bargain for a family with kids that might otherwise have to rent two or more motel rooms. Condos, by definition, come with fully equipped kitchens and dining areas, offering considerable savings on the food budget. What's more, condos often offer additional amenities like swimming pools, tennis courts, and golf courses at no (or moderate) additional expense.

■ By working through a packager or a consortium, you can offer your client a lower rate than they would be able to get directly from the resort or condominium developer.

■ Commissions are often easier to track and collect.

■ Condominiums offer you the opportunity to target vacationers who seldom deal through travel agents, namely families who drive to resort destinations for their vacations and make their own lodging arrangements.

■ When booking many condominium vacations, it is possible to deal directly with the supplier and receive the entire commission.

In fact, condominiums offer so many advantages that many independent travel agents are specializing in this lucrative leisure travel product. Many hotel consolidators offer condominium and villa rentals. LeisureLink, mentioned earlier, specializes in this type of rental. It's also becoming increasingly easy to find private condo and villa rental opportunities on the Internet — for example, try doing a Google search for "Orlando villa" — raising the possibility of forging business relationships with their owners.

If you are specializing in a destination, you should make an effort to identify as many private owners as possible and discuss "representing" their properties. Not many travel agents are doing this — yet.

Foreign hotels

The discussion so far has pretty much assumed we were booking domestic hotels. The picture can change, however, when it comes to booking hotels overseas. First of all, it should be said that there are a great many hotels in far-flung parts of the globe that can be booked just like a Holiday Inn in the next state — through a toll-free number here in the States or on the Internet. These are, for the most part, hotels that are part of an American chain, although a growing number of excellent but little-known (at least to Americans) chains are now available online. Still, there are many hotels around the world, that, for the time being at least, haven't been gobbled up by the major American chains.

If you are used to selling American hotels, you will find foreign hotels, especially European hotels, will take a little getting used to. For starters, many well-regarded European hotels will not pass muster with many of your American clients, who are used to the high, but cookie-cutter standards of American hotels. This can mean small rooms, odd bathroom plumbing and fixtures, bathrooms down the hall, and limited amenities. It's the bathrooms down the hall that really seem to spook Americans, so make sure you look for "en suite" facilities, which simply means that the bathroom is attached to the room. On the other hand, many travelers love the "charm" these quirky hotels offer. You can, of course, find hotels that meet the highest American standards, your clients will just have to pay more for the feeling they haven't really left home. In Asia, where hotels catering to tourists are a relatively new phenomenon, standards tend to be more "American" and more uniform.

Another thing to bear in mind is that, whereas most American hotels charge by the room, European hotels tend to charge by the person. So a double in Rome might cost 20 to 80 percent more than the same room occupied by a single person.

Hotel representatives

Foreign hotels are just as eager to market their services as anyone else. Many of them have turned to "hotel representatives" to make their properties more accessible to American travelers. (You will find contact information for many hotel representatives in *The Travel Agent's Complete Desk Reference*.) A hotel representative, as the name implies, represents a foreign hotel chain, a number of foreign hotel chains, or a collection of independent foreign hotels. Usually a hotel representative will deal with both travel agents and the general public.

The advantage of booking through hotel representatives is convenience. You call them up (many have toll-free numbers), make your booking, and, down the road, collect your commission. The disadvantage, as I have found, is that their rates are much higher than those you can obtain directly from the property itself. I have found this true for hotels in Venezuela ($35 vs. $20) and the south of France ($240 vs. $170). Now, if your client doesn't mind paying these rates, I suppose that's fine. There are, however, other alternatives.

Booking direct

In these days of global communications, there is no reason you cannot make bookings directly with hotels in foreign countries. Many guidebooks list local phone numbers for the hotels they cover, most foreign hotels (even very small ones) have faxes and many have web sites. I have also mentioned the possibility of booking at least some foreign hotels on the Internet.

I have found that the best way to book is by fax. You can call whenever you wish — even program your fax to dial in the middle of the night — and not worry who will answer the phone. Language is less of a barrier; most hotels will have someone on staff who reads English or will be able to find someone who does. The hotel can confirm the reservation and provide information about any deposits that might be due by return fax. If the client's trip is far enough away, you could also do this by mail.

As for getting paid, you have two choices:

- Rely on the hotel to pay you. This is risky, and the hotel may not have the facilities to pay you in U.S. currency.
- Charge the client a booking fee to pay for your time and the cost of faxing overseas. Most clients will accept this, especially if you can point out to them that the cost of the hotel plus your fee is less than you were quoted by a hotel rep. You will often be able to back this up by printing out a web page showing a much higher rate. In other cases, this will be the only way you could have made the booking.

Booking direct will probably be most attractive to outside reps who become destination specialists. They will gain an in-depth knowledge of the area, may have language skills, and may even be able to develop special relationships with unique and charming inns that will offer special value to their clients.

Voucher programs and packages

Mention should also be made of voucher programs, which allow the traveler to purchase a book of coupons that can then be redeemed at participating hotels or bed & breakfasts throughout a country or region. Ireland is one example of a country that has a well-established voucher program. The best source of information on programs like these is the tourist bureau of the foreign country. When you call, remember to identify yourself as a travel agent and ask how you can collect a commission on the sale of these products.

It also may be possible to get your client a "hotel package" through a tour operator. Typically this would involve a stay of several nights or a week at a set price. See *Chapter 15: Booking Tours & Packages* for more information on dealing with tour operators.

Summary

Hotels may seem like an afterthought, but they can represent a significant profit center for your home-based business if you approach selling them in an organized fashion. Better yet, more and more hotels are dealing directly with home-based agents, few or no questions asked. Once you have your own IATA number, you can book virtually any hotel, often on the Internet, and earn a full commission. If this idea appeals, you will want to read *How to Get Your Own IATA Number*. If you purchased this book as part of my home study course, you already have it. If not, you can order it at:

http://www.HomeTravelAgency.com/getiata.html

Generally speaking, clients are less price-resistant when it comes to hotels than they are with airline tickets. Hotels can be sold as a nice way to pamper the client. You never want to talk a customer into spending more than he or she is comfortable with, but within a given customer's budget range, hotel bookings offer a certain amount of leeway.

Hotel consolidators are a growing force in the hospitality industry and are usually open to working with home-based travel agents. Vacation condos and villa rentals are another profitable and, until recently at least, overlooked profit opportunity. Marketing these types of properties can mean reaching a segment of the market that doesn't often use travel agents. If you specialize in a destination, you should make an effort to forge private relationships with the owners of this type of property.

Niches in the lodging industry, such as foreign hotels and b&bs, offer special opportunities for the home-based agent, because "traditional" travel agencies have done a generally poor job of addressing these markets. Booking these types of properties can sometimes mean charging fees because of the lack of commissions or the difficulty in collecting them.

Action steps

Here are some things you can do to put what you have learned in this chapter into action:

- Visit the web sites of hotel chains with which you are familiar. Look for links to special travel agents' sections and determine whether the site allows online booking by travel agents and, if so, what is required of the travel agent in terms of industry identification. Be sure to check the commission rate and the payment terms.
- Visit the web site of *Hotel and Travel Index* and familiarize yourself with what it has to offer. (www.hoteltravelindex.com)

- Call a few hotels and, posing as either a consumer or a travel agent, see what sort of rate you can negotiate. Ask about corporate rates, special promotions, AARP rates, and so forth — be creative. This will give you a better appreciation for the elasticity of hotel pricing.
- If you are currently working with a host agency, familiarize yourself with its guidelines for making hotel bookings. Pay special attention to online booking opportunities, either on the host's own web site or elsewhere, and preferred supplier relationships.
- If at all possible, make some real, commissionable hotel bookings. Write down a step-by-step account of what you did to make the booking(s). Refer to this as you make additional bookings, refining your instructions to yourself. Make special note of new things you learn on each booking.

Chapter Fourteen:
Booking Rental Cars

What you will learn

After you have completed this chapter you will be able to:

- Gather the information you need from your client to make a rental car booking.
- Research rental car options using a variety of techniques.
- Understand the variables that go into making the right car booking for your client.
- Book rental cars with confidence.

Key terms and concepts

This chapter involves the following key terms and concepts:

- Rental cars are often overlooked by home-based agents, which is too bad because they can represent a small but steady stream of income.
- Knowing why your client is traveling can lead you to the "right" car and often a better commission.
- Most rental cars can now be booked on the Internet, without a GDS.
- The best commissions are earned on non-discounted "leisure" rates, that is on trips by people who are on vacation and, therefore, less price-conscious.

Introduction

Rental cars are a small, and therefore often overlooked, niche for the home-based independent agent or outside sales rep. Like hotels, they are something that travelers will often book for themselves prior to the trip or select upon arrival.

"Will you be needing a car?" is a question you should train yourself to ask your customers whenever you are making a reservation for airline tickets. Often they will not; relatives will be picking them up or they will be relying on shuttle buses and taxis while away. When customers do need a car at the destination, however, booking one for them is a relatively painless process that can result in a small but steady stream of additional income.

Small because car rentals are generally not a high-ticket item to begin with and many travelers are price conscious when renting cars. Steady because the major car rental companies have a good track record on paying commissions. They also pay pretty decent commissions, all things considered. Generally speaking, they will pay ten percent on non-discounted "leisure" rates and five percent on discounted or promotional rates. A few pay a flat five percent. Most companies have stopped paying any commissions on negotiated corporate and government rates, but it's unlikely most home-based agents will be dealing with those anyway.

Another overlooked advantage of rental cars from the travel agent's perspective is that there are relatively few rental car companies. That means that, with a little effort, you can get to know most of the major companies in depth and become a real rental car expert.

Gathering information

As with any travel booking, make sure you have a clear grasp of why the customer is traveling and what he or she plans to be doing on the trip. Is it a humdrum business trip or a romantic getaway? That knowledge can help you guide the customer to wise decisions in renting the right car.

The key ingredients of a car rental are fairly straightforward:

- *Place, date, and time of pickup.* Typically, the customer will pick up the car at the airport upon arrival. Sometimes, the customer will want to pick up the car later in the trip, at a different location. Be alert to the possibility that the place and time the customer requests may not be optimal.
- *Place, date, and time of return.* Most car rental rates are based on the assumption that the car will be returned to the location at which it was picked up. Deviations from this rule can result in significantly higher base rates or the addition of a "drop-off fee." Some rental companies will allow a car that was picked up at the airport to be returned to a downtown location in the area without penalty (or vice versa). Most will charge more when a car is rented in one city and returned in another.
- *Type of car.* The size and model of the car affect the rental rate. The standard categories are subcompact, compact, midsized, and full-sized. There are any number of other options, from luxury cars, to RVs, to vans, to pickup trucks. Some companies even offer, in selected markets, "fantasy" cars like vintage Corvette convertibles or Rolls Royces.
- *Type of rental.* In other words, is it a daily or a weekly rental?
- *Mileage charges.* Are unlimited miles included in the rental fee, or is there a per-mile charge added?

You may already know some of this information if you are making air arrangements as well. In addition to this basic information, there are some other things you will want to know about your client.

- **Brand preferences.** Many clients will have a preferred car rental company. This preference will be based on factors such as the customer's perception of the company's quality and reliability, frequent flyer mileage tie-ins, or even the car company's frequent-renter program (which offers various perks to members). You should, of course, familiarize yourself with this information and record membership numbers on the *Client Profile Form*, which you will find at the end of *Chapter 20: Qualifying*.
- **Car preference.** Some people will insist on at least a mid-sized car. Others want nothing but the cheapest subcompact. It's a good idea to ask what the customer wants you to do if the preferred car size is not available.
- **On-terminal or off.** Airports have a limited amount of space for car rental companies. Those that have counters and pickup points inside the terminal pay dearly for that privilege. The other companies are relegated to satellite locations, outside the terminal, reached by a free shuttle bus. Obviously, the on-terminal locations are more convenient and quicker for the traveler. Often (but not always) that will mean a higher rate.
- **Price.** If the customer has a preferred company and a preferred car type, then price becomes a non-issue in most cases. If price is a concern or becomes an issue, you will want to ask the customer how much convenience can be sacrificed in the interests of economy. Then you'll have to do some comparison shopping in your research phase.

Less frequently, you will need some additional information:
- **Additional drivers.** If more than one person will be driving the car, it can be helpful to know their name(s).
- **Driving record.** Some of the major car rental companies are now doing routine checks of the driving records of all renters at pickup time. If the renter has any moving violations or too many points on their license, they can be denied a car. You may want to alert your clients to this new policy. If it is a problem, you may want to suggest alternatives — a different driver in the same party or a different company that doesn't do such checks.
- **Dreams and wishes.** Sometimes clients can be influenced to pick a more expensive rental if it can satisfy their curiosity or provide ego satisfaction. For example, a client may be considering buying a Lexus someday. Why not rent one for an extended test drive? Or they may be curious what a hybrid car feels like or have a hankering to drive a Hummer.

At this point, you should analyze the customer's request to see if you can make any money-saving recommendations. Many customers will "overbook" a rental car, thinking that their only option is to pick up and return the car at the airport. Consider this alternative scenario:

- Day One: The customer arrives at the airport and takes a shuttle bus to her hotel.
- Day Two: The customer picks up a rental car from a downtown location.
- Day Three: The customer returns the car to the same location.
- Day Four: The customer takes a shuttle bus back to the airport.

A four-day rental has become a two-day rental. Alternatively, the customer might pick up the car at the airport and return it downtown or vice versa. Be aware, too, that an increasing number of airports levy "facility charges" that are passed on to the renter. Using a free hotel shuttle and renting from an in-town location can result in a much lower rental fee (although not always).

Or a customer might want to use his preferred rental car company overseas, when a local firm might offer a much better rate. Or perhaps you are aware of a special promotional rate that might be attractive to your customer. Being aware of the possibilities, and being able to counsel your customers, will result in their loyalty and repeat business.

Research

If your customer is intensely loyal to a particular company, your job is easy. If not, things quickly become more complicated. Car rental rates are extremely competitive and volatile. Rates go up and down, policies change, promotional rates come and go. So if you are looking for the best deal, prepare yourself for some serious comparison shopping.

Car rental information is available on all the major GDSs. If you do not use a GDS, you can turn to the Internet and the web sites of the various rental car companies.

Another option is to use the online travel agencies (or booking engines) like Expedia and Travelocity to research car options, although I have found they favor the major car rental companies and higher priced rentals. Of course, higher prices mean higher commissions, but if your client wants the cheapest deal, you may have to try out a number of online agencies to see which offers the best selection.

Of course, you could also do this research by calling up all the car companies via their toll free numbers, but I would discourage this approach. It takes up valuable time, creates an untidy mound of notes, and gets confusing very quickly.

Using the online booking engines is not an ideal solution, but at least you should be able to get some basic information. Among the things you might be able to find out (depending on the booking engine) are:

- Which companies serve that particular airport or city, although many booking engines do not include all the companies that serve a given airport.

- Whether the company is on or off terminal. You also may be able to find out if a company has other local rental sites besides the one at the airport.
- Whether certain categories of car are still available or are sold out — a not too uncommon occurrence at holiday times.

You will find that different booking engines will give you different rates for exactly the same car, from exactly the same company, in exactly the same city, on exactly the same date and time. But it's a start. With comparative information in hand, you can then log on to the company's web site or call the company directly for more information and to make reservations. Of course, finding the exact same rate you found on Expedia or Travelocity on the rental car company's web site or from the reservationist can be tricky.

That's why most beginners will find it easier to call the car rental companies directly to begin with. For one thing, a live reservationist can help you find the rate you saw on the Internet. In this case, it's probably easiest to place the "blame" for your call on the client. For example, you might say, "My client says she saw a rate of $95.99 on the Internet. Can you match that?"

Before you make your calls, create a simple grid or table on a piece of paper to record the information you collect from the various companies. This will make it easy to compare and will give you all the information you need when and if you go over alternatives with your client.

Factors influencing your choice

As with any booking, you will have to weigh a number of factors when considering car rental companies. Some of them may be at odds with others.

- *Client preference.* The customer is always right and should be booked with the company he or she prefers, unless availability is a problem. Or if price becomes an issue.
- *Price.* Price is usually expressed as a type of car rather than a dollar figure. Generally speaking, if a customer wants Avis, they will not be particularly concerned that an Avis compact car costs $5 more than one from Budget. On the other hand, if the customer is looking for the absolute lowest cost, don't assume that "big" companies with on-terminal locations will automatically be more expensive than "little" companies with off-terminal locations. Always check.
- *Convenience.* All things being equal, book your client with a car company that has on-terminal pickup. If their preferred company is off-terminal at a particular airport, see if they want to shift allegiances in the interests of convenience.
- *What's in it for you?* As with hotels, it can be hard to track special promotions, contests, commission rates, and so forth.

But they exist with car rentals, just as they do with other travel products. If you have the leeway, you might want to steer your customers to rent with a company that will provide you with some advantage. As always, balance your self-interest against the client's best interests and make the right decision.

Making the sale

Most car rentals are straightforward enough that you should be able to discuss the client's needs and simply make the booking. The client will trust you to make the best decision based on his or her preferences. If you have to get back to the client to discuss alternatives, you may want to make bookings to hold the car; reservations can always be cancelled. In this case, try to limit the variables as much as possible. In other words, the client can have car A with car company B for price C or car X with company Y for price Z. Once you introduce too many variables, the customer (and you) will become hopelessly confused and the discussion will wander around in circles. Present the customer with a clear choice; be able to discuss the pros and cons; then let the customer decide.

Making the booking

If you have opted for a host agency that requires GDS connectivity, then you will be following whatever procedures apply to the GDS you are using. Once you get the hang of it, booking rental cars via a GDS becomes a quick and painless process. But there are other situations and other options:

Booking on the Internet

Most, if not all, of the domestic rental car companies give travel agents the option of booking on their web sites and earning a commission. In addition to the majors you might want to consider Car Rental Express (www.carrentalexpress.com), which serves as a booking portal for small, regional, discount car companies. It, too, pays commissions.

In every case I've seen, you will need to have an IATA number or another unique industry identifier to make these bookings. If you don't have one, you can always try to set up a "pseudo ARC number" with the car company in question, which can be a long, frustrating, and probably futile process. For guidance on how to get one, read *How to Get Your Own IATA Number*. If you purchased this book as part of my home study course, you already have it. If not you can order it at:

http://www.HomeTravelAgency.com/getiata.html

If you are working through a host agency and plan to use their IATA number, check with them to make sure your booking will be trackable when you book on a rental car site. Your host may have special pages set up on its own web site to facilitate bookings at some companies. It may also have special arrangements with a consortium or with preferred suppliers. Whatever, the situation, your host will be able to guide you — at least, it should.

The good news is that virtually all rental car sites offer online booking capabilities to travel agents. (Of course, that could change at any minute, but I think that's unlikely.) The bad news is that it's not always easy to find the travel agent portal; sometimes you have to go to a separate web site set up just for travel agents. However, if you poke around a bit or make a few phone calls, you should be able to figure it out. After that, it's point and click.

Booking on the phone

Most rental car companies will let travel agents book on the phone. If the reservationist tries to steer you to the GDS (which for the sake of this discussion I am assuming you don't have), try saying, "The GDS is down." You'll seldom get an argument to that one. Here's how this scenario will most likely play out.

First, identify yourself as a travel agent. You might say:

> *"Hello, this is Martha with Anytown Travel
> Agency. I'd like to make reservations for a
> client, please."*

This is the only way you will be able to collect your commission. At some point during the booking process, the reservationist should ask for your agency's IATA number, address, or some other identifier. Don't conclude the booking until you have given this information!

Information to give

First, tell the reservationist that you are a travel agent making a booking. Then, provide the basic booking information as outlined earlier:

- Place, date, and time of pickup.
- Place, date, and time of return.
- Type of car.
- Type of rental.

It's probably also a good idea to ask the reservationist if there are any special offers or promotions available that might give your client a better deal. Often car companies will have free upgrades or similar promotions going, but will only give them to you if you ask.

Make sure you provide the information that will assure your commission. That could include all or some of the following:

- Agency name, address, and phone number.
- Agency IATA number.
- Your name.

Information to get

There is also some very important information you will want for your client and for your records on each booking you make:

- **Confirmation number.** Like the record locator number in an airline booking, this is a unique identifier for this booking. You will want to give this number to the client, just in case there is any misunderstanding when they go to pick up the car.
- **The location** of the rental car counter in the airport or directions on how to get to an off-airport location.
- **Rules of the reservation.** For example, is there a penalty for no-shows?
- **The name of the reservationist.** It's also a good idea to ask for the name of the reservationist. If a problem arises later, it's good information to have.

Relaying the booking

When confirming the booking with the client, simply repeat the key booking information and the confirmation number. That's all the customer should need. Then be sure to cancel any extra bookings that you may have made to hold cars while the customer was deciding which company to use.

Foreign car rentals

Many of the companies that you deal with for domestic rentals have international operations that can provide your clients with cars in many foreign countries. These reservations can be researched and made exactly as you would a booking in the next state.

However, you should be aware that a better deal might be available from a company that specializes in overseas rentals. Firms like Kemwel and Auto Europe offer very attractive rates to the leisure traveler. Some of these rates require airline tie-ins; that is, the traveler must arrive on a certain airline to qualify for the rate.

Most domestic bookings are simply reservations — a car is held for the customer's arrival and the customer pays for the rental by presenting a credit card at the time of pickup. Many foreign bookings, however, require prepayment of some sort, especially the budget ones. These bookings are treated more like a tour element (see *Chapter 15: Booking Tours & Packages*) than a domestic car rental. In these cases, the car company will provide your customer with a voucher that the customer will present upon arrival overseas. The traveler will also be required to present a credit card at that time to cover any additional or unforeseen expenses (and there always are some), along with a valid driver's license, passport, and visa, if one is required to enter the country.

In some countries, especially Italy and Spain, an International Driver's Permit will be helpful or even required. The same holds true for less well traveled corners of the world, where officials prefer seeing a license in their own language, or at least one they can understand. International Driver's Permits must be obtained before leaving home; they are inexpensive and, even if not absolutely necessary, a fun thing to have. Your clients can get them at any local office of the American Automobile Association

(AAA), even if they are not members. The cost was $10 at press time and applicants must supply two passport-sized photographs. More information is available on the AAA web site, www.aaa.org.

Be sure to check the driver's age when booking foreign rentals. It's not just the minimum age you need to worry about. Some countries have laws that prevent renting cars to people over a certain age. The company you book with will be able to fill you in on any applicable laws.

Getting paid

Rental car commissions, like hotel commissions, are paid only after the trip has been completed. In the case of foreign car rentals, the commission payment is not due until 30 days after the car is returned. It may not be paid until some time after that.

Making sure you get what's coming to you will require careful record-keeping and persistent follow-through. A complete discussion of making sure you get your commissions will be found in *Chapter 9: Getting Serious*.

Summary

While booking rental cars will not make you rich, it can represent a fairly steady stream of income. When booking air, you should always ask whether the client will need a car at the destination. Car rentals also offer "upselling" opportunities for the alert agent who takes the time to ask why the client is traveling. Renting a flashy car is a relatively inexpensive way to make yourself feel special.

For the independent home-based agent with his or her own IATA number, one of the most attractive aspects of rental cars is that all the major companies (and some minor ones) now allow Internet bookings that let you avoid sharing the commission.

Foreign car rentals are a special case and can often be booked as if they were an element in a tour, complete with prepayment and better commission rates.

Action steps

Here are some things you can do to put what you have learned in this chapter into action:

- Visit several car rental web sites and explore their travel agent sections. Check to see what qualifications and identifying numbers are required to book on their site. Some rental car sites offer downloadable or printable information for travel agents. You may want to collect some of this material and file it for future reference.
- If you are currently working with a host agency, familiarize yourself with its guidelines for making rental car bookings. Pay special attention to online booking opportunities, either on the host's own web site or elsewhere, and preferred suplier

relationships.

- If at all possible, make some real, commissionable rental car bookings. Write down a step-by-step account of what you did to make the booking(s). Refer to this as you make additional bookings, refining your instructions to yourself. Make special note of new things you learn on each booking.

Chapter Fifteen:

Booking Tours & Packages

What you will learn

After you have completed this chapter you will be able to:

- Gather the information you need from your client to book the right tour for them.
- Use a variety of research tools to find the right tour.
- Understand the basic process of presenting a tour product to a client.
- Book tours with confidence.

Key terms and concepts

This chapter involves the following key terms and concepts:

- The word "tour" has several different meanings in the travel industry, depending on the context. To most people in the industry, it refers to an escorted trip in which ground transportation, lodging, at least some meals, and guide services are provided. More generically, it refers to any travel product that combines two or more elements.
- Selling a package usually results in a higher commission.
- The key challenge in selling tours is matching the tour to the client.
- When choosing a tour product, you must take sensible precautions to protect both yourself and your clients from any unpleasant surprises.

Introduction

"Wouldn't you like to make $200 on every phone call?"

That was the headline used by one tour wholesaler in its trade advertising aimed at travel agents. Two hundred dollars, it turns out, was the average commission paid out on the tour products the wholesaler offered at the time the ad ran. If you booked directly, that $200 would be yours. As an outside agent, you would only be in line for a portion of that $200 — $100, $120, even $140. Still not a bad payout for a single phone call.

That is why tours are so attractive to travel agents in general and why they should be especially attractive to you, the prospective home-based travel agent. In addition to the high per-sale income that tours offer, there are a number of other attractions to this particular travel product:

■ Tours are, by definition, a leisure product. That is, people take tours when they are going on vacation. Consequently, they are less price sensitive. Unlike the business traveler or the short-hop airline passenger, people shopping for tours are not looking for the absolute lowest price. They are looking for value within their budget. A good travel agent will be able to find out exactly what that budget is.

■ Because tours combine a number of separate elements, much of the travel agent's work is already done. You have far fewer worries about messing up the airline reservations because the tour operator has taken care of them for you — unless, of course, the tour is land-only.

What is a 'tour'?

For many of us, the word tour conjures up images of the "if-this-is-Tuesday-it-must-be-Belgium" type of experience. We picture harried tourists being shunted from place to place at a maddening pace, stuffed on buses, whisked past historical sights, rushed through museums, and dumped, exhausted, at the end of the day into hotels with mysterious plumbing fixtures. Some tours are like that, no doubt. But for the travel agent, the word tour has developed a much more generic meaning.

Some travel agents may quibble about definitions but, for all practical purposes, a "tour" is any combination of travel products that can be booked and sold as a single unit. Some operators use the word "package" to distinguish offerings that don't include the more "traditional" elements of a tour, such as group travel and a guide. In their parlance, airfare to London combined with four nights in a hotel and two theater tickets would be a package. Two weeks of sightseeing in England with a guide and group motorcoach travel from site to site would be a tour.

"Tour" or "package," the key point to remember is that a number of ingredients are bundled together and sold for a single price.

The power of the package

One reason that I put the discussion of tours and packages here, after airline tickets, hotels, and car rentals, was to make the following point: Packages, which are nothing more than a tour product, allow you to combine airfare, hotel, and rental car into one pre-priced product that is not only cheaper for your customer than the three elements booked separately but that pays you, the travel agent, a higher rate of commission. In fact, it is possible to book a package that saves your client money, while putting more money in your pocket than you'd have earned had you booked each element separately. Even if you never become a home-based travel agent, this single booking strategy can save you hundreds of dollars a year just on your own travel, both domestic and foreign.

Packages are an often overlooked option in domestic travel. For example, clients traveling to another city to attend a professional conference would typically think of getting an airline ticket and reserving a hotel room as two separate bookings. You might think that way, too. But put together a package for your clients, and you may be able to offer them the same air-hotel combination at a better price. Or, for only a bit more, you may be able to add a rental car to the package.

Domestic packages are not available everywhere. You will generally find them offered only to larger cities with a steady tourist trade — cities such as Boston, New York, Orlando, Miami, New Orleans, Las Vegas, Los Angeles, San Francisco, and Washington, DC. But packages are sometimes available to smaller markets as well. Some tour wholesalers may even be able to create a package for you; just call them up, tell them what you're after, and ask what they can put together for you.

Overseas, you will find a package to just about any major destination, and quite a few minor ones as well. Even tour operators who advertise escorted, all-inclusive tours will often be able to provide you with just air, a car, and a hotel if that's what your client wants.

Packages can even be good products to sell to clients who insist, "We're not interested in a tour." Say, a couple wants to fly to Paris and explore the chateau country on their own. They are perfect candidates for a "fly-drive" package, combining air and a rental car. You can probably even find a package that has hotel vouchers thrown in, so your clients can pick hotels or b&b's along their route or choose alternate lodgings as the spirit moves them. Packages can offer such good value that clients like them even when they don't use all (or any) of their vouchers. It's also a lot easier to get your commission when you're working with one U.S.-based supplier rather than a string of foreign hotels. So, as you begin serving your new customers in your new travel agent business, keep in mind the power of the package to save your clients money while making money for you.

Gathering information

You will probably find that there are three kinds of tour customers:
- Those who know exactly what they want.
- Those who have no idea of what they want.
- Those who are somewhere in between.

Obviously, the first type of customer is easiest to serve. For the others you will have to do some careful probing about their expectations — what they like, dislike, and so forth. This is what is known as "qualifying the customer" and a complete discussion of the techniques you can use will be found in *Part III* of this book. For now, let's look at some of the more obvious things you will need to know:
- ***Who, what, where, when, and why?*** These questions pro-

vide the basics. Family or couple? What sort of things are they hoping to do? Where would they like to do them? When do they want to go? And, for all of the above, why? Often the "why" can be the key element in making the right choice. A couple looking to "get away from the kids" should not be steered toward Disney World!

- ■ ***How?*** People looking into a tour-type vacation usually fly to the destination and then get around by rental car, escorted motorcoach, or local transportation. However, there are many vacationers who want a train experience. Others want to bike, pony trek, sail, or hike. Still others want to cruise. Since cruises are a whole separate category of travel experience, we will discuss them in the next chapter.

- ■ ***Budget.*** Try to get as specific information as possible about how much the customer is willing to or can spend. "We don't want to spend a lot of money," doesn't really give you what you need to go on. Some people will be very forthcoming. Others will hedge, perhaps worrying that you will try to sell them something 20% more expensive than the figure they provide. More suggestions on qualifying budget will be found in *Chapters 20: Qualifying* and *22: Handling Your Customers' Concerns* in *Part III* of this book.

- ■ ***How do they prefer to pay?*** Payment terms can make a big difference to many clients. Some people simply won't book unless they can pay with a credit card. Others will pay more on a credit card than they would if they had to pay by check. Since most tours require deposits (unless the departure date is very close, in which case the entire amount will be due), showing a willingness to work with the client to spread out payments can help you book more tour business. Even a deposit of as little as $10 is an important psychological commitment from the customer. You may have a week or longer to get the rest of the deposit.

- ■ ***Past experience and present expectations.*** A good benchmark for what people will like in the future is what they liked (or didn't like) in the past. Ask your clients about their past vacation experiences (especially ones similar to the one they are now planning). "What was your last trip to Hawaii like? Where did you stay? How did you like it?" Their comments will help you determine what to keep the same and what to change. Again, you will find a much lengthier discussion of this in *Part III*.

Research

Learning about tours and tour products is an ongoing responsibility for the serious travel agent, part-time or no. You should begin your research even before you start working on your first tour booking. The research itself can be fun; it can also save you time when that first booking comes along. Just be aware that you will never be able to know everything there is to know about tours; there are just too many, and the players and particulars keep changing.

If you have decided to specialize in a destination, you are way ahead of the game. In that case, you actually may be able to know all there is to know, or at least come close to it.

Here are some research tools and strategies you may want to follow:

- ■ ***Official Tour Directory (OTD).*** In my humble opinion, this tool is indispensable. It used to be available in print, a sort of Yellow Pages of the tour industry (and about the same size, too). Now it's available free, online, at www.TAedge.com. Free is nice, but I must say I miss the old print edition.

  You will have to register at TAedge, but it's simple and painless. Once you have access, you can search for tour operators by destination, activity, name, keywords. You can even search alphabetically. The listings do not give detailed information about all the tours offered by each operator. Rather they give you the address, web site, and phone number (usually toll-free) to call for more information. The listings will also alert you if the supplier is currently offering any special promotions. Don't be shy. If something catches your eye, call and ask for a brochure.

  Caution: The fact that a tour operator is listed in the *OTD* may tell you something about its seriousness as a travel provider, but it is not an absolute guarantee that the company is reliable or provides first-rate experiences to tourists.

- ■ ***United States Tour Operators Association (USTOA).*** Here is another free online resource. USTOA's members include most of the major tour operators. One nice thing about dealing with USTOA members is that, as a condition of membership, they are required to post a $1 million bond, specifically to reimburse travelers in the case of bankruptcy or other unpleasantnesses. At the site, you can browse through what members have to offer and download a complete current membership list. As with the *OTD* on the TAedge site, you will not find in-depth information, but you will be pointed to the companies that can provide it.

- ■ ***Your agency's preferred suppliers.*** Of special interest to you will be those tour operators listed in the *OTD* who are also preferred suppliers to your agency. There are a number of reasons for this. The most important, perhaps, is money. Your agency's preferred suppliers pay higher commissions, which presumably will be passed along to you. Another reason is that, by concentrating on selling the products of your agency's preferred suppliers, you will develop a growing familiarity with their offerings. That, in turn, will save you time (and therefore make you money) when it comes to doing re-

search for your one-hundredth tour customer. (For more on preferred suppliers, see *Chapter 9: Getting Serious*.)

- **The trade press.** Another source of information about tours is the trade press. Even though the *Official Tour Directory* is on the Internet, it can never be completely up-to-date. Tour companies are constantly offering new tours, amending existing ones, and phasing out old ones. New tour companies come into being all the time. The trade press documents this constant parade of products.

  Some publications, like *Travel Weekly* and *Jax Fax*, conveniently divide their coverage into sections. That makes it easy to find information about specific destinations. Many publications, *Travel Weekly* and *Travel Agent* among them, regularly publish separate supplements that focus on a specific destination (Hawaii, Europe, Southeast Asia), activity, or special interest (skiing, golf, honeymoons).

  The trade press will also keep you posted on which tour operators are no longer in business or seem to be headed for the dustbin. While it may seem unfair, any indication in the trade press that a tour operator may be in trouble is sufficient reason to stop booking with them. (See the discussion on "Protecting yourself" in *Chapter 9*.)

- **Clipping files.** It's a good idea to maintain a clipping file of destination and tour operator information that is of particular interest to you. This becomes a relatively easy task if you specialize in a destination or type of travel. If you are trying to be all things to all people, you may start to contemplate the benefits of specialization as your clipping file threatens to take over your house. I would especially recommend that you hold onto the special supplements in the trade press covering destinations and activities. These involve no clipping, usually provide a wealth of information on a number of suppliers, and are easy to store and refer to.

  Other sources of clippings are travel magazines and the travel section of the Sunday paper. The articles in them invariably focus on the destinations themselves rather than on specific tour operators. But it is a simple matter, using the *OTD*, to locate an operator that offers tours to a destination mentioned in *Travel & Leisure*, say, or a wholesaler who can book your client into that luxurious hideaway mentioned in *Conde Nast Traveler*.

Brochures

If there's a tour, there's a brochure. In most cases, it will be difficult, if not impossible, to sell a customer on a tour without showing a brochure. This is not a problem. In fact, a good brochure can be an excellent sales tool for you. Sometimes, an attractive brochure will sell a tour even when the agent is a less-than-compelling salesperson. This means, of course, that you should plan on having the appropriate brochures when selling tours. Whether you have the right brochures on hand when you need them is another matter. Here are some thoughts on getting brochures:

- **Your agency.** If your agency is local, you may be able to go to their office and put your hands on the brochures you need.
- **Your own brochure collection.** If you have decided to specialize, it's a good idea to start amassing a collection of appropriate brochures, especially from your agency's preferred suppliers.
- **Tour companies.** You can request brochures from tour companies. This can raise a number of problems, however. Some tour companies will only send brochures to the agency itself. This will slow things up considerably if your agency is out of town. Also, your agency may charge you postage to forward the material. Most do. If you are not working through a host agency, of course, the brochures come directly to you. Even when you can get the brochures sent directly to you, the wait can seem interminable. Tour companies vary widely in their responsiveness to requests for information. You may receive brochures so long after requesting them that you'll forget why you asked.
- **Fax.** Some companies will fax information on certain tours. Sometimes you can call a tour company and get them to fax brochures to you. They aren't quite as effective as the real things when it comes to presenting the tour to the client but they are a lot better than nothing.
- **The Internet.** You can sometimes use information on a tour company's web site as a sort of brochure. In fact, some companies have pretty snazzy slide shows on their sites. It is possible to talk to a client over the phone while each of you has a web site open on the computer screen in front of you. This can be a powerful and effective selling strategy, as you guide the client through the site. However, be careful. I would recommend using this only with tour companies that will not sell directly to the consumer. That way, you are protected from the tour operator poaching your prospect.
- **Other agencies.** If worse comes to worst, you can always go into another agency in town, pose as a tourist, and collect the brochures you need. The downside, of course, is that they will be stamped with the name of the agency from which you got them! Carefully apply a mailing label over the other agency's name and stamp on your own name.
- **Trade shows and seminars.** Suppliers are constantly exhibiting at trade shows and holding free seminars for the agency community. When you attend, come home with a bagful of brochures. For more on free seminars, see *Chapter 9.*
- **Other options.** If all else fails, you can use guidebooks, ar-

Booking Tours & Packages

ticles clipped from newspapers and travel magazines, even your own holiday snapshots as brochure substitutes. In fact, material like this can add extra punch to your presentation even when you have brochures.

Brochures are not just glossy sales aids. They contain crucial information about the terms and conditions of the tour. This is information you must have to do your job properly. It can be very dangerous to sell a tour without a brochure. So if you can't get the brochure itself, at least get the tour operator to fax you the terms and conditions and the pricing information.

Brochures can also help you pin down appropriate tours for customers who are indecisive or come to you with only a vague idea of what they want. After talking with them a bit, give them a bunch of brochures and say, "Here are some tours that might be right for you. Why don't you look them over. Then we can sit down and go over the ones that appeal to you."

When you are giving brochures to customers to take away with them, make sure that your name and phone number go with them. Most brochures have a blank space on the back page where the travel agency can print or stamp its name, address, and phone number. Staple your business card there. Or have a rubber stamp made.

What to look for

At first you will be matching up a client's stated desires with likely sources that can fulfill those desires. Let's say the client says, "I want to go somewhere warm and lie on a beach for a week," or "I'm attending a conference in Cannes and my wife and I would like to get a car and explore Provence." *OTD* and your host agency's list of preferred suppliers will quickly tell you who does the Caribbean and who rents cars in Europe.

That could be quite a long list; so you will need more information to winnow out the most appropriate choices. Give some thought to the specific type of tour product your client is looking for. That will determine which operator you call. And, again, just because the client says, "We're not interested in a tour," doesn't mean that a tour operator isn't the best source to call. Remember the "power of the package."

- *Fully escorted tours.* Some travelers are most comfortable with the type of tour where they travel with a group, are met at the airport by someone who knows where they'll be staying and eating, and have a guide to shepherd them along at every stop of the journey. This is a huge market. If this is what your client is looking for, you will most likely be able to satisfy their needs through one or more of your preferred suppliers. Tours in this category are sort of like blue-plate specials in a restaurant; the prices are very attractive but you can't make substitutions.

- *Customized tours.* Some companies specialize in putting together special tours that go beyond the blue-plate special model of the fully escorted tour. If your client has specialized requests, you may have to deal with one of these companies. Chances are you will still be able to deal with a preferred supplier.

- **Specialized tours.** The more offbeat your clients' interests (birding in Borneo or hiking in the Hebrides), the more likely you will have to deal with a small, specialized tour operator. Ecotourism and "soft-adventure" traveling are perfect examples. Usually this means dealing with someone who is not a preferred supplier or a major operator.
- **Wholesalers.** Many of your agency's preferred suppliers are probably wholesalers as well as tour operators. It's a malleable distinction. It means that, in addition to offering fully escorted tours and standard packages, they can put together special combinations for your clients on an ad hoc basis. A good example would be when your client has heard from a friend that such-and-such a resort in Jamaica is a good place to stay. A Jamaican tour wholesaler will be able to put that resort together with an air ticket, and perhaps a rental car, and quote you a single price for the package.

Tours can be seen as representing an entire spectrum of travel experiences. At their simplest, tours may be an airline ticket and a single hotel. At the other extreme, they can be months-long journeys through several countries, involving planes, trains, motorcoaches, several guides, many hotels, and specialized activities. What you look for in a tour operator will change somewhat as you move along this spectrum.

Here is a list of criteria offered by one tour operator in its advertising materials. While these points don't apply universally to all tour operators — and many of them don't apply at all to simpler types of tour products — they are a good place to start:

1. How much experience does the tour operator have in handling the destination to which clients are traveling?
2. Does the tour operator have its own offices in the destination?
3. Is the tour operator offering standard government-controlled tour packages (where applicable)?
4. Can the tour operator choose from a range of accommodations in given cities?
5. Are meals a la carte at local restaurants or are they set menus in hotels?
6. Will the tour group include only Americans, or will other nationalities be part of the group?
7. Can clients vary the itinerary as they travel?
8. Are departures set on fixed dates or is some flexibility allowed?
9. Has the tour organizer actually visited the destinations?
10. Can the tour operator handle all necessary arrangements including air ticketing, visas, and ground services in multi-destination trips?

11. Are air and visa services included in the advertised price?

12. Are prices subject to change, or are they guaranteed?

13. What background information can the operator provide concerning health, safety, and other practical matters?

14. Can the operator provide references from past clients?

15. Can the operator make special arrangements, such as overland crossings or visits to remote villages or archaeological sites?

The fine print

Somewhere on every brochure, often in teeny, tiny type, are the "Terms and Conditions" or "General Conditions" under which the tour operator sells the tours listed in the brochure. The customer will sometimes ignore this information. You never should. Before you recommend a tour to a client, read the terms and conditions and make sure you understand them, agree with them, and can justify them, if necessary, to the customer.

The Terms and Conditions can also serve as a helpful reminder to you about what's important. Among the things they cover are:

- *Deposits.* It's the rare tour that doesn't require them. Usually they are required within seven to ten business days of making the booking. You will also be told when final payment is due. It can range from 30 to 60 days prior to departure.

- *Late booking fees.* Because tours are generally planned well in advance, most tour operators penalize those who book shortly before departure.

- *Revisions/changes.* Tour operators do not like to make changes to bookings once they're made, so they'll often build in a penalty for doing so.

- *Cancellations/refunds.* Tour operators will refund money in the case of cancellations, but they don't like to do it. Therefore, they build in elaborate rules and restrictions concerning when and under what conditions refunds will be issued. Typically, there is a penalty for cancellations; that is, you don't get all the money back. Sometimes, the cancellation penalty is graduated; the closer the departure date, the less the client gets back. In either case, no money will be refunded after a certain point, sometimes as much as 30 days prior to departure.

- *Insurance.* Because of cancellation hassles, most companies will recommend that your client take out insurance. Very often they will follow up this suggestion with an offer to sell that insurance. This insurance may be commissionable to you, although the brochure (since it is intended for the client's eyes) probably won't say this.

- *Responsibility/liability.* This will probably be the longest section of fine print. Here the tour operator presents a long litany of things that are beyond its control and for which it will accept no liability. These are things like airline delays, hotels going out of business, natural disasters, and international terrorism. Presumably they pay some lawyer a lot of money to draft these sections to protect themselves from lawsuits. Of course, if something goes wrong, some other lawyer will make a lot of money by suing them anyway. Go figure.

Form of payment

There is another aspect of the "fine print." It won't show up in the brochures, but it is very important for you to know. That is the form or forms of payment the tour operator will accept. The way in which the operator chooses to handle payment may affect your decision on whether to use them or not.

There are two basic ways a tour operator will accept payment:

- ■ ***Credit cards.*** Most of the larger tour operators will accept credit cards. This makes it easy on everyone, and many customers prefer to use plastic because of the flexibility and protection the cards provide. You may have to time your booking carefully so that the charge shows up on next month's bill instead of this month's. That can mean instructing your host agency not to submit the card before a certain date.

  All things being equal, you're better off if the customer uses a credit card. That way, if a problem develops with the supplier, the customer has some recourse — he can tell the credit card company he's disputing the charge. The argument becomes one between the customer and the supplier, not between the customer and you. *Chapter 9* offers important advice on dealing with credit cards.

- ■ ***Agency check.*** This is a business check with the name of the agency on it. If you're an outside agent, that means the name of the host agency through which you book and not your own business name. If you are dealing with the tour operator directly, it would be your business check. If you can collect a check from the customer, this arrangement sometimes (but not always) has the advantage of allowing you to deduct your commission up front and pay the tour operator a "net" amount. The trouble is, many customers don't want to pay by check and won't understand or particularly care about your problems in dealing with the tour operator. If this is going to become an issue, it's better to find it out during the research phase — before you get the customer all excited about taking the tour.

Some tour operators who prefer agency checks will accept credit cards for an additional charge intended to cover the fees the credit card company charges the tour operator. This, too, can cause problems with customers, who won't understand when their $1,000 tour costs $1,030.

You also may find that, for one reason or another, your host agency doesn't like issuing agency checks. So even if your customer is willing to pay by check, you still have a problem. Check to make sure you know your agency's policy on this score before you find yourself in an embarrassing situation with your customer or the tour operator.

As your business grows and your horizons expand, you may find yourself dealing with tour operators located in a different country. In this case, making payment presents additional challenges. The standard method is by wire transfer. That is, funds are sent electronically from your bank to the supplier's bank. This service is not free and, as I mentioned earlier, you might want to take wire transfer fees into account when choosing a bank for your business checking account. A $40 fee will seem low when you are paying for several bookings at once, but when your total commission on a booking is $100 or so, $40 represents a big hit. If you need to make a wire transfer, your banker can walk you through the process. It is not difficult.

Factors influencing your choice

Unless the client has made a specific request for a tour operator (or unless you know that the client has had a bad experience with a particular tour operator), you have wide latitude in recommending the best tour product to meet your client's needs and desires.

- **Client preferences.** First and foremost, of course, is giving the client what he or she wants. In other words, the tours you suggest should match as precisely as possible the list of wants and needs the client has given you. Getting the match right is a matter of getting to know your customers, asking them the right questions, and listening closely to their answers. Those skills will be discussed more completely in *Part III* of this book. However, we should note here that, in the area of client preferences, you will want to pay particular attention to:

- **Budget.** Ideally you will begin your research and selection phase knowing what the customer's budget is. (Again, this will be discussed fully in *Part III*.) Unless there is a compelling reason for doing so, you will not want to recommend anything that is over the client's stated budget — except, perhaps, as a "just in case" alternative. The best choice is a tour that is sufficiently below the client's stated price that he or she will feel that you are providing an especially good deal. If the client has suggested a range of prices, coming in at the middle to low end of that spectrum is a good idea.

  I am assuming, of course, that you will be able to meet the customer's expectations at the price you will quote. The client must understand the relationship between price and value. It may be important to make clear to the client what is possible given the budget. It may even be appropriate to suggest to a client that, for the price they want to pay, a stateside vacation might be more appropriate than the trip to the French Riviera that they envision. While it may be possible to send them there at their price by booking them into the Chateau Fleabag, you will not wind up with a happy customer.

The issue of client preference and budget aside, there are other equally important factors that will govern your choice of the products you will present to your client. They are as follows:

- **Preferred suppliers.** I am a firm believer in using your agency's preferred suppliers wherever possible — especially those with whom the agency has a direct relationship (as opposed to those with whom the agency gets a higher commission because they joined a consortium). This enhances your income, makes you more valuable to the agency, and provides you with a body of information and experience that makes you more efficient and therefore more valuable to your customers. When you can't find a match between your client's needs and your agency's preferred suppliers, you can always use other suppliers. Or you can decide that you sell only the products of your preferred suppliers and direct your clients elsewhere.
- **The "personality" of the tour.** This applies primarily to fully escorted tours, where the personnel involved and the choices of sightseeing options can directly affect the quality of the experience. Three fully escorted tours, provided by three different operators, can cover the same ground yet provide radically different experiences — none of them necessarily bad. Knowing which tour operator's personality best matches your client can be tricky. As you gain more experience, debrief more and more returning clients, and go on fam trips yourself, you'll begin to get a sense of the styles of the various operators.
- **Required form of payment.** As noted above, the form in which the tour operator requires payment may influence your ability to do business with them.
- **The reliability of the tour operator.** Things go wrong when people travel. Flights get canceled. The reserved hotel room is unavailable when the traveler arrives. Tour operators strand people in far-off lands. In the first two examples, travelers are likely to blame the airline or the hotel. In the last example, they are likely to add you to the list of guilty parties. They might even sue you! I go into this ghastly possibility a bit more in *Chapter 9*. For now, just remember that it is a good idea to guard against the possibility that the tour operator will go belly up or otherwise make your client's life miserable.

Sensible precautions

Since the viability and reliability of a tour operator are such important considerations, let's take some time to consider ways in which you can protect yourself (and your clients) from disaster. Just remember that none of the things suggested here offers an absolute guarantee that something won't go wrong. There is always that possibility. Still, some sensible precautions will increase your odds of being able to provide your customers with carefree vacations on a consistent basis.

- *Preferred suppliers.* Your agency's preferred suppliers will tend to be the older, bigger, more stable companies — thus the ones least likely to leave your clients stranded. This is especially true of companies that are members of consortiums. It may be less true of suppliers with whom your agency has a direct relationship.

- *The trade press and other media.* As mentioned earlier, it is a good idea to keep an eye on the trade press for distant early warnings that things may be amiss at certain tour operators. The letters to the editor columns in travel magazines and travel sections of newspapers may also contain horror stories about certain operators or destinations. Take heed and avoid them.

- *The Internet.* The Internet can serve as a distant early warning system of tour operator problems. Sites like TripAdvisor.com and Epinions.com carry reviews of hotels and other travel products. You might also do a Google search for the tour operator you are considering or search the online archives of the travel trade magazines, which you can access at sites like TravelWeekly.com and TravelTrade.com.

- *Your own clients.* In *Part III* we will discuss the importance of follow-up with your customers. One thing you want to find out is which suppliers your customers like and why. All things being equal, you're better off sending a client off with a supplier another client likes than trying out someone new.

- *Credit cards.* As I mentioned earlier, using a credit card can offer the client some protection if problems develop later.

- *Built-in tour insurance.* One of the reasons I mentioned the membership of the United States Tour Operators Association (USTOA) earlier is that the Association has a program that indemnifies travelers against the failure of its members. The American Society of Travel Agents (ASTA) also has a program whereby tour operators insure the travelers' trip. Booking with these suppliers can provide an added level of assurance.

- *Optional tour insurance.* If insurance isn't built in, encourage your clients to take some out. You can choose to sell the limited insurance the supplier provides or (a better alternative) third party travel insurance that offers broader protection and, often, higher commissions. If they choose not to buy insurance, document that fact on an insurance waiver (see *Chapter 9*).

Making the sale

Three basics that we've discussed in the previous sections about "making the sale" apply to tours as well:

- Present the client with three choices — your recommendation and two fallbacks.
- Be prepared to discuss the tradeoffs and differences among the choices.
- Lay out all the relevant facts about the booking.

Tours, however, differ from the products we've discussed so far (airlines, hotels, and rental cars) in a number of ways. Thus they require even more careful presentation to the client. You want to be absolutely sure that the client understands all the "rules of the game." Otherwise, you and the client may have some unpleasant surprises down the line.

Presenting the tour to the customer

"Presenting" is a very specific sales skill, which we will discuss in detail in *Part III* of this book. For now, it's important to remember that recommending a specific tour to a customer and asking that customer to make a decision to part with his or her hard-earned money to go on that tour is a serious business, which you should conduct in a thorough, orderly, and professional manner.

Our primary concern here is that the customer understand just what she will receive for her money. That means you have to make sure the customer understands, among other things, the following:

- **What's included.** One reason to be thorough in this area is to present the product you are offering in all its glory; "A champagne cocktail reception on arrival" has a nice ring to it. On another level, it is plain common sense; you owe it to your customer to explain exactly what she is getting.
- **What's NOT included.** Your list of what's included implies that everything else is not included. If the tour provides "some meals" that implies that most meals are on the client. If the tour includes "a half-day excursion to Tulum," that implies that it does not include "a half-day excursion to Chichen Itza." Still, it is often a good idea to spell out what the client can't expect, especially when there is the slightest possibility of a misunderstanding. Many people, to cite one small example, don't know what a "Modified American Plan" is. (It's breakfast and dinner but no lunch.) Similarly, if the brochure tells the customer he is going to "the Caribbean's biggest and best scuba diving resort," it might be a good idea to point out that the tour he is contemplating does not include any scuba diving, although it is available on-site for an additional charge. Telling customers what is not included can sometimes en-

courage them to add elements to the tour — which are commissionable, naturally!

- ***Payment terms.*** This one is crucial. Make sure the customer knows when deposits are due (see "Get the check," below), when additional payments are due, and when the final payment is due. If there is enough lead time, you may be able to work out an installment payment plan.
- ***Restrictions and penalties.*** You have to give the bad news along with the good. Make sure the customer knows what will happen if she backs out later. It is a good idea to point these items out in the fine print of the brochure, explain them to the customer, get her agreement that she understands, and then make a mark in the margin (a check mark or "OK") to indicate that the point has been covered.

'Get the check'

Years ago, when I was preparing the original manuscript of this book for publication, I ran it by some friends in the travel industry. One Certified Travel Counselor (CTC) kept writing in the margins of the previous chapters, "Ask for the check...Get the check!... Don't be shy. Ask for the check... Always get the check!"

I decided to save his sage advice for here. With airline tickets, most clients pay by credit card and are pretty certain they're actually going to make the trip before they get in touch with you. With hotels and car rentals, customers usually don't pay until they get there. Tours are another matter.

Because tours are relatively high-ticket items and because they are usually a discretionary purchase (no one *has* to go to the South Pacific!), there is always the risk of "buyer's remorse." This is common in all sorts of selling situations, and travel is no exception. Once the customer has made a buying decision, he immediately starts thinking, "Oh no, what have I done? I've parted with my hard-earned money. Maybe it wasn't the right decision. Maybe I could have gotten a better deal somewhere else. Maybe I can't really afford this. Maybe I better not go." If the client hasn't actually given someone a check, backing out becomes a very easy option. Moreover, because there are so many tour operators and travel agents out there seeking your clients' business, there is always the possibility that they may find a better deal — or at least a different deal that appeals to them more.

Those are just two good reasons to "get the check." Another is that the tour company demands it. Most tour operators want to get a deposit no later than seven days after the booking is made: No deposit, no booking. If the client decides to "firm it up" later, the price may have gone up — assuming, of course, there's still space left.

That is why it is always a good idea to conduct this phase of the booking process face-to-face with the client. That way, you can not only ask for the check, you can get it in your hot little hand. More on the nitty-gritty details and techniques of handling this kind of situation will be found in *Part III.*

Of course, the "check" may be a credit card. If that is the case, you will have to make arrangements to comply with your agency's policy on handling credit cards. This was discussed in *Chapter 9.*

I am not suggesting that you "trap" or "hoodwink" or "pressure" your customers in any way. Even if they give you a check, they still have the option to cancel within the rules laid out by the tour operator. By asking for the check, you help your customer see the true nature of the decision you are asking him or her to make. Suppose you say to your customer:

> *"Would you like to take the Grand Tour of*
> *Italy?"*

A customer's "yes" answer to this question does not mean the trip will take place. The customer probably wants to do a lot of things, very few of which will actually get done. Suppose, on the other hand, you say:

> *"If you'd like to take the Grand Tour of Italy,*
> *I'll need a deposit of $500 today to reserve*
> *your space. Shall we go ahead and do that?"*

If the customer responds affirmatively and writes a check, there is a much higher probability — not an absolute certainty, but a higher probability — that he or she will actually go.

Another way to handle this is to institute a "plan-to-go" fee as discussed in *Chapter 9.* That way, you already have the client's deposit (or a good chunk of it) in hand and the client has an added incentive to firm up the booking.

Getting help

Most tour operators are more than happy, even eager, to help you in any way they can, especially when you have an interested prospect you are trying to get to sign up. This is especially true if you are working on a group booking. Don't hesitate to contact the tour operator's regional sales manager (RSM) if you feel you need some assistance. They might be able to give you some hints or provide you with additional sales materials that will help you close the sale. If a big enough booking is involved, the RSM might even make a trip to meet with you and the prospect.

Making the booking

You may have made a booking with the tour operator before getting the final go-ahead from the client. You would do this for the same reason you would book a hotel room before getting the client's okay — to hold the space. Many tour operators will give you a price quote which they will then guarantee for a certain period of time. Bookings can always be canceled — and frequently are.

There are so many tours, types of tours, and tour operators that it is almost inevitable that there are many different permutations, combinations, and subtleties in how individual companies operate. Fortunately, like the airlines, most of the larger tour operators have well-trained reservationists whose job it is to make it as easy as possible for you to book your clients on their tours.

Smaller companies, for their part, are often willing to walk you through the process of booking, even if it means calling in the owner to explain the procedures. So, if you have any worries or uncertainties about making your first tour bookings, I would encourage you to remember the "magic words." If you can't remember what they are, here's a hint: They're at the end of *Chapter 11: The Basics of Booking*.

Above all, don't let your uncertainty or embarrassment keep you from asking what you might think are "dumb" questions. It's possible to make mistakes when booking tours, and you want to avoid that at all costs.

GDS and Internet bookings

Many tour products can be booked on the GDS if you are using one. More and more of the larger tour operators are providing travel agents with an online booking engine. However, I would recommend that you stick with the phone until you really know your way around the tour marketplace. There are so many variables that it is always helpful to have the reservationist's expertise to fall back on.

In the case of the online booking engines, I find that they work best for the simplest, plain-vanilla products. Once you gain some experience, you may find them a time saver for certain bookings.

Information to give

Booking a tour is, in many respects, like booking an airline ticket. The reservationist will want to know:

- The name of the tour, as given in the brochure. Sometimes a number of code will be used (see "IT number," below).
- The passenger(s) *exact* name(s). In other words, their name as it appears in their passport.
- The departure date.
- The city of departure.

If your customer wants any add-on options (excursion to the ancient ruins, scuba diving package, tennis lessons, etc.), the reservationist will need to know about that, too. Some tour products will have an extensive list of options, so make sure you cover all the bases — with your customer and with the reservationist.

The reservationist will also want:

- Each passenger's address and phone number.
- The IATA number of your host agency. If you are dealing directly with the tour operator you may be using your own or a "pseudo ARC or IATA number." You will find more on this in

How to Get Your Own IATA Number. If you bought this book as part of my home study course, you already have it. If not, you can order it at:

http://www.HomeTravelAgency.com/getiata.html

- Information about the passengers' citizenship and whether they have passports and any necessary visas.

Information to get

Among the things you will want from the reservationist are:

- *Airline schedule.* If the tour operator takes care of the air as well as the land portion of the trip, get a complete rundown of the customer's flight itinerary: airline, flight numbers, dates, and times of departure and arrival. You may even be able to get seat assignments at this time.
- *Confirmation number.* As with other types of bookings, this specific tour booking will be identified by the tour operator with a unique confirmation number. You will need this for any future communication with the operator about the booking.
- *IT number.* The IT number is a number that identifies the tour product in the various global distribution systems (GDSs). The same systems that carry all the data on airline schedules and fares can also be used to book many tour products, especially those of the major operators. If the tour you are booking is one of these, you may need the IT number to identify it to your host agency and make it easier for them to claim and process the booking.
- *Reconfirmation of payment schedule and amounts.* Make sure you know when the deposit and the final payment are due. Usually, payment is a two-step process, but the routine may differ from operator to operator.
- *When and how tour documents will be delivered.* Documents are usually delivered after final payment and about two weeks before departure. It's best to have them delivered to you, if possible. Otherwise you'll have to make arrangements with your agency to pick them up there or have them forwarded to you in plenty of time to present to your client.

Relaying bookings & getting documents

Assuming that you are booking the tour in your capacity as an outside sales representative (as opposed to dealing directly with the tour operator under your own business name), you will have to relay the booking to your agency. Most agencies will give you a form they have developed specifically for this purpose. Your agency will need the information to process the booking properly (if that's necessary on their part) and to identify you as the appropriate person to pay when the commission comes in.

The term "tour documents" is used to refer to a grab bag of things sent to the passenger by the tour company. They include:

- Airline tickets.
- Coupons or vouchers for various elements of the tour such as meals, reception parties, excursions, vehicle rentals, etc.
- A printed itinerary and/or instructions for the tour. This information may be included in something with a fancy name like "Tour Membership Certificate."
- Guidebooks or pamphlets covering areas to be visited.
- Luggage tags and stickers with the tour company's name and logo.
- Shoulder bags, passport wallets, and such, also boldly emblazoned with the tour company's name.

If the trip is a fully escorted tour, items like luggage tags and stickers may be more than "little extras." They are often used by the people conducting the tour to identify luggage and people who belong to the tour. Consequently, using them isn't optional. Make sure your customers know the importance of displaying these tags and stickers — even if they are ugly and garish, which many of them tend to be.

When the tour documents arrive, examine them carefully against your written records to make sure everything is in order — correct dates, flights, number of vouchers, etc. You may want to prepare your own additions to the package. Here are some suggestions:

- Your own list of things to see and do, restaurant recommendations, special instructions, and so forth.
- Brochures about the destination from the country's tourist office.
- Maps.
- A guidebook you feel will be especially helpful.
- A gift from you that will prove helpful on the trip.

Remember, you may be receiving several hundred dollars in commission on this trip. Spending a little time and a few extra dollars is an excellent investment in goodwill.

Getting paid

Tour commissions are typically paid to the travel agency about 30 days after the customer returns from the trip, and certainly not before departure. How soon the agency passes your share of the commission on to you depends on the agency's policies, efficiency, and goodwill.

Tour operators do not have the best of records when it comes to paying commissions. Delays, especially when credit card payments are involved, are widespread. Some agencies report waiting seven to eight weeks after the client's trip before receiving their commission.

To protect yourself, make sure you know the tour operator's policy on paying commissions. Knowing when the agency should receive the commission lets you know when to start bugging them about getting your share. Here again, good record-keeping is essential. Tours are often booked many months before departure. If you don't keep on top of what's coming due when, you run the risk of missing out on what's owed you. Remember, no matter how nice the folks at your host agency are, their primary duty is to run their business, not yours.

Summary

The word "tour" has various meanings, but in the travel industry it's most often used to refer to any travel product that has two or more elements that could be sold separately. By selling a "package" or "tour," you can sometimes earn a higher commission than you would if you had sold the elements separately. A package combining air, hotel, and rental car is a good example of this phenomenon.

Selling tours requires the same attention to detail as selling other travel products, but the issue of personality — both of the client and the tour — plays an equally important role. The better you can match the client to the tour, the more successful you will be and the more repeat business you will earn. Because there are so many tour operators, it makes sense to concentrate on selling the products of major operators that you know to be financially sound or that have bonding or insurance policies in place.

Tour brochures are not just a great source of information; they can be valuable selling aids. It is rare to sell a tour without a brochure. You should have a good supply of brochures on hand for those tour products you sell most often or in which you have decided to specialize. Always read the fine print of the brochure and do not neglect to instruct the client about the tour's Terms and Conditions.

Because tours are relatively high ticket items that require time to research and sell, you should always ask for a deposit at the earliest possible time. A good way to do this is with a so-called "pay-to-go" fee.

Action steps

Here are some things you can do to put what you have learned in this chapter into action:

- Familiarize yourself with the TAedge and USTOA web sites. You might start by using a real or made up request from a potential customer ("I'd like to take one of those African safaris.") and then seeing how easy (or difficult) it is to locate some solutions that might work for the customer.
- Collect some tour brochures and pay particular attention to the Terms & Conditions (the fine print). If you find something that is unclear or you have any questions, call the tour operator and ask them to explain it to your satisfaction.
- If you have a host agency, look into the tour operators that are preferred suppliers. Try to familiarize yourself with what they have to offer and ask yourself which ones would work best for you. That is, which do you think have products that

would appeal to the people to whom you will most likely be selling.

- Download the current membership list of the USTOA, browse through it, and investigate any tour operators that you feel might fit in with your business plan for your travel business. Circle the ones that are preferred suppliers of your host agency (if you have one).

- If at all possible, make an actual tour booking, even if it is an extremely simple one (a package, for example). Keep step by step notes of what you did to make the booking.

Chapter Sixteen: Booking Cruises

What you will learn

After you have completed this chapter you will be able to:

- Gather the information you need from your clients to make a cruise booking.
- Use a variety of questioning techniques and research sources to choose the cruise that is right for your client.
- Understand the importance of your "drive market."
- Book cruises with confidence.

Key terms and concepts

This chapter involves the following key terms and concepts:

- A home port is any port from which a particular cruise ship departs. Cruise ships can change home ports once or more during the course of a year.
- A "drive market" is a geographical area within driving distance of a home port from which cruises depart. If you live in a drive market, you should concentrate on the cruise lines that serve its home ports.
- Cruising is more about the overall experience than the specific itinerary. Cruise customers are especially loyal, with more than 85 percent of them taking another cruise.
- Cruising is perhaps the most popular and profitable travel product you can sell.

Introduction

"The Lo-o-o-ve Boat!"

There can't be very many people who aren't familiar with that theme song. In fact, one cruise line bought the rights to it and used the song in its commercials.

Cruises are a great travel product for the home-based travel agent to sell: They have broad "name recognition," as they say in the ad game. On top of that, they're a lot of fun. Cruise lines get phenomenal repeat business because the people who like them, really like them. The Cruise Lines International Association (CLIA) says that nine out of ten people who take a cruise report that their expectations were met or exceeded and two thirds of them rate cruising as superior to other types of vacations. Even those who have never cruised are thinking about it — six in ten, according to CLIA.

According to another source, 85% of those who take one cruise take another. Many people cruise twice a year, regular as clockwork. Moreover, cruise bookings have a wonderful way of being (or becoming) multiple bookings. One person in four cruises with friends, says CLIA.

Some other facts about cruising may surprise you. Half of all cruise passengers are under 40. First-timers are even younger, and fully one-third are single.

From the travel agent's standpoint, a cruise is like a tour, only more so. It's like a tour in that it combines a number of different elements in one package at one price. Many cruise bookings combine airfare to the port of embarkation and back, a berth, all meals, and all entertainment. I say "only more so" because when you book a cruise you are, in effect, earning a commission on things (like meals and night club shows) you wouldn't share in otherwise.

While land-tours are very dependent on the destination, cruises are more about that elusive something called "the cruise experience." Just because someone loved the tour of Italy you sent them on last year, doesn't mean selling them a tour to China this year will be any easier. If someone loved their cruise of the Caribbean, however, selling them a Mexican Riviera cruise can be a snap. This aspect of cruises makes it easier to sell "cruising" as the product itself, without waiting for a customer to express an interest in going to a certain destination. You simply select a specific cruise that you think will appeal to your market and then go out and sell it through direct mail or email solicitations and "cruise nights" — gatherings to which you invite a sizable group of people interested in cruising and sell them on the benefits of this specific cruise, usually with the aid of videos and brochures from the cruise line.

In short, cruises are a great product — high-ticket (yet economical for the traveler), easy to explain and sell, and an excellent source of repeat business. Once your cruise business gets going, you should be able to look forward to a steady stream of cruise customers each year. Many will be repeaters who will require little selling.

Important Note: By this time, you should have a pretty good idea of the process of gathering information and booking travel products. So in this chapter, I am going to concentrate more on the elements that make cruises different from other travel products. I will also discuss them more as an off-the-shelf product you can actively sell than as customized packages that you put together on an ad hoc basis to meet a particular customer's needs. Of course, if you specialize in a destination, you can sell tours in much the same way. (If you are skipping around in the book, you will find a lot of information in the previous chapters that will be useful when booking cruises.)

Gathering information

As with any travel product, it is important that you do a thorough and efficient job of debriefing your customers for the key information you need to match them with the perfect cruise. Assuming that someone comes to you expressing an interest in taking a cruise, you will want to know:

- ***Who's going where, for how long, and why.*** This is not always as obvious as it might seem. Are they planning on taking the kids? (Cruising is a great family getaway!) Are they considering going with friends? (If so, you will want to make a strong case for handling the friends' bookings as well.) Cruises range in length from one day to several months, with four- and seven-day cruises being the average. The Caribbean is the stereotypical cruise destination for Americans, but Alaska, Hawaii, and the Mediterranean also offer wonderful experiences.

  Asking "why" the customer wants to cruise can give you valuable insights into what the customer is looking for in terms of budget and overall experience. If the customer is new to cruising, you will want to explore their preconceptions and misconceptions about cruises to help you sell them the right product.

- ***Past experience and preferences.*** If they have cruised before, they may have a specific cruise line in mind. At the very least, their past cruising experience (what they liked and what they didn't) will tell you the type of cruise line and cruise experience that is most likely to appeal.

- ***Preferred and alternate sailing dates.*** Cruises tend to sell out. The availability of berths on any given cruise, however, is somewhat fluid until shortly before sail time. That's because reserved space gets canceled when no deposit is forthcoming. Thus, a cruise that's all booked up today may open up tomorrow. Still, it's best not to count on that when booking. Holding confirmed space is always preferable to being on a wait list.

- ***Budget.*** What the customer can pay is an important factor in determining the kind of experience you will be able to provide. With cruises, more so than with other travel products, you get what you pay for. So don't be afraid to "stretch" the budget a bit by presenting a cruise that's at the upper end of the customer's price range. While the cost may seem high at first glance to first-time cruisers, you'll be able to show them that cruises are actually very economical when you take into account their all-inclusive nature. Generally speaking, it's better to provide a great cruise at the upper range of the client's budget than to provide a disappointing experience at the bottom end of that range. If you know the kinds of cruises your customers have taken in the past, you will be able to ballpark their budget, even if they are reluctant to give specifics.

- *Client preferences.* Under this heading are things like inside or outside cabins (the inside are cheaper), a range of cabin categories they will accept (if they are experienced cruisers), the kinds of things they want to do (frequent port calls or more days at sea, for example), and preferred cabin layout. Along with budget, client preferences will tell you what cabin categories (see "Making the booking," below) you'll be looking at when selecting a specific cruise. For example, if your customers will not or cannot tolerate upper and lower berths, that will cut them out of the cheapest categories.

As I mentioned earlier, cruises can be marketed much more readily than many other travel products. Typically, a travel agent or agency will pick a sailing date for a specific ship and build a marketing campaign to sell berths on that cruise to as many people as possible. (We'll talk more about how that works a little later.) That means you can begin today to gather the information you will need to make decisions about which cruise lines and which cruises you might want to market to your customer base.

This is not as big a job as it might be with tours. Although the number of cruise options grows every year, the total number is still manageable, especially since you will probably narrow your search to a few key cruising areas — Alaska, the Caribbean, and the Mexican Riviera, for example. Here are some things you will want to consider as you look around for cruises to sell:

- *Your own personal preferences.* It's always easier to sell a product you know well and feel enthusiastic about. So if you are an old hand at cruising and you have a favorite cruise line, it makes a lot of sense to start your cruise business with that line. If you are new to cruising or don't have a strong preference, you will be well advised to follow your interests. If naturalist cruises to the Galapagos, Alaska, and Antarctica appeal, pushing the Caribbean may not be your best bet.
- *What's popular.* You can get a quick idea of what's selling in your market by looking at the ads in the travel section of the Sunday paper. The cruise destinations that show up again and again are "hot" in your market.
- *The drive market.* The term "drive market" refers to the geographical region within driving distance of a cruise line home port. What constitutes "driving distance" will vary from client to client, but it is probably farther than you'd imagine. A great many people are willing to drive a long distance to avoid taking a plane. Recognizing this trend, the cruise lines have increased the number of home ports they are using.

Cruising will be very attractive to your drive market, as it holds out the promise of exotic ports of call without the hassle (and in some people's minds the risk) of an airline trip. Take the time to familiarize yourself with home ports within a day or so's drive from your location and the cruise lines that serve them.

- *Marketing help.* Many cruise lines offer marketing assistance to help you sell their product. Knowing which lines provide the best backup may well affect your decisions. In fact, this consideration can be crucial when selecting a specific cruise to market.

- *Preferred suppliers.* Take a close look at the cruise lines with which your agency has a special relationship, either directly or through a consortium. If there's a match between what they offer and what you want to sell, then the added commission is an additional incentive.

Research

Long before the first customer asks you about cruises, you should be doing your research into this lucrative area. There are many good sources of information about cruising, cruise lines, and their individual ships. Among the sources are:

- *The cruise lines themselves.* I find that cruise line brochures make for wonderful reading. You can get booklets that cover all cruises in a specific area, brochures about a particular ship, and itineraries for individual sailings. Many cruise lines also provide videos that do a beautiful job of making the cruise experience come alive. Not only do they make superb marketing tools but the cost is so modest that they are worth buying just for your own research and viewing pleasure.

- *CLIA.* The Cruise Lines International Association can provide you with a wealth of information about cruises and how to sell them.

- *Books and industry references.* My favorite is the *Berlitz Ocean Cruising and Cruise Ships*, but there are many others available. *The Travel Agent's Complete Desk Reference* has more listings. If your purchased this book as part of my home study course, you already have it. If not, you can order it at:
  http://www.HomeTravelAgency.com/deskref.html

- *The Internet.* There are a growing number of web sites that cater to the cruising public, posting detailed reviews from actual cruisers. Among them are CruiseCritic.com, CruiseOpinion.com, Epinions.com, CruiseMates.com, CruiseAddicts.com, and Cruises.About.com. One I especially like is CruiseDiva.com, which also offers excellent articles that can help educate you about the cruising experience from your customers' point of view.

- **Personal experience.** Nothing substitutes for first-hand, on-the-spot experience. If you don't have it, you can get it by taking a low-cost cruise-seminar sponsored by an organization like OSSN. Get out on the high seas, let the salt air blow through your hair, relax by the pool, take in the floor shows, graze at the midnight buffets — learn all you can about cruising. Like exploring destinations, it's a tough job. But someone has to do it, and it might as well be you.

These sources will help you decide which cruise lines might have a product line that is ideal to go out and sell to your customers and your marketplace. Once you have a live customer sitting in front of you asking specific questions about specific dates, specific cruising areas, and even specific cruise lines, however, you will have to narrow your research to the most appropriate sources. You'll find them by checking:

- **Your own "preferred suppliers."** If you have a number of cruise lines that you, personally, like to recommend, your first step would be to see if their offerings match the customer's needs and wants.
- **Books and industry references.** These are excellent sources of information when you need to respond to specific requests.
- **The trade press.** A good way to stay on top of what's currently available is through the trade press. *Travel Weekly*, for example, publishes a Cruise Guide supplement every few months, with a complete listing of sailing dates and itineraries. Some trade publications even specialize in cruises.

As soon as you spot likely cruises for your marketplace, go straight to the cruise lines themselves. The cruise lines' reservations departments will be able to tell you what's currently available and answer whatever questions you have. The reservationists I have dealt with have invariably been friendly, helpful, and patient. Don't be afraid to ask questions about anything that is unclear to you. And don't forget the "magic words." (See "Making the booking," below, for more information on the booking process.)

Here are some things to keep in mind when researching fares and availability:

- **Pricing.** Cruises are usually priced on a per-person, double-occupancy basis; that is, the fare quoted is for each person when individuals stay two to a cabin. A single person in one cabin pays a premium known as the "single supplement," usually considerably higher than the double occupancy rate but less than the cost for two people. Some, but not all cabins, can accommodate additional people. The third person in a cabin pays a lower fare and the fourth person a still lower rate. Many cruise lines have "guaranteed share" programs whereby a single passenger will be paired with a roommate of the same gender at the normal per-person, double-occupancy fare. If the ship can't make the match, the passenger travels solo at no extra charge.

In addition to the fare, there are the inevitable "port charges," taxes levied on departing passengers and something over which the cruise lines have no control, although a recent class-action lawsuit charged the cruise lines with overcharging for port fees. At least partially as a result of that case, the cruise lines are now including port charges in their quoted fares. Port charges are not commissionable. There may be additional, noncommissionable fees incurred at stops along the itinerary, which will also be passed on to the passenger. Usually, these will be lumped together with the fare so that the passenger has the convenience of paying for everything at once. Finally, some cruises will have optional shore excursions, which are priced separately and may be commissionable. Check with the cruise line.

- **Cabin categories**. Just as airplanes have first-class, business-class, and coach, cruise ships have various cabin categories. A ship's cabins are typically divided into four to ten or more categories, usually indicated by letters of the alphabet. Typically. "A" will designate the best, most expensive category, with the following letters designating progressively cheaper accommodations with progressively fewer amenities. Usually, all the cabins in a given category will be either inside or outside cabins. This should be obvious if you have the ship's layout in front of you (it will be in the brochure). If for some reason you do not have this information available to you, make sure you know what the category designation means.

- **GG rates.** Most cruise lines have negotiated special rates, called "guaranteed group rates" or "GG rates," with certain travel agencies or consortiums. In simplified terms, the cruise line is saying to the agency, "We will give you the same, lower fare we offer to large groups for single bookings." One of the first things you will want to find out, then, when talking to the cruise lines is what is the best fare they will give you. That can mean identifying yourself (or, more likely, your host agency) as a consortium member or part of a larger chain of agencies that qualifies for a better fare.

- **Fending off the competition.** Cruises are a competitive field — competitive among travel agents, that is. Don't be surprised if your customer books with you and then shops around, finds another agency that offers the same cruise for a lower fare, books with it, and calls you back to cancel your booking. One way to prevent such cancellations is to ask the reservationist, "Will you protect my booking?" In other words, if you book Mr. and Mrs. Smith on this cruise today, will the cruise line guarantee to match, through you, any fare another agency quotes the Smiths? In effect, you are asking the cruise line to give you its lowest fare — but only if you'd lose the booking otherwise. This won't always work but it's certainly worth asking at this stage of the game. Presumably, you are looking at a number of different alternatives for your client. Guaranteeing the booking will help the cruise line secure your business. If you do get a verbal guarantee, remember to ask for the reservationist's name so you can later say, "Carmen guaranteed this booking on January 7th."

- **Option dates.** As with tours, cruises are typically paid for in two stages. First a deposit is due by a certain date — the "option date" — to guarantee the booking. Missing the option date doesn't always mean loosing the berth, but it usually means having to rebook. Make sure you are very clear on what is due when, and in what form, to avoid embarrassment later on.

- **Airfare alternatives.** Once you get to the point of researching fares, you may want to check the cruise-only pricing. This is a lower fare for passengers who will get to the port city on their own. Most cruise lines have a laundry list of air-inclusive fares that vary according to the passenger's departure point for the port city. In today's highly competitive airfare environment, you may be able to find an airfare that beats the air-inclusive fare quoted by the cruise line.

- **Always make a "just in case" booking.** Cruises have a way of selling out. There are only so many berths on a ship; when they're full, they're full. Always make a booking if you have gotten to the point of actually talking with a reservationist. You can cancel it if you don't sell it or the clients change their mind. In fact, you will probably find yourself canceling many more bookings than you confirm with a deposit. The cruise lines are used to this, so don't worry about it. Just make sure that you cancel the booking immediately, as soon as you know it's not going to happen, rather than waiting for the cruise line to "get the message" when the option date rolls around.

Picking the 'perfect cruise'

There's no such thing as the perfect cruise. There are so many options available that one person's dream cruise will be another person's nightmare. Here are just a few of the variables that have to be weighed and sorted to determine which cruise will be right for which person:

- **The ship's "personality."** Every cruise line has a carefully designed and nurtured image, style, or personality that it hopes will appeal to a fairly specific slice of the marketplace. Some cruises go for upscale "mature" folks, others for "swinging singles," still others for families with small children. In theory, then, different cruises should appeal to very different people. In practice, people of very different backgrounds, with very different tastes, can go on the same cruise and all have a wonderful time. They may even meet and discover they get along famously — even if they'd never dream of speaking to each other on shore. Still, the general rule is valid, and you should take care when matching cruise line with customer.

■ ***Cruising area.*** Different cruise lines cruise in different parts of the world. Consequently, they appeal to different interests and pocketbooks. Cruises to the Caribbean on the East Coast and the so-called "Mexican Riviera" on the West Coast are the most accessible to the greatest number of people and, therefore, appeal to the broadest range of tastes and budgets. But there are numerous other possibilities. There are cruises to Alaska and among the Hawaiian islands, and newer, so-called expeditionary cruises to places like the Galapagos and Antarctica. Tours of the real Riviera and the Greek islands have long been a romantic staple. Finally, riverboat cruising has recently come into its own in the U.S., thanks largely to relaxed state laws allowing casino gambling on board.

A rather specialized type of cruise is the "crossing," a cruise that goes across an ocean and is typically sold on a one-way basis with either the return or the outgoing leg on a plane. In this category are "repositioning cruises," which occur when a cruise line is moving a vessel from, say, the Mediterranean (at the end of the summer season) to the Caribbean (for winter cruising). Crossings and repositioning cruises are for those who relish long periods on the open seas.

■ ***Gambling, alcohol, and other "sins."*** Cruises have always been seen as a way to let loose and have a little fun. Trouble is, people's ideas of a good time tend to differ. Gambling is now pretty nearly universal on the larger cruise lines, as is the sale of alcoholic beverages. There are people who shun cruises for precisely this reason.

Consequently, a growing number of cruises are being designed to cater to this "lost" customer base. You can even book your clients on cruises with support groups, seminars, and regular "AA" meetings.

Other cruises cater specifically to single people in search of a mate — and another, and another. A growing number are being designed for gay and lesbian cruisers (no pun intended). If you, or your clients, are likely to be offended by booze, gambling, or alternative lifestyles, book with care.

■ ***Solo passengers.*** We're not talking here about those in search of companionship necessarily but those who, by chance or choice, are traveling alone. Many solo travelers never consider cruises in the mistaken belief that cruises are designed specifically for couples. But, in addition to the "meet and mate"

type of singles cruises, many cruise lines have programs that cater to the solo traveler — from guaranteed-share programs, to attractive single-supplement rates, to activities designed with the single person in mind.

- ■ *Size.* The nature and quality of the cruise experience can differ rather remarkably depending on the size of the ship. Some people prefer the big ships; others like something a bit less hectic. There are two ways to gauge size: by total number of passengers and by the ratio of the number of passengers to the vessel's gross registered tonnage (GRT). Dividing the GRT by the ship's capacity results in a "space ratio," which can be used as an indicator of the "elbow room" available on a ship. The higher the space ratio, the roomier the ship. In an example given by CLIA, a ship with a GRT of 38,000 and a capacity of 1,116 passengers would have a space ratio of 34. A ship with a GRT of 21,000 and a capacity of 1,100, on the other hand, would have a space ratio of 19. The first ship then is much roomier, despite the fact it carries slightly more passengers. According to CLIA, a space ratio in the 20's or higher is an indicator of a spacious ship.

Making the booking

As I have mentioned before, which comes first — the booking or the sale — is not always clear. Sometimes you book a cruise (or a tour, or a hotel room) just as if the customer were actually going and then "sell" it to the customer (that is, get their okay to spend the money). Sometimes you will get the customer's firm go ahead and only then make the actual booking. Sometimes the two processes will go on in tandem — a little selling, a little conversation with the supplier, a little more selling, a little more talking with the supplier — until everything is finalized.

In previous chapters, I placed "Making the sale" before "Making the booking." I am reversing the order here because of the annoying tendency of cruises to sell out or become overbooked months in advance because other travel agents are holding space. So the rule of thumb in booking cruises is, "Book first, ask questions later."

While there are not as many differences among the policies and procedures of the various cruise lines as there are among tour companies, there are some. Eventually, you will find yourself dealing with the same handful of cruise lines again and again, and it will all become second nature to you. Until you become familiar with the way each works, however, throw yourself on the mercy of the reservationist; ask questions about anything that seems confusing to you.

Information to give

Booking a cruise is in many respects like booking an airline ticket, except that you get a cabin number instead of a seat assignment. Here's what the cruise line reservationist will want from you:

- **The name of the ship, the date of sailing, and category.** This is the first order of business. This information allows the reservationist to get the proper information in front of him to continue the booking process.

  Categories have a maddening way of being fully booked when you ask for them, so it's a good idea to have some flexibility when it comes to picking the category. This will only happen if you have thoroughly debriefed your customer. In some cases, however, you may have to do quite a bit of checking back and forth before the booking is finalized. The more you can do to avoid this, the better. Sometimes, the entire ship will be sold out (or the affordable cabins will all be booked, which amounts to the same thing). This is where alternate dates come in. Of course, you can wait list your passengers. But all things being equal, you are better off booking your people on a sailing you know they can take than risking their eventual disappointment.

- **The fare basis.** Will this be an air-inclusive booking or do you want the cruise-only price?

- **The names, ages, and nationalities of the passengers.** If there is a group of people involved, you might begin by telling the reservationist the total number of cabins you will need. Then you can go on to break down the list of names into standard double, or triple, or single cabins.

  If there is more than one cabin involved, you will have to know who goes in which cabin. Age becomes important with minors; many cruise lines will not let teenagers stay in a cabin without an adult. The nationality of passengers is important, too. Many cruise lines call at foreign ports, and the documentation required by the various governments involved varies widely.

  American citizens will not absolutely require passports for most cruises to Mexico or the Caribbean. They can get by with an original or certified copy of their birth certificate *and* a government-issued photo ID such as a state driver's license. However, with security getting tighter every day, you should encourage your clients to obtain and use a passport. Not incidentally, once your customers have passports, they become prospects for a much wider variety of vacation options.

- **Who's paying.** In the case of a group of people, each cabin may be paid for by a different person. Or three cabins may be paid for by one family member and two additional cabins by another.

- **Odds and ends.** On larger ships, the reservationist will want to know which seating the passengers prefer at meals. (To accommodate the large number of passengers, cruise lines usually serve meals in "shifts." Typically, the first seating is at six and the second at eight.) Will they want an assigned

table or general seating (if available)? There may be other items of information needed to complete the cruise line's records. If you don't have all this information, you will still be able to make the booking. However, you will have to get all the required information straight well before the sailing date.

- **Your agency information.** The reservationist will want to know who you are, who your agency is, and what its ARC, IATA, or CLIA number is, if appropriate.

Information to get

Among the things you will want to get from the reservationist are:

- **Booking details.** This would include such things as the precise cabin numbers (the customer will no doubt have the brochure and be able to find his or her cabin on the ship's layout), the exact pricing — after all the port charges and any add-ons have been figured in, and the payment schedule. Sometimes cabin assignments will be TBA (to be assigned).
- **Option date and payment procedures.** Even if you think you know, double-check when deposits and final payments must be received. If a credit card will be used, make sure you understand the procedure.
- **Confirmation numbers.** Most cruise lines book by the cabin and treat each cabin booking as a separate reservation with a separate confirmation number. Once issued, this number becomes the point of reference for all subsequent communication with the cruise line about the booking. In addition to the confirmation number(s), it is always a good idea to get the name of the reservationist who took the booking.
- **Airline schedule.** If this is an air-inclusive booking, you will want to know the precise air itinerary information so that you can pass it on to the customer. You will also want to know what arrangements will be made to get, or "transfer," the passengers from the airport to the cruise ship. Usually, the cruise line takes care of that with air-inclusive bookings. Conversely, if this is a cruise-only booking, you will have to make a mental note to deal with the issue of getting the passengers to dockside.
- **When and how the travel documents will be delivered.** As with tours, documents are usually delivered to the travel agency after final payment and about two weeks before sailing. Again, you will have to make arrangements to get them from the agency and to the customer.

Making the sale

Everything that was said about making the sale in *Chapter 15: Booking Tours & Packages* applies to cruises. You will be well advised to reread that section. Here we will confine the discussion to some points that are peculiar to cruising or which bear repetition.

I am assuming that you have made at least some form of tentative booking with a cruise line before you get to the point of actually asking the customer to make a firm buying decision — by writing a check or making some other form of deposit. You may be able to confirm all of the details of the completed booking with the client in the process of making the sale. Or you may have to make additional arrangements or changes with the cruise line after making the sale. Or you may do a bit of checking back and forth before everything gets ironed out. Whatever the particular situation, it's always a good idea to recap the booking details with the customer after the booking is complete in the cruise line's records (in other words, after you have crossed all the t's and dotted all the i's with the reservationist).

A good way to present the cruise and ask for the sale is with a brochure of the cruise ship. On it, you can circle the customers' cabin and point out the various amenities they will be enjoying. You should also circle, underline, or highlight key portions of the "Terms and Conditions" of the cruise line to make sure the client knows what to expect. If you are selling to a couple, make sure you have a copy of the brochure for each person. This way you avoid "insulting" one or the other by making assumptions about who the real decision-maker is.

Among the things you will want to cover are:

- **Payment schedules.** Make sure the customer understands the payment process and all deadlines. Ideally you already have the deposit in hand, or perhaps you collected a pay-to-go deposit at the start of the sales process. Make arrangements to get the rest of the money as well. You may even want to consider some sort of installment payment program (assuming the sailing is far enough off). If a credit card is to be used, get a signature guarantee (see *Chapter 9: Getting Serious*) and agree with the client on which day you will submit the credit card number for final payment.
- **Cancellation policies.** Review the fine print with the client. Make sure everything is understood. This can be a good time to pitch cancellation and other travel insurance, either the cruise line's or that of another provider.
- **Travel documents.** Since your customers may not be receiving any travel documents (airline tickets, etc.) at this point, be sure to review exactly what they can expect to receive and when. This will keep them from undue worry as the sailing date draws near.

Dealing with price resistance

One thing to be aware of when making a cruise sale is that the quoted cost of the typical cruise is very often noticeably higher than the quoted cost of a comparable land-tour of similar length. This is due to the all-inclusive nature of cruise pricing. Essentially, out-of-pocket expenses on a

cruise are limited to alcoholic beverages, soft drinks, tips, casino losses, shore excursions, and any souvenirs you buy. The land-tour passenger — in addition to the above — may be paying for all or some of his meals, local transportation, admission to attractions, entertainment such as nightclubs, and even a rental car. So while the total cost of the tour may be higher — even much higher — than the cost of the cruise, the cruise may appear more expensive when you quote the price.

Consequently, you should be prepared for some resistance, especially from first-time cruisers. Make a point of underlining the many, many features of the cruise package when you present the cruise. That way, your customers are fully aware of just how much they will be getting for their vacation dollar. To emphasize that value, you may want to break down the total costs. For example:

"The first two people in the cabin are $679 each. The fare for the third person is just $449. That includes..."

Additional tips for dealing with price resistance, whenever and for whatever reason it occurs, will be found in *Part III*. Fortunately, when you are dealing with repeat cruisers, price resistance becomes much less of an issue, which is why you should be prospecting for regular cruisers and constantly seeking to turn your current cruising customers into repeat business.

Bear in mind, too, that the steps outlined in "Making the sale" and "Making the booking" may take place in a different order. In other words, you may make the booking (that is, the reservation with the cruise line) after you make the sale (present the cruise to the customer and get his or her acceptance). Conversely, you may have to go back and change or refine the booking after making the sale.

Finally, remember the wise advice given in the last chapter: "Get the check."

Relaying bookings & getting documents

While it is possible to develop a direct relationship with a cruise line, it is most likely that as a beginner you will have to route this booking through a host agency to be able to collect a commission. This will be especially true if a credit card payment is involved, as it frequently is. If cruises become a major part of your business, however, you may want to consider joining CLIA and becoming a "cruise-only" agency — at least as far as the cruise lines are concerned. This would enable you to collect commissions directly from the cruise lines.

As with tours, most host agencies will have a simple form that you can use to transmit your cruise bookings. Also as with tours, you can expect travel documents to arrive after the final payment has been received and about two weeks before the sailing date.

When the travel documents arrive, be sure to double-check them for accuracy. If this is an air-inclusive arrangement, instruct the customer to reconfirm the airplane reservations directly with the airline in case of any schedule changes.

In addition to airline tickets, cruise passengers receive a ticket for passage on the cruise itself. These tickets spell out the major details of the booking and usually have a sea of fine print on the back. Immigration forms, if required for ports of call, will also be provided and must be filled out by the passenger. Be sure to go over these points with the client to avoid misunderstandings later on.

GDS and Internet bookings

As with tours, many cruises can be booked on the GDS if you are using one. Depending on which host agency you have affiliated with or which consortium you have joined, you may also have access to a cruise-only booking engine that allows you to book via the Internet. More and more cruise lines are providing travel agents with an online booking engine on their web sites. The cruise line booking sites require registration and, in many cases a pre-approval process. And bear in mind that just because you are approved and are dealing directly with the cruise line does not mean that you will be making more money than you would be if you were funneling your bookings through a host agency that has a pre-ferred supplier relationship with the cruise line. Consequently, I recommend that you stick with the phone until you really know your way around the cruise marketplace. There are so many variables that it is always helpful to have the reservationist's expertise to fall back on.

Once you have gotten your feet wet in the cruise business, so to speak, and know you will be making a fair number of bookings with a particular cruise line, then it may make sense to sign up with that cruise line's web site. You may find the online booking engine a time saver for certain bookings. However, I would encourage you to discuss this move with the regional sales manager (RSM) for your region. He or she should be able to tell you if the move will make financial sense for you.

Getting paid

Arrangements for cruise commissions vary widely. If the passenger is paying by check, you or your agency can sometimes take the commission out directly. It works like this: The passenger writes you (or your agency) a check for the deposit. You (or your agency) deposit it and immediately write another check for the same amount to the cruise line. When the passenger gives you a check for the final payment, you (or your agency) deposit that check and write a check for that amount less your commission.

Be aware that even if the whole transaction is handled by check, you cannot necessarily bypass your normal ticketing agency. In other words, the cruise line may be willing to accept a check from your agency, which has an IATA or CLIA number and with which, presumably, the line has been dealing for years. But it may not accept a check drawn on your personal account, or even your business account. One way around this is to ask the cruise line if they will accept a money order. Most will.

Sometimes, the cruise line will want to get the full amount and wait until the actual sailing date or later (just to make sure the person doesn't cancel) before paying your commission. In the case of a cancellation, even though the cruise line keeps part of the payment, the agent usually gets no commission. The exception is when there is some "commission protection" deal with the agency. Usually this will be in place if the agent has sold the passenger the cruise line's own trip cancellation insurance.

If payment is by credit card, you will have to ask the reservationist for the correct procedures and what sort of documentation the cruise line requires. They may require an MCO ("miscellaneous charge order"), which means that payment will be processed much as an airline ticket would be and run through ARC. Commissions on credit cards are invariably paid after the fact, typically 30 days after the passenger returns from the cruise.

Cruise lines have been getting better about paying commissions promptly, thanks to an aggressive lobbying campaign on the part of the travel agency community. According to ASTA, 60% of cruise lines pay the agency commission within two to three weeks after final payment is received. Of those that wait until the ship has sailed, many have taken to paying up within a week to ten days of the sailing date.

On the other hand, cruise lines have taken note of what the airlines have been doing in reducing and capping commissions and some are beginning to follow suit. Make sure you know — and are comfortable with — the commission policies of a cruise line before you decide to sell their product. There is plenty of competition in the cruise marketplace and a good salesperson will be able to direct customers to lines that provide a great experience for the client and fair compensation to the agent.

Summary

Cruises are such a popular travel product that they have developed their own specialty agencies — the cruise-only agencies. Many home-based agents make the same choice. One reason cruises are so popular with travel agents is because of the strong loyalty of cruisers; nearly 85 percent of people who cruise once cruise again. This can add up to serious repeat business and virtually guaranteed income for the savvy travel agent.

Beginner travel agents will do well to concentrate on their drive market. That is, they should familiarize themselves with and promote cruises that depart from home ports within driving distance of their customers.

Like tours, cruise ships have personalities and different cruise lines attract a different clientele. Consequently, there is no "perfect cruise." The travel agent's challenge is to match the client with the cruise line, the cruise itinerary, and the cruise theme. Like tours, cruises come with a fair amount of "fine print." It is important that the agent help the client understand the Terms and Conditions.

The best way to sell cruises is through your own personal experience. That's why cruise-oriented travel agents cruise so often and is perhaps yet another reason cruises are so popular with agents.

Price is an important issue when selling cruises because to the uninitiated cruises can seem expensive. A good travel agent will point out and prove how the all-inclusive nature of cruise pricing can actually make them a better value than land-based vacations of similar length.

Cruise vacations can now be booked on the Internet, but beginning travel agents are well advised to use the telephone and the services of the cruise lines' highly trained reservationists.

Action steps

Here are some things you can do to put what you have learned in this chapter into action:

- Research your "drive market." That is, identify the home ports that people in your area might drive to to take a cruise and learn about the cruise lines that sail from them. If you do not live in a drive market, research the most popular cruise ports for people in your area. You can get this information by monitoring the ads in the Sunday travel section or by asking the RSMs of a few cruise lines.

- Collect brochures from a variety of cruise lines and study them, paying particular attention to the Terms & Conditions.

- If you have joined the Outside Sales Support Network (OSSN), sign up for one of their low-cost cruise-seminars to learn more about the cruise business and gain some first-hand experience. You'll probably find it's tax deductible! (But check with your professional advisor to make sure.) If you have not yet joined OSSN, you can download a discounted application form at www.HomeTravelAgency.com/ossnapp.pdf.

- Contact a number of cruise lines and identify the regional sales manager (RSM) for your area. Note that if you are working with a host agency, you must deal with the RSM who serves your host agency's geographical region, not yours. Contact this person and ask what educational support they provide to beginning agents such as yourself. Take advantage of what they have to offer.

- If at all possible, make an actual cruise booking. A good goal to shoot for is to round up a few friends for a cruise you'll all enjoy taking together.

338

Home-Based Travel Agent

The Fine Art of Selling Travel

Chapter Seventeen:
The Art & Science of Selling

What you will learn

After you have completed this chapter you will be able to:

- Distinguish between old-fashioned, hard-sell techniques and a sales approach that puts the customer first.
- Understand the importance of focusing your attention on your customers' needs, not your own self-interest.
- Set goals for yourself in such a way that you have a high probability of achieving them.

Key terms and concepts

This chapter involves the following key terms and concepts:

- Selling is a normal and natural human activity that does not have to involve high-pressure tactics or deception.
- Salespeople prosper when they stop focusing on their own needs and concentrate on what is best for their customers.
- To be effective, goals must be challenging, realistic, measurable, time-limited, and written down.
- It is up to you to decide how big your business will be. But no matter how big your business or how much time you devote to it, you should approach it professionally.

Introduction

Monty Python, the British comedy group, once featured a skit about an enterprising encyclopedia salesman with a novel approach. He rang the doorbell of a suburban home and announced that he was a burglar. The suspicious housewife on the other side was unconvinced; she was certain he must be an encyclopedia salesman. No, he assured her, he was simply a burglar who wanted to come in, ransack her home, and steal a few things. Finally, convinced that he wasn't an encyclopedia salesman, she let him in — whereupon he launched into a high-pressure sales pitch for "a really fine set of encyclopedias."

The joke, of course, is that people would rather have their homes burglarized than talk to a salesperson. Like all humor, it has some basis in fact. There is an old-fashioned, down-the-street kind of selling that's not too far removed from the tactics employed by that encyclopedia salesman. Here are some of the distinguishing characteristics of what we might call the "traditional" approach:

- The product being sold is treated as a commodity — that is, it is seen as basically the same as other products in its category.
- The concerns of every customer are seen as being identical.
- Or worse — the concerns of the customer are *ignored*. Selling someone something they don't want or need is considered the height of success. (Have you ever heard the phrase, "He could sell iceboxes to Eskimos?")
- Every sales presentation involves a "pitch." The same words are used over and over, for every customer.
- Salespeople use flattery, glad-handing, and insincerity — and call it "building rapport."
- Salespeople like to describe themselves as "closers," who won't take "no" for an answer.
- The salesperson's goal is to intimidate the prospect and gain a position of superiority.
- The mastery of hard-sell techniques is considered a sign of an excellent salesperson.

[handwritten: Wrong!!]

High-pressure, in-your-face salespeople still exist. You may have some idea that if you ever get involved in selling you will have to become one of those people. Nothing could be further from the truth. Selling is actually a very normal human activity — something we all do at one time or another whether we know it or not.

Avoiding the 'screaming me-me's'

I'm assuming you don't see yourself as a high-pressure salesperson. I'm also assuming you have no desire to transform yourself into one. My guess is that you are simply someone who loves to travel and sees an opportunity to benefit both yourself and others by sharing your enthusiasm for seeing more of the world. But even if you have the best intentions in the world, it's easy to fall into a trap I call the screaming me-me's.

Many people who start a new business venture — like becoming a home-based travel agent — are so excited about what they are doing that they can talk of little else.

> "***I'm*** a travel agent! ***I*** can get you great rates on hotels anytime you want them! ***I*** can book you on a cruise! ***I*** know all about these great tours! ***I've*** found a great island resort!"

Or they get so excited about the prospect of making a sale (and getting that commission) that they focus only on the end result.

*"Let **me** book it for you. You're going to go to
a travel agent anyway, why not let **me** do it.
Come on, what's the difference, give **me** your
business. You'll love this cruise! Take it! Do
it for **me**!"*

They make the mistake of thinking only of themselves and forget that it is their customer who makes all things possible. Now there's nothing wrong with getting excited about what you can do and how you can benefit in this new career field. But when you're in front of a potential customer, you will do well to remember: They don't care what's in it for you!

The only thing your customers care about — think about it — is what's in it for them. That doesn't mean that people are selfish beasts. Far from it. It's just human nature that when your customers are considering a decision that may eventually involve parting with some of their hard-earned cash, their charitable feelings toward you are not foremost in their minds.

As long as the question foremost in your mind is "What's in it for me?" you will never reach your full potential as a provider of travel services.

Take a 'you' turn

I have had the opportunity to study hundreds of high-performing salespeople in a range of industries. If there is one characteristic that links them together it is their single-minded focus on the customer — on what the customer's situation is, on what the customer needs, on what the customer thinks, on what the customer will feel comfortable with.

These are people who have stopped thinking "me, me, me" and started living "you, you, you." By committing themselves completely to servicing the best interests of their customers they have, at the same time, reached truly amazing sales goals. You can do the same.

So, if you are single-mindedly pursuing your own selfish interests, slow down and take a "you" turn. The next time you are with a potential customer — and in this business that means virtually anyone you happen to meet — get to know him or her.

*"Tell me about **yourself**. What do **you** like to
do when **you're** on vacation? Where do **you**
like to go? What are **your** favorite sports?"*

Getting to know your customers means not just asking questions but really *listening* to the answers — and then remembering them. Take the time to truly get to know your customers before you even begin to think about "selling" them something. You may decide that you have nothing to offer them!

As a general rule, the more questions you can ask and the longer you can go without pulling out a brochure or suggesting that they book a trip with you, the more successful you will be. That may seem odd now, but it will make more and more sense as you read the chapters that follow. For the moment, remember that the secret to success in sales is to concentrate as fully as possible on your customer. If you do, your needs will have a wonderful way of taking care of themselves.

The importance of goals

Selling is a goal-directed activity. Even though much is made of the importance of "motivation" in sales, you must have a clear idea of where you are going and what you want to accomplish to be a success at selling. All the motivation in the world will do you no good unless it is directed toward a goal. Goals, on the other hand, can get you going even in the absence of obvious motivation. Goals, in fact, are great motivators.

To be effective in producing sales results your goals must be:

- **Challenging.** Set yourself a goal that will give you a feeling of genuine pride when it is achieved. Something you can do with one hand tied behind your back is an excuse, not a goal.
- **Realistic.** On the other hand, don't set yourself up for crushing disappointment. Be wary of any tendency you may have to set your goals too high as a subconscious way of proving to yourself that something is impossible.
- **Measurable.** If you can't put a precise number to your goal, how will you be able to tell you've reached it?
- **Time-limited.** Good goals come with a deadline. A real deadline. A *drop dead*line. If you give yourself forever to accomplish your goals, that's exactly how long you'll take.
- **Written.** By writing your goals down, you reinforce your commitment to meeting them and create a record that will, over time, remind you of your steady progress.

Start now to set yourself some challenging, realistic, measurable, time-limited goals. Set them for the near term (what you'll accomplish tomorrow), short term (what you'll accomplish this week or month), and long term (what you'll accomplish this year). Keep them simple and remember that they can always be adjusted, up or down. Indeed, that's the whole point. Goals should constantly be adjusted so that you are always doing just a little bit more than you did last time.

Start with activity-based goals such as:

- Contacting ten suppliers this week.
- Introducing yourself as a travel agent to 50 friends and acquaintances this month.
- Subscribing to two trade papers before Wednesday.
- Going to the library to research the industry reference books listed in the *Resource Section*.

Then, move on to results-oriented, or sales-based goals such as:

- Making three bookings this week.
- Making 20 bookings this month.
- Earning $500 in commissions in one week within the next two months.

At first, setting your goals will take a bit of guesswork. As you gain experience, you should become quite adept at setting reachable goals that will keep you energized and excited about your new home-based business.

What 'Part III' is all about

In *Part III*, I will attempt to provide you with a comprehensive look at the specific selling skills, tools, and techniques that can help make your home-based travel agent business a success. I'll begin at the beginning ("Where do I find my first customer?"). Then I'll proceed through the selling process in more or less logical steps, from your first contact with a customer, through making the sale, to following-up. These steps are discussed in the following chapters:

- ***Chapter 18: Prospecting.*** Before you can sell anything, you have to find someone to sell it to. In this chapter, I'll tell you how to find your best prospects.
- ***Chapter 19: Spreading the News about Your Travel Business.*** To be successful, you need an ongoing program for identifying and approaching people who are likely to become your customers. In this chapter, I'll provide you with a rich menu of possibilities for reaching your customers.
- ***Chapter 20: Qualifying.*** Once you have a prospect in front of you, you have to learn enough about that person to know what he or she is likely to buy and for how much. In this chapter, I'll show you how to get to know your customers and create a treasure trove of information that will pay you dividends for years to come.
- ***Chapter 21: Presenting the Wonder of Travel.*** Travel products don't often sell themselves. They depend on you to present them in such a way that your customers are eager to buy. In this chapter, I'll show you how to present your wares professionally and persuasively, whether it's to one person across the table or to dozens of people at a time.
- ***Chapter 22: Handling Your Customers' Concerns.*** People are naturally hesitant about making a buying decision. They have questions and need reassurance. In this chapter, I'll show you how to turn all sorts of objections, stalls, and excuses into closed sales.
- ***Chapter 23: Closing the Sale & Follow-Up.*** Selling travel is a repeat business. In this chapter, I'll show you how to turn customers into customers-for-life.

Some general considerations

Some of you may want to keep your home-based travel agent business quite small, while others may be looking for a regular part-time business that occupies 20 or more hours a week. Still others will want to go whole hog and make this new career their sole source of income. In order to make this part of the book useful to the greatest number of people, I have had to make some decisions about how best to present the material. I have chosen to make the discussion in *Part III* more, rather than less, inclusive — that is, I am operating on the assumption that you will want to maximize your opportunities in the travel business.

Therefore, although the basic principles will apply to everyone, some of the specific strategies and tactics I'll discuss will be inappropriate for some of you. It shouldn't be too difficult to pick and choose the suggestions that are best for you or to modify strategies to better suit your needs. Here are some things to bear in mind:

- **The scope of your business.** Your business need only be as big as you want it to be. Don't feel you have to try *everything* I suggest. Do just as much as you feel comfortable doing.

- **Computers.** I have already suggested the wisdom of acquiring a computer if you don't already have one. Computers are the gateway to the Internet, the World Wide Web, and email, all of which have become virtually indispensable business tools for every home-based business.

- **Cost.** Even simple expenditures can add up. For example, if you have a customer base of a thousand people and you send each of them a small postcard four times a year, you will spend about $1,000 on postage alone, which is why more and more businesses are seeing the wisdom of email marketing. You can — and should — promote your business only to the extent you feel it will pay off in additional business. Don't be afraid to start off small and then add elements as your confidence increases and your income grows.

Action steps

Here are some things you can do to put what you have learned in this chapter into action:

- Using the suggestions in this chapter (and your own imagination), write some goals for yourself that meet the criteria of being challenging, realistic, measurable, and time-limited. Create a list of short-term as well as long-term goals. Don't worry too much at this point. Since you will be revisiting your written goals regularly (you will, won't you?), you will gradually become more skilled in setting goals that will motivate you to ever greater success.

Chapter Eighteen: Prospecting

What you will learn

After you have completed this chapter you will be able to:

- Distinguish between suspects and prospects.
- Institute a professional prospecting program for your travel business.
- Track and determine your sales ratios and begin to gather the data that will, in time, tell you the lifetime value of a customer.

Key terms and concepts

This chapter involves the following key terms and concepts:

- Prospecting is the constant and ongoing process of finding new people to add to your list of satisfied clients.
- A *suspect* is anyone who might become a customer. A *prospect* is anyone who meets minimum requirements for becoming a customer.
- The sales pipeline is a metaphor that reflects the fact that it takes time to move someone from suspect, to prospect, to customer.
- Sales ratios help you gauge your level of sales skill.

Introduction

If you are new to sales, the word "prospecting" probably conjures up images of a grizzled old desert rat and his heavily laden pack burro heading into the Sangre de Christo Mountains in search of the mother lode. Salespeople, of course, know that prospecting refers to the constant and never-ending process of finding new people who might become customers. When you start your home-based travel agent business, prospecting will be your top priority. "Nothing happens 'til somebody sells something," the old saying goes, and to sell something you need someone to sell it to.

Where do these prospects come from? The beauty of the travel business is that virtually everybody travels at least every once in a while. That means that your potential supply of prospects is limited only by your get-up-and-go and, to a certain extent, by geography. But as you will quickly discover, just because everyone travels doesn't mean that all of them will become your customers. All prospects are not created equal. That is one reason why many sales professionals like to distinguish between "suspects" and "prospects."

Using this approach, you would look at your "territory" (the geographical area in which you want to practice your travel agent trade) and first eliminate all those who don't travel for one reason or other. Everyone else is a suspect.

Start with your friends

If you're new to the travel business and new to selling, the best place to begin looking for customers is among your friends and family. In fact, even if you aren't new to travel or selling, it's still a pretty good place to look! Why? For a lot of reasons. You know who your friends are. You know where they are and how to get in touch with them. You already know something about them, their likes and dislikes. You have a built-in reason to contact them and start a conversation. They like you and are probably going to be willing to give you the benefit of the doubt. Some of your friends actually love you and will be willing to put up with your bumbling first efforts and give you their business anyway. And, finally, there are probably enough of them to keep you busy for a while and give you the practice you need to hone your selling skills.

The first thing you will want to do as an organized salesperson is to make a list of prospects. You need to start keeping track of people in a somewhat more organized, professional manner than you may be used to. Start with your address book. Transfer every name in it to your prospect list. Rather than use a piece of scrap paper or a yellow pad, put your prospects in a computer database. This way you will be able to sort them into categories and move them around later.

For now, keep it simple. Name, address, and phone number will do. Your task is simply to get some idea of how many people *might* become your customers. Later I'll show you how to build up a veritable gold mine of information about your prospects and customers.

Once you've transcribed your address book, you have identified your hard-core prospects — family, friends, and associates. These are people important enough, for one reason or other, for you to record their phone numbers. If you're thinking, "Gee, I don't have that many friends," wait. You're not finished.

Now go through the list again. For each person, ask yourself, "Whom do I know through this person?" For example, when you look at Aunt Matilda's card you may realize that you also know her three grown children, your cousins. Add them to the list. Or when you look at the Smiths' card, you may remember the Joneses whom you meet every time the Smiths have a barbecue. Add them to the list. Your doctor and dentist have receptionists and nurses. Add them to the list.

You know more people than you think

By now you should have assured yourself that you do have a lot of friends. It's just that not all of them made it into your address book. The fact is that we all know many more people than we think we do.

Let's take this prospect-finding game a step further. Consider for a moment your acquaintances and associates. These are people you either come into contact with on a regular basis or with whom you have some point of connection. A good way to identify these people is to mentally walk through your daily activities. Where do you shop? You probably have a nodding acquaintance with many store owners and their employees. Whom do you meet at church or synagogue? Whom do you see everyday when you drop your kids at the day-care center? Who works in your office with you? Who are you in contact with in other parts of your company? Keep asking yourself questions like this until you think you've identified everyone you could possibly know. Then ask some more. If you and your spouse are thinking of working together in your home-based travel business, make it a game; see which one can come up with the longest list of prospects.

You've probably got a pretty long list by now. And everyone on it is someone who, if they don't know your name, at least recognizes you on sight. In other words, these are all people who are not going to put up automatic defenses when you speak with them. But don't stop now. There are a lot of other people whom you may not know by name, and who may not recognize your face but whom you can contact easily and talk to openly after just a short introduction. These people might include:

- High school or college classmates.
- Fellow club members.
- Fellow parishioners or congregants.
- Neighbors on your block or in your apartment building.
- Parents of your children's classmates.
- PTA members.

These are people to whom you can say, for example, "Hi, we're in the same congregation," and expect a friendly smile in return. The goal, at the beginning, is to make life as easy as possible by concentrating on people you will have no trouble approaching and talking with about your services as a travel consultant.

Other sources of prospects

To begin with, I would recommend sticking to folks you know and can approach easily — especially if you are new to the selling game. It's just easier that way. Eventually, however, you will probably have to or want to widen your search for prospects to include people you've never met before and who will not be immediately predisposed to chat with you about their travel plans. Here are some ideas about how to find these people. Along the way, you may get some ideas you'll want to put to use sooner rather than later.

- **Everyone you meet.** From now on, everyone you meet for the first time is a potential customer! Use the "Three Foot Rule" — If you find yourself within three feet of someone, you have an opportunity to strike up a conversation.
- **Advertising.** Not the glossy, four-color, full-page ads you see in magazines but the simple ways of getting your name out there — by circulating your business card, for example.
- **Engagement announcements in the local newspaper** are a great source of prime prospects for you. These are people who will be taking honeymoons, remember. That means cruises, resorts, foreign destinations — big commissions!
- **Small town papers** sometimes feature chitchat about who's doing what, including where folks have been on vacation. These columns not only give you the names of potential prospects but valuable information about the kind of travel that appeals to them.
- **Lists of associations, clubs, organizations.** These are excellent prospects for group travel opportunities.
- **Referrals.** Everyone who becomes a customer knows people they think might benefit from your services. But there's a catch: They won't tell you who they are unless you ask them!

How many prospects do I need?

Good question. The answer is, "It depends. . ." Among other things, it depends on how many customers you want, which travel products you choose to sell, how much money you want to make, how much time you want to spend making it, and how good you are at converting prospects into customers. Assuming you're just getting started, you won't have the answers to all those questions; in fact, you won't have them for quite some time. But now is the perfect time to lay the groundwork for answering them.

Begin by asking a question you probably can answer now: "How much money do I want to make?" The answer might be $5,000 a year, $15,000 a year, $50,000 a year, or a free trip with an educational tour. Don't be afraid to dream a bit here. No one's going to hold you to it later.

The next step is to figure out what each sale is worth to you. In the case of the educational tour operator who gives you a free trip for every person you sign up, the answer is simple — each sale is worth one-sixth of a free trip. In other situations, it's more complicated, especially if you sell a variety of travel products. For example, today you may book your friend Susie a hotel room in Orlando and earn a commission of $15. Tomorrow you may book a retired doctor and his wife on a luxury cruise and earn a commission of $1,000. Over the course of time — three months, six months, a year — you can add up all your commissions, divide the sum by the number of bookings you made, and arrive at an average. This is what each sale is worth to you. Obviously, the number will fluctuate. Some months are better for sales than others. But after your first year in this business, you should have a pretty useful figure to work with. You should expect to make at least this much per sale in your second year, hopefully more because your skills will be improving.

Starting today, I strongly urge you to keep meticulous records of your sales activities — how many people you talk to each day, what you talk about, and the results. If you do that, it's a relatively simple matter to work backwards from each sale and determine what you had to do to make it. To keep things simple, let's assume that you have decided to specialize in selling cruises. Over time, you may learn that to make one booking you have to give a formal presentation to three couples. To find those three couples you have to invite 16 people to a "Let's Take a Cruise" party at your house. To get those 16, you may have to invite 32 people you have determined are good prospects. And to locate those 32 prospects you might have to chat with 100 different contacts. In other words, you'll need 100 prospects to make one sale!

If you want to make $30,000 a year and each cruise booking brings you $500, then you have the answer to the question "How many prospects do I need?" — 6,000!

If that scares you, good! In my experience, more salespeople fail because of poor prospecting habits than from any other reason. We can see why by looking at the two major metaphors that salespeople use to illustrate the importance of constant prospecting — the "funnel" and the "pipeline."

You can look at the sales process as a funnel, but a funnel with holes in it. You put in lots of prospects at the top but only some come out the bottom as customers. The others slip through the holes: They decide not to take a vacation this year; they get a better price somewhere else; whatever. This image brings home the importance of having many more prospects than you need customers.

The pipeline metaphor illustrates the importance of planning. If you put oil in one end of a pipeline, you'll get oil out the other end. But it takes time to get from one end to the other. To the salesperson, this means that if you want sales next month, you have to start filling the pipeline *this* month. If you are happy to rely just on "walk-in" business, fine. But if you want a steady income, and you know that selling a tour or a cruise takes two months from first contact to the actual booking, then you have to get busy in April to guarantee you'll have bookings in June.

There is another lesson to be learned from the made-up example we just used. If you don't like your numbers you can change them! For example . . .

- If you can't imagine digging up 6,000 prospects in the course of a year, maybe you've set your earnings goal too high. Adjust it downwards until things look a bit more doable.
- If, on the other hand, you *must* have that $30,000, you now have a pretty good idea of what kind of activity level you will have to maintain to reach that goal. That knowledge in itself

Prospecting

can be a powerful motivator.

- In the example given, you had to present to three couples to make one sale. What if you could increase your presentations skills so you'd be making two sales for every three couples? Or what if you could throw better parties and wind up presenting to four or five couples instead of three? The more you improve your basic selling skills the fewer prospects you will need to make each sale.
- You can also examine your sales strategy and see if making changes might improve things. It might be that "Let's Take a Cruise" parties are not the best way for you to sell in your market.
- Finally, you might want to change your "product mix" and sell travel products other than cruises, or sell different types of cruises that might provide a higher commission or have greater appeal to your clientele.

What's a customer worth?

Before you start thinking that the cards are stacked against you, consider the value of repeat business. Yes, it may be difficult to get the 60 couples you need to make $30,000 selling cruises. But the good news is that people who take cruises love the experience and do it again. According to one source, 85% of people who take one cruise take another. That means that of the 60 couples you book this year, some will cruise again next year. Another percentage will cruise the following year, and still another group will cruise in year four.

Only experience will tell you exactly how many. But let's say 20% of them will cruise again in year two. That's 12 couples or $6,000 in commissions. You're already well on your way to your $30,000 a year goal before the year has even started! That means that to earn the same amount of money, you will need to add fewer prospects to your pipeline.

The travel business is a repeat business and, dollar for dollar, it repeats more frequently than most. There are people who will buy a $15,000 car once every five years who will spend $4,000 a year on leisure travel. Many people take a cruise twice a year. Some couples seek out a different foreign destination each year. Others prefer all-inclusive resort vacations in the States. Many business people make at least one business trip each month, requiring a plane ticket, a hotel, and a rental car.

The patterns will differ with each individual, but once someone becomes a customer you will have a fairly good idea of how much business to expect from them each year. As time progresses, you will start to get an idea of how long the average person remains a customer. (Remember, people die, relocate, stop traveling for one reason or another, or shift their allegiance to another provider.) Now you know the lifetime value of a customer.

The cyclical nature of prospecting

Prospecting does not just mean identifying potential customers, it means contacting them. Moreover, you need to contact them again and again, until calling on you for all their travel needs becomes a reflex. Marketing guru, Dr. Jeffrey Lant, preaches what he calls the Rule of Seven. By that he means that a prospect must be contacted seven separate times before they make a buying decision.

While you may not have to contact everyone on your prospect list seven times before making a sale, you will be well advised to be persistent. Otherwise, you'll lose easy bookings that might otherwise have been yours.

Here's a typical example: You run into your old acquaintances Bill and Marilyn in June. You tell them all about your new career as a travel agent. They're impressed. Naturally, you tell them that whenever they need to make any travel plans they should call you. They assure you they will. The next time you hear from Bill and Marilyn is when you get their Christmas card. "We're off on a cruise to the Bahamas in early January!" they announce.

Cruise? What cruise? Why didn't you hear about it? What happened? Well, it's probably a safe bet that the reason Bill and Marilyn failed to call you wasn't because they don't like you. If that were the case, they wouldn't send you a Christmas card would they? There is a very slight possibility that they didn't book through you because they think you're an incompetent ninny who would have just screwed up their booking. It's more probable that they didn't book with you because they already have a travel agent with whom they are perfectly satisfied and to whom they are very loyal. But my guess is that the *real* reason they didn't book with you is that they forgot you were now a travel agent! Had you contacted them in the early Fall, reminding them that the cruise season was fast approaching, you might have snagged the booking you lost.

One of the challenges of your new identity as a home-based travel agent, then, is going to be finding ways to keep reminding folks that you exist and that you are ready, willing, and able to assist them with their travel needs. This is true not just of people who have never booked with you but with people who have as well. In fact, your present customers are your best source of new business.

An excellent way to keep your travel consulting services fresh in your customers' and prospects' minds is with regular email newsletters. Keep it short and chatty and use a mix of general travel tips and special offers that you are currently promoting. Be sure to get people's permission before adding them to your email list; nothing turns off prospects faster than unsolicited email.

Managing your prospecting activity

A professional prospecting program, because of its cyclical nature, requires careful management. You'll need to set up a prospect-management system to ensure that you make calls, mail out letters, and follow

up every lead in a timely manner. The best way to do that is with your computer.

There is a growing supply of so-called "contact management" programs, a subset of database programs, which are specifically designed to help salespeople keep in touch with their prospects and customers. Essentially, these database programs are Rolodexes on steroids. In addition to basic information about your clients and prospects, these programs allow you to record key demographic information, follow-up dates, client history, and a wealth of other data.

Once you've entered basic data about a client, you can go back into the program and pull up the information in a variety of useful ways. Most programs will automatically alert you when a follow-up call is due. Or you can search the database for things like people who are interested in cruising or people who have wedding anniversaries coming up.

In *Chapter 20: Qualifying* I will introduce you to a *Client Profile Form* that you can use to record a wide variety of information about your customers. It, too, can be computerized, although you will probably have to put it into a separate database program: Contact management programs usually aren't designed to hold as much information as you will want to have on each of your customers.

If you are not computerized, you can create a simple prospecting system using index cards and a box with 12 dividers, one for each month of the year. Most well-stocked business stationery stores will carry index file-boxes and dividers with the months printed on them. The cards carry the names, addresses, and phone numbers of your prospects. As you contact them, you record the date and results on the card and then place it two, three, or four months back in the pack, where it will serve as a reminder that the time has come to contact this person again. In a computer program, this task is automated.

Summary

At this stage of the game, you shouldn't worry too much about how many prospects you'll need. This is no time to get caught in the "paralysis of analysis." The important thing is to get out there and start.

If you followed the suggestions earlier in this chapter, you probably have a list of 50 people, maybe 100 or more. You certainly don't need more than that to get started spreading the word about your new venture. For some ideas on how to do that, turn to the next chapter, *Spreading the News about Your Travel Business.*

Action steps

Here are some things you can do to put what you have learned in this chapter into action:

- Start the process, outlined in this chapter, of drawing up a
  list of suspects and prospects. Enlist the help of your spouse,

even if he or she will not be working with you in your new travel business.

- Begin to sort your prospect list into categories using the A-B-C method, with A prospects being the most likely to produce business for you. At this point you will be guessing to a greater or lesser extent, but don't let that bother you. The important thing is to get yourself used to the concept that not all prospects are of equal financial value.

- Start entering your prospect list into a computer database. You may eventually upgrade to a more specialized database program later, but don't worry. Virtually every database program allows you to export data from one program to another.

- Create a system, in your appointment book or elsewhere, to begin tracking the data that will yield your sales ratios. You will want to keep track of the number of people you contact, the number of sales presentations you make, and the number of bookings you make. You will also want to keep track of how many times you have to contact an individual before a booking occurs. Of course, some bookings will "just happen." People will contact you. Keep track of this, too, since it will give you, over time, an idea of how much business just falls into your lap and how much you have to work for.

356

*Home-Based
Travel Agent*

Chapter Nineteen:

Spreading the News about Your Travel Business

What you will learn

After you have completed this chapter you will be able to:

- Better understand your market.
- Make your first sales call using a time-tested, professional, four-step process.
- Distinguish between general and specific benefits.
- Create a direct mail campaign to promote your new business.

Key terms and concepts

This chapter involves the following key terms and concepts:

- Advertising, as it is commonly understood, is not usually a viable option for the home-based agent.
- Understanding your market is one of the keys to success.
- A general benefit is one that might logically apply to anyone; a specific benefit is one that appeals to the needs of the person you are addressing.
- Direct mail marketing is an effective way to introduce yourself and new travel opportunities to people you know as well as to those you don't yet know.
- Email should *never* be sent without first obtaining the permission of the addressee. Therefore, email is *not* a tool for introducing yourself to people you don't know.

Introduction

Once you have allied yourself with an agency as an outside sales representative, the time has come to begin letting the world know that your new venture exists and that it is there to make their travel dreams come true. You have entered the world of advertising and marketing.

Advertising and marketing have a variety of definitions, depending on who's using the terms and in what context, so the definitions I give here may vary from the ones you have in your college marketing textbook. Don't worry about it. They will serve for our purposes in this chapter.

Advertising is the process of announcing the availability of a product or service to the greatest possible number of people. By definition, it is virtually impossible to predict who will see or respond to your advertising. Advertising your travel business may provide you with great customers, but it may just as easily provide you with poor customers (buyers of cheap travel, for example) or time wasting tire-kickers.

Marketing is the process of defining very precisely to whom you will sell and then devising strategies to reach that well-defined market. Marketing weeds out the unwanted customers and the tire-kickers. Unlike advertising, it never reaches out to them in the first place.

My recommendation is that you do very little advertising and a great deal of marketing. The two most obvious forms of advertising for a small retail business are the Yellow Pages and space ads taken out in local publications. Both of them are poor bets for the home-based travel agent. A business phone (a prerequisite for a listing in the Yellow Pages) is a useless expense for the beginner. Space ads are an equally frivolous expenditure. Advertising gains power only through repetition, and that's neither cost-effective nor, for most people, feasible at the outset of an outside travel-agent career.

Another form of advertising with which most of us are familiar is the flyer, one-page ads, cheaply printed on colored paper and posted on bulletin boards, slipped under windshield wipers, slid under doors, handed out on street corners, and so forth. While advertising of this sort might seem to make sense if, for example, you are trying to sell a large block of cabins on a cruise, it can better be used in the context of a direct marketing campaign, which I will describe a little later.

Your business card

The one form of advertising which I wholeheartedly recommend is the broad distribution of your business card. As I mentioned in *Part I*, the best place to splurge when setting up your travel business is in the design and printing of your business card. A well-designed card should sell you, sell your business, and sell the excitement of travel.

Make it one of your goals to get your business card in the hands of as many people as possible. From now on everyone you meet should receive one. In fact, give them several with the suggestion that they pass the extras along to friends, family, and business associates. Many people put a business card in every piece of mail they send out, including their monthly bills. Don't be stingy with your card. If you meet someone four times in a month, they should get your card each time.

Giving business cards is also a great way of gathering information because it puts you in a position to ask for one in return.

Observation: Many stores, especially office supply stores, have bulletin boards on which folks can post their business cards. While it can't hurt, my experience is that these boards produce next to no response, and the people who do respond are going to be more likely to want to sell you something than to travel.

Defining your market

We discussed the importance of defining your travel business in *Chapter 2: Defining Yourself*. Much of that discussion was about making marketing decisions; you might find it helpful to review that chapter from time to time. As you gain more experience in the travel game, you will bring new insights to the discussion.

There are two major ways to define your market:

- *Geographically.* While it's possible to have clients scattered across the country, you will probably want to restrict yourself to a manageable geographic territory, centered on where you work or live. The key idea is accessibility to your clients. That might mean concentrating on the five-mile radius around your home and the five-block radius around your current place of employment.

- *Demographically.* Within your geographic market are any number of demographic markets, although several will probably predominate. Demographics is the science of grouping people by factors such as age, income, interests, ethnicity, and so forth. If your community is composed primarily of older people, your travel business will (or should) take on a different emphasis than if your community is primarily young marrieds. One of the most important demographic indicators for the purposes of your travel business is income. The bigger the paycheck, the greater the disposable income. Professionals with incomes of $50,000 or more do a lot more cruising than laborers with incomes of $18,000.

The geography and demographics of your area are givens; there's nothing you can do to change them. In a very real sense, they determine what is possible and not possible in your area. You can examine the demographics of your geographic market and make shrewd decisions as to which travel products will sell best and how best to market them. Or you can decide to run your travel business according to what appeals to you and pretty much ignore the message of the market. There's nothing wrong with that. But be aware that, unless there just happens to be a match between the market in your area and what you want to do, your business will be less prosperous than if you had consciously tailored it to the needs and wants of your neighbors.

The other major way to define your market and guide your marketing efforts is through segmentation. By this I mean that you will subdivide (or "segment") your larger geographic and demographic markets by concentrating on selling such things as cruises, a specific destination or destinations, or travel built around a special interest such as golf, scuba diving, hiking, archaeology, art, music — the list is virtually endless.

If you go this route, your own personal likes and dislikes will undoubtedly take precedence over the numbers (that is, what the demographics tell you). Again, there's nothing wrong with that. Just be aware that if you want to sell cruises in an area that doesn't generate much cruise business, you'll have to dig a lot harder.

Learning about your market

Very few people who get involved in the travel business rationally analyze their market. So don't feel too bad if you don't either. However, if you'd like to learn a bit more about your market — who lives there, how old they are, how much money they make, and what they like to do — help is at hand. There are two great sources, both eager to help you.

- *The library.* The reference librarian at the main branch of your public library is the best person to contact first. Tell the librarian you'd like to study the demographics of the area; get to know more about the income and spending habits of the various neighborhoods; and so forth. Don't be shy about explaining why you want this information. The librarian may know just where to find a market study on the travel habits of your neighbors. He or she will certainly be more than happy to point you in the right direction. (And don't forget: The librarian is a prospect!) If you live near a business school, the library there might also have good, targeted information about the local area.

- *The Chamber of Commerce.* This alliance of local businesses is dedicated to growing the local economy. They will be happy to share information with you.

- *The Internet.* There is a large and growing repository of demographic information publicly available on the World Wide Web. Use a search engine like Google to explore your territory. For example, type into the search box "ZIP code data 00000," where "00000" is your ZIP code. Or use so-called reverse telephone directories available on the Web to get the names of everyone who lives on your street or in the ritzier neighborhoods in your area. Using Internet tools like these and a little imagination, you can gather a surprising amount of useful information.

Doing this kind of research will not necessarily make you rich. But it can be fun in itself and it might offer some valuable insights that you can put to work for yourself.

Your first sales calls

As I mentioned earlier, from now on, everyone you meet is a prospect and should receive your business card. That means that every meeting you have with your friends and family in the coming weeks is going to be (or should be) a sales call. That doesn't mean it has to be anything less than informal, friendly, and fun. Indeed, the best sales calls are always just that. All it means is that these meetings will have a purpose.

Generally speaking, these initial meetings or encounters are not about selling travel. Of course, you never know a person's situation until you ask, so you may walk away from some of these meetings with a booking. However, that is not your main purpose. The primary purpose of these first attempts is to sell the idea of establishing a client/consultant relationship with you.

You want to let this person know . . .
- You are a travel agent.
- Using your services makes sense.
- You are serious about making the person to whom you are talking a customer.

Like any good sales call, these first meetings with your prospective customer should have a structure and an agenda. Here's a time-tested strategy I urge you to use:

Step One: Introduce yourself and your company

If you're approaching a friend or family member (as I strongly suggest you do at first), they will obviously know who you are. What they will not know is that you have a new identity as a travel agent. Don't be shy. Share the good news.

> *"I just wanted you to know that I've become*
> *a travel agent with the Very Big Travel*
> *Agency. I'm going to be specializing in tours*
> *and cruises, but I'll be able to book any kind*
> *of travel you might need.*
> *Here's my card."*

That tells people what you are doing and with whom. It also gives them a rough idea of the scope of your business. Or you might say:

> *"Hey, I've just started a new job as a travel*
> *agent. I'll be working as an outside rep,*
> *which means I can come to you, or you can*
> *call me, anytime you need some travel ad-*
> *vice. Here's my card."*

Step Two: Generate interest with a benefit statement

It's possible that your friend will reply, "Say, that's great! Susie and I want to take a cruise in November. Can you handle that for us?" There's a greater chance he won't. So, your next challenge is to create some interest in speaking with you a bit more about what you can do for them.

You do that with something known in the sales business as a "benefit statement," any interest-generating statement that offers a potential pay-off (or benefit) to the listener. There are two kinds of benefits, general and specific:

- **General benefits.** A general benefit is one that would be of interest to most people who travel.

> *"Very Big is part of the Mega Chain of agencies; so we can offer you terrific savings on most tours and cruises."*

> *"To celebrate my new venture, I'm offering free rides to the airport to everyone who books with me this month."*

> *"Since I'm an outside rep, I'll be hand delivering all tickets and travel documents directly to my customers."*

- **Specific benefits.** If you know something about your prospect, you can often tailor your benefit statement to their specific needs, desires, or interests.

> *"Very Big has super rates on all Circus Line Cruises. That's your favorite cruise line, right?"*

> *"So the next time you want to visit your daughter, you can call me and I'll bring the tickets right to you."*

Step Three: Deal with skepticism, if necessary

I would be less than honest with you if I didn't point out that not everyone will fall all over themselves to turn over their travel business to you. Some people will be skeptical. Some people will reflexively put you off because they sense this is a sales call. These are what are known as stalls by professional salespeople. They do not necessarily mean that the person speaking will never do business with you (although that may eventually prove to be the case). Most often they are simply subconscious requests for more information.

Be prepared to respond when you hear a stall. Here are some examples of stalls and responses:

> **"Come on. You? A travel agent?"**
> *"That's right. I've been accepted as an outside rep by a $20-million a year agency. I'm in training now."*

*"**Don't you need a license or something
to do that?**"*
*"Absolutely. And my agency is fully accred-
ited and a member of ASTA, the travel
agency association."*

*"**You don't know anything about being
a travel agent.**"*
*"Actually, I've learned quite a bit. And I have
someone in the travel business [that's yours
truly!] showing me the ropes."*

*"**I already have a travel agent.**"*

This last statement may be a stall, but it is an important one. I will deal with the best way to respond a little later, in *Chapter 22: Handling Your Customers' Concerns.*

Step Four: Ask for a commitment

No sales call is worthy of the name unless the salesperson "asks for the business." That doesn't always mean asking for a booking or getting the prospect to hand over his or her hard-earned cash. But is does mean asking the prospect to make some decision or commitment that will carry the selling relationship forward.

To do that, you have to ask a question that will be answered "yes" or "no." What you ask for will depend on the situation, how well you know the person, and so forth. However, here are some things you might ask. In fact, you might ask several of them.

*"Do you have any immediate travel plans?
Can I handle those for you?"*

*"Will you be willing to book all your travel
through me?"*
*"Would you be willing to fill out this travel
survey so I can learn a little more about your
travel preferences?"*

*"I'd like to start a Client Profile Form on you
so when you make your first booking, I'll
have all the information I need at hand. It'll
take just a few minutes. What do you say?"*

All of these are what are known as "closes" by professional salespeople. Any question you ask of a prospect that requires a "yes" or "no" answer is a close. To distinguish them from the final close, which asks for the check, these earlier questions are sometimes referred to as "trial closes." You are

simply asking the prospect if they are ready and willing to move to the next phase of the selling relationship.

The trial close you use here must be a genuine request for a genuine decision. Offhand remarks like . . .

> *"So if you ever need anything, you know
> where to find me, right?"*

or

> *"So, I'd be happy if you'd think of me next
> time you need something, okay?"*

. . . are just that — offhand remarks. People can say "Sure" or "Will do" without feeling they have made any commitment, because they haven't.

If you didn't hear a stall before, you might hear one when you make this trial close. In fact you may hear a bona fide concern or objection. Those will be discussed in *Chapter 22*. For now, let's assume that you will get a positive response. If you do, you will have a very tentative commitment or a very firm commitment, or something in between. Unless the prospect has immediate travel needs, you will need to contact them again on a regular basis until the commitment you got today evolves into an actual booking.

You don't have to rush through the four steps I've just outlined. In fact, going through them one after the other is not a good idea at all. Instead, they should occur naturally, in the course of conversation. For example, you might spend some time chatting about why you decided to get involved in selling travel between steps one and two or between steps two and three. Don't rush it. Let it happen naturally.

After each of these initial contacts, run a little review. Ask yourself:

- How comfortable did I feel? Why?
- Did I use all four steps?
- What stalls did I hear? How well did I answer them? Could I have responded better?
- What benefit statements seem to work best for me?
- What should I do differently the next time?

The point is not to beat yourself up about your failures. Instead, you want to identify what went right so you can do it again, and what went wrong so you can change it next time.

You also may have noticed that many of the trial close questions above solicited more information from the prospect, either about their future travel plans or about their travel interests in general. This is the beginning of a process known as "qualifying."

I will discuss the all-important subject of qualifying, along with travel surveys, questionnaires, and the *Client Profile Form*, in the next chapter.

Direct mail marketing

Direct marketing is marketing aimed directly to the specific person you wish to address. You can market directly by mail, by phone or fax, or through a computer network. When direct marketing is done through the mail it is called — surprise, surprise — direct mail.

Direct mail can be an excellent and efficient way of letting the people on your prospect list know that you are in business. It is not a substitute for face-to-face selling. Instead, the two complement and reinforce one another. When you send out a mailing to a large number of people, you should plan on following up within a reasonable period of time with a sales call, either in person (preferable) or on the phone (okay, but not great).

Contacting friends

A direct mail piece (to use the jargon of the direct mail industry) to your friends and family should be informal and chatty, just like a personal note — which it is. You can type it on the letterhead of your new business (if you've become an outside rep for a distant agency), or use the letterhead of the local agency you've hooked up with (if that's okay with them), or just use your personal note paper. In any event keep it simple.

> Dear Jim,
>
> Hi! Just wanted to share the great news. I'm now affiliated with the Very Big Travel Agency as an outside sales representative. Very Big covers the entire world, but offers some extra special good rates on Caribbean resorts and cruises.
>
> I'm enclosing several of my new business cards. I hope you will pass them along. I'm also enclosing a brochure for the January 18th sailing of the *Fantasia II*. Thought you and Sharon would love the chance to get away.
>
> But whatever your travel needs, feel free to call me, day or night. Providing personal service is what my new business is all about.
>
> All the best,

This is just a sample. Feel free to use it or adapt it. The Outside Sales Support Network (OSSN) provides its members with sample direct mail letters you might want to consider. Or just use your imagination to create a letter that sounds like you.

Including a brochure with your initial letter is not necessary. But it does provide a built-in reason for contacting the prospect to follow up:

"What did you think of that cruise? Not interested? Well, what are your vacation plans this year?"

Here are some other thoughts on contacting your friends:

- You can automate the process on your computer. If you do, be sure to craft a letter that will apply to everyone on your list. Or be clever and design it so you can use the computer's "mail merge" functions to personalize each letter.
- Form letters and computer-generated stick-on labels are efficient and time-savers but they lack that personal touch. In fact, if you send friends a letter on your new stationery using a stick-on label on the envelope, they may just toss it in the trash, without ever knowing it came from you.
- By handwriting or typing each letter and hand-addressing the envelope, you increase the odds the letter will be opened, read, and well-received. This, of course, is more time-consuming; but that may actually be a benefit. . .
- If you stagger your letter-writing (as opposed to sending out hundreds of letters at once) you make the job of follow-up easier. For example, send out 20 letters this week and make 20 follow-up calls in two weeks. That way, you get into a routine: 20 letters and 20 follow-up calls each week.

Contacting people you don't know

One advantage of direct mail is that it is an excellent way of getting in touch with people you don't know, but who should know you. For example, the doctors, dentists, lawyers, and other professionals who have offices near you are excellent prospects. What's more they are easily located just by picking up the Yellow Pages or walking around the neighborhood.

A letter to people with whom you do not yet have a relationship should be a little more formal than one to your friends.

Dear Dr. Harris,

I am writing to announce a new and innovative travel service that can save you time and money.

As a Travel Consultant with the Very Big Travel Agency, I specialize in bringing the services of a full-time travel agency to you. Now you can make all your travel arrangements in the comfort of your own home or office and have tickets and travel documents hand delivered to you.

I am enclosing several business cards for you to keep and share with your friends and colleagues. I am also including a brochure for a Winter sailing of the M/S Colossal, for which I can provide very attractive rates.

Whether you are traveling to a professional confer-

ence or looking for that very special getaway, please
call me for all your travel needs at [phone number].

Sincerely,

H.B. Agent
Travel Consultant

P.S. I am adding your name to my list of preferred
clients. This will assure that you are alerted to special
travel opportunities and always receive the best fares
on all your travel.

A letter like this will benefit immensely from a nicely printed letterhead, either your own travel-business letterhead or that of the agency
with which you are affiliated. If you are using the agency's letterhead, be
sure to include your own business address and phone number and let re-
cipients know that they should contact you directly. If a prospect contacts
the agency, there will probably be no way of knowing that your letter was
the cause; so the client will become the agency's and not yours.

As with the letters to your friends, a letter like this requires follow-
up. If you are mailing only to professionals in your immediate area, a
personal visit will not only be advisable but easy to handle. The sooner
your prospects can put a face to your business the better.

When making this type of call on a doctor or dentist (it's called a "cold
call" in the selling business), try to drop in at off hours — before the office
opens or just as it's closing. The doctor is more likely to have time to chat
with you then. Your time together is likely to be short, however, so plan on
using the four initial-call steps outlined above —and plan on using them
quickly.

Take care with your appearance during these calls. A good rule of
thumb is to dress as your prospects do. In this case, that would mean
dressing like a highly-paid professional person, in business attire. A
good-looking briefcase to carry brochures and other materials is also a
nice touch.

It is appropriate to ask a series of closing and qualifying questions
during this follow-up call. Some of the things you might want to know
include:

- When is the doctor planning her next vacation?
- How does she book travel now? Would it be more convenient
  to have someone come to her office?
- Is she planning on attending a conference in the near future?
  Where? When? Can you do the booking?
- Would her patients enjoy some travel brochures left in the
  waiting area (with your business card attached, of course)?

Don't worry about seeming pushy. Doctors and other professionals
receive regular visits from salespeople selling them things. If anything, a

call from a travel agent will seem a novelty and perhaps a welcome change of pace, especially if you bring along brochures or even travel videos that you can lend. Remember, too, that you will likely encounter other potential prospects during these calls — the doctor's staff and patients. Be prepared to give something to them as well. In return, attempt to get their names and addresses for your mailing list. At a minimum, you should record the names of the doctor's secretary and assistants. You can always reach these staff people at the office.

Email marketing

Email, as you probably know, stands for "electronic mail." So it's easy to think that email marketing and direct mail marketing are exactly alike, except that one doesn't require postage. Nothing could be farther from the truth.

While there are definite and obvious similarities between the two methods, there are also profound differences. The most important of these, perhaps, is the fact that the etiquette of the Internet (or *netiquette*) demands that you ask permission from people before you send them anything that might remotely resemble "unsolicited" email.

In the process of collecting information on prospects and customers, you should always ask for their email. If they provide it, you may think they have given you permission to send them a monthly newsletter about your travel services and special alerts about last-minute specials. Not necessarily. When you ask for someone's email address, you should explain what you will use it for. If you have or plan to have a newsletter or send out special-offers alerts, you should ask people if they want to receive them. If they do not, then by all means honor their wishes. It can take time and effort to separate out the people who want to hear from you regularly from those who only want you to email them when absolutely necessary (about bookings they have already made with you, for example), but it will pay dividends in good will.

One result of this peculiarity is that email is *not* an acceptable method for contacting people you don't know for the first time. This is true even when the practice seems "innocent." For example, you have probably received broadcast emails from friends or local organizations that reveal the email addresses of everyone else who got that message. Those email addresses are off limits. Just because a local law firm posts the email addresses of all its lawyers on its web site does not mean you have permission to send them a solicitation about that cruise you're promoting. You must always have permission before using someone's email address!

The same problem does not exist with direct mail (the stuff you send through the Post Office). People may not like getting unsolicited commercial notices in the mail, but they accept it as part of life. Most of us are used to throwing out the vast majority of the mail we receive. Email is something else again. It sometimes amazes me how irate people get over unsolicited email and the lengths to which they will go to retaliate. So do yourself a favor and bend over backwards to observe proper netiquette.

Be aware, too, that just because someone told you it was okay to send them email doesn't mean they'll remember that when they receive your first newsletter months later. They might accuse you of "spamming" them and even report you to your Internet service provider! One way to lessen (but not entirely eliminate) this possibility is to use a "double opt-in" system. For the new home-based travel agent, that could mean sending a brief email to someone who has just given you their email address. You might say something along the lines of "Thanks for chatting with me the other day about cruising the Caribbean. You were kind enough to give me your email address so I can keep you updated with new cruising opportunities as they arise. If that was not your understanding, please let me know and I'll take your name off my 'Cruise Bargains Alert' list."

While there are drawbacks to email and some pitfalls to avoid, email marketing can still be a very powerful tool for the home-based travel agent.

Using email marketing

Here are some tips and thoughts on how to put email marketing to work for you.

- **Create a signature that sells.** Email programs allow you to create a "signature" that is automatically added to every email you send. In fact, you can create a number of signatures to use in different situations. So create one that "sells" your services. Signatures can contain links to your web site or promote your regular email travel newsletter.

- **Use every email.** From now on every email you send should advertise something. It could be a cruise that's months away or a last-minute special you know about through your host agency. No matter what the subject is, sell travel.

- **Start a newsletter.** This is not a must-do, but it has proven effective for many agents, especially those who have a well-defined specialty. The idea is to keep both your services and the benefits of travel alive in your customers' and prospects' minds. Monthly newsletters are the norm but they can be more or less frequent. I strongly suggest that you use a third party service to send out your newsletter rather than trying to do it all yourself.

- **Build lists.** As you add more and more names to your customer and prospect databases, you will find more and more ways to "segment" those lists. (The *Client Profile Form* in *Chapter 20: Qualifying* will help you do this.) This means you can send out highly targeted emails (with permission, of course) to the people most likely to respond.
  One of the most powerful examples of this is promoting last-minute specials to people who are interested. Because of the short-fuse nature of these offers, you get immediate response and a quick commission payoff. If your list is large enough, you can build a highly profitable business using just this one strategy.

Summary

You have begun what will (or should) become a regular practice — contacting people in your customer base to let them know you are a professional travel consultant and to ask for their business. In this way, you turn your liability as an outside agent into an advantage. Here's what I mean:

The traditional agency, with its storefront offices and windows filled with alluring travel posters, may seem to have the advantage over you. But it is hampered by its lack of mobility. Like the Venus' flytrap, it depends on people wandering close enough to be attracted by its displays and coming through the door. Very few traditional agencies do the kind of active selling I just discussed. For many of them, meeting the high costs of their overhead and their investment in newspaper advertising leaves precious little money for any kind of direct marketing campaign.

You, on the other hand, are free to roam your territory — meeting people, getting to know them, inquiring about their travel plans and interests, and offering your services on a regular basis. The simple act of "keeping in touch" will be a major ingredient in your success.

Ultimate success demands that you:

- Ask for the business, and
- Ask for the business, and
- Ask for the business, and
- Ask for the business, and
- ASK FOR THE BUSINESS!!

Action steps

Here are some things you can do to put what you have learned in this chapter into action:

- If you do not yet have a business card, get one. Follow the suggestions in *Chapter 8: Getting Started*. If you have not yet settled on a business name, get the cheapest cards you can, because you will be changing them. Then start passing them out, each time trying to get basic contact information (including email address) in return.

- Spend some time learning about your market. What do the demographics tell you? Where are the upscale neighborhoods? Can you identify the people who live there?

- Practice some sales calls using the method outlined in this chapter. For each one, write down a brief summary, noting what went well and what didn't go so well. Ask yourself how you can improve.

- Draft a direct mail letter to introduce yourself and your new travel business. Solicit feedback from family and friends. If you know someone in the business world, their opinion will be especially valuable.

Chapter Twenty: Qualifying

What you will learn

After you have completed this chapter you will be able to:

- Name the various stages of qualifying.
- Begin the process of determining the most important qualifiers for your specific travel business.
- Ask productive qualifying questions in a professional manner.
- Use the *Client Profile Form* to build a comprehensive customer database.

Key terms and concepts

This chapter involves the following key terms and concepts:

- Qualifying is the logical, structured process of getting to know more about potential customers and current clients.
- Qualifying saves you (and the client!) time and enables you to make more money faster.
- Qualifying the situation is the process of gathering the information that will allow you to *precisely* match the right travel product with a customer's needs and desires.
- Open questions get your prospects talking freely; reflective questions delve more deeply into what the prospect has told you; closed questions gather very specific details.
- Questionnaires and surveys can be great time-savers, but they need to be used and handled with discretion.

Introduction

When you believe in the products and services you provide, you want to see to it that the greatest possible number of people become aware of and experience the many benefits they offer. You may even begin to think that *everyone* should do business with you.

Enthusiasm is a tremendous asset, but not when it blinds us to certain bedrock business realities. The truth is that no travel agent can possibly do business with every person in his or her potential market. Instead, every travel agent in a given geographic market will do business with a certain percentage of the potential market. That's what's called *market share*, and it's a natural (and healthy) byproduct of competition.

It follows that of all the people who *could* become your clients, only a certain percentage will. Some won't become your clients because you will choose not to work with them. They might include:

- People who shop you to death, calling back several times a day to ask for a lower fare or have you research yet another itinerary.
- People's whose needs outstrip your capabilities, such as business clients who need the services of someone extremely well-versed in the area of corporate meetings.
- People who need short-haul airline tickets, when you have decided to specialize in cruises, tours, or a specific foreign destination.

In some cases you will simply discourage business from certain people (politely, I would hope). In other cases, you will refer people to a more appropriate source, sometimes, perhaps, for a commission (as when you refer a corporate account).

Then there are those people who will choose not to work with you. They will make that decision for any number of reasons:

- They may have an ongoing relationship with a travel agent they like and see no need to switch.
- They may not trust you, as an outside rep, to provide the same level of service they have come to expect from "traditional" travel agencies.
- Some people don't like mixing business with friendship, on the theory that if something were to go amiss with their travel arrangements, the friendship would be jeopardized.
- They book all their own travel. Always have, always will.

Those of you with sales experience may look on this list as a list of objections and not as a list of valid reasons not to do business with you. Fair enough. But for now let's acknowledge that not all objections can be overcome. There will be some people who won't become clients.

Between these two extremes there are a great many people who will become your customers. Some will become better, more frequent customers than others. Your challenge, as a salesperson, is to separate the wheat from the chaff — to eliminate the people who won't or shouldn't be your customers, concentrate on those who will or should, and identify the real winners in that group. This is the process that's known as qualifying. It is something that begins when you start compiling the list of prospects we discussed in *Chapter 18: Prospecting* and continues throughout your business life.

What is qualifying?

Qualifying is the logical, structured process of getting to know more and more about your potential customers and your current clients. It is not something you do once; you are constantly qualifying — or should be. The major stages of qualifying are:

- **Pre-qualifying.** Sometimes you can pre-qualify suspects before you make contact with them. Presumably, you did that as you drew up your list of prospects by eliminating people you felt were very poor candidates and making sure to include those who travel frequently.

- **Qualifying.** When sales professionals speak of "qualifying," they are most often referring to this phase of the process. In this stage of qualification you make contact with the prospect to determine whether or not the person should remain on your client list. You can determine that by asking a handful of questions. Just how much specific information you will need to know will vary from situation to situation and from client to client. Note that qualifying is not entirely selfish on your part. You will be saving the prospect's time as well as your own by eliminating those who aren't real prospects from your list of potential customers.

- **Qualifying the situation.** Just because it proves worth your while to talk to a prospect does not mean that you will succeed in making a sale every time you approach them about a particular travel opportunity — or even every time they approach you, expressing a desire to take a trip. That is why, for each individual sale, you must take your qualifying a step further. You must know the prospect's specific needs to provide appropriate travel solutions.

  Exploring and analyzing needs is sometimes called "qualifying the situation." This process is what I was referring to under the heading "Gathering information" in the chapters on booking various types of travel products. (*Chapters 11 through 16* in *Part II*.)

- **Long-range qualifying.** Qualifying is an ongoing process and is crucial to the success of your long-term relationship with customers. In a very real sense, you can never know too much about your clients. That is what the *Client Profile Form*, at the end of this chapter, is all about. This type of long-range qualifying will enable you to compete effectively against larger, traditional agencies. Too many people in the travel business make the mistake of taking current accounts for granted. Always be on the lookout for changes in your clients' situations that might create new travel needs for them and opportunities for you. It never hurts to review your basic information about your current customers every six months. If you have established a good working relationship, you should have no problem in getting your clients' help in expanding and updating your records.

Why qualify?

The simple answer is: To save time — your own and your customers'. In the early stages of your home-based travel agent career, you will want to know who, out of the several hundred people who may be on your prospect list, are most likely to deal with you, so that you can concentrate your efforts on them. When you are dealing one-on-one with potential customers, you will want to know enough about their needs and wants to select the right products for them. That way, to use a small example, you will not research and present a resort property without tennis courts to a tennis player. Later on, when your client list has grown large, the qualifying you have done and recorded on your *Client Profile Forms* will let you quickly select those people who are the most likely to be interested in a special cruise or in staying at that all-inclusive resort that is running a special promotion for travel agents.

Remember that travel is a repeat business. Once the people on your "prospect" list become "customers," they are still "prospects" — prospects for a cruise next year, prospects for a European tour and a trip to their kid's college town the year after, and so on, and so on. Never stop qualifying.

Who's qualified?

You will no doubt take on all comers in the early days of your new career as a home-based travel agent. As you gain experience and learn the ropes of selling and booking, however, I would encourage you to look on your business as an exclusive club to which only those meeting certain qualifications can belong.

Qualifying is sort of like a scoring system. Those with higher scores go to the head of the class, as it were, and become your best prospects, your best customers. Many professional salespeople like to rank their prospects using an A-B-C method. "A" prospects (or customers) get the most attention, "B" prospects a little less, and so on. In adapting that system to selling travel, we must distinguish between those people you might sell travel to in the future and those people to whom you are speaking at this very moment. Once a customer is in front of you asking you for help on a trip to visit relatives, attend a conference, or whatever, they become your primary concern. On the other hand, when you look at the ever-growing list of people who have booked through you before or who have yet to book through you, you can begin sorting them into categories.

Early in your travel career, you will probably want to score people against some or all of the following qualifying criteria:

- *An immediate travel need.* Someone who has an immediate need for travel advice and bookings is a far better prospect than someone who may take a trip sometime next year.
- *A willingness to work with you.* Don't kid yourself. You will meet with some skepticism at first. That is why it is important to find those people who are willing to give you the benefit of the doubt and start booking through you. As you

gain experience with these people, you will gain credibility with others.

- **Straightforward travel needs.** In other words, don't try to land a corporate account, or send a group of 127 on a ten-country independent tour of Europe, your first week out. Armed with the information in *Part II,* you should be able to handle most normal requests.

As your travel business grows, you will start to notice differences among your customers and prospects. You will start qualifying and categorizing them according to certain demographic and lifestyle criteria. For example:

- **Frequency of travel.** Those who travel three times a year are better prospects than those who travel once a year.
- **Budget.** This could mean the average amount of money spent per trip. If your records show that the Bakers spend an average of $5,000 each year to take a vacation, while the Coopers spend $2,000, it doesn't take much figuring to know which family is the better prospect for that $6,000 cruise.

  It could also mean annual income. Those who earn over $50,000 a year are better leisure travel prospects than those who earn less. Those making over $100,000 are better prospects still.
- **Price sensitivity.** People who will trust you to get them a good deal within their budget are better customers to have than those who nickel and dime you to death.
- **Life situation.** Many retired people are active travelers, while young families may be limited in their discretionary income. A small business owner may make travel decisions for several members of his or her staff in addition to her own leisure travel, while an executive at another company may be so snowed under that he never has time to get away.

These are only some of the ways in which you can qualify and rank your customers and prospects. You no doubt will develop your own criteria that will apply to your market, the type of business you run, and the types of travel products you sell.

The importance of qualifying the situation

So far we have been discussing qualifying primarily as it relates to money — whether prospects will part with money, how frequently they will part with it, and how much they'll part with. That is only part of the qualifying picture. Once your prospects are sitting in front of you to make a buying decision about a trip, you must qualify the situation — gather the information you need to match this specific prospect with the right travel product or combination of products.

At this stage of the game, the actual sale may not be in doubt. Of course, the customer might decide that what you ultimately present is not suitable and take their business elsewhere. This is especially true with leisure travel, when the customer may be speaking to several different travel agencies and suppliers. (In fact, one of the most important things to qualify is whether the customer is talking to other travel agents or if they have made a decision to book through you.)

Let's assume, for the sake of discussion, that the sale is not in jeopardy, that the customer has made a firm decision to book their business trip or vacation through you. While qualifying the situation will not affect whether or not you make the sale, it is still vitally important to the future health of your travel business. Travel is a repeat business: Every sale you make has a direct impact on your ability to make more sales in the future. Provide people with a wonderful travel experience and they will come back. Book them into an overpriced fleabag hotel on a filthy beach and they'll go elsewhere to book next year. That's why all the qualifying information you gather at this stage (aisle or window, smoking or non smoking room, ocean view or garden view, tennis or golf, and on and on) is crucial to matching this prospect with the ideal travel product.

Not only will this produce a happy client who will bring you a continuing stream of business, but it will create a walking advertisement for your business. People have a way of talking about their good experiences (especially if you encourage them to do so). Also, the information you gather during this process can be recorded on the *Client Profile Form* for easy reference the next time you work with this customer. Your efficiency and in-depth knowledge of the person's preferences will be noticed. It will further establish your reputation as a professional and reliable travel agent with whom it is a pleasure to do business.

Asking qualifying questions

In certain situations — such as when you are trying to determine just which tour product is right for a particular customer — qualifying can involve gathering a great deal of information. That is why it is helpful to approach the task in an orderly and professional manner. These four steps should suffice in most situations:

1. ***Explain the need for qualifying.*** Avoid any possible misunderstanding by letting the customer know what you are doing and pointing out that there's something in it for them.

   > *"What I'd like to do is get a general idea of the sort of things you like to do on vacation. That way, we'll be sure to pick just the right tour for you. Okay?"*

2. ***Keep the questions friendly and conversational.*** When you are gathering a lot of information, there's a danger that customers will feel like they are being interrogated. This is

especially true if you are working with a form — the *Client Profile Form* included. There is a tendency to just go down the list, firing questions at the customer. A far better strategy is to start a wide-ranging, general conversation, noting down specific facts as they emerge naturally. You can always go back later and fill in the blanks. See the discussion of types of qualifying questions, below, for more tips.

3. ***Handle stalls as necessary.*** There is a slight possibility that the customer may be hesitant about providing certain information or may not understand the purpose of some questions. If so, you will have to reassure the customer and proceed. (See "Handling stalls," below.)

4. ***Thank the customer.*** Always acknowledge the customer's role in what is, in fact, a joint effort of investigation and information gathering.

> *"Thanks a lot. You've certainly made my job a lot easier. And I think I'll be able to come up with just the sort of vacation you're looking for."*

As a general strategy, you should begin with the big picture and then progressively narrow the focus until, finally, you are dealing with the small details. There are three basic types of questions you can ask to facilitate this process. Ask them in order, as you move from the very general to the very specific.

■ ***Open questions.*** Although, technically, an open question is any question that cannot be answered "yes" or "no," some open questions are more productive than others. Try to begin with broad, open questions to get the customer talking freely about their situation and their needs. The broader and more general the better.

> *"Why don't you tell me a bit about what you have in mind?"*

> *"If you could design the perfect vacation, what would it look like?"*

■ ***Reflective questions.*** Reflective questions bounce off what the customer has already said. They are designed to encourage him or her to share more information. They can be very simple questions like "Uh-huh?" "And . . . ?" "What else?" or "Could you expand on that a bit?" Sometimes, you may want to be more specific.

"You said you like to 'learn a little about the culture' on a trip. How have you done that on previous vacations?"

- **Closed questions.** These are the ones that can be answered "yes" or "no" or with a simple one- or two-word answer. For example:

"Smoking or non?"

"Do you have any dietary restrictions?"

"Would you like me to look into theater tickets in London?"

Don't ask these kinds of nitty-gritty, closed questions until you have to. The answers to a lot of the questions on your list (or in the *Client Profile Form*) will emerge naturally in the course of the conversation. Be alert for them and record the information as the client provides it.

Handling stalls

Prospects or customers will sometimes show some resistance to answering qualifying questions. Usually this is a reflex reaction and not a serious objection. Sometimes it may signal that the conversation has gone on too long. Most of the time, you will not have a problem if you have remembered to give a reason for asking a series of qualifying questions. But if you hear a stall or a put-off, follow this simple process:

- **Respect the prospect's position.** Don't try to brush aside or belittle the resistance. Instead, say something like,

"I can understand how you feel."

"I certainly don't want to waste your time."

- **Give a good reason.** If you are a professional, you will have a number of excellent reasons why asking these questions is a benefit *to the prospect.* But first, ask a clarifying question.

"Is there a problem?"

"What's your concern?"

The answer will allow you to select the *precise* reason, or to reassure the prospect.

- **Ask again.** As soon as you have provided a good reason for asking your qualifying questions or soothed a concern, *immediately* ask another question that will move the process forward.

If the customer still shows resistance, don't push it. You may be able to get the information at a later time. Remember that this prospect will become your customer for many years. You will be able to pick up more and more information over time.

Surveys and questionnaires

Asking questions in the course of a conversation is not the only way to gather qualifying information about your prospects and customers. Many travel agents use surveys and questionnaires of one form or another to speed up the qualifying process.

Surveys and questionnaires have the advantage of saving time for the agent and allowing a large number of prospects to be qualified at once. On the downside, they run the risk of alienating or offending some people. Handle them with care and carefully consider what information to request, how much information to request, and under what circumstances to request it.

Conducting a travel survey

One way to introduce yourself to your market and gather some valuable pre-qualifying information at the same time is with a Travel Survey. This is nothing more than a short form requesting a modest amount of information, which the prospect can fill out and return to you. One of the most effective forms a travel survey form can take is a self-addressed postcard (addressed to you, that is) that the prospect can simply fill out and drop in the mail.

You can include a Travel Survey card in every introductory letter you send out. Invite your prospects to fill it out and send it back, but don't be surprised if very few do. A return of 1% is considered excellent in the direct mail business. Since your initial list will be heavily front-loaded with the names of friends and family, you may get a higher return.

The very fact that someone has taken the time to fill out a survey form and return it is itself an important qualifier. The fact that this person has taken some action to further the selling relationship with you indicates that they are more likely to book with you than others who received the card and didn't return it.

In addition, the travel survey can be used to gather simple information that will start to tell you who your best prospects are. What information you solicit is up to you. There are no hard and fast rules. Gary Fee, Chairman of the Outside Sales Support Network (OSSN), in his *Official Outside Sales Travel Agent Manual*, which is included with membership in the organization, suggests asking the following questions:

- Are you planning a vacation this year?

- Does anyone in your family travel on business?
- Have you ever taken a cruise vacation?
- If so, where and on what ship?
- What was your favorite vacation spot?
- If you could choose to travel anywhere in the world, where would that be?
- Where did you go on your last vacation?
- Where did you stay?

These are all good questions. There are not too many of them and they are not threatening in any way (unlike a question such as "How much money do you spend each year on travel?"). They solicit information about upcoming needs ("Are you planning a vacation this year?"), possible regular bookings ("Does anyone in your family travel on business?"), and a lot of information about likes and dislikes. To an experienced agent, the answers to these questions will speak volumes. For example, a person who has never taken a cruise vacation is less likely to take one than someone who has. If the person cites a particular ship, the agent will have a good idea of their budget range and tastes. The same applies to questions about past vacations and hotels in which they've stayed.

To encourage prospects to reply, be sure to put a stamp on the reply card. Once your business grows large enough, you may want to consider applying at the Post Office for Business Reply Mail privileges. These are the preprinted post cards and envelopes you receive all the time from companies soliciting your business. In the place where the stamp usually goes, they say "No Postage Necessary If Mailed In The United States."

Using questionnaires

Another way to gather qualifying information is with a questionnaire. Handing a prospect a questionnaire usually implies that he or she has already committed to entering into a business discussion — that is, the prospect has become a customer who is actively looking for your assistance in making a booking. A questionnaire allows you to gather accurate information quickly and the customer may actually prefer that to being asked a series of questions.

Your questionnaire might include some of the kinds of questions listed earlier, but it also might solicit other, drier information that will prove helpful now that the prospect has become a customer. That might include such intelligence as frequent flyer programs to which the prospect belongs; airline seating preferences; preferred hotels, rental car companies, and airlines; etc. In short, it would ask for the kinds of information you will want to record on your *Client Profile Form*.

I do not recommend that you simply hand a *Client Profile Form* to every prospect. There may be a few people (your best friend, your mother) who will sit still and fill one out just to oblige you. Most people will have better uses for their time. Besides, there is some information on the *Client Profile Form* that, while having no sinister purpose, might raise questions in your prospects' minds. Instead, you should create a separate questionnaire that excerpts key information from the Form. You may even want to create several questionnaires for different occasions (for example, one for tour booking, one for cruises). Of course, there's nothing to prevent you from creating a long questionnaire from the *Client Profile Form* and using it with people you think will have the patience to fill it out completely.

You can use a questionnaire the first time you sit down with a prospect to discuss a booking. You can use it as a sort of "assumptive close." In other words, you are acting on the assumption that the prospect fully intends to become a long-term client and won't hesitate to provide you with information about his likes, dislikes, and frequent flyer numbers. If he cooperates, terrific; you have just further qualified this prospect. If he hesitates, no problem. You simply explain that the questionnaire is optional and move along to other matters. Another occasion on which you might use a questionnaire is when you have developed an ongoing client-consultant relationship. You could send a questionnaire in the mail along with a short letter or note, and a stamped, self-addressed return envelope.

Dear Bill,

First of all, let me thank you for letting me handle your travel needs this past year. Serving you has been a privilege — and a great deal of fun as well.

I am sending you a short questionnaire that will help me serve you even better in the future. I hope you will be able to take a few minutes to fill it out and return it in the enclosed stamped, self-addressed envelope.

As a small way of saying "Thanks" I am also enclosing an upgrade coupon from Acme Rent-A-Car, which is valid until March 31st.

Best wishes,

H.B. Agent
Travel Consultant

Whether you use questionnaires and, if so, in what circumstances, is entirely up to you.

Summary

Qualifying is one of the key skills in selling travel, or anything else for that matter. Developing your qualifying skills will pay many benefits, in time saved, in travel booked, and in commissions earned.

Until you gain more experience (and even then) you should use checklists as a reminder of what key qualifying information you need to gather from new prospects. The guidelines provided in the chapters on booking specific travel products (*Part II*), can help you qualify the situation in the case of individual bookings.

The information you gather about prospects and customers should be collected and stored in a meaningful and systematic way for future reference. The *Client Profile Form* can assist you in doing this.

Action steps

Here are some things you can do to put what you have learned in this chapter into action:

- Using the list of prospects you have developed, pick some of the people you know best and, to the best of your ability, qualify them. That is, try to determine which of these people are the most likely to produce commission income for you. By doing this, you will begin the process of determining which characteristics are most important in your prospective customers.

- Try sorting your prospect list into A, B, and C prospects. Do this in such a way that it can be easily undone, as this is a very preliminary sorting. The goal is to get you used to thinking in terms of focusing on the most productive business first.

- Practice the method for asking qualifying questions outlined in this chapter. You can do this with an actual prospect or you can enlist a friend or family member to role play the part of the prospect. If possible, record your practice session and count the number of open, reflexive, and closed questions you ask.

- Familiarize yourself with the *Client Profile Form*. Photocopy it or convert it into a computer database. Begin to fill out the form for those prospects you know the best.

The Client Profile Form

Qualifying

On the following pages you will find the *Client Profile Form*. It is intended to serve as the definitive repository of all the information you will collect about your customers over the years. The information it contains will help you sell to them more effectively and satisfy their needs more fully. It contains a great deal of information. Obviously, you will not gather it all at one time. Even if you could, doing so would probably not be advisable; you'd end up sounding like the Grand Inquisitor

You should feel free to use the Form just as it is. Or you can adapt it in any way you see fit, dropping or adding sections to better reflect the way you do business with your clients.

I also suggest that you either computerize the entire Form or the key portions of it. By entering this data into a database program you will be able to do some revealing analyses of your customers and their travel habits. You also will be able to identify the ideal prospects for special deals that come your way. A database program will allow you, for example, to produce a list of all those customers who play golf and have expressed an interest in visiting Hawaii. Many database programs can be designed to print out the information in any variety of ways, including a complete form that will look very much like a filled-in version of the one on the following pages.

Notes on the Client Profile Form

Most of the information on the Form is self-explanatory. However, some elements may require further explanation.

Will Refer? Make a note of whether this client is willing to serve as a "proof source" for you. In other words, will they be willing to talk to other people about the benefits of a cruise or a tour or a resort they booked through you.

Birth Date. Get the precise day and year of birth. You can use this information, for example, to chat with a wife about taking her husband somewhere special for his 50th birthday.

Marriage Date. Again, get the day and year in which they were married. Recording this information (as opposed to just the anniversary date) lets you market a splurge trip for those very special 10th, 20th, and 25th anniversaries.

Honeymooned in. Most people are sentimental about the place they honeymooned. It can be an ideal destination for an anniversary trip.

Children. Don't overlook the possibility of "Sweet Sixteen" trips or other gift vacations that can be tied to a child's birthday.

Income. You'll probably be guessing here but the data can prove useful when marketing high-ticket cruises or tours.

Memberships. Tracking this kind of information will prove helpful when you start going after group business.

Personal Interests. Keeping track of this information will help you look good when describing potential destinations. It will also help you avoid miscalculations like recommending a resort with no golf course.

Travel History. Keeping this section up to date can be troublesome, but an in-depth knowledge of a client's past travel history is an excellent tool for predicting future travel destinations.

Business Travel. Note that some people must book their business travel through a company-approved agency.

Leisure Travel. Knowing your clients' leisure travel patterns will help you market to and service them better.

Airlines, etc. Keeping track of frequent flyer, frequent lodger, and other affinity programs will save you and the client time in subsequent bookings and aid you in selecting travel vendors.

Booking History. Taking the time to make a brief note here each time you book a client will tell you, in due course, who your best customers are. It will also give you a very accurate gauge of their budgets for various types of travel.

Client Profile Form

Personal Data

Name: _____ Will Refer? _____

Address (home): _____

(office): _____

Phones/Email: _____

        (home)   (office)   (fax)   (email)

Birth Date: _____ Marriage Date: _____ Honeymooned in: _____

Spouse (age & DOB): _____

Children (ages & DOB): _____

_____

Profession: _____

Income: ❑ <$25K   ❑ $25-$35K   ❑ $35-$50K   ❑ $50-$100K ❑ >$100K

Memberships in professional organizations and clubs: _____

_____

_____

Health considerations when traveling: _____

_____

Personal Interests

	Self	Spouse		Self	Spouse
Music/Dance	❑	❑	Hiking	❑	❑
Art	❑	❑	Golf	❑	❑
Antiques	❑	❑	Tennis	❑	❑
Theater	❑	❑	Skiing	❑	❑
Opera	❑	❑	Swimming	❑	❑
Museums	❑	❑	Snorkeling	❑	❑
History	❑	❑	Scuba diving	❑	❑
Archaeology	❑	❑	Surfing	❑	❑
Genealogy	❑	❑	Windsurfing	❑	❑
Religion	❑	❑	Rafting	❑	❑
Gourmet food	❑	❑	Sailing	❑	❑
Cooking	❑	❑	Cycling	❑	❑
Wine	❑	❑	Spelunking	❑	❑
Sightseeing	❑	❑	Ecotourism	❑	❑
Gambling	❑	❑	Soft-adventure	❑	❑

Travel History

	Has visited	More than once	Would return	Will never visit	Would like to visit
Northeast	❑	❑	❑	❑	❑
Cities: _____					
Florida/South	❑	❑	❑	❑	❑
Cities: _____					
Midwest	❑	❑	❑	❑	❑
Cities: _____					

	Has visited	More than once	Would return	Will never visit	Would like to visit
Mountain States	❏	❏	❏	❏	❏
Cities: _____					
West Coast	❏	❏	❏	❏	❏
Cities: _____					
Alaska	❏	❏	❏	❏	❏
Cities: _____					
Hawaii	❏	❏	❏	❏	❏
Islands: _____					
Canada	❏	❏	❏	❏	❏
Cities: _____					
Caribbean	❏	❏	❏	❏	❏
Islands: _____					
Mexico	❏	❏	❏	❏	❏
Cities: _____					
West Europe	❏	❏	❏	❏	❏
Countries/cities: _____					
East Europe	❏	❏	❏	❏	❏
Countries/cities: _____					
Middle East	❏	❏	❏	❏	❏
Countries/cities: _____					
Africa	❏	❏	❏	❏	❏
Countries/cities: _____					
Asia	❏	❏	❏	❏	❏
Countries/cities: _____					
Central America	❏	❏	❏	❏	❏
Countries/cities: _____					
South America	❏	❏	❏	❏	❏
Countries/cities: _____					

Other: _____

Future Travel Plans

"Dream" Destination(s): _____

_____

Is there anywhere you NEVER want to go? _____

_____

Business Travel

How Many Trips/Year: _____ Average Length: _____

Destinations: _____

_____

❏ Pre-paid by company ❏ Paid by client & reimbursed ❏ Company-approved agency

Comments: _____

Leisure Travel

Time of Vacation: ❏ Winter ❏ Summer ❏ Spring ❏ Fall ❏ Varies
Length of Vacation: ❏ 1 week ❏ 2 weeks ❏ 3 weeks ❏ 1 month ❏ Longer ❏ Varies
Preferred Destinations: _____
Type of Leisure Travel:

	Always	Sometimes	Never
Independent	❏	❏	❏
Fly/drive	❏	❏	❏
Escorted tours	❏	❏	❏
All-inclusive resorts	❏	❏	❏
Cruises	❏	❏	❏

Travels on Vacation with: ❏ Solo ❏ Spouse ❏ Girl/boyfriend ❏ Children ❏ Friends ❏ Varies
Type of Vacation: ❏ US ❏ Foreign ❏ Warm in winter ❏ Cool in summer ❏ Beach
❏ Mountains ❏ All-inclusives ❏ Sightseeing ❏ Active sports ❏ Skiing ❏ Tennis ❏ Diving
❏ Sailing ❏ History ❏ Archaeology

Airlines

Preferred Airline(s): _____
_____

Frequent Flyer Information (airline, number):
_____
_____
_____
_____
_____

Seating: ❏ First ❏ Business ❏ Coach ❏ Aisle ❏ Center ❏ Window ❏ Smoking ❏ Non
Special Requests: _____
_____

Car Rentals

Preferred Companies: _____
_____

Frequent Renter Programs (company, number):
_____
_____
_____

Type of Car: _____
_____

Comments: _____

Hotels

Preferred Hotel(s): _____
_____

Frequent Lodger Programs (hotel, number):
_____
_____
_____

Preferences for general and business travel:

	Required	Preferred	Optional
All-suite	❑	❑	❑
Non-smoking room	❑	❑	❑
"Green" room	❑	❑	❑
King	❑	❑	❑
Double	❑	❑	❑
Two beds	❑	❑	❑
Suite	❑	❑	❑
Junior suite	❑	❑	❑
Wheelchair accessible	❑	❑	❑
High floor	❑	❑	❑
Low floor	❑	❑	❑

Preferences for leisure travel:

	Required	Preferred	Optional
Deluxe	❑	❑	❑
Moderate	❑	❑	❑
Budget	❑	❑	❑
"Old world charm"	❑	❑	❑
Modern facilities	❑	❑	❑
Resorts	❑	❑	❑
Villas, castles, etc.	❑	❑	❑
Inns, b&bs	❑	❑	❑
All-suites	❑	❑	❑
Ranches, farms	❑	❑	❑

Comments: _____

_____

Cruises

Preferred Cruise Line(s): _____

_____

Preferred Cruise Area(s): _____

_____

Ship Type: ❑ Large ❑ Medium ❑ Small ❑ Windjammer

Cabin Location: ❑ Forward ❑ Midships ❑ Aft ❑ Upper deck ❑ Mid deck
❑ Lower deck ❑ Suite ❑ Outside ❑ Inside

Comments: _____

_____

Booking History

Date	Booking Details	Total Cost

Chapter Twenty-one:

Presenting the Wonder of Travel

What you will learn

After you have completed this chapter you will be able to:

- Develop needs through the process of gathering information or "qualifying the situation."
- Distinguish among features, functions, and benefits.
- Present your travel recommendations powerfully and persuasively using a time-tested presentation technique.
- Use visual aids professionally.

Key terms and concepts

This chapter involves the following key terms and concepts:

- Most travel agents meet their customers' basic needs. The truly great travel agents sell to their customers' higher-order needs.
- A feature is any element of a product. A function is what the feature does. A benefit is the positive result the customer experiences from the feature.
- Sales are made by benefits, not just features and functions, but many salespeople have difficulty in distinguishing between functions and benefits.
- Probe-Present-Prove-Close is a presentation technique that has been proven effective because of the way it actively involves the prospect in the decision-making process.
- Visual aids are only as good as the skills of the travel agent using them.

Introduction

Some travel selling situations are pretty straightforward. A customer calls you up and says, "I'm going to Fort Lauderdale for a medical conference. I have to leave the third of March and return the sixth. I want to stay at the Marriott Harbor Inn Resort, and I'll need a mid-size car." You pull the client's *Profile Form*, make the bookings, and that's that.

In other situations, you'll have to do some selling. When a client has asked your help in selecting a tour or a cruise, or when you have decided to go out into the marketplace and actively promote a specific tour or cruise, you will be faced with the challenge of presenting your wares in such a persuasive and professional manner that the prospect will be convinced that this is the right buying decision.

While this chapter covers the skills and techniques of making professional — and successful — sales presentations to a single person or a couple, the techniques discussed can be applied when you are presenting to a small group in your living room or to dozens of people at a formal sales meeting.

Gathering information, developing needs

In *Part II*, we discussed the process for booking airlines, hotels, rental cars, tours, and cruises. Each of the chapters devoted to these products discussed the importance of gathering information from the client so that you would know which specific product to book. By now, you should also realize that, by gathering this information, you are qualifying the prospect. You are learning about her likes and dislikes in general and you are also "qualifying the situation," learning what specific elements must be in place for this *specific* journey. In addition, you are finding out what the prospect *needs*.

In the strictest sense, no one buys anything they don't need. I know you can immediately think of exceptions to this supposed rule — how about that candy bar you picked up yesterday? Or the fourth drink you had at the bar last night? You didn't need those. True, perhaps. But something inside you, the "inner shopper," convinced you that you *did* need those little luxuries. So you bought them.

When selling travel, everything that the prospect tells you he or she wants — a non-smoking, a subcompact car, and so forth — is a need. Successful sales are concluded when the seller (you) matches the customer's needs with the right products. The customer needs a non-smoking room and a subcompact car. You provide it. Sale made. Everybody's happy.

Determining needs and satisfying them is not always that simple. With complex travel itineraries or higher-ticket discretionary purchases (like tours and cruises), more complex needs come into play. It's no more a matter of room selection or the right car. The traveler, for example, might have a need to be reassured that connections will go smoothly and that all aspects of the itinerary have been taken care of. A would-be cruiser may have a need to achieve total relaxation and freedom from care.

Those are a higher-order of needs than the basic elements of the booking. If it's true that meeting needs earns sales, then it is also true that the more needs you meet and the more important those needs are, the greater the likelihood of making the sale.

Most travel agents do a pretty good job of meeting the basic needs (the right seat on the right airline, for example). What distinguishes the great travel agents from the rest of the herd is their ability to identify and

(sell to their customers' higher-order needs.)

What are those higher-order needs and how do you find out about them? Higher-order needs tend to be very personal, emotional, and specific to the individual. Some of them may apply in most or all travel situations. For example, some people have a need to feel they are always getting the best deal available. Others may want to use travel as a sort of "fashion statement," spending a little (or a lot) extra to get the very best. Still others have a need to be made to feel special, a need that you might meet by hand delivering tickets, providing them with extensive notes on what to do in Singapore, driving them to the airport, and so forth.

Other needs are specific to a particular journey and are best discovered by asking, "Why are you taking this trip?" The answers you receive will provide you with your most valuable information on how to sell this trip to *this* customer. For example, if a customer is taking a business trip to try to close a major deal, you may have uncovered a need for a first-class hotel and a full-size rental car to impress the people he's meeting. If you learn that someone is inquiring about a trip to the Caribbean to celebrate a twentieth wedding anniversary, you have probably uncovered a need for a very special, romantic experience. Of course, you will have to ask the right questions to uncover and pin down specific needs. But once you have this powerful information in hand, you will be able to tailor a highly persuasive presentation for this client, as we shall see.

Features, functions, and benefits

One of the keys to successful selling is understanding the difference among features, functions, and benefits and how they relate to needs. Let's start off with some working definitions.

- ⬛ *Needs.* A need is something for which a prospect or customer *has expressed a desire.* Strictly speaking, if a prospect hasn't told you that he needs a beachfront room, he has no need for a beachfront room.
- ▪ *Features.* A feature is any aspect, element, or part of a product. It is also the name given to that element. In the case of a travel product that means things like an "oceanfront room," a "tour guide" on the motorcoach, an "optional excursion to the archaeological ruins," "first class" on the airline, and so forth.
- ▪ *Functions.* A function is what the feature does. The function of "transfers" (a feature of a tour) is to provide transportation from the airport to the hotel and back.
- ⬤ *Benefits.* A benefit is the positive outcome the prospect will enjoy from the feature. *Every feature offers a benefit!* Many features offer more than one benefit. It is the benefit that fulfills the prospect's need and convinces the prospect that this is the right product.

That last point bears repeating, so let's repeat it.

It is the benefit that fulfills the prospect's need and convinces the prospect that this is the right product.

Qualifying the situation, as I just mentioned, is a process of developing needs. Of course, there are such things as unexpressed needs. The problem is, from your point of view, it is very difficult to sell to an unexpressed need. If the client wants to play tennis on vacation and hasn't told you, then you may present a tennis-less resort, lose a sale, and never know why. Now you might say, "If she wanted to play tennis, why didn't she tell me?" The answer is, "Because you didn't ask." *It is the travel agent's responsibility to elicit complete information about the client's needs.* That is what you get paid for.

The features of any travel product are the suppliers' answers to the needs of the traveling public. The Modified American Plan, to cite just a single example, is a feature of a resort hotel. Its function is to provide vacationers with breakfast and dinner every day for a set price. The benefit is that vacationers don't have to worry about where they will eat breakfast and dinner or what it may cost them, leaving their days completely free for sightseeing and shopping at their leisure.

The selling power of benefits

Unless you're flat out lying to your customers, a feature is always a feature and a function is always a function. Yes, this hotel does have five pools. Yes, the Modified American Plan at the hotel does provide breakfast and dinner every day. That's the plain truth and nothing can change it.

But is a benefit always a benefit? The answer is, "No."

Unlike features and functions, which are defined by the product, a benefit is defined by the customer and the customer alone. Consequently, what is a benefit for one customer may actually be a drawback for another. For example, an oceanfront room may seem like a dandy idea. It has the benefit of giving immediate access to the beach. But if the room faces East, the sun will come pouring in at dawn. To a late-riser that could be a drawback.

That is why only benefits make sales. Not features. Not functions. Benefits!

Still, many travel agents make the mistake of overloading their prospects with features. One reason for this is that features are easy to find. The brochure lists them for you. It requires no particular skill or imagination to simply rattle them off. Professional salespeople have a term for this tendency to fling features at a customer — "feature vomit." Avoid it like the plague. Just remember that:

- Features alone provoke little interest.
- Features and functions spur moderate interest.
- Features and functions linked with specific benefits create high interest and lead to successful sales.

Choose specific benefits

Any given travel product may have literally dozens or scores of features. Each of those features may have several benefits, depending on the customer. You simply don't have time to present all the benefits of a given cruise or tour. Even if you did, it would be a terribly inefficient way to sell to your customers.

So what benefits should you present? How many should you present?

You should present only those benefits that fulfill specific needs expressed by the customer. You should present them in the order of their importance to the customer. And you should present only enough of these benefits to make the sale.

Caution: You will remember from the chapters on booking travel products that there is important information you must relay to the customer. Much of this information concerns the features and functions of the travel product. I am not suggesting that you stop providing information once the sale is made. What I *am* suggesting is that when you sense the client is ready to make a buying decision (write a check, for example) you should stop presenting and conclude the sale. Then you can continue to provide information about the product the customer has just purchased. Only now, you can do so in a somewhat abbreviated fashion because the sale is no longer in doubt.

How will you know which specific benefits to present? You will know because you have taken the time to qualify the situation.

Distinguishing features, functions, benefits

I am convinced that selling benefits is the key to all successful selling, whether it's travel products or anything else. Unfortunately, not everyone can distinguish a feature from a function, or a function from a benefit. I have seen example after example of cruise and tour sales materials that claim to list "benefits" and actually list "features." Take it from me, "great service, spacious cabins, elegant decor, and an early booking discount" are features and not benefits!

I have also learned from training hundreds of salespeople, many of them accomplished professionals, that distinguishing among features, functions, and benefits is not always easy. One way to do so is to use the "So what?" test. If you state what you consider a benefit and the prospect can plausibly reply, "So what?" you haven't gotten to the real benefit yet.

Many travel agents continue to offer their customers features. Some offer functions, in the mistaken belief that they are benefits. Some offer generic benefits when they could very easily tailor the benefits to the specific, expressed needs of their clients. Truly creative travel agents — and I hope you will become one of them — offer their customers powerful benefits that match and meet very specifically the customers' expressed needs and desires.

Because I feel so strongly about the importance of selling benefits, as opposed to features or functions, and because I want you to succeed, I am going to take a moment to further illustrate the point with the following table of features, functions, and benefits. I have chosen the features more or less at random. The functions, hopefully, are self-explanatory. In the final column, I have listed *possible* specific benefits. In other words, much of this is made up. Some benefits listed may be benefits for one person but not another. You can probably think up additional benefits for most of these features (in fact, I encourage you to do so). Just remember, you can never know if a benefit is appropriate for a particular customer until you have thoroughly qualified the situation and developed their needs through artful questioning. The number of possible specific benefits is limited only by your customers' needs.

Feature	Function(s)	Possible Specific Benefits
Escorted tour	Provides a guide throughout the trip. Handles check-in, check-out, and all details of the trip. Explains sights and attractions.	• Learn more about the culture than you could on your own. • Make sure you see all the highlights of the museums and castles you visit. • No worries about speaking the language. • No dragging your bags around, so you can concentrate on having a good time.
"Cashless" cruises	All on-board expenditures are signed for. You get one bill at the end of the cruise.	• You can forget about money for a week. • You can wear nothing but a swimsuit if you wish because you don't need pockets. • You'll know exactly what you spent and for what (final bill).
"All-inclusive" pricing	Lodging, meals, and activities included in a single price. Very few extra expenditures.	• You can forget about money for a week. • You can wear nothing but a swimsuit if you wish because you don't need pockets. • You know what the trips costs *before* you go, not after you get back and count up the bills. • Easy to budget, pay for.

"

Feature	Function(s)	Possible Specific Benefits
Day at leisure" (tour)	Provides a day when no activities are scheduled. You are on your own.	• Lets you get the benefit of an independent tour at a package tour price. • Not tied down to someone else's schedule. • Private time for you and your spouse. • Perfect opportunity to splurge on a 4-star restaurant or go shopping. • You can visit attractions, museums, theater, or sporting events not on the regular tour. • Lets you take a break and sleep late. • Lets you and your spouse enjoy different activities without inconveniencing the other.
First Class (airline)	Provides more comfortable, spacious seating, free cocktails, better food, higher level of service.	• Pamper yourself. • Reward yourself for a successful business year. • Surprise your new bride on your honeymoon. • Arrived relaxed and "psyched" to do business. • Be more productive because you'll be able to work in flight.

This is just a start. There are literally thousands of features associated with the travel products you will be selling. However, I hope this table serves to illustrate the differences among features, functions, and benefits. I would encourage you to practice making these distinctions. Take a hotel or tour brochure at random and make your own table. For each feature, describe its function. Then ask yourself, "So what?" Use your imagination and come up with as many possible answers as you can. Envision different types of travelers and imagine what would be a specific benefit *to them*.

The more skill you develop in translating features into powerful, *specific* benefits for your customers, the more successful you will be as a travel agent, especially when it comes to booking those high-ticket, high-commission tours, honeymoon packages, and cruises.

A presentation model

As with so much of what we discuss in this book, presenting the wonderful benefits of the travel products you sell will be a lot easier if you approach the task in a professional and orderly fashion. Over the years, sales professionals have developed a highly effective way of providing information to their clients in such a way that the client sees — even experiences — the wisdom of making an immediate buying decision. This method is built around a simple, four-step process:

Probe — Present — Prove — Close

This method works best if you fully qualify the situation first, research available travel products, and then present your solutions to the client. It works in both informal settings and formal group presentations. Let's take a look at each step in turn.

- *Probe.* Ask a question — preferably one to which you know the answer — that addresses an expressed, known, or strongly suspected need of the customer. Obviously, expressed needs will be the strongest motivators. But you may know about your customers' needs based on past experience with them. Also, some needs can be inferred; for example, it is reasonable to assume that a need to escape the chill of winter to a Caribbean island is shared by an audience in upstate New York that is attending a Cruise Night you sponsored. When the customer answers the question, he will be reinforcing the need in his own mind, conjuring up a mental picture of whatever it is in his life that is lacking.
- *Present.* Your question sets the stage for you to present a specific benefit or group of benefits of the travel product you are offering.
- *Prove.* While not always necessary, your presentation of benefits will be stronger if you have some way of backing up what you say with proof. That proof can take the form of your own personal experience with a cruise line, that of other satisfied customers, the pictures in a brochure, or slides or a video you can show the customer.
- *Close.* Once you have presented the benefit and proved its worth, you should make a trial close to test that the customer has accepted the benefit as valid.

Let's take a look at how this process might be played out in a typical selling situation.

Travel Agent:	Now, you said that peace and quiet was important to you, right? ***(Probe)***
	[The agent, we can assume, has elicited the customer's feelings about peace and quiet while qualifying the situation.]
Customer:	Is it ever! Work's been a madhouse lately. I just want to get away from everything and chill out for two weeks.
Travel Agent:	***(Present)*** Then I think there are some things about the Ends of the Earth Resort that you'll find particularly appealing. It's located on 478 acres of private land, with the nearest town over 25 miles away *(Feature)*. Unless you leave the resort itself there are absolutely no signs of civilization *(Function)*. You're completely removed from the cares of the world *(Benefit)*. The individual cabanas are spread around the grounds, separated from one another by lush tropical vegetation *(Feature)*, so it's impossible to see or hear anything from your neighbors *(Function)*. You'll have absolute quiet *(Benefit)*. Best of all, the rooms have no telephones *(Feature)*. So if there's an emergency at the office, that'll be just too bad. No one will be able to reach you *(Benefit)*.
Customer:	Wow!
Travel Agent:	Here's a map of the resort. See how the cabanas are spaced? And there's the beach. It's possible to go for hours without seeing another soul. ***(Prove)***
Customer:	That's great.
Travel Agent:	Is that the sort of peace and quiet you had in mind? ***(Close)***

As you can see, in this example the travel agent bases the presentation of the resort's quiet, out-of-the-way atmosphere as a benefit that addresses a specific need — the customer's expressed desire to get some real peace and quiet.

In theory, you could carry on a dialog like the one above for every element of the booking. ("Now, you said you wanted an aisle seat, right?") In practice, you will want to go into this depth and detail only for those aspects of the product that address the customer's major needs. That could mean the higher-order needs uncovered when you asked "Why are you taking this trip?" Or it could mean those benefits that, through the process of qualifying, you have determined are the most crucial to making this sale.

The example above suggests a benefit by benefit approach, and there's nothing wrong with that. You can continue to probe, present, prove, and close, covering one benefit after another, until you have made your most persuasive case. This, however, is not your only alternative. For example, you might begin a presentation to a couple looking for a winter vacation this way:

"As you asked me, I've been researching some vacation possibilities in the Caribbean. And I think I've come up with three choices that fit the bill. Today, we can choose the one that's best for you and put down a deposit to secure your booking. Now you told me there were three major considerations for this trip: You wanted something sophisticated, without a lot of honky-tonk or loud, raucous people. You were also looking for something that would give you the widest choice of activities and allow you to try out some new sports activities. You also said that some of your previous trips wound up costing a lot more than you'd anticipated so you wanted to budget very carefully on this one. Does that about sum it up?"
[They agree that it does.]
"Is there anything else you'd like to add to this list?"
[They say there isn't.]
"Fine. Then let me start by presenting what I feel is the preferred choice for you. But, remember, the decision is yours. You pick the one you like best."

This approach isolates the three major benefits that will make the sale — sophistication, a wide choice of activities, and good pricing. Presumably, if the travel agent can make a persuasive case that these criteria have been met, then the customers have no real reason not to put down a deposit. (By the way, notice how the agent made it very clear that the purpose of this discussion was to make a *buying* decision, not just to chat. I like that.) That doesn't mean the agent will ignore the other benefits of the packages he recommends. But the prime thrust of the presentation will be aimed at fulfilling those three major needs.

The cost/value ratio

One of the major considerations for just about anyone considering a major leisure travel expense such as a tour or a cruise is the cost/value ratio. In other words, is this product worth what they are going to charge me for it? This consideration is separate from, but related to, budget. A customer may have the budget for (be able to afford) a specific tour but not be convinced that the trip is worth the price (the cost/value ratio doesn't make sense). On the other hand, many people will be willing to pay a little more than they had anticipated if they are convinced that the extra money will provide an enhanced travel experience. I am convinced that more travel sales fall through because the cost/value ratio isn't there than for any other reason.

The problem is, the cost/value ratio is a slippery concept. It can't be found in any reference book. It exists only in the minds of your customers. It changes from person to person and it can change from day to day or minute to minute for any individual. One of your goals in presenting travel products, then, is to create the most favorable cost/value ratio possible in the customer's mind. You want the prospect to feel, after your presentation, that the several thousand dollars he is being asked to part with to finance this cruise is the bargain of the decade.

Think of the cost/value ratio as an old-fashioned balance scale with two trays. On one side is the cost, tipping the scale down. On the other side is a tray for all the benefits you will provide. Each one evens the scale just a little more. At some point, the cost on one side and the benefits on the other will become even. Keep adding benefits, or add "heavier" ones, and the value becomes much greater than the cost. That's your goal.

Obviously, this can be taken to absurd extremes:

"And on the flight down you will receive the soft drink of your choice, served by an attentive and highly trained flight attendant. Each soft drink will be accompanied by a beautiful foil-wrapped portion of the finest mustard-dusted pretzels — all at no additional cost to you!"

Still, the point is valid. The more value you can build into your presentations with specific benefits, the less the cost will seem.

Visual aids and how to use them

One nice thing about selling travel is that the suppliers do such a good job of helping you out with eye-popping brochures, videos, slides, and posters. Depending on the kind of travel business you eventually evolve, you may even create your own visual aids — for example, slide shows of tours you have led in the past.

While there is no doubt that visual aids can be of immense help to the travel agent, they do not relieve you of the responsibility to be in charge of the presentation. In this section, I will discuss the most common forms of visual aids and give some pointers on how to use them to best advantage.

Whatever visual aids you use, you must use them *interactively*. That is, they are not a substitute for talking with your customers but a spur to further discussion. So get the prospect involved with the visuals you use. Ask questions about the pictures or slides you show. Have prospects choose among alternatives ("Which of these hotels looks the nicest to you?"). Have them point to the pictures that most appeal. Encourage them to *imagine* themselves in the photos or in the video.

Studies have shown that people remember 25% of what they hear and 50% of what they see. But they remember fully 85% of what they see, hear, and interact with.

Brochures

When you are using a brochure to make a presentation to a client, there are two salespeople involved — you and the brochure. You (presumably) are constantly working to improve yourself, but the brochure, once printed, will never get any better. In fact, it will get worse with age as it becomes dog-eared from use, or as the information it contains becomes outdated, or as the hairdos on the models in the photographs grow out of style. Unfortunately, the brochure is one aspect of the presentation over which you have no control. Well, almost no control. You can control which brochures you choose to present to your clients.

To help you make good choices, here are some insights gleaned by the Martin Agency of Richmond, VA, in focus groups with travelers. Use them to evaluate the brochures that come across your desk.

- The photographs are the most important single aspect of a travel brochure. The more beautiful and evocative the pictures, the more interest your customers will have. But no matter how beautiful they are, the pictures must also look recent. If they appear to be years or decades old, the customer will become suspicious that the property can't stand up to current scrutiny.
- The quality of the travel experience is also conveyed to the customer through such seemingly minor details as the quality of the paper on which the brochure is printed.
- A simple, open layout, with large, easy to read type will convey the idea that going there will also be a relaxed and pleasurable experience.
- Brochures with lots of information are appreciated because many people take the brochures with them on their trips and use them as guides.

You can factor in your evaluation of the brochure when you make your decisions about which resorts, hotels, and destinations you will be recommending to your clients. Jamaica (to cite a random example) is chockfull of resorts. Why not sell only those which make the best impression on would-be guests with sleek, professionally designed and produced marketing materials? Of course, we all know that photos can lie and your clients won't be comforted by the knowledge that the brochure looked lovely when the actual trip is a horror show. You'll have to assure yourself that the brochure adequately reflects the reality — that's what fam trips are all about. But all else being equal, a fine resort with a fine brochure will be an easier sell than a fine resort with a mediocre brochure. It's a small point perhaps, but one worth bearing in mind as you choose properties to recommend to your customers.

Using brochures as part of a sales presentation requires a modicum of care and attention to details. Here are some tips:

- Don't simply hand your customers copies of the brochures at the beginning of your presentation. They will read the brochures while trying to listen to you. As a result, neither you nor the brochure will communicate effectively.

- Use the brochure as a sort of slide show, to illustrate points you are making, as you make them. When talking about the beach, have open the page with the beach picture. When talking about the amenities of the hotel room, point to the photo of the typical suite or a map of the resort's layout.

- If presenting to a couple — a fairly typical situation — sit between them, with the brochure on the table in front of you. That way, you can all see what you're pointing out. You can present the brochure across the table, with the brochure facing the clients and you behind it, but that requires a certain amount of practice.

- Highlight, underline, circle, or otherwise mark key elements in the brochure as you cover them in your presentation. This is especially important when discussing such matters as cancellation policies (the "fine print"). It serves as reminder to both you and the client (see below) that these matters were explained. Keep this copy for yourself.

- At the end of the presentation, hand out fresh copies to the client, containing appropriate highlightings and marginal notations that you've made in advance. For example, next to the cancellation policy you might write, "Very Important!" If you are presenting to a couple, give each of them a copy; that way you avoid insulting the "decision-maker" by giving the brochure to the wrong spouse.

- Practice your presentations so that you become comfortable using the brochure. Enlist a spouse or friend or use the always accommodating mirror.

Videos and slide shows

Many tour and cruise suppliers will provide you with video cassettes at very modest cost. Videos may also be available from foreign tourist bureaus, commercial suppliers, or your local public library.

Video cassettes can be given to a prospect to be viewed at home, shown in your own living room to a group of friends, or used as the centerpiece of a presentation to a larger group. Here are a few simple things to bear in mind when using videos with a group.

- ***Always pre-screen the video.*** This may seem obvious, but some agents forget to do it. You want to make sure you can answer any questions that the video might generate from your audience. You also want to make sure that you can deliver on everything that the video promises, or seems to promise. If there are parts of the video that don't apply or that may be

misleading you may want to stop the video in midstream rather than risk confusing your audience.

- ***Make sure the screen is visible to everyone.*** In a living room, this might mean moving the set so that it is at shoulder height. When arranging seating, it is better to place people a little farther back than too far to the side.
- ***Dim, but do not completely turn out the lights,*** when showing videos. Try to position yourself in such a way that you can observe reactions during the screening.
- ***Adjust the volume.*** Set it slightly higher than you would if you were watching for your own enjoyment. The somewhat louder soundtrack will help focus attention squarely on the video (much as it does in a movie theater). Of course, the sound should never be so loud as to be uncomfortable.
- ***Introduce the video.*** Tell people what they are going to be seeing. You might, for example, give a brief summary of the video's highlights. Or suggest that, as they watch, viewers pick out which of the locales shown is their favorite. Or pose a question, the answer to which will be found in the video. Strategies such as these will encourage audience attention to and involvement in the video.
- ***Schedule a short break before playing it*** if the video is longish (say, over 20 minutes). That way people can help themselves to refreshments or make that important visit to the rest room.

Much of the advice that applies to videos applies to slide shows as well. However, there are few items that are peculiar to slide presentations:

- ***Position yourself correctly.*** If you are going to be speaking as you present the slides, stand in front of the audience to the left of the screen (from the audience's point of view). Since people read left to right, positioning yourself to the left puts you in a stronger position. Use a remote control device to advance the slides, or have an assistant do it. Standing at the back of the room and advancing the slides yourself is not a good idea; you and the slide show become two separate elements in the minds of the audience.
- ***Check your materials.*** Always check your slides, their order, and orientation just before each presentation. I don't why it is but practical jokers seem to have a special affinity for slide trays.
- ***Know your equipment.*** The best slide machine is the one you know intimately and bring yourself. If you are using rented or borrowed equipment, get there early, test it out, do a couple of dry runs, and have a back-up plan in case of emergency.
- ***"Clear the visual."*** If your slide show includes slides that

contain nothing but text, be sure to "clear the visual" immediately whenever such a slide appears. In other words, read the text aloud before proceeding, because your audience will do so whether or not you allow time for it. Typically, a text slide will have a major subject heading and three or so bullet points. Once you have read through the material on the slide, you can return to the beginning and expand on each point separately, knowing that your audience is with you.

Selling through visual imagery

Don't think that just because you have all these wonderful visual aids at your disposal, you have all the pictures you need. Some of the best pictures that travel agents use are the ones they create in their prospects' heads through the use of visual imagery and powerful, evocative words. Here are some of the ways you can paint those pictures:

- *Modifiers.* Adjectives, adverbs, and short phrases are all modifiers; that is, they define or describe other words. Select modifiers that are particularly evocative yet still describe your products and services accurately. Can you offer savings or tremendous discounts off the regular fare? Do you provide fast delivery of tickets or personal delivery to your customers' homes? Do you book cruises or glamorous cruises of the sunny Caribbean?

  The optimum adjectives and descriptive phrases for you will, of course, depend on your area of specialty and the mix of travel products and services you are offering. They will also depend on what you feel comfortable with. Make an effort to search them out. Once you have found them, use them!

  Using vivid adjectives and descriptive phrases will add power to any sales presentation. One caution: Avoid adjective pollution. You can overdo it if you're not careful. Don't use three adjectives when one will do nicely. Check yourself periodically to make sure that the words you are using accurately convey your meaning. For example, which is bigger — "huge" or "colossal?"

- *Romance words.* Certain words are especially romantic. In fact, the word "romantic" is one of them. People who sell travel often use the term "romance words" to refer to those adjectives that do a special job of capturing the allure of the products and experiences they are selling. You can find plenty of romance words in the brochures and videos put out by the various suppliers. Which of them will work for you is a matter of taste; what sounds great on the page may sound corny or trite coming out of your mouth. Nonetheless, you should start searching for romance words that will work for you. Find words and phrases that you can use convincingly and unselfconsciously to describe and promote your travel products.

■ ***Setting the scene.*** If people buy benefits (which reflect their selfish interests), it follows that helping them envision those benefits working for *them*, on *their* trip or vacation, providing the specific benefits *they* are seeking, will make it easier for them to make the right buying decision.

So, when presenting the wonder of travel, set the scene: "Remember, that tour of Italy you told me about when . . . ." Now the prospect is seeing that pleasant episode in his mind's eye. When you present your tour of Ireland, he will automatically "see" it as providing a similar, even superior, experience.

■ ***The telling detail.*** Another way to bring your presentation to life in the prospect's mind is to use crucial information that you gathered while qualifying the situation. Suppose your client had told you that she was looking for a vacation where she could "sit on a beach, sip a margarita, and watch the perfect sunset." During your presentation of a resort brochure, you could linger over a photo of a picture-perfect beach and say, "Wouldn't this be the perfect spot to relax, sip a margarita, and watch that perfect sunset?" Whether the prospect remembers her earlier remark or not, she will be subconsciously reminded of her desire for the perfect getaway and move one step closer to firming up her booking.

■ ***The sizzle, not the steak.*** There's a line from the world of advertising that you may have heard: "Sell the sizzle, not the steak." The idea is that people are looking not so much for the product itself but the *feelings* that are associated with it — the benefits, if you will. The word pictures you create, then, should evoke the emotions and feelings rather than the nuts and bolts. "Like an elegantly furnished country cottage" is more evocative than "a one thousand-square-foot junior suite" although both may describe the same thing.

The power of words

While we're on the subject of words, let's take a moment to consider how they affect another important aspect of your success as a travel agent.

Some 80 years ago, Benjamin Whorf, a language scholar from Yale, discovered that the way people talk actually affects the way they think and act. He was studying the language of the Native American Hopi tribe, but his insights have implications for present-day travel agents and other salespeople.

Your choice of words affects not only your prospects' view of you but, even more important, your view of yourself. Listen to these two travel agents:

Agent #1:   Gee, I'm really not too sure. Would this be okay? I'll try to find out; and if I can get the information, I'll try and get back to you.

Agent #2: I don't have that information, but I'll be happy to get it for you. I'll call you back tomorrow morning at eleven, or would two in the afternoon be more convenient for you?

Not only will Agent #1 *seem* tentative, uncertain, and indecisive, the odds are overwhelming that he or she will *behave* in precisely the same way. Agent #2, on the other hand, not only comes across as decisive and proactive but he or she is committed to a plan of action.

So, speak positively! If you do, you'll act positively!

Summary

Travel is fun, exciting, and romantic; at least it should be. The skill and enthusiasm with which you present the wonder of travel will help your prospects and customers experience that excitement at every stage of the process, from consulting with you on their travel options, to selecting just the right travel experience, to the trip itself, to their return, when they are sharing their good experiences and fond memories with you.

Mastering the art of presenting means being a good qualifier. That way you'll know *what* to present. You must also be able to distinguish among features, functions, and benefits and understand the selling power of benefits. That way you will know *how* to present.

Presentations are best done in a consistent, professional, and structured fashion. The Probe-Present-Prove-Close model can be used in many situations throughout the sales cycle. It has proven to be a powerful tool for salespeople who take the time to master it.

One of the great advantages you have in the travel industry is that suppliers provide you with stunningly beautiful sales aids, either for free or at very low cost. Spending the time to learn how to use them effectively will make them even more powerful and productive. Even so, nothing will prove more effective than your own enthusiasm and the skill with which you convey it. So make a commitment to develop and hone your presenting skills, now and throughout your travel marketing career.

Action steps

Here are some things you can do to put what you have learned in this chapter into action:

- Choose some supplier brochures that appeal to you, that is ones that feature travel products you would like to sell. Read through them and identify the features, functions, and benefits you find in the text. You might use different colored highlighters to call out the features, functions, and benefits. If you find there are very few benefits in these brochures, it's probably not your fault. Most travel brochures do a great job of listing features and functions, but a poor job of selling benefits.

- Get some supplier videos and DVDs or, failing that, borrow some destination- or activity-specific videos from the library. Screen them and think about ways you could use them to sell the kinds of travel products that interest you.
- Practice the Probe-Present-Prove-Close model. At this point, you will probably have to call on the services of a friend to role play the part of the prospect. Make the situation as realistic as possible and record your practice session. Review it to see how well you implemented the model.
- As you develop your client base, use the model to present to clients. Again, try to review your performance, noting things you did well and things on which you need to improve.

Chapter Twenty-two:
Handling Your Customers' Concerns

What you will learn

After you have completed this chapter you will be able to:

- See customer concerns as an opportunity, not an obstacle.
- Distinguish among different types of concerns.
- Use a time-tested four-step process to deal with customer concerns in a friendly, non-confrontational, and professional manner.
- Use a variety of techniques to answer customer concerns within that four-step process.
- Justify the cost of the travel solutions you recommend and handle any concerns about cost that might arise.
- Handle with confidence any customer concern that might arise.

Key terms and concepts

This chapter involves the following key terms and concepts:

- Concerns (or objections as they are sometimes called) are natural. They are not a sign of failure on your part, but an opportunity to present more information, enhance your relationship with the client, and move closer to a sale.
- The key to handling concerns successfully is to recognize the customer's right to question your presentation and to empathize with their feelings.
- Empathizing with the customer does not mean agreeing with a customer's negative perception, which may be the result of a misunderstanding.
- Concerns about cost are usually the result of poor qualifying. If you have done a good job of qualifying the prospect's budget then you should meet no resistance when you present the price.

Introduction

Nothing puts fear into the heart of a novice salesperson like the sound of a customer saying, "Yeah, but . . . ." To many beginners, this signals the arrival of an "objection," an "obstacle" to the sale that must be "overcome." They are on the defensive. Their products or, even worse, their honesty and integrity are being called into question. The customer is fighting them.

Nothing could be further from the truth. If anything, these so-called "objections" signal the prospect's high level of involvement in the selling process. After all, if a prospect is truly uninterested, why would she bother asking questions about the tour or cruise you are presenting?

By and large, travel agents don't have to face the heavy resistance that some other salespeople must contend with. There are a number of reason for this:

- **People come to you.** In many cases, the only reason you are talking to someone is because they have decided to take a trip. The sale is never in doubt. All that remains to be done is iron out the details.
- **The product range is vast.** Most salespeople are limited to a greater or lesser degree by their product lines. Not so the travel agent. If your customer *hates* escorted tours, you can arrange a fly/drive package, an all-inclusive resort package, or a cruise.
- **Qualifying avoids objections.** Another bonus you receive from your huge product line is that you can eliminate most objections through the qualifying process. In other words, you avoid an objection to escorted tours by learning the customer's likes and dislikes and recommending something else.
- **Your customers are in a buying mood.** Most of the people you deal with are actively looking for reasons to take the trip, not searching for excuses to avoid going.

In spite of everything you have going for you, I would be doing you a disservice if I were to suggest that all will go smoothly from first contact to final sale. The selling process runs into a variety of hitches, bumps, and glitches along the way. Very few of them are full-fledged, sale-busting objections, in the sense that most salespeople use the term. Therefore, I prefer to call them concerns. But whatever we call them, and no matter when or why they come up or how serious they may be, there is a way to handle them — as we shall see in this chapter.

One note of caution to those of you who have decided to specialize in any way or have made a conscious decision to restrict your product offerings for any reason: Because you cannot easily shift to a product you don't usually offer, you may have to be a bit more aggressive in selling the products you do offer. Here's an example:

Vacation getaways to the Caribbean are a huge market. Some home-based travel agents may decide that rather than sell the hundreds (even thousands) of resorts in the Caribbean, they will specialize in a dozen or so properties that offer a good selection, covering most tastes and budgets.

When a client requests a Caribbean holiday, they select the one or two most appropriate destinations and present those. For these agents, having the customer pass on both choices presents something of a problem. Of course, the agents can always research another, more suitable property for the client, but that defeats the purpose of specializing. Therefore, these agents have a built-in incentive to push just a little harder to sell the properties of their choice.

The same goes for the person who decides to specialize in Scandinavia. While she *could* sell a tour to Spain, she'd rather not. Her goal is to convince people that Scandinavia offers the kind of vacation experience they're looking for. A travel agent in this kind of situation may want to handle customer concerns a bit more aggressively.

The truth about customer concerns

Because a certain amount of . . . well, *concern* . . . exists about concerns, let me make a few of points up front:

- Concerns don't mean you've failed. Just the opposite. The expression of a concern by the customer usually means that they are seeking more information, in the hope that the answer will provide them with the reason to make a positive decision.
- Concerns don't slow down the selling process, they accelerate it. Once you have successfully handled a customer concern, you are closer to the sale than you would be had the concern not been expressed.
- Concerns signal involvement. Whatever else, an expression of concern by the customer at least means they are listening and engaged. They are not dismissing you out of hand.
- Concerns often tell you the final decision is close at hand. Always be ready to close for the booking after handling a concern.
- Concerns expressed early in the sales cycle are not really concerns at all. They are reflex reactions, and you shouldn't try to close on them. Once interest is aroused, these stalls and excuses tend to melt away.
- Handling concerns can be fun. It's really all about solving problems and helping people. What can be bad about that?

Handling customer concerns

Concerns cannot be ignored, brushed aside, or minimized. To the customer, *every* concern is a serious matter and should be treated as such. Nor can you hope to make much headway by meeting your customers' expressed concerns with a burst of cheery enthusiasm. That will just raise their hackles and reconfirm all their prejudices against pushy salespeople.

Here is a simple, time-tested, four-step method that you can use to answer just about any customer concern, whenever and for whatever reason it comes up.

- ■ ***Clarify the concern.*** Make sure you *really* know what the customer's concern is. Even if you're sure, it's a good idea to encourage the customer to expand on their thinking.
- ■ ***Empathize with the concern.*** Show that you respect the customer's point of view, even if you don't necessarily agree with it.
  Note: Sometimes these first two steps can be reversed. It depends on the situation and your personal style.
- ■ ***Answer the concern.*** Solve the customer's problem. If necessary, provide appropriate proof that what you are telling the customer is actually true.
- ■ ***Check for agreement.*** If the customer doesn't agree that the concern has been satisfied, then it hasn't.

Step One: Clarify the concern

Many travel agents make the mistake of responding to concerns they do not fully understand. Avoid this trap. Never assume you know what the customer means. Even if you are "right" you will lose a valuable opportunity to build rapport and trust with your customer.

Ask questions that probe beneath the surface. There are a number of reasons to do so:
- ■ You want to understand the customer's feelings as well as the facts of the situation.
- ■ You want to know if this is a mild concern or a serious problem.
- ■ You want to know if it is something that arises from a misunderstanding or incomplete information, or if it involves a real drawback that you can't easily solve.
- ■ Questions give the prospect a chance to talk through his or her own thinking. Many times, the customer will handle the concern for you!
- ■ You gain valuable time to choose your best strategy and formulate an effective response.

For example, you can ask questions like:

"Could you explain that a little more?"
"Why do you see that as a problem?"
"What do you think would be the result?"
"How would that make you feel?"
*"I'm not sure I understand exactly what
you're concerned about."*

Step Two: Empathize with the concern

Once you know the nature of the concern and see how easily you can explain it away, there is a great temptation to jump ahead and explain it with a smile and a flourish. This is a mistake. Instead, take a moment to show that you understand and accept the customer's feelings.

This does not have to involve an elaborate show of concern on your part. Indeed, you should avoid anything that would strike customers as inappropriate to the situation. You can express empathy in a number of simple but effective ways. Just paying attention — nodding your head and saying, in a sympathetic tone, "Uh-huh." — will tell customers you are on their side.

The important thing here is to signal to the customer that you are not going to fight them on this point. If they were raising their defenses, they will lower them now. They will become receptive to your point of view and give your response a fair hearing. Here are some things you might say to convey empathy for the customer's point of view:

> *"That's a good point you've brought up."*
> *"Well, I can certainly understand why you'd*
> *feel that way."*
> *"We certainly wouldn't want that to happen."*
> *"I see what you mean."*
> *"That's only fair."*
> *"A lot of people feel just as you do."*

Anything you say that tells the customer you are listening, you are open, you are fair-minded, sends a powerful message that encourages trust and rapport.

Just remember that empathizing with a concern does not mean agreeing with it. You wouldn't want to say something like. . .

> *"You're absolutely right. The fares are outra-*
> *geous. But, hey, what can you do? That's*
> *what cruising is all about — spending a lot*
> *of money."*

Remember, too, that you can sometimes empathize before clarifying the concern.

> [Empathize] *"No one wants to pay more than*
> *a tour is worth.*
> [Clarify] *What is it, specifically, that makes*
> *you feel the tour is overpriced?"*

Step Three: Answer the concern

By empathizing with and clarifying the customer's concern, you have not only made the customer receptive to your point of view, you have gathered the information you need to effectively answer the concern.

Sometimes simply providing an answer is not enough. You may also have to *prove* to the customer that your solution to their problem is in fact a solution and not just a glib response meant to put them off. There are any number of ways to offer proof.

- Your own word should suffice in most instances. Assuming the customer trusts you (and they should), they will be willing to accept your reassurance on minor concerns. More serious concerns will require — indeed, demand — proof.
- Citing an authority can serve as a proof source, even if you don't have actual documentation. For example, the customer should accept your statement that a particular cruise ship received a sanitation score of 99 from the U.S. Public Health Service even if you cannot produce the actual report.
- Materials from the supplier can be used to clear up concerns where a misunderstanding or lack of information is the cause.
- Your own experience and that of other customers can also reassure clients that their concerns are unfounded. If you can suggest that the customer call Joe Smith to ask how his vacation went, it can be a very powerful proof source.
- Some concerns respond well to paper and pencil. For example, jotting down pricing comparisons between travel alternatives is a good way to reassure customers that they are, in fact, getting the better deal with the product you are promoting.
- Finally, some serious concerns may require a bit of research on your part to produce proof that will be acceptable to the customer.

We will deal with some specific ways of answering concerns a little later.

Step Four: Check for agreement

Finally, make sure that the customer is satisfied — that the concern has been handled to their satisfaction. Ask questions like:

> *"Does that answer your question?"*
> *"That doesn't seem to be a problem, then,
> does it?"*
> *"Are you more comfortable now?"*
> *"Are you reassured on that point?"*

If the customer doesn't respond positively, all is not lost. She is simply telling you that the concern has not yet been handled to her satisfaction. Use the same process to find out what you missed and deal with the situation accordingly.

Some additional points

Before we continue, let's make a few additional observations about concerns and how to handle them:

- The process outlined above can be abbreviated. Many low-level concerns or misunderstandings can be cleared up without using the complete four-step process. This is a judgment call. However, should you discover that you've miscalculated and the customer *does* have a serious concern, switch to the four-step method immediately.

- Don't try to pound square pegs into round holes. Some concerns are valid objections that mean the particular travel product you are trying to sell is not appropriate for this prospect. Don't fight the inevitable. It is far easier to go back to the qualifying phase and find the right product for this person than to try to talk them into something they don't want or need.

- Handling concerns is about helping people not hoodwinking them. If you find yourself in a struggle with a customer over a booking, your problem does not really lie with the customer. It lies with your qualifying skills. Figure out where you went wrong in the qualifying phase and apply the lessons learned. If you do, you will sharply decrease the odds of a similar situation arising in the future.

Types of concerns

One of the keys to knowing how to answer a customer's concern is knowing what type of concern it is. Sometimes you know this immediately. Other times you will have to clarify the concern to get a better handle on it. Here are the major types of concerns:

- *Stalls.* A stall, putoff, or excuse, as I have noted elsewhere, is usually a reflex reaction rather than a valid concern. Stalls are an expression of that quirk of human nature that doesn't enjoy change. If the customer is not in a sales discussion he would rather not start one (even if he knows there might be something in it for him). If a customer has not yet made a deposit, she will tend to postpone doing so (even if she really wants to go).

- *Misunderstandings.* Most concerns you will deal with will arise because the customer is working with incomplete or faulty information or has misunderstood the information you have provided. These are the easiest concerns to deal with.

- *Drawbacks.* Some concerns revolve around drawbacks in your offering. The customer wants something you can't provide. Or an otherwise acceptable offering contains an element the customer doesn't like. Drawbacks may be minor and easily resolved, or they may be major and hold the potential of killing a booking. Concerns in this category require creative solutions.

- *Cost concerns.* Concerns about cost may be the result of misunderstandings or they may be real drawbacks. Because they tend to come up late in the sales process and can be troublesome to customer and agent alike, we will discuss them separately at the end of this chapter.

Answering customer concerns

There is an "answer" to every objection.

Sometimes the answer is that the prospect is quite right, the cruise or tour you are offering is not for them. In that case, your best strategy is to recommend an alternative that does meet the prospect's needs and make that booking. You haven't lost a sale, you have gained a friend. You can rest assured that the next time they need the services of a travel agent, you will be likely to get the call.

Sometimes the "answer" is a snow job. By cleverly twisting words, telling half truths, or outright lying, the agent tricks prospects into believing their concerns have been dealt with. Travel agents who use such tactics tend to have a high turnover of customers.

Most of the time, however, the prospect has been well qualified by you. You know the prospect has a need for the tour or package you are presenting. In these cases, your challenge is to guide the prospect to a favorable decision — favorable for them; favorable for you.

The successful travel agent has at his or her disposal a number of techniques to answer customer concerns. Here are some of them:

Explain it away

Many objections are the result of simple misunderstandings. You haven't explained something well. The prospect hasn't heard what you said. The prospect has heard something from another source that is not true. Some important piece of information is missing. By following the four-step method outlined above, you will be able to spot these misunderstandings. In that case, it is a simple matter to explain the objection away.

> *"Mr. Jones, you'll be happy to know that all
> the hotels on this tour have fully functioning
> modern toilet facilities and not just a 'hole in
> the ground out back.'"*

Here are some other examples:

Prospect:	I dunno. All that shuffleboard and bingo. I'm not sure a cruise is for me.
Travel agent:	I know what you mean. I don't much care for bingo myself. You know, they have bingo right here in the city.
Prospect:	Yeah. But I never go.
Travel agent:	Well, that's pretty much how it is on a cruise ship. Just like a city. There's an awful lot going on, and you pick those things you like to do. What are some things you think you might like to do on a cruise?

* * * * *

Prospect:	I'm a diabetic. I couldn't handle all those big, rich meals.
Travel agent:	You're right to be concerned, and I certainly wouldn't want you to put your health in danger. That's why you'll be happy to learn that the M/S Big Ship's kitchens can cater to all dietary requirements. I'll just make a note of your special needs and you'll get the same superb cuisine, except tailored to your diet. How does that sound?

Outweigh it

Sometimes your prospect will point out a real drawback in your offering. It may not seem like a drawback to you, but that's hardly the point. It is the customer who must be satisfied. In this situation, you must attempt to outweigh the negative of the tour's (or cruise's, or package's) shortcomings with the many positives of its strengths.

> *"Well, Mr. Jones, it's true that none of these hotels have microwave ovens in the rooms. However, wouldn't you agree that doing without microwave popcorn is a small price to pay for seeing the wonders of the Himalayas from the back of an elephant?"*

Here are some other examples:

Husband:	Looks like there's a lot of museum-going on this tour.
Travel agent:	Is that a problem?
Wife:	Oh Harry, don't be such a slob! Pay no attention to him. I *love* art. That's one of the main reasons we're going to Paris.
Husband:	Look, I'm just as cultured as the next guy, but a little art goes a long way with me.
Travel agent:	Well, I can see both your points. Perhaps there's a way to keep everybody happy. What would you like to do, Harry?
Husband:	I'm more of a people watcher. I could have a good time just sitting at a sidewalk cafe, sipping a glass of wine, and watching the gir . . . watching the world go by.
Wife:	We are going to the museum!
Travel agent:	Well, you know, one stop is the Pompidou Center, which not only has a great collection of modern art . . .
Husband:	I *hate* that crap.
Wife:	Harry!

Travel agent:	. . . but it also has a great street scene outside. There are singers, and mimes, and jugglers. It's like a free circus. Now I'm sure you'll want to give Martha the benefit of the doubt and check out the museum, Harry. But if you decide you don't like it, you can wait outside and have a terrific time.
Husband:	Hmm.
Wife:	Well . . .
Travel agent:	And another thing you'll be happy to know: The Louvre has a *terrific* cafe. Great wines, very reasonable prices, and some of the most interesting people in Paris. So it would seem that you can stick together and both be happy, wouldn't you say?

* * * * *

Prospect:	I dunno. It's a little more than I'd hoped to spend.
Travel agent:	Really? About how much over is it?
Prospect:	About 500 bucks.
Travel agent:	Well, that's certainly a consideration, especially when you were expecting to pay less. On the other hand, let's look at what we're getting for our money.
	[The travel agent would then list all the *agreed-on features and benefits* that had been elicited during the qualifying process. At each step, she would check for agreement. The client did want a golf course so he could play every day, didn't he? He had specified a junior suite so he wouldn't feel cramped, correct? And so on.]
	And on top of all the amenities, wouldn't you agree that the El Luxo Magnifico qualifies as the sort of special anniversary trip you were looking for?
Prospect:	Well, it certainly is fancy.
Travel agent:	And when you think about it, the extra money comes to less than $50 a day. Doesn't it seem worth it to pay a little bit extra to assure you get the vacation you want?

Feel-Felt-Found

Sometimes prospects' objections are the result of doubt, uncertainty, or fear. They've never experienced the benefits of a cruise, for example, and just aren't sure it will be as much fun as everyone says it will. You can help reassure them by pointing out that others have been in the very same position, taken the plunge, and are now very happy.

"Mr. Jones, I understand exactly how you

*feel. That's exactly the way I **felt** before I took my first cruise. And I **found** that there was so much to do that I was hardly in my cabin at all, except to change clothes and sleep."*

This "feel-felt-found" technique is not only one of the simplest ways to handle your customers' concerns, it's also one of the most effective. The technique works well because you express empathy and understanding for the client's point of view. You make it all right for the client to feel the way he does. By sharing with the client that you felt the same way once, you become equals in discussing the matter. Now you have an attentive audience for your presentation of the benefits of cruising.

You don't always have to use the exact words feel-felt-found to use the technique. For example, you might say,

"I can understand why you say that. I hear that a lot from first-time cruisers. But when they get back they can't stop talking about all the things they found to do on the cruise. They were hardly in their cabins at all!"

You can add some extra punch to this technique if you can refer the client to a third party. For example:

*"I know just how you **feel**. One of my best cruise customers is Joe Smith and he **felt** the same way you do before he took his first cruise. He **found** it wasn't a problem at all, and now he's one of the biggest cruising fans in the city. Why don't I give you his number? I'm sure he'd be happy to talk to you about it."*

Talking to Joe Smith may give the client an extra level of assurance. After all, Joe has no financial interest in the sale. Of course, you should make sure that Joe is willing to chat with reluctant cruisers before you give out his number to people.

And if you don't already have a list of satisfied customers willing to answer questions for other would-be travelers, start compiling one now!

'I already have a travel agent'

Early in your career as an independent travel consultant, you may hear those words a lot. One way to deal with them may be to say, "Okay. But if you're ever interested in changing agents let me know." I don't particularly recommend that you take that stance, but if you do, I won't hold it against you. You may feel that it's easier to find people who will be eager to deal with you rather than try to change somebody's mind about a travel agent with whom they have an ongoing and presumably satisfactory relationship. It may be that you will find plenty of people who don't already have a travel agent and that they will bring you all the business you want to handle.

You should be aware, however, that just because someone already has a travel agent doesn't mean you can't become their new travel agent. The statement "I already have a travel agent" is, technically speaking, an objection. As such it can be dealt with using the four-step method outlined above. Here's how:

Prospect:	I already have a travel agent.
Travel Agent:	Great. Having a regular travel agent is important. [Empathize] Which agency do you use? [Clarify]
Prospect:	The Traditional Travel Agency down on Main Street.
Travel Agent:	I've heard good things about them. [Empathize] How do you like them? [Clarify]
Prospect:	They're okay.
Travel Agent:	Who do you deal with down there?
Prospect:	No one in particular. Just whoever happens to be free.
Travel Agent:	Uh-huh. What is it you like about them?
Prospect:	Well, they seem to know what they're doing, and I've been pretty happy with the fares I get.
Travel Agent:	I see. So a knowledgeable travel agent and good prices are important to you then? [Clarify]
Prospect:	Yeah. Of course.
Travel Agent:	Are they easy to work with? I mean, how do you usually book through them? [Clarify]
Prospect:	I call up and tell them what I need and if I need to look at brochures or something I go down and check 'em out. Then they tell me when the tickets are ready and I go pick 'em up, or they mail them to me.
Travel Agent:	Well, let me ask you this: Say the Traditional Agency assigned you your own personal travel agent, so you'd be dealing with someone who really got to know you and how you like to travel. And say they came to you with the brochures, instead of your going all the way down to Main Street. And say they hand-delivered the tickets to you. Would you be likely to continue doing business with them? [Clarify]
Prospect:	Well sure.
Travel Agent:	I'm glad to hear that because that's just the level of service I want to provide for the neighborhood. My agency has access to all the same suppliers

and brochures as Traditional, so with the help of my agency I can answer any travel question you have. Plus, I make a personal commitment to gain an in-depth knowledge of all my clients' travel preferences. And I can come to your house when it's most convenient for you and Martha to look at brochures and discuss your plans, and I'll hand-deliver your tickets. [Answer the concern] Isn't that the kind of service you'd like to get from your travel agent? [Check for agreement]

Prospect: Well, when you put it like that . . .

Travel Agent: Will you let me handle your next booking? [Check for agreement]

Let's analyze what happened here. First, the agent — let's call her Sue — empathized with the objection by noting that it's a good idea to have a regular travel agent (which it is). Then she began a process of learning more about the prospect's situation and how strongly attached he is to his current agent.

Asking the name of the agent can provide Sue with some valuable information. She may know quite a bit about the Traditional Agency, how big it is, what its specialties are, and so forth. She may even have looked into becoming an outside rep there. Also, by asking questions like this, she will start to get an idea of who her main competition is. At the very least, she will get an idea of how far the prospect has to go to get travel assistance; convenience, after all, is one of the biggest things the home-based, neighborhood-based travel agent has to offer.

In further clarifying the objection, she learns that the prospect's loyalty to his agency is not particularly strong. "They're okay," he says. And the fact that he doesn't have a personal, ongoing relationship with a specific person there also speaks volumes about the strength of his commitment. If it turned out that the prospect had a much stronger relationship with the agency, Sue might well decide not to push so hard for his business.

In the process of clarifying the objection, Sue tries to find out what is important to this prospect when it comes to dealing with a travel agent. She also finds out the basic nature of the prospect's dealings with Traditional. Reading between the lines here, we can determine (as can Sue) that this prospect deals with Traditional not so much because of their great level of service but because he hasn't found anything better. Many people continue dealing with the same travel agency year after year out of simple inertia. If you examine your own buying habits, you may find you do much the same thing. All of this leads me to the conclusion that, most of the time, when you hear the words, "I already have a travel agent," you are not hearing a super-serious objection.

Sue next asks a question to which there is only one answer: "Say the Traditional Agency assigned you your own personal travel agent, so you'd be dealing with someone who really got to know you and how you like to travel. And say they came to you with the brochures, instead of your going

all the way down to Main Street. And say they hand-delivered the tickets to you. Would you be likely to continue doing business with them?"

What's he going to say? "No?"

Of course, the prospect may see exactly what Sue is doing here, and that's just fine. After all, she is merely feeding back, in slightly different form, what the prospect has told her. She is restating Traditional's negatives as positives. That puts her in a position to state her case for her own travel consultancy. She is offering the prospect features his current travel agency doesn't offer. These are all perfectly good reasons for switching agencies, at least on a trial basis.

Not only does Sue check for agreement ("Isn't that the kind of service you'd like to get from your travel agent?"), she does it twice. The second check is a strong closing question — "Will you let me handle your next booking?"

Overcoming initial skepticism

Ideally, the prospect will say, "Sure, Sue, I'll let you handle my next booking. In fact, Martha and I are thinking about a Caribbean cruise this winter. Why don't we talk about that?"

On the other hand, the conversation might not go so smoothly. It could very well continue along these lines:

Travel Agent:	Will you let me handle your next booking?
Prospect:	We-l-l-l. I dunno, Sue.
Travel Agent:	Is there a problem?
Prospect:	I dunno. You're kinda new at this, right?
Travel Agent:	About a month now. Are you concerned that I might not have the knowledge and experience to handle your bookings?
Prospect:	Well, I'd hate to put it like that.
Travel Agent:	Phil, don't worry. It's a perfectly valid concern and I understand completely. Believe me, the last thing I want is for you to be left in the lurch because of a mistake on my part.
Prospect:	I'm sure you're very good. It's just that . . .
Travel Agent:	Well, I certainly haven't gone into this half-cocked. I did a lot of research and training before I started asking for business, and I continue to go to seminars and association meetings to build my knowledge. And the agency I book with double-checks all my bookings for accuracy, so there's very little chance of things getting fouled up. Does that help reassure you?
Prospect:	A little.
Travel Agent:	I can see why you'd be hesitant. Let me ask you this: How did you find out the Traditional Travel Agency was right for you?
Prospect:	I just tried 'em out a few times and they seemed pretty good.

Travel Agent: Sounds sensible. Why don't you do the same with me? Try me out a couple of times and see how you like the service. How about letting me book your next vacation?

Once again, we can see how Sue applies the same four-step process — clarify, empathize, answer, check for agreement — and then asks a strong closing question to move the sales relationship forward.

There are some other lessons about how to handle your customers' concerns to be learned from this little exchange between our travel agent, Sue, and her prospect, Phil.

- ◾ ***Respect the prospect's position.*** Sue always showed that she respected Phil's point of view: "Having a regular travel agent is important." "It's a perfectly valid concern." These reassurances will make Phil comfortable, so he'll be receptive to Sue's ideas. Notice, too, that when she found that Traditional was lacking in certain areas, she didn't try to make Phil feel bad about it by saying something like, "Come on! You call that service? They probably don't even know your name!"

- ◾ ***Don't knock the competition.*** If Sue had said something like, "Traditional!? That fly-by-night outfit? How can you deal with them?" she would have, in effect, been calling her prospect a jerk. Sometimes you may have to point out why you feel a particular travel product is inappropriate for a customer. When that's the case, do so objectively — with facts and figures and proof — rather than with a sweeping condemnation.

- ◾ ***Don't be afraid of concerns and objections.*** Phil was reluctant to come right out with his concern, but Sue wasn't afraid to bring it into the open. The only objection that can hurt your sales is the objection that remains hidden and is never identified or discussed.

- ◾ ***Be persistent.*** Many people might have walked away from this discussion as soon as Phil said, "I already have a travel agent." But Sue persisted past several expressed concerns on Phil's part. She was successful because she kept her cool, focused on Phil's point of view and his needs, and remained polite. Polite persistence will invariably be respected. But let the discussion degenerate into an argument ("Traditional is a lousy agency and I can prove it.") or a shouting match ("I'm better than they are any day!") and you have lost.

- ◾ ***Don't beg.*** Sue kept the discussion on a professional level, giving solid, businesslike reasons for doing business with her. Don't succumb to the temptation to say things like, "Come on, Phil. I'm your *friend*. How do you expect me to get any business if my own friends won't work with me? Ple-e-e-ase!"

Concerns about cost

Concerns about the cost of travel products are troublesome — to the customer as well as the travel agent. They are often times hidden from the travel agent because most people feel uncomfortable about discussing their financial situation or have difficulty being forthright about how much money they consider to be "too much." Consequently, cost concerns tend to crop up late in the selling process, after you have invested a fair amount of time and energy. Worse, they have the potential to sink the sale and, for that reason, can be stressful.

Here are some thoughts on dealing with your customers' concerns about the cost of travel.

The best way to handle cost concerns — avoid them

If you have done a good job of qualifying the situation, cost concerns should not be a problem — in theory. In practice, people get cold feet at the last minute and use cost as an excuse. Still, the theory is valid. Once you know the prospect's budget range, you can present only products that fall within that range. Elsewhere, I recommended that you try to propose something in the middle to lower end of the customer's range, holding in reserve a higher-priced alternative. That remains good advice.

The problem, then, is how do you determine the prospect's price range? First, you need to establish a feeling of trust between yourself and your client. If someone feels relaxed and confident in your ability to serve their needs, they will tend to be more forthcoming. Once this trust has been established, you need to ask the right questions. "How much do you want to spend?" is a good place to start, but it will not always get you the best answer. Here are some other things you can say. Try them out and see how they work for you.

*"What did you pay for your last cruise?
Would you like to spend about the same this
year, or upgrade a bit?"*

*"As a rule of thumb, I figure that a trip like
this costs $1,000 per week per person. Is that
about what you had in mind?"*

*"I can serve you best if I have a clear picture
of what you want to spend. That way, I can
make sure you're not in for any unpleasant
surprises."*

*"Tours of this type tend to range from $2,000
to $5,000. Where would you like to be on that
scale?"*

*"Are you looking for a splurge, or would you
like to keep the costs down?"*

"Without doing a lot of research, my guess would be that this will come in at about $3,500. Would you like me to look for something a little fancier or shall we keep it at the $3,500 level?"

"Is there a price level above which you definitely don't want me to make any recommendations?"

Through careful, polite, and persistent questioning, you can usually arrive at a pretty clear idea of what the prospect is willing to spend. Armed with that information you can select the right product, a product that might even be seen as a bargain.

In presenting that product, you will want to follow the suggestions in *Chapter 21: Presenting the Wonder of Travel* to create the most favorable cost/value ratio in the prospect's mind. In this way, you can nip cost concerns in the bud.

Compared to what?

If a customer thinks the price you've quoted is too high, the first thing you will want to know is, "Compared to what?" Clarify the concern to make sure the customer is comparing apples to apples instead of apples to oranges, which is more often the case.

- *What's included?* Sometimes the concern occurs because the customer has not taken into account all the things that are included in the price. This is especially true of cruise vacations and all-inclusive resorts. Take the time to list all the things that might cost extra on a "regular" vacation but are included in this product's quoted price.

- *What level of quality?* This is the apples to oranges problem. If the customer tells you they've seen "the same" tour advertised at a lower price, clarify the source. Usually, they are referring to a discount tour operator's product. There may be some differences in the itinerary ("What's included?"), but this is more often a matter of quality. Some tour operators specialize in lower-priced tours. They do this by using smaller, less luxurious hotels, skimping on meals, using older buses, and hiring cheaper tour guides who may be less qualified. It's not necessarily that the lower-priced tour is *bad*. It's just been designed for a different market, much as Motel 6 attracts a different traveler than the Hyatt Regency chain.

- *Adding it up.* Sometimes you'll have to prove the value of what you're offering by doing a side-by-side, pencil and paper comparison. You might, for example, compare the cost of air, hotel, and car booked separately to the cost of a package. Or you might ask a couple to estimate what they actually spent on last year's independent trip through Europe ("About how much did you spend each day on restaurants? How about gas for the car?") to illustrate that the cruise they are now considering may actually cost less, even though it seems more expensive at first blush.

Cushioning the blow

Not all major travel expenses have to be paid all at once. Typically, customers pay a deposit for tours, cruises, and many packages followed by a final payment-in-full some time later. Stating the total cost as two separate payments due at different times can sometimes lessen the potential for "sticker shock." Here are some other ways of either making the cost seem less oppressive or spreading out the burden.

- **Point out the self-financing opportunities.** If the customer is paying by credit card, they don't have to pay the entire amount at once. Sometimes, you can arrange that two (or more) payments appear on the customer's credit card bill in different months. Some resorts let guests charge the final payment to their credit card at checkout, postponing the day of reckoning until well after the trip has taken place.

- **Put it in perspective.** Point out that a $2,000 trip costs just $200 a day, or a mere $100 a day for each person, or even less if a child is sharing a room for free. If this is an annual vacation, point out that it's like setting aside just $40 a week ($2,000 divided by 50). If it's a *paid* vacation, point out that their boss is, in effect, offsetting some of the expense of their holiday. Compare the price to the event — it's your honeymoon; it's your anniversary; it's the only time in your life you'll visit China.

- **Spread out payments.** Depending on the timing, you might want to consider getting the full payment in installments, a few hundred dollars each month. Usually, this will mean the client is paying by check. Make sure the client understands that if the full payment is not made for any reason, the deposit may well be forfeited.

- **Get financing for the customer.** It is also possible to arrange financing for your customers. Some cruise lines are now offering loans. Or you can approach a local finance company and explain that you would like to offer your clients financing on their vacations. If the finance company is willing to work with you, they will provide you with applications you can give your clients. If their credit is approved, the finance company will pay for the trip and the client will then be responsible for monthly payments to the finance company. It is also possible to set up arrangements like this with the savings department of a bank (a "Cruise Club"), although finance companies seem to be more receptive to dealing with folks like you and me. Of course, you can always suggest that the customer set up his own savings program to pay for a vacation or cruise. Setting up a savings program requires forethought, however. It is seldom a good solution to a last-minute cost concern.

Summary

Objections, concerns, call them what you will, can arise at any point during the sales process. Far from being a "bad sign" or an interruption, they are an indication that your prospect is actively engaged in the decision-making process and is eager for more information. By handling customer concerns promptly, cheerfully, and professionally you create greater rapport with your customer and move the sales process closer to a final decision and a booking.

There are many ways to handle concerns and answer objections. A good salesperson will develop a variety of different techniques to use within the context of the four-step process — Clarify-Empathize-Answer-Check — outlined in this chapter.

The most troublesome concerns for most travel agents are those that arise around the issue of cost. The best way to handle these concerns is to avoid them altogether, by doing a good job of qualifying the customer's budget and presenting only those options that fit within that budget range. Creating a powerful cost/value equation during the presenting process can also help avoid last-minute concerns and stalls over price.

Action steps

Here are some things you can do to put what you have learned in this chapter into action:

- Begin to develop a written list of possible objections to the travel products you will most likely be selling. If you have started actively selling travel, make of list of the objections and concerns you have heard from prospects and customers. For every concern, write down a number of possible ways of handling it.
- Pick a relatively high-priced travel product such as a cruise or an overseas tour. Write down all the things that justify the price of the product, from the most trivial to the most important. (You may want to review the section on the cost/value ratio in the last chapter.) List as many things as you can think of. The goal is not to develop a long list you can "throw at" a prospect; you would only use a small portion of the items on this list in an actual sales presentation. Rather the goal is to help you develop an appreciation that in a very real sense "you get what you pay for." This exercise will help you better understand the cost/value ratio in travel products and avoid cost concerns.
- Practice the four-step process for handling concerns outlined in this chapter. You will probably have to enlist a friend or

family member to role play the part of the customer. If possible, record your practice session and review it, making notes of what you did well and what you still need to work on. As soon as you can, start to use this method with actual prospects and customers.

Chapter Twenty-three:
Closing the Sale & Follow-Up

What you will learn

After you have completed this chapter you will be able to:
- Build agreement throughout the sales process through trial closes.
- Ask for the order with confidence.
- Use effective follow-up both before and after the sale.
- Ask for referrals in a confident and professional manner.

Key terms and concepts

This chapter involves the following key terms and concepts:
- Closing is asking any question or taking any action that requires the prospect to make a decision.
- A trial close is any closing question or action that occurs before the final close, in which you ask for the order and complete the booking.
- Effective and efficient follow-up, both before and after the sale, is what distinguishes exceptional travel agents from the rest.
- Referrals from satisfied customers are your best source of highly qualified prospects.

Introduction

For those of you who are new to sales, the word "closing" and terms like "trial closes" and "close the sale" may be unfamiliar. So let's start this chapter with some definitions.

Closing is any question you ask or action you take that requires the prospect to make a decision. At the end of the sales process, that decision will be whether or not to give you a deposit or a credit card number and authorize you to make a booking. Earlier in the sales process, you will be asking the prospect for any number of decisions — whether they

prefer an inside or outside cabin, whether an all-inclusive resort sounds like a good idea for their vacation, and so on. Closing, then, is the simple process of reaching an agreement with another person and confirming that agreement.

Building agreement with trial closes

Many travel agents truly believe that they don't close until they actually ask for the deposit. That is because for most of the sales process they gather information, answer questions, show the customer a selection of brochures, or arrange to send the customer more information. Yet, whether they know it or not, they are constantly closing throughout every conversation they have.

If you think you only "close" at the end of the sales process, consider this. . .

- When you say, "May I ask you a few questions for my records?" you are closing.
- When you say, "Do you want me to check availability?" you are closing.
- When the prospect says, "Do they have triple rooms?" and you respond, "Do you want a triple room?" you are closing.
- When you finish reviewing a brochure by saying, "Is that the kind of resort you're looking for?" you are closing.

Any question you ask or action you take that requires the prospect to agree or commit to continuing the conversation is closing. These preliminary closes are called "trial closes" because they tell you how close you are to the "real" close: asking for the order. Don't underestimate the importance of trial closes. They are the glue that cements your relationship with your customers.

Creating a sense of urgency

In many industries, salespeople qualify their prospects by the *urgency* of their need. In other words, someone who needs a new widget immediately because theirs just broke is a better prospect than someone whose widget is six months old and still working well (even though it will eventually need replacement).

The same principle holds true in the travel industry. But the nature of the travel business works in your favor because a sense of urgency is built into virtually every product you sell. When the cruise is full, it's full. When the airline sells all its seats, there aren't any more. Most airfares aren't guaranteed at all. The price quoted today could go up 20% tomorrow. Other fares expire 30, 14, or seven days before flight time. With other products (like widgets), the factory can simply add another shift and crank out some more to meet increased demand.

One of your responsibilities as a travel agent is to remind your customers of these built-in deadlines. Don't think of this as a high-pressure sales tactic. You are doing your customer a favor by pointing out that you can nail down this airfare or this stateroom *now*, but might not be able to get it at all tomorrow. You can often use the sense of urgency to secure at least a tentative booking by making a reservation (which you might have to cancel tomorrow). This is a trial close, and signals that the customer is more likely to go through with the booking than would be the case had he decided against making the reservation at all.

The greater the sense of urgency you create, the more likely the customer will make a buying decision. There is an art to this, however. Reminding the customer of deadlines is one thing, hounding the customer is something else again. If you cross the line and harp on it too much, then it really does become a high-pressure tactic. The customer will get annoyed and simply start dealing with another travel agent who doesn't put him under so much stress.

Asking for the check

Asking for a deposit or the customer's credit card doesn't have to be a difficult or stressful event. It is, in fact, the natural conclusion to your sales conversations. Closing the sale should be easy for a number of reasons, some of which have been mentioned before:

- ▪ ***People come to you.*** Why would they be here if they didn't want to give you money? At the very least, they are open to the *possibility* of giving you money.
- ▪ ***Qualifying avoids the odds of hearing "no."*** By qualifying budget and selecting appropriate travel products, you should be able to make the sale a "sure thing."
- ▪ ***Your customers are in a buying mood.*** Most of the people you deal with are actively looking for reasons to take the trip, not searching for excuses to avoid going.
- ▪ ***People expect you to ask.*** No one is going to be surprised or feel "waylaid" when you ask for a deposit.

Still, no matter how easy it might be for travel agents (as opposed to other types of salespeople) to ask for the order, the fact remains that you have to ask. You can't finish a presentation and then hope that the customer will just naturally reach for her checkbook.

I am a big advocate of setting up the eventual close by making it clear to the client (and yourself!) at the very beginning of the meeting that the meeting's purpose is to reach a definite buying decision.

> *"As you asked me, I've been researching some
> vacation possibilities in the Caribbean. And
> I think I've come up with three choices that
> fit the bill. Today, we can choose the one
> that's best for you and put down a deposit to
> secure your booking."*

If that opening seems familiar, it's because you read it in *Chapter 21: Presenting the Wonder of Travel*. While a statement such as this puts the prospect on notice, I think the psychological effect on the travel agent is just as important.

Starting the call is one thing. Ending it with a clear, unmistakable request for the check is another. Let's turn our attention to how to ask for the order.

The alternate-choice close

Elsewhere, I have recommended presenting the customer with two or three choices. This is actually a form of alternate-choice close. The question is not whether the customer is going to take a tour. The only thing to be resolved is which tour she will take. But presenting three tours is only part of the process. You still have to ask:

"Which of these tours shall we book?"

"You seemed most interested in the Trafalgar Tour. Shall I book that, or would you prefer the Tauck Tour?"

"Which of these hotels shall I book?"

"Will you be putting that on a credit card, or would you prefer to write a check?"

The direct close

Sometimes the best way to ask for the check is . . . to ask for the check.

"I'll need a check for $150 to hold the cabin."

"Which credit card number do you want to use?"

The assumptive close

In this close, you *assume* that the answer is "yes" and proceed accordingly.

"I'll book the room and put it on your Amex card."

"I'll go ahead and firm things up with Mega Tours. I'll need the full $200 deposit by Monday."

You can also use the assumptive close for add-on business. For example, if a customer has booked a flight to Cleveland, you might say:

> *"Which hotel would you like? What size*
> *rental car will you be needing?"*

The booking-form close

This is a type of assumptive close. You can use paperwork provided by the supplier or your own form. Here's how it works.

Travel agent:	So you prefer the May 16th sailing?
Prospect:	Yeah, that looks like the better deal.
Travel agent:	Okay. Let me just get my booking form. Ah, here it is. Now which name will you want on the booking, yours or your husband's?
Prospect:	Use Bill's name.
Travel agent:	And I have the address. And the phone. Okay. That was an outside cabin in Category C, right?
Prospect:	Right.

Simply go down the form, whatever it is, and fill in the blanks, asking for input from the prospect as needed. You are operating on the assumption that the sale is closed. The more information the prospect lets you fill in, the surer the sale.

Eventually, of course, you will have to deal with the deposit. Perhaps an alternate-choice close would work nicely.

> *"Now the minimum deposit is $200. Or shall*
> *I put down $300, so your final payment will*
> *be smaller?"*

Follow-up

Perhaps this chapter should have been called "Follow-Up & Closing The Sale & Follow-Up." Follow-up is a constant activity for travel agents not only because success in selling travel depends a great deal on repeat business but also because travel agenting is above all a service business. You have to follow up before the sale and after the sale, with prospects and with customers.

Follow-up involves activities that can be classified as sales, marketing, and customer service — and some that are a blend of all three. In this section, we will discuss some of the many ways you can use follow-up to power your successful travel business.

Follow-up before the sale

Not all sales happen with one phone call or meeting. Some sales take weeks, even months to conclude. And there are some sales you might begin plotting years in advance — a twentieth anniversary "second honeymoon" or landing the group business of a local fraternal organization or church group. Making sales happen requires persistent, creative, but always polite and professional follow-up on your part. Here are some of the things you will find yourself doing, along with some tips on how to do them.

- **Nailing down dates.** Before you can book anything, you need firm dates of departure and return. Some prospects can be maddeningly vague about just when they are going to take that vacation they need so desperately. Call periodically with tantalizing references to great packages you have been finding. When they ask for specifics, say that you really need to know when they want to book before you can proceed.

- **Following up on brochures.** Sometimes you will send clients a selection of brochures. Follow up to find out which ones appealed. Close for a meeting to discuss their favorite choices and finalize the booking. An alternate-choice close works well here.

> *"I'm glad you narrowed it down! We should
> pick one and book it before it's too late. I can
> stop over tonight at eight or would tomorrow
> night be better for you and Phil?"*

- **Mailings.** Periodic mailings to your client base are an excellent way to generate a steady flow of bookings. Each card, letter, or email they receive reminds your clients of your travel business (people do forget, believe it or not) and can get them to pick up the phone if they have an immediate or short-range need. Your mailings can also be used quite effectively to promote specific tours and cruises that offer a high payback to you.

- **Following up on mailings.** Most mailings deserve a follow-up call — either in person or over the phone (unless of course your client list has grown so large that this is impossible). In *Chapter 19: Spreading the News about Your Travel Business*, we talked about sending out a mailing announcing your new travel consultancy. That mailing definitely requires follow-up. And within a reasonable time, too. Calling three months later to say, "Remember that letter I sent you?" won't suffice. Follow-up calls like this are sales calls. They should end with a closing question.

- **Keeping your promises.** If you tell your customer that you will research available Hawaii packages and get back to him in three days, do it! If a client has a question you can't answer immediately, get the information as quickly as possible and get back to the customer. Developing a reputation for quickly fulfilling requests and meeting promised deadlines will go a long way to building a loyal repeat following.

- **Servicing your customers.** You can take care of your clients even when you are not selling them travel. Alert them to articles about their favorite destinations. Pass along upgrade coupons that might come your way. Send a free informative brochure (the government and trade associations print this kind of thing all the time). The ways of keeping in touch are limited only by your imagination and determination to follow up.
- **Never stop prospecting.** One thing that requires constant follow-up is your prospecting program. Review *Chapter 18: Prospecting* and recommit to making those calls, turning out those letters of introduction, making new contacts, getting referrals (which we will discuss in more detail shortly), and keeping your pipeline full of prospects who will turn into bookings next month, the month after, and every month of the year.

Follow-up after the sale

Once you have made a successful booking, it is not time to relax. There is still a lot of work to do. What you do after the sale can be your most effective marketing tool. It can certainly differentiate you from run-of-the-mill travel agents who make the booking and promptly forget the customer exists. Here are some of the things you will (or could) do *after* the sale is made.

- **Deliver tickets.** If at all possible, hand deliver the tickets and other travel documents. It's a level of service most people are not accustomed to. It also gives you an opportunity to review the details of the booking with the customer in person.
- **Review the details of the booking.** Now is not the time to make false assumptions. Make sure the customer understands everything about the booking. This is especially true of tours and cruises and doubly true when it's the first such experience for the traveler. Go over what will happen, step-by-step. Make sure the client is comfortable with the procedures and feels secure that everything has been taken care of.
- **Provide pre-trip assistance.** Your client may need assistance and guidance with things like passports or visas, even immunizations or other health concerns. In some cases, you may even want to volunteer to go shopping with the client for that special dress she'll wear on the cruise.
- **Customize the trip.** You may be able to add value to the tour or package you have booked by providing personal advice, based on your actual experience or research — a list of romantic restaurants in Paris; tips on using public transportation in Rome; your own guide to the sights of Vienna, complete with your personal observations and insider's secrets. Even if you can't write your own mini-guidebook, you may be able to recommend guidebooks, historical accounts, even novels that will add to the client's travel experience.
- **Market to their interests.** Once a client shows a predilec-

tion for a certain type of travel, he or she should be on the "A" list to receive notices for any future opportunities that might come up. A prime example would be the retired couple who goes cruising once a year. Once you have their business, you should make it a priority to keep it by attentive and creative follow-up.

- *Monitor the booking.* Things change. It's the agent's responsibility to make sure the client is kept posted about changing schedules and the like.
- *Give them a going-away present.* A bouquet in their stateroom, a bottle of champagne in their hotel room — gestures like these are appropriate when you've secured a major booking. They will also be appreciated and remembered.
- *Be a chauffeur.* Some agents build fantastic customer loyalty by driving their clients to the airport and picking them up on their return.
- *Keep the home fires burning.* Why not volunteer to keep an eye on the clients' home while they're away? Pick up the mail, change the position of curtains to deter intruders, feed their pets.
- *Debrief them after the trip.* Once your clients have returned from a trip or cruise, give them a call to ask how things went. Not only is this a welcome way for you to keep in touch, it will give you valuable intelligence for your own use and that of future travelers. Get their opinions about hotels, restaurants, sights, the trip in general. What did they like and what could they have done without? Far from feeling put upon, most clients will welcome the opportunity to provide you with a complete and detailed report on their trip.

Asking for referrals

Referrals are the hallmark and the lifeblood of any first-class sales organization — and a travel agency is no exception. There are several times during your sales relationship with a client when you can ask for a referral:

1. When you've failed to make a sale.
2. When you've made a sale.
3. When the client returns from the trip.

You will find that the quality of referrals you solicit will get better as you move from 1 to 3.

Of course, you can always ask for referrals by saying, "Know of anyone else who might be interested?" But the odds are that this approach will produce very few names. You will do better if you repeat the benefits of the product. For example. . .

"I can understand how this cruise might not be right for you. But perhaps you know someone else who is just itching to spend thirteen peaceful days away from everything on a cruise to Lisbon."

This approach still has the problem of asking the client to draw a name or two out of a very big group of people — everyone he knows or might be acquainted with. Many salespeople find that both the quantity and quality of their referrals increase when they narrow the field. You might say, for example,

"I bet there are some folks you know down at the legion hall who'd be interested in a tour of Normandy. Can you think of anyone?"

If the client shows a willingness to search his or her mental database for you, you can keep probing.

"How about down at the office?"

This way, your clients can focus in on a small group of people and begin to visualize faces and personalities. When that happens, there's a better chance they will see a match between someone they know and the travel product you're offering.

The best time to get high-quality referrals is immediately after a client has returned from a positive vacation experience. This is also the appropriate time to ask if they'd be willing to share their enthusiasm with other people who might be considering taking the same type of vacation or visiting the same destination. If they're willing, be sure to ask how many calls from would-be travelers they'd like to answer. Don't push it. Better to have 12 people who'll talk to reluctant cruisers once a month than one person who'll have to answer 144 calls a year!

Folks like this are called "champions." They have a genuine love for the experience and relish the chance to share it with others. Ideally, you should have a number of champions for each travel product in which you specialize — champions for Alpine ski trips, champions for cruises, champions for escorted cultural tours, and so forth.

Once you've located a champion, take care of him or her. If you refer another client to them for a chat, follow up to see how it went. If they show any signs of wearying of the task, back off. Show your appreciation for their assistance by giving them first crack at special fares and discounts. If someone has produced a lot of business for you through their enthusiastic recommendations, you should consider rewarding them with a tour conductor slot if you can.

Following up on what you've learned

We are ending this discussion of the art and science of selling pretty much where we began — prospecting for new business, this time through referrals. The cycle has come full circle. The process begins anew.

And although much more on-the-job training lies ahead, you have come to the end of this course manual. But, like selling travel, learning about the travel business is not something you do once. It is something you do over and over again for as long as you remain in this fascinating, romantic, and rewarding career.

So now that you have come this far, I urge you to follow up. Follow up on what you have read here. Follow up on the ideas that leapt into your mind as you read. Follow up on the excitement that thinking about your new home-based business has generated. Follow up by reading more. Follow up by joining a professional association. Follow up by subscribing to the trade publications. Follow up by attending the many informational seminars offered by suppliers.

This book is also a resource for your future development. I urge you to use it as a ready reference. Return periodically to the text and reread it. If you are new to the travel industry, to sales, to self-employment or to all three, things that you breezed over on the first reading will take on new meaning once you have some experience under your belt. A colleague and I have also put together *The Travel Agent's Complete Desk Reference* so that you can have a one-stop source for the inside information — supplier contacts, airport and airline codes, industry jargon, and so on — you will need to book travel and work smoothly with the suppliers' reservation departments. If you purchased this book as part of our home study course, you already have it. If not, you can order it by going to:

http://www.HomeTravelAgency.com/deskref.html

However, the real job is yours. I can tell you about the wonderful opportunities that exist in this fabulous industry. Only you can make them happen.

Remember, a dream is just a dream.

A dream you act upon is a reality.

Action steps

Here are some things you can do to put what you have learned in this chapter into action:

- First, do something special to celebrate your completion of this course. Go to a movie, take that special someone out to dinner, or better yet, take a trip! Treat yourself. You deserve it!
- Look back at whatever sales activities you have conducted so far. That could mean something as simple as telling people you were now a travel agent and asking for their business. What closing questions did you ask? Write them down.

- If you have made any recent sales, contact those customers and (if you haven't done so already) ask them for referrals. Assuming you are just getting started, from now on, whenever you contact friends, family, or acquaintances to add them to your prospect list, ask them about other people they know who might be interested in the travel products you will be selling.
- Follow up on what you have learned in this course by putting your newfound knowledge to work. Go out and get active selling travel. Pick and choose the techniques, strategies, and leads you have picked up from this course and start putting them into action. As you do, you will find more and more things "falling into place" as your business develops.
- Refer back to this manual frequently as you start putting your business in motion. Reread chapters and use the *Index* to answer questions as they come up.
- Above all, have fun!

*Home-Based
Travel Agent*

Index

Index